W9-BXR-936

ON THE
PERIPHERY OF
NINETEENTH-CENTURY
MEXICO

ON THE PERIPHERY OF NINETEENTH-CENTURY MEXICO

SONORA AND SINALOA
1810-1877

STUART F. VOSS

THE UNIVERSITY OF ARIZONA PRESS

TUCSON, ARIZONA

About the Author . . .

STUART F. VOSS, an associate professor of history at the State University of New York at Plattsburgh, has been interested in the dynamics of regional history throughout his professional career. He has carried out extensive research projects in Mexico on the interrelation between regional and national historical experiences and on the role of family networks in shaping the course of modern Latin American history. He earned his Ph.D. from Harvard in 1972 and was appointed coordinator of the Latin American Studies Program at SUNY-Plattsburgh in 1978 and again in 1981.

972.17
V960
1982

THE UNIVERSITY OF ARIZONA PRESS

Copyright © 1982
The Arizona Board of Regents
All Rights Reserved

This book was set in 10/11 IBM MTSC Times Roman.
Manufactured in the U.S.A.

Library of Congress Cataloging in Publication Data

Voss, Stuart F.
   On the periphery of nineteenth-century Mexico.

   Bibliography: p.
   Includes index.
   1. Sonora (Mexico : State)–Politics and
government. 2. Sinaloa (Mexico : State)–Politics
and government. 3. Sonora (Mexico : State)–
Economic conditions. 4. Sinaloa (Mexico : State)–
Economic conditions. I. Title.
F1346.V69   972'.17   81-21983
                              AACR2

ISBN 0-8165-0768-6

To the Children of

La Orfandad de la Esperanza
(Tijuana, Mexico)

and

La Escuela Ibarra
(Pátzcuaro, Mexico)

Contents

Preface   xi

1. Prolonged Prelude   1
    (1530-1810)

Mission Society: Inclinations to Permanency (1530-1700)   2

Missions, Settlers, Tribes: Whose Frontier? (1700-1767)   9

Blowing the Whistle: Decisive Royal Intervention (1767-1810)   18

Urban Notables Lay Claim (1770-1810)   24

2. Borrowed Time   33
    (1810-1831)

Independence and the Future: Economics   34

Independence and the Past: Problems of Security   48

Independence and the Present: Politics   52

3. Visions on the Periphery   62
    (1831-1837)

Sonora: How to Sustain Progress   64

Sinaloa: How to Corner Progress   74

National Connections: Aligning Realities With Visions   80

4. Visions Gone Awry   95
    (1837-1854)

Sonora: Progress No Longer a Promise   95

    From Vision to Lamentation   105

    External Panaceas   113

Sinaloa: The Rivalry of Two Cities   121

5. Somos Mexicanos   130
   (1854-1866)

New National Visionaries   132

Adjustment to the Ayutla Aftermath   135

Sonora: An Overture to Progress   148

Sinaloa: Theme and Variations   161

The Intervention: Commitments Finalized   168

6. The Burden of Recovery   176
   (1867-1875)

Recurring Insecurities and Shortages   178

Limited Economic Recovery   186

The Municipios in Regression   196

7. The Liberal-National Contradiction: Progress   204
   (1867-1875)

The Responsibility for Progress   206

The Sonoran Governor's Initiatives   209

Assessing Blame for Stagnation in Sonora   221

Sinaloa: Mazatlán at Odds   227

Common Binds   230

8. The Liberal-National Contradiction: Politics   233
   (1867-1875)

The New Liberal Order: Ill at Ease   233

Sonora's Liberal Trustee: Increasingly Out of Favor   237

A Constitutional Challenge in Sonora   246

Altered Configurations in Sinaloan Politics   256

The Federal Dimension in Sinaloa   262

9. Cross Purposes: The Tuxtepec Revolution   272
   (1875-1877)

The Tuxtepec Coalition   273

Electoral Imposition   275

Armed Resistance Seeking Outside Assistance   281

Testing Linkages   287

Striking a Deal With Don Porfirio   294

Bibliography   301

Acknowledgments   309

Index   311

MAPS
  Political Composition of the Region of Sonora and Sinaloa   36
  Sonora, 1854   120
  Sinaloa, 1854   122

Preface

An important legacy of the colonial period in Latin America was regionalism. The collapse of conquest society in the late sixteenth century, the steady erosion of royal authority and direction in the New World thereafter (reinforced by the isolating tendencies of Latin American geography), the varied mixes of racial elements, and—in many cases—economic contraction, all led to the creation throughout Spanish America of distinct regional societies with historical experiences largely separate from a general colonial norm. The return of an aggressive royal presence in the Bourbon dynasty after the mideighteenth century did not arrest that development. Indeed, the reorganization of administration into the intendancy system and the liberalization of trade within the empire stimulated regionalism even further.

With independence, the external imperial overlay was replaced by nation-state structures of varying size and complexity. The empire had been able to coexist with regionalism, because its unity could be reduced to respect and loyalty to the Crown. The new nations could not. They inherently embodied a commitment to the realization of unified, uniform institutional structures that extended to all areas within the national boundaries. Some failed quickly, breaking down into national entities that corresponded closely to colonial regional societies: Uruguay, Paraguay, Ecuador, and the Central American republics. Others divided into smaller groupings of regional societies, which spent several decades trying to work out a reconciliation between national and regional interests. Argentina, Peru, Colombia, and Venezuela are noteworthy examples.

Mexico alone within the former Spanish Empire kept its colonial boundaries almost intact (only the already largely autonomous presidencia of Guatemala broke off from the viceroyalty of New Spain). This fact made the divisive effects of regionalism there even more formidable, for political accommodation involved not only a large number of regional interests in a national structure, but also an extensive periphery, twice removed from the central core, that might gravitate toward another historical experience on its other borders unless thoroughly integrated into the nation. Texas did so, as did New Mexico and California, though under more forced circumstances. The Yucatán almost joined them. The Northwest (and some of the north-central states) considered doing so.

By the late nineteenth century the national entities that survived the frag-mentation of the post-independence years were able to create the permanent beginnings of national societies, economies, cultures, and identities, though degree of participation varied from region to region within each country. A crucial underlying theme of nineteenth century Latin America is how the regional historical experiences inherited from the colonial period became part of such a national experience. In Mexico, the extensive periphery made the process more problematical. On the periphery it was less a question of accom-modating regional and national experience, than of realizing a common iden-tity between them.

A related development was the transformation of family-based politics into a nationally oriented, institutionally based political structure. Local colonial politics was largely dominated by powerful families, often interrelated, who exercised official control through the *municipio* (the municipality included not only the incorporated town but also the surrounding countryside, which was often an extensive area). Politics at the viceroyal level was almost always external in the sense that local communities did not participate directly, but only petitioned distant royal officials for favors or satisfaction of grievances. In between, the intermediate levels of imperial government were generally nebulous in their lines of authority and weak in their initiative powers. The Bourbon intendancy system was devised to correct this situation, but it came too late and was in operation too briefly to do so effectively.

With independence, a political vacuum arose. The imperial (continental) realm became nonexistent. The viceroyal level was defunct, except in Mexico. The provincial and district levels were even more nondescript. Into this vacuum moved two forces: those with extralocal interests, who set about creating institutional political structures at the national (and often state) level, thereby to impose their will downward to the localities; and prominent families, who sought to extend their local domination upward to the district and state levels through alliances with other families or through the sheer weight of their expanding economic domain. Each had its own concerns, its own pressing problems and desired ends, its own visions of what society should be like and what direction it should follow to fulfill these visions.

The nineteenth century in Mexico, and Latin America generally, to a signif-icant degree centered on the issues of the how and who of governance at the state and district levels. National politics in great part hinged on the resolu-tion of these questions. In the process the familial orientation of politics gradually gave way to an institutional basis, though it was never totally sup-planted. In most cases, local "elites" reached a *modus vivendi* with national political interests, whereby the former received support in the retention of their control of local society and in the promotion of their economic interests in return for cooperation with national ruling groups. The share of power at the district and state levels, and the economic benefits thereby derived, varied.

Sonora and Sinaloa illustrate well these important themes in nineteenth century Mexico, and Latin America generally. Since this region was on the periphery, the relation between regional and national historical experiences was less clear, less certain, and the integration between the two was more arduous. The centripetal forces were not as strong there. The centrifugal forces had to be reckoned with seriously, especially in view of the aggressive, expanding United States society on the Northwest's border. Geography fostered isolation from the rest of the country and contact with the world beyond. The colonial legacy also played an important role, distinguishing society in the Northwest from that elsewhere in Mexico.

The late development of a permanent hispanic society in what became the states of Sonora and Sinaloa resulted in the control of the region's society by clusters of interrelated, prominent families located in the numerous towns scattered throughout the area. It left the Northwest a more enterprising, urban society after independence than that in Mexico in general. The founders of such families, mostly immigrants from northern and eastern Spain, came to Sonora and Sinaloa at the end of the colonial period. They readily made their fortunes in the midst of the Bourbon effort to pacify permanently that frontier area and to promote vigorously the establishment of enlarging, productive hispanic communities. These "notables," as they referred to themselves, intermarried with one another and fostered the rise of small urban centers, which they dominated.

The late settlement provided an alternative to the more general hierarchical colonial patterns elsewhere in the viceroyalty. The ecclesiastical establishment had been precluded by the Jesuit mission society, and, with that order's expulsion in 1767, the church's presence was quite weak. The Jesuit missions had also forestalled the creation of large landed estates. The military had considerable influence, but it was composed of professionals oriented towards making possible the rise of a new society; it was not a militia reflecting an established local society and committed to preserving it.

This enterprising, urban society inherited from the colonial world was, at the same time, one whose foundations were quite vulnerable in the absence of external support, as the post-independence years revealed. This vulnerability was especially evident in Sonora. Urban notables in the Northwest sought to enlarge their family holdings and bring progress to their states and the society whose public affairs they dominated. The word *progress* is employed here with caution. The prominent families of Sonora and Sinaloa's urban centers did not use the term until the late nineteenth century. Yet what they meant by it then was only a less sophisticated form of a world view or vision they commonly shared at least from independence, and most probably from even a generation before that. Their expectations involved a future in which the economic activity begun under the Bourbons would expand, bringing with it a more stabilized society and a more refined culture. It was not the all-encompassing twentieth century concept of modernization, or of development. Rather, it was a more limited sense of steady improvement and growing refinement. It was progress, without positivistic capitalization. In their search for such progress, these notables acted far more as part of a larger cluster of similar families than singularly in promoting their interests at the district and state levels. The identity of interests between town and family were closely linked.

For two generations, however, the notables were unable to accomplish their aim, to realize their vision for the region. The tribal Indians in their midst and the Apaches on the frontier—whose subjection and pacification, respectively, the Bourbon Crown had succeeded in achieving—stubbornly resisted their enterprising efforts. Sonora and Sinaloa were effectively cut off by rugged mountains from all but the Pacific coast, so economic ties with the rest of Mexico were slight. They provided little stimulation for the expansion of economic activity. The special provisions to support mining undertaken by the Bourbons lapsed. Instead, contact with external markets and investment became the immediate alternative. But that contact remained transient, cautious of the region's security problems, always ready to withdraw for more profitable ventures. At the same time, increasing foreign contact brought the prospect of outsiders trying to seize the states' potential for themselves: North American and French filibusters, annexationist-minded United States administrations, and colonial-dreaming French imperialists.

The urban notables initially sought to work out their own future, little concerned with the Mexican context into which independence had thrust them. They expected to extend the society their parents and grandparents had recently begun. Soon, however, they were confronted with the problems resulting from the decline of external support and economic stimulation. Their own proclivity for in-fighting about the predominance of one district over the others in state politics only aggravated these problems. Realizing soon that being part of a larger society that could provide assistance was requisite for the resolution of the problems confronting them, they nonetheless insisted that such support be wholly on their terms. Under those conditions, it was not forthcoming on anything more than a sporadic basis. Finally, through the shared experience of nationwide war, first civil (the Reforma) and then quasi-foreign (resistance to the Intervention), permanent links of political commitment and identity were forged. Nevertheless, the integration of the Northwest into the Mexican nation was not thereby conclusive.

For a decade after the Intervention, the notables of Sonora and Sinaloa wrangled among themselves and with national interests, trying to work out an acceptable place in the national framework, one which would resolve the protracted problem of impeded progress, while reserving to them local control and prerogative. They were unable to do so. Then, in the late 1870s, political circles arose in each state offering a solution, one which the great majority of notables accepted or to which they accommodated themselves in the succeeding decade. The two circles premised their control of state government on the determination that the realization of progress required the forging of close, working connections with those who directed the nation's politics in Mexico City. Only with such direct federal assistance could the region's security be assured, its transportation greatly improved, its politics stabilized (in their hands preferably). The price was an increasingly closed politics at the state and, in time, local levels. These were the terms of finding a place in the national framework then taking shape under the supervision of Porfirio Díaz. The growing economic benefits with the passing of time pleased them, though the rising political cost left them increasingly disgruntled.

The nearly seventy-year process by which the region of Sonora and Sinaloa found its place in the larger Mexican society, by which its own particular experience became part of the larger national experience, constitutes the dynamic of its history in the nineteenth century. The interpretation of this process has been derived from multifarious sources. Some have been amply revealing, in particular the numerous geographies and travel accounts, and the newspapers for the third quarter of the century. Others have been a source of frustration in the smattering character of their availability: family papers, the state archives of Sinaloa, economic and demographic statistics. The few monographs published on the Northwest have been either too restricted in their subject matter or chronological framework, or too unwilling to consider larger historiographical questions to be of significant assistance in reaching a satisfactory interpretation for the nineteenth century as a whole. It is hoped that this general interpretation will serve as a catalystic framework for further research and as a basis for understanding how a region on the periphery of Mexico in time became not only an ongoing part of the nation, but eventually its center.

1

Prolonged Prelude
(1530-1810)

Colonial society in New Spain, as generally in the Indies, was not the result of Spaniards implanting a single, homogeneous society in a virgin environment after the destruction of its pre-Columbian predecessor. The Spaniards and their descendants were one neither in mind nor purpose; nor were the native inhabitants. Colonial society was instead a continuing competition of sub-societies, held together by the Crown. Elements within the larger society were enmeshed in a constant, often bitter struggle, each trying to assert and impose its subsociety on the others, to mold the colonial world around it to its own liking. In the midst of this competition was the Crown. As royal arbiter it enforced the rules and periodically altered them to suit its own purposes, disrupting the equilibrium among the subsocieties in the process. The interests of some were favored, those of others undermined.

The mix of subsocieties, the relative success of one or more of them as compared to the others, and the degree of royal intervention combined to produce varying regional patterns. Environmental conditions were important, but they only presented possibilities, favoring the subsocieties in varying degrees. They did not in themselves determine the outcome of the subsociety competition. Northwest New Spain experienced such competition for nearly three hundred years before the outcome became clear and a distinct regional pattern emerged. The competition there was more intense, more violent than was generally the case elsewhere.

The region in northwestern New Spain encompassing the future states of Sonora and Sinaloa was on the periphery of Colonial Mexico. Geographically, it was on the edge of the viceroyalty, cut off overland from the rest of New Spain by the rugged Sierra Madre Occidental, so the forces from within were stronger than those from without. Though climate ranged from dry basin and range country in the north to gradually less arid coastal plains that became tropical lowlands in the south, the region was given unity by a succession of river valleys that originated in the Sierra to the east, flowed down through mineral-laden foothills, and emptied into the Gulf of California. Communication overland from one river valley to the next was not difficult; nor was that by coastal navigation.

Culturally, the several indigenous societies that inhabited the region before the conquest were on the edge of the sophisticated pre-Columbian world of Middle America. The complex district town societies of the Tahue tribes in the south, under the cultural influence of the Tarascans of central Jalisco and Michoacán, gave way to more localized tribes of sedentary village farmers to the north: the Cahitas, the Pimas, and the Opatas.[1]

Administratively, until the end of the colonial period the Northwest was at best of peripheral concern to the Crown and its viceroyal representatives. Before then, what external direction there was came from across the Sierra in the person of the governor of Nueva Vizcaya in Durango and the audiencia of Nueva Galicia in Guadalajara.

Being on such a periphery, the subsociety competition was more freewheeling, less determined in its eventual outcome than that in the heartland of Mexico. The existing native peoples were less malleable to the colonial pattern shaped in the central core of Middle America. Geographical isolation and royal disinterest left the various subsocieties almost entirely to their own resources, and the competition was consequently less distracted or influenced by external considerations. Not until the late eighteenth century were external forces and royal intervention significant enough to favor one of the subsocieties and thus to produce a distinct, lasting, regional society.

MISSION SOCIETY: INCLINATIONS TO PERMANENCY (1530-1700)

Two conquest expeditions in the sixteenth century—those of Nuño de Guzmán in 1530-1531 and Francisco de Ibarra in 1564—established only a precarious foothold in the Northwest. By the 1590s the Spanish community there consisted of two scant settlements (Culiacán and San Sebastián in central and southern Sinaloa respectively) and two ephemeral mining camps (Pánuco and Copala, further inland from San Sebastián). There was a scattering of *encomiendas* (grants of tribute in goods and labor in return for Christianization) particulary around Culiacán. However, there were no real markets for their production and the Indian population which rendered tribute had been declining markedly. The killings and dislocations of the conquest, the periodic epidemics, and the retreat of many Indians into the nearby Sierra Madre had all left the *encomiendas* greatly depopulated. The resulting scarcity of labor, the hostility of neighboring mountain tribes, and the almost total isolation from the rest of the viceroyalty had likewise combined to discourage what mining had been commenced. The few Spanish settlers were

---

[1]Carl Sauer, *Aboriginal Population of Northwest Mexico*, Ibero-Americana, No. 10 (Berkeley, 1935), 22-54.

forced to eke out a meager existence. They farmed on a subsistence level and sold fish and salt when they could to the Nueva Vizcaya settlements on the other side of the Sierra.[2]

In the 1590s, when the generally successful system of conquistadores and their mendicant auxiliaries (Franciscans) had clearly proven to be a failure in the Northwest, the Crown turned to the Jesuits, recently arrived in New Spain. In doing so, it was not shifting to a preconceived alternative. The Northwest (and the other unpacified regions in the New World to which they came) was just as much a frontier for the Jesuits as for the other hispanic elements. The European mission concept of itinerant preachers purifying those already converted to the faith, based in urban *colegios* (seminaries), was applicable to only a small portion of the population. Hispanic population centers were still, in the late sixteenth century, like islands in a native-speaking, pre-Columbian sea. This new world was almost wholly uncharted as one moved north out of the traditionally sophisticated, culturally complex, Meso-American heartland. The Jesuits soon found that knowledge of the native language was a prerequisite; that—given the less organized, rarely ur-banized character of the Indian peoples to the north—sophisticated, central-ized, seminary bases were out of the question in the immediate future; and that, hence, Jesuit itinerant preachers would have to create their own bases of operations among the Indians themselves, in a village context. The concept of itinerancy was reduced to a very limited sense.[3] The outcome was the mis-sion, which in time evolved into a system and even a society.

The Crown saw the Jesuits as transitional figures, spearheading the new colonizing effort. Pacifying the Indians by converting them to Christianity and adapting them to European culture, they were to prepare the way for later Spanish settlers. Small military garrisons were to accompany the Jesuits as auxiliaries, protecting the missions from hostile Indians without and from

---

[2]Luis Navarro García, *Sonora y Sinaloa en el Siglo XVII* (Sevilla, 1967), 11-16, 28-32, 35-36, 51. For detailed accounts of the conquests of the sixteenth century in Northwest New Spain, see Hubert H. Bancroft, *The History of the North Mexican States, 1531-1800* (San Francisco, 1884) and Miguel O. de Mendizabal, *La evolución del Noroeste de México* (México, 1930), 15-19, 43-48.

In the coastal plains of southern and central Sinaloa, the two conquest expeditions encountered the Tahue tribes, whose level of population and culture compared favorably with the Tarascans of central Jalisco and Michoacán. The conquistadores, however, were stopped by the Cahita tribes, who inhabited the coastal valleys of northern Sinaloa and southern Sonora. The Cahitas, sedentary farmers, were at a less sophisticated cultural level than their neighbors to the south, but they were more tenacious fighters.

Southern and central Sinaloa were initially a part of Nueva Galicia. In time, these areas and the territory north into southern Arizona that was added in the seventeenth century became part of Nueva Vizcaya under its governor. However, judicially they remained under the audiencia of Nueva Galicia in Guadalajara.

[3]Charles W. Polzer, S.J., "The Evolution of the Jesuit Mission System in Northwest New Spain, 1600-1767," (Doctoral dissertation, University of Arizona, 1972), viii-ix, 1, 24-33.

any rebellious converts within. It would be a considerable time before the divergence between this royal understanding of the Jesuits' temporary assignment and the missionaries' own evolving need and commitment to a far more permanent calling became readily apparent and a source of growing conflict. With consistent (though somewhat limited) official support and continued royal blessing, Jesuit missionaries achieved considerable success in pacifying the Northwest through the course of the seventeenth century.

The initial beachhead was the Sinaloa valley (in modern northern Sinaloa), where the Jesuits arrived in the 1590s. From there they moved steadily north, pacifying the Cahita tribes of the Fuerte, Mayo, and Yaqui valleys; the Lower Pimas in central Sonora; and the Opatas in modern northeastern Sonora. These tribes, settled along the river valleys that cut through the foothills of the Sierra Madre, comprised the large majority of the native population and were most sedentary, socially organized, and materially advanced. Expanding the mission system elsewhere met with increasing difficulty and limited success. The slow, circumscribed establishment of missions among the mountain tribes of the Sierra to the east revealed the problem, and the efforts to push into the desert and semi-arid basin and range country to the north and west in the last two decades of the century made it all too clear. The Seris of western Sonora and the Papagos further north rejected the missions. Those established among the peoples across the gulf on the Baja peninsula led a tenuous existence and required continual provisioning from the mainland missions. Only among the Upper Pimas, dispersed along the river basins of northern Sonora and present-day southern Arizona (then called Pimería Alta), under the remarkable leadership of Padre Eusebio Kino, did the Jesuits approach their earlier success to the south.[4]

The mission system that evolved through the sixteenth century created a structure that isolated the Indians from would-be settlers and kept the new converts under the direct, supervising hand of the missionaries. The padres were encouraged in this direction by the loosely organized, unsophisticated manner of the Northwest tribes' lifestyles.[5] The missionaries immediately consolidated the Indians, who had previously lived in scattered rancherías, into compact pueblos to facilitate worship, instruction, and joint labor. Each male was given a plot of land, which he worked in order to support his family. Three days a week, however, he was required to work for the mission: tilling the community fields, whose production went to the mission; tending the herds of livestock, also belonging to the mission; or providing other

---

[4]*Ibid.*, 34-37; Eduardo W. Villa, *Historia del Estado de Sonora* (Hermosillo, 1951), 93. Bancroft, *North Mexican States,* contains a detailed account of the Jesuits' pacification of the Northwest, and Peter M. Dunne, *Black Robes in Lower California* (Berkeley, 1968), details that of the Baja peninsula.

[5]Polzer, 33.

special services, such as escorting travelers, contructing mission buildings, or defending against any enemies threatening the mission.[6]

Each mission was integrated economically into an emerging larger network of Jesuit institutions and related to various local and regional economic markets which could enhance the mission's assets. Part of the mission's production went to feed those working on it and part to stock and supply newly established missions—in particular those in Baja, which had to be provisioned on a permanent basis, owing to acute climatic obstacles and the nomadic traditions of the tribes there.[7] The remainder was used to supply provisions to the military garrisons and to the settlers who began to trickle into the region. Supplies were sold even as far away as in the Parral mining district on the eastern side of the Sierra.[8] With the proceeds from these sales, and from the annual Crown allotment to each mission of three hundred pesos, the mission came to carry on an active commerce with the interior of the viceroyalty through the growing Jesuit commercial network, centered in a buying agent and warehouses in Mexico City. The padres provided the Indians with clothing, trinkets, knives, needles, and other tools. European goods were purchased for resale to soldiers and settlers, as well as for consumption by the missionaries themselves.[9] Decorations and liturgical items for the churches were also bought in considerable quantities.[10]

Administratively, the Jesuits reduced the Indian chiefs to the role of subordinate officials, though they remained titular heads. Their authority was confined to settling disputes occurring within the mission villages, seeing that the laws (spiritual as well as secular) were obeyed, and punishing transgressors.[11] However, in time the Indian leaders' governmental role was enlarged in response to the growing threat from without. The outbreak of incursions by the Apaches on the northern border after 1680, soon joined by the raids of the intransigent Seris of western Sonora, necessitated a permanent defense

---

[6]Ignaz Pfefferkorn, *Sonora—A Description of the Province,* translated by Theodore E. Treutlein (Albuquerque, 1949), 274-275. Pfefferkorn, a German, served in the missions of the Pimería Alta from 1758 to 1767.

Those Indians who provided personal services for the missionary were to receive remuneration; however, continual complaints to the Crown reveal that this rule was frequently not observed. Navarro García, *Sonora y Sinaloa,* 181-182.

[7]Dunne, 111, 354.

[8]Navarro García, *Sonora y Sinaloa,* 22, 172; Pfefferkorn, 273-274.

[9]Pfefferkorn, 275-276; Dunne, 354-371.

[10]Pfefferkorn, 272-273. Though usually built of adobe and flat-roofed, ". . . the churches were decorated with beautiful altars, images, paintings, and other ornaments. On important feast days in practically all missions, the utensils used in the altar service were generally of hammered silver, sometimes beautifully gilded, . . . and the garments of the priests were correspondingly costly. Even on common work days, silk vestments having gold or silver borders were always worn . . . . Although wax was very expensive in Sonora, it was nevertheless used without stint during public feasts."

[11]Ibid., 266-267.

establishment.[12] The missionaries supported the development of a centralized military hierarchy among various tribes to defend the pueblos and lead punitive expeditions.[13]

Until the mid-seventeenth century, very few Spanish settlers followed in the Jesuits' footsteps as the Crown had expected and planned, largely because the mining failures of the previous century had fostered a reputation of poverty for the Northwest.[14] But with the development of the mining districts in Nueva Vizcaya on the eastern side of the Sierra Madre, white and *casta* (those of mixed Indian-black-white blood) settlers were once again interested. This time they were not disappointed. Mines were discovered in numerous areas throughout Sonora, while the old mining districts (*reales*) of southern Sinaloa were reactivated and some new mines discovered.[15] Some Spanish farms and haciendas sprang up to support the mines, and soon began to intrude among the mission pueblos in Sonora and northern Sinaloa.[16] The settlers began to encroach on mission lands and increasingly sought to lure the Indians to work on their estates and especially in their mines. Merchants were quick to follow.[17]

The mining districts consequently provided the motor of expansion for Sonora and Sinaloa after 1650 and fostered the permanent, though itinerant, presence of the hispanic population there. This expansion was reinforced by the Franciscans' pacification of the northern part of Nueva Vizcaya east of the Sierra Madre, by the development of mining in the eastern slopes and foothills of this range, and by the settlement of New Mexico. All brought an end to the Northwest's virtual isolation from the interior—especially in Sonora and northern Sinaloa. Roads were developed, facilitating the flow of population into the region and of commerce within and out of it.[18] By 1678 the

---

[12] Laureano Calvo Berber, *Nociones de historia de Sonora* (México, 1958), 96-97; Clara Manson, "Indian Uprisings in Sonora, Mexico" (Master's thesis, University of Southern California, 1963), 12-15, 22-24, 49-51.

[13] Mendizabal, 121.

[14] Ibid., 118-119.

[15] James Rodney Hastings, "People of Reason and Others—The Colonization of Sonora to 1767," *Arizona and the West*, 3 (Winter, 1961), 327-330; Antonio Nakayama, *Documentos para la historia del Rosario, Sinaloa* (Culiacán, 1955), 7. The largest and richest silver veins discovered in the last half of the seventeenth century were those of the Real de Alamos in the hills southeast of the Mayo valley in the early 1680s, and the Real de Rosario in southern Sinaloa in 1655.

[16] Hastings, 326,331.

[17] Navarro García, *Sonora y Sinaloa*, 60-61; Sauer, 27-28.

[18] Navarro García, *Sonora y Sinaloa* 42-43, 68, 172, 255, 259-263; Bancroft, *North Mexican States*, 207, 276 fn. One of the primitive roads opened went east from the Opata country to the Franciscan missions in northwestern Chihuahua, there connecting with roads to New Mexico and to points south; another connected the mining districts of central Sonora with the large mining center of Parral, to which the Jesuits sent large droves of livestock:, Population flowed over these trails into the region, especially after the general Indian uprising in New Mexico in 1680.

The Pimería Alta was the name given to the areas of southern Arizona and northwestern Sonora inhabited by the Pimas Altos and Pápagos.

report of a Jesuit inspector placed the hispanic population at five hundred families (about three thousand people), sparsely settled, scattered, and quite mobile, following the new mining discoveries.[19]

The settlers who began trickling into Sonora and Sinaloa in growing numbers after 1650 came with the conviction that the foundation laid by the Jesuits was theirs to build upon—that they would be the architects of the area's future. The colonists generally acknowledged the usefulness of the missionaries in preparing the region for their own habitation. A good many believed their presence was still necessary for a while longer, but by the late seventeenth century a growing number of settlers began publicly to contend that the padres should move on in accordance with the Crown's secularization law. In theory, the law required mission secularization after ten years, on the assumption that after such a length of time a frontier area should have been sufficiently civilized to allow the missionaries to transfer their work to new lands.[20] Nevertheless, the practice of the law became universally contrary to its original premise: missionaries were expected to retain control until royal and ecclesiastical authorities judged the missions capable of self-sustaining participation in the larger hispanic colonial society.[21]

And there was the rub, the source of a growing fester among missionaries, settlers, and authorities. If the law was not strictly adhered to in practice, the question of a mission's readiness for secularization was wide open to interpretation and debate. Resolution of the question involved theological consideration of whether the Indians had reached the state of firm, instructed believers in the faith; material acculturation (hispanization) was also deemed essential to their integration. With the passage of time, it was on this latter consideration that the Jesuits' argument for the delay of secularization increasingly hung.

The padres out in the field came to understand well the relation of material acculturation to the primary task of conversion and instruction. Material benefits were primarily responsible for first attracting the Indians to mission life and then retaining them, as a number of Jesuits acknowledged in their writings,[22] including the noted Padre Kino.[23] The pressures moving the missionaries toward the creation of a strong, stable, prosperous economic structure to undergird the mission system grew steadily. The missionaries more and more reached the conclusion that they could not move on, at least not for a considerable time. They made this pointedly clear to the settlers, though

---

[19] Hastings, 331.

[20] Dorothy Boe Shull, "The History of the Presidios in Sonora and Arizona, 1695-1810" (Master's thesis, University of Arizona, 1968), 50-51. The military commanders held the principal civil positions with the coming of settlers.

[21] Polzer, 119-120.

[22] Dunne, 59, 118-119; John L. Kessell, *Friars, Soldiers, and Reformers—Hispanic Arizona and the Sonoran Mission Frontier, 1767-1856* (Tucson, 1976), 5, 8-9, 14.

[23] Polzer, 102, 204-205.

more subtly to the Crown. To secularize, they argued, was to abandon unprepared native peoples to widespread exploitation and the dissolution of their acquired faith.[24] The evolving mission society protected the Indians from such misfortunes by separating them from the settlers and maintaining them under the exclusive, benevolent supervision of the padres.

The material well-being of the missions depended upon their control of economic resources and the labor of neophytes. The missionaries became so occupied with economic matters because, as noted above, they understood the integral role of material benefits in the process of evangelization and the full integration of the Indians into hispanic society. They also came to know from experience that economic relations were the first and fundamental basis of Indian-settler contact and that this contact increased the difficulty of evangelization and hispanization. The result was a growing and increasingly bitter conflict between the Jesuits and the settlers. The center of contention was control of the Indian population.[25]

Initially, the Jesuits were nearly complete masters of the situation, owing to the priviliged and isolated conditions under which they pacified the Indians of the Northwest and to the well-developed system they had evolved in establishing the missions. Administratively, the military commanders periodically tried to restrict the Jesuits' prerogatives,[26] but they had no effective means to make their orders stick. The few soldiers under their command were scattered in small detachments over wide areas, and they had little hope of aid from distant superiors. In contrast, the missionaries could call upon hundreds of mission neophytes, led by Indian officials who could usually be removed if they did not comply with the padres' will.[27]

Economically, through the Indians the Jesuits were the masters of most of the productive lands of Sonora and northern Sinaloa. They controlled not only the primary production from the land (the crops and livestock), but the derivative products as well.[28] They had trained many of the mission Indians (especially the Opatas, Yaquis, and Mayos) in such crafts as spinning and weaving, the building trades, wood carving, and tanning.[29] Dominating the production of this large region, they were able to corner a considerable share

---

[24]Kessell, 8-9, 14; Polzer, 204-205.

[25]Polzer, "Mission System"; Navarro García, *Sonora y Sinaloa;* and John A. Donohue, S.J., *After Kino—Jesuit Missions in Northwest New Spain, 1711-1767* (St. Louis, 1969) provide numerous examples of such conflicts between settlers and missionaries.

[26]Shull, 45-51.

[27]Navarro García, *Sonora y Sinaloa,* 180-182. According to Navarro García, the Indian officials, though elected by the pueblos and nominally confirmed by the Spanish authorities, obeyed the missionaries because "they believed in the superior authority the power of excommunication gave the Padres."

[28]*Ibid.,* 204-209.

[29]Pfefferkorn, 244-246.

of its commerce as well, supported by the Jesuit commercial network based in Mexico City. The Jesuits also employed a number of measures to combat the growing encroachment of hispanic settlers. To prevent them from securing Indian labor, the missionaries warned the Indians of falling from God's grace through contact with the scandalously sinful Spaniards. They threatened and dispensed punishment through Indian officials beholden to them. They refused to recognize official requests for Indian labor in mines and on haciendas short of workers. Moreover, they tried to discourage the settlers from occupying lands in their mission domains by underselling the settlers in supplying the mines, often by as much as fifty percent. Underselling was also a prime Jesuit weapon against the merchants. In addition, the missionaries had their own stores to trade with the Indians and impeded the tribes' attempts to sell their individually-produced goods directly to the settlers.[30]

MISSIONS, SETTLERS, TRIBES: WHOSE FRONTIER? (1700-1767)

The rivalry between settlers and the missionaries for control over the Indians, and through them the power to determine the Northwest's future, became increasingly aggravated through the early eighteenth century. There was less room, theoretically as well as physically, in which the conflicting colonial groups could maneuver. The assumption of an expanding frontier was now little applicable.

The missionaries' advance became stalled by the turn of the century. A series of uprisings by the Lower and Upper Pimas in the 1680s and 1690s, added to the increasingly hostile Seri resistance, had bred caution. The War of the Spanish Succession (1701-1714) precluded any substantial royal financial support and initiative. Avoidance of competition with the Franciscans in New Mexico provided additional discouragement. The most formidable obstacle to expansion was the outbreak of Apache raiding along the northern frontier at the close of the seventeenth century. With Padre Kino's death in 1711, vigorous leadership ceased at the time and in the place it was most needed.[31]

While the padres's option of moving on was diminishing markedly in the early 1700s, the influx of settlers continued, assisted by the establishment of

---

[30]Navarro García, *Sonora y Sinaloa,* 207-209, 214-215, 218-221. As the population and purchasing power of the mining districts grew, the missionaries increased their plantings proportionately, even installing horse-driven mills in some pueblos to supplant the far less efficient thrashing by hand. So effective were the Jesuits in commercial competition that the *colegio* at Matape (in central Sonora) in the 1670s every year sent more silver to Mexico City than all of the merchants in that province combined.

An example of the Jesuit commercial network was the annual cattle drive of approximately 5,000 head in the late seventeenth century from the missions in Sonora through Sinaloa to the order's sugar haciendas in central Mexico. Polzer, 170-172.

[31] Hastings, 332; Donohue, 9; Luis Navarro García, *José de Gálvez y la Comandancia General de las Provincias Internas del norte de Nueva España* (Sevilla, 1964), 35-36, 43-44.

a permanent presidio garrison in northeastern Sonora at Fronteras (1695) to contain Apache penetration.[32] The consequences of secularization were now far more serious for the missionaries; hence, they felt the need to extend, elaborate, and justify its prerequisites. For the settlers, secularization became more imperative as the alternative to a solidified, permanent mission society which spelled a restriction of opportunity. The Northwest frontier was becoming far more defined. The question of whose frontier it was and for what purposes was neither as remote nor as simple as it had seemed previously.

In the 1720s, when the long War of Succession was over and the Bourbons were beginning to get a handle on the vast bureaucratic machinery inherited from the Hapsburgs, the Crown revived the intention of expanding the frontier. The independence and rising profiteering of presidial captains and local officials prompted a royal inspection by Pedro de Rivera in 1724. Underlying this immediate cause was the growing concern of the Crown at the threat of foreign aggrandizement of the vast territory to the north, claimed by Spain, but as yet uncontrolled. Royal interest was increasingly directed toward consolidating and expanding the northwestern frontier to help foreclose this threat. Rivera reported that the Jesuit missions, especially those of Sonora, were an important component of that process. Not only would the existing missions serve as supply bases for the new ones to be erected, but they would provision the presidial companies with food and livestock, and their neophytes would act as armed auxiliaries on campaigns against the Apaches and as armed escorts for travellers. Rivera's report effectively dispelled proposals for secularization.[33]

The new Bishop of Durango, Benito Crespo, enthusiastically endorsed missionary expansion on the frontier. The new presidial capitans and alcaldes mayores lent firm support. Jesuit superiors in Mexico City began a renewed effort, assigning three new missionaries to the Pimería Alta in 1732. Through Padre Jacobo Sedelmayr's half-dozen excursions, the Jesuits undertook independent exploration of uncharted territory in the 1740s. To further promote expansion, Jesuit superiors in 1745 proposed secularizing twenty-four of the southern missions in Sinaloa (especially those in the Sierra) in return for additional finances and manpower to push north and west. Cultural assimilation was still minimal at best, they acknowledged, yet secularization was required if expansion were to continue. The new king, Philip VI, agreed and the lengthy implementation process began.[34]

The intentions of Jesuit superiors in Mexico City and Rome concerning the northwestern frontier were not too dissimilar from those of the Crown. In the

---

[32] Shull, 10-11.

[33] Donohue, 13-15, 43-58; Navarro García, *José de Gálvez y la Comandancia General*, 48.

[34] Polzer, 220-226; Donohue, 61, 67-70, 74-75, 112-118.

second quarter of the eighteenth century there was even a meeting of minds of sorts. Ironically, there seems to have been a greater divergence between Jesuit superiors and their own missionaries out in the field. The order's hierarchy in the viceroyal capital from very early on had worried over the by-products of the missionaries' inclinations toward the creation of a prolonged mission society: fractious relations with the settlers and abuses in the order's commitment to an ascetic life. They anxiously watched the evolving mission system entangle the missionaries more and more in temporal affairs. Difficulties in communication made supervision all the harder.[35]

In the early 1660s, one provincial (the order's head in New Spain) had attempted to arrest the developing system, to move toward secularization, and to return to the missionary approach of urban colegios and itinerant missionary work in the countryside then practiced in central Mexico. But the missionaries had argued that their neo-Christian communities needed buffers until the neophytes were acculturated adequately to compete and survive in colonial society. The order's general meeting in 1662 had acquiesced to their views, and the resulting revision of the 1610 code had focused on confronting situations then commonly arising on the frontier. Jesuit superiors had yielded to the missionaries' request for permission to expand economic activities to supplement the royal stipend of three hundred pesos so as to ease their temporal burdens, in particular the gap between their living standard and that of their colleagues in the urban seminaries. Yet they then had sent out new rules to curb the resulting affluence of the missions and their increased dealings with the settlers. In the 1690s, the mission of Matape, an important center for distribution and assistance, had been ordered to liquidate most of its extensive assets, which included a mining operation. Compliance in this instance had been generally fulfilled, but owed more to the changing needs of the mission system than to clerical obedience, for by 1700 missionaries had begun to ignore rules and precepts and to criticize their inconsistency, impracticality, and uselessness in the ever more complex frontier society in which they had to work.[36]

The pressures toward paternalism mounted steadily in the early eighteenth century. With evangelization and conversion complete in most missions, the padre's function became that of protector and preparer of the Indians for eventual full participation in hispanic society.[37] However, the reality in colonial New Spain was that the Indians did not have full participation, but were the near bottom rungs of the ladder in a rigid socio-economic hierarchy. The mission system was, thus, a subsociety that was increasingly irreconcilable with the expansion of hispanic society, represented by the settlers.

---

[35]Donohue, 44, 136-137; Polzer, 203.
[36]Polzer, 51-52, 58-84, 129, 136-144, 178-187.
[37]*Ibid.*, 117-119.

Paternalism also stemmed from another source. With the passing of years, a growing pessimism among the missionaries had begun to take hold beneath the surface as expectations were not met and discipline was increased to compensate for it. The visible, marked decline in the mission population between the 1670s and 1720s was indication enough that all was not nearly as well as it should have been. And the decline was not arrested thereafter in most districts. Disease was the major culprit, but many neophytes simply drifted away.[38] This manifestation of a general problem of the Indians straying from the straight and narrow path was attributed by the padres to the neophytes' ignorance, laziness, and irresponsibility. Nevertheless, the real snake in their Garden of Eden was the settlers, who, with increasing success, tempted the Indians with the material goods of European culture in exchange for their labor. The missionaries viewed most settlers as un-Christian, greedy people, who so lusted after gold and silver that they would resort to the vilest means to discredit the padres and lure the mission neophytes to work for them, disseminating their immoral habits in the process.[39] "Without the evil examples of these godless people," Padre Pfefferkorn was convinced, "Christianity would have been just as flourishing in Sonora as it was in Paraguay and in all other places to which the Spaniards did not have free access."[40]

The settlers saw themselves as the principal architects of frontier society, setting its tone and determining and dominating its institutions. Nevertheless, they disagreed among themselves over how great an impediment the Jesuit missions were to the development of such a society. For many, the awareness of their dependence on the missions—through economic dealings or essential services provided—overrode whatever feelings of envy and frustration they might have had. Often their defense of the missions in their disputes with other settlers and officials added to the delay in secularization. However, this position became harder and harder to maintain as the eighteenth century wore on, as the number of settlers steadily grew, and as horizons of potential opportunity expanded but went unfulfilled. This was especially the case in areas where mines were discovered.[41]

The fixation of a growing number of settlers was on what seemed to be a Jesuit monolith. They contrasted the uncertain situation of their often transitory presidio communities, mining camps, and haciendas, which (save in the windfalls of periodic bonanzas) experienced generally lean times, with the solid, stable prosperity of the missions—and found it wanting. The mission

---

[38] Dunne, 38, 40, 66.
[39] Navarro García, *Sonora y Sinaloa*, 211-212; Pfefferkorn, 175, 241-242, 280.
[40] Pfefferkorn, 241-242.
[41] Donohue, 19-21, 39, 56; Polzer, 202.

system, they believed, increasingly denied them access to the region's resources, to which they felt they were entitled. They were deterred from agriculture and stock-raising for want of adequate labor and by the competition for markets. As a result, the colonists said, they generally were forced to try their fortune in mining, carry on a difficult commercial trade in the face of the prevailing low purchasing power of their fellow colonists and the stiff price competition from the Jesuits, or settle for a steady, though meager, wage as a soldier in the expanding presidial garrisons.[42]

Settlers with such views painted a none too rosy future, but they had some tactics of their own, which they employed with increasing frequency and success. Growing numbers alone meant the Jesuits were faced with more encroachments. More settlers in time brought more soldiers for their protection, which in turn meant more interference from royal officials in the missions' operations.[43] The most effective device was the lure of the colonists' material goods for the Indians, which became a rationalization and justification for their penetration of the mission areas. The padres were stifling the Indians' individual initiative, thereby holding back their hispanization, the settlers believed and wrote in periodic letters to the Crown. By leaving the missions and going to live among and work for *them*, would not the Indians be able to purchase with their wages a better living than they now were paternalistically given by the missionaries? [44] An increasing number of neophytes left the missions to find out whether such a freedom did yield a better living. Most, however, seem to have found life among the colonists little better, if not worse.[45]

While the Crown and Jesuit superiors were negotiating the expansion of the frontier, and settlers and missionaries were quarreling over the degree to which the existing frontier should be secularized and who should manage its Indians, there slowly had emerged among the tribes themselves the vision of another alternative for colonial society in the Northwest: their own independence from both colonists and padres. The settlers treated them as economic

---

[42]Navarro García, *Sonora y Sinaloa,* 214-215; Donohue, 22-30.

[43]Shull, 10-13, 45-48. The presidial garrisons were frequently quartered near, or even in, the mission pueblos, and the soldiers often employed the Indians, at about half their regular pay, to do the menial tasks of building construction or attending livestock assigned to them in addition to their military duties. The presidios also provided the settlers with a way to penetrate the pueblos by encroaching on the Indians' land and water supplies under the protective wing of the garrison.

[44]Fernando Ocaranza, *Los Franciscanos en las Provincias Internas de Sonora y Ostimuri* (México, 1933), 63-64.

[45]Donohue, 41; Calvo Berber, 102. Soon after the Jesuit expulsion (1767), Franciscan Padre Antonio de los Reyes noted efforts by settlers to woo neophytes on such premises. Antonio de los Reyes, "Sonora Manifiesto" (1772), *in* Albert Stagg, *The First Bishop of Sonora: Antonio de los Reyes, O.F.M.* (Tucson, 1976), 37. The Reyes report was first published in the *Boletín del Archivo General de la Nación,* 9 (México, 1938), 276-320.

objects; the missionaries as children. The mounting contention between the two only made this fact even more evident to the Indians, and they increasingly chafed at either form of subjection. Moreover, the Jesuits' creation of a centralized political-military hierarchy, sanctioned by the Crown, had been fostering among the Indians a growing tribal consciousness and resulted during the 1730s in the emergence of a group of leaders in the various tribes who had risen to prominence and official position in the pueblos through military service against the Apaches and Seris.[46] They heard the escalating grievances of the people and increasingly saw the solution to them through native autonomy under their leadership.

The Indians' toleration of Jesuit paternalism by this time was wearing quite thin. The missions had been in existence for more than a century and it seemed more and more to the Indians that the padres, not they, had received the lion's share of the benefits. The missionaries still freely disposed of the ornaments and liturgical items of the churches, the crops of the mission lands, and the livestock of the pueblos—all of which the neophytes with the passing of time had come to view as their own. Indian officials were almost always underlings of the missionaries.[47] Sometimes imported Opatas, whom the padres trusted and lauded as the most Christian and civilized of the tribes, were placed as leaders over other tribes.[48]

The diffuse intentions emerging on the northwestern frontier came into bitter, even violent conflict after 1730, brought on in the immediate sense by a failure of local officialdom to maintain a semblance of the royal function of arbiter. Royal officials at all levels in the New World were generally pragmatic. They were quick to size up the balance of power in the region or district over which they were given authority and cast their lot accordingly, favoring the element of subsociety which currently held the upper hand. Those who went against the grain found their stay in office considerably shortened. The pragmatic official had not only to read correctly the power balance in his domain, but also to keep his bureaucratic ears attuned to the shifting whims and attentions of the Crown for alterations in the rules which regulated competition among the various subsocieties under his jurisdiction. The official's position became most difficult when the local balance of power

---

[46]Manson, 13-15, 22-24, 45 fn. To defend the mission pueblos, the Jesuits had fashioned a military hierarchy—captains, lieutenants, sergeants, and corporals—whose responsibility it was to keep vigil over each village, muster the Indian warriors in case of danger, direct the defense of the pueblos, and lead punitive expeditions. As the excursions grew in number and destructiveness, the expanding military operations of the diverse mission forces obliged the Jesuits to create the position of captain-general of each tribe, who became recognized by the Crown as head of the tribe.

[47]Navarro García, *Sonora y Sinaloa*, 180; Stagg, *First Bishop of Sonora*, 84.

[48]Pfefferkorn, 243-247, 264-265.

and the purposes of the Crown were shifting simultaneously. If he lagged behind the political and administrative change of direction, or got too far out in front of it, his days were numbered and his domain was prone to disorder. The new governor of Sonora and Sinaloa, Manuel Bernal Huidobro (appointed by the Crown in 1732), was too forward.

The year before, the area had been granted separate government as a new administrative entity called Sonora and Sinaloa. The new province was created in response to the gravity of Apache and Seri incursions on the northern frontier and to the steady increase in the white and *casta* population.[49] The balance of power on the frontier had begun to shift away from the Jesuit missions. Yet the Crown, through its inspectors' report and its promotion of frontier expansion in close cooperation with the Jesuits, had indicated that the question of secularization was still open. Huidobro, however, interpreted the creation of the governorship to mean that the settlers and their civilian authorities were now to set the tone of colonial society in the Northwest. As a result, Huidobro considered himself governor not only of the settlers, but of the mission Indians as well. They were now his charge, not the Jesuits'. Accordingly, he determined that royal taxes such as the *tributo* (the head tax on non-whites) and the *alcabalas* (consumption taxes) be extended to the mission pueblos, that the communal lands of these villages be measured and adjudicated, and that the pueblos be governed by native officials truly elected by the villagers and free of missionary control. Buoyed by the governor's official attitude, the colonists stepped up their penetration of mission lands and labor supplies. The padres perceived Huidobro's intentions correctly as a fatal threat to their mastery over the mission pueblos. They fought back tenaciously, tightening their grip over the Indians.[50]

With the challenge to their control escalating sharply, the missionaries' intensifying paternalism was becoming unbearable for native villagers and their leaders. The alternative of domination by the settlers was also growing intolerable. Hacendados and miners tried to tighten their control over Indian

---

[49]Calvo Berber, 99; Donohue, 70; Bancroft, *North Mexican States*, 520-521. Donohue dates separate government at 1734; Navarro García, Calvo Berber, and Bancroft at 1732.

The new administrative entity of Sonora and Sinaloa at this time also included Lower California. In the latter part of the century, Upper California was added as the mission frontier was extended there. In 1792, in one of the numerous realignments within the recently created Provincias Internas (1776), the Californias were put under the direct control of Mexico City, where they remained through the end of the colonial period. With independence, they became territories under the supervision and control of the national government. For details, see Robert C. Stevens, "Mexico's Forgotten Frontier: A History of Sonora, 1821-1846" (Doctoral dissertation, University of California at Berkeley, 1963); and Ernesto Lemoine Villicana, "Historia geográfica-política del Estado de Sonora," *YAN–Ciencias Antropológicas*, No. 1 (1953), 60-63.

[50]Berber, 99; Luis Navarro García, *La sublevación del Yaqui en 1740* (Sevilla, 1966), 20-23.

laborers. It was now being reported that some even had jails and employed torture to coerce their Indian laborers to work without pay. Extortion by settlers (and some civilian authorities) against their Indian laborers and mission villagers in general was becoming common.[51] Furthermore, the imposition of royal taxes in place of Jesuit control over the resources of the pueblos was the substitution of one heavy burden for another.

Seeing the rapidly growing resentment of their people caught in the ever tightening vise of Jesuit paternalism and settler avarice, and impelled by their own vision of autonomy and personal ambition, the Indian leaders decided it was time to assert their independence. In doing so, they found general support among the mission villagers.[52] In 1737, some Pimas Bajos tried to desert their mission before being forcibly returned by presidial troops.[53] Three years later there was a general uprising among the Yaquis and Mayos. Though the revolt was put down the following year (1741), the Jesuits' prior degree of control was not restored, nor was the penetration of the settlers, whose haciendas and farms were burned and mining operations shut down in the Yaqui and Mayo valleys.[54] The Pimas Altos rebelled in 1751 in alliance with the Papagos on the northern frontier. A formal peace, more purchased with gifts than achieved by force of arms, soon gave way to a series of uprisings over the next two decades.[55]

The promotion of frontier expansion was shelved. The Crown turned to defensive protection, centering on the erection of additional presidios.[56] Jesuit superiors had second thoughts about their secularization proposal and delayed initial implementation until the Pima uprising of 1751; then resistance of the Indians in a couple of targeted Sinaloan missions to submission to seculars embarrassed and alarmed them into securing the viceroy's suspension of the plan. Thereafter, they adhered to the view of their missionaries in the field that acculturation was indeed a long-term process.[57] Despite efforts

---

[51] Calvo Berber, 102-103. The Jesuits opposed the royal decree requiring that up to four percent of all able-bodied males in each pueblo take work in the mines when privately recruited labor was insufficient. Stagg, *First Bishop of Sonora,* 8.

The missionaries received numerous complaints from their village parishioners that settlers were obliging them to leave their fields to work for others; some officials were doing so, claiming to be acting in accordance with the king's order. Stagg, *First Bishop of Sonora,* 16.

[52] Calvo Berber, 99; Hastings, 736.

[53] Donohue, 84-86.

[54] *Ibid.,* 89-104. For a detailed and well-documented account of the Yaqui-Mayo uprising in 1740-1741 (in particular, the accumulation of events and circumstances after 1732 that brought it about), see Navarro García, *La sublevación del Yaqui.*

[55] Donohue, 131-133. For narrative surveys of these and other eighteenth century uprisings, see Manson, "Indian Uprisings in Sonora," and Bancroft, *North Mexican States.*

[56] Navarro García, *Jóse de Gálvez y la Comandancia General,* 124.

[57] Polzer, 225-230.

to enforce stricter discipline, the missionaries nevertheless saw their neo-phytes shrink more rapidly in number through disease and raiding, which also inflicted stock and crop losses.[58]

By the mid-1760s conditions had gone from bad to worse for the settlers. The five additional presidios established to meet the crisis had been largely ineffective.[59] Those on the frontier (Terrenate in 1741, Tubac in 1752) had been unable to contain the marauding Apaches, whose growing incursions were now reaching as far south as the Río Sonora. In addition, the two presidios further south (Horcasitas in 1741, Altar in 1753) could not contain the Seris' raids or pacify the Pimas Altos, who were again in revolt, forcing the abandonment of the Pimería Alta by most of the settlers. The garrison at Buenavista (1765) at best only kept the Yaquis, Mayos, and Pimas Bajos nominally submissive. The Opatas alone remained obedient.[60] For northern and central Sonora the prospects of ruin were ominous. Mines, haciendas, and farms were abandoned.[61] Most settlers relocated around the presidios, "where they were forced to get along wretchedly on a small farm[s], and with little stock remaining to them, or to exist on earnings from gold and silver mines or from trade." Others sought haven in the missions, but only among the Opatas and some Pimas Bajos "did they seek and receive a friendly reception."[62] Further south economic activity contracted.[63] It was now no one's frontier, with the possible exception of the tribal Indians.

---

[58] Donohue, 140.

[59] Shull, 14-17.

[60] Padre José Ortega, *Historia del Nayarit, Sonora, Sinaloa y ambas Californias* (México, 1887), 541-544; Stagg, *First Bishop of Sonora*, 7, 17, 23-24.

[61] Padre Juan Agustín Morfi, *Descripción (1778) por Padre Morfi, sobre Arizpe, Sonora, capital que fué de las Provincias Internas* (México, 1949), 17-18; Donohue, 139-140. Hastings disputes the accepted interpretation (first presented by Bancroft) that the period from 1740 to 1770 was one of depopulation, abandoned mines and ranches, and empty settlements. He contends that though there was a general deterioration of the colonial effort in the Northwest after the death of Padre Kino in 1711, the non-Indian population of Sonora actually increased quite markedly: from approximately 3,000 in 1678 to 17,000 in 1763. According to a detailed account in the latter year by the Bishop of Durango (whose diocese then included the province of Sonora and Sinaloa), there were even five settlements with more than a thousand inhabitants: Alamos, 3,400; El Fuerte, 1,886; Soyopa (San Antonio de la Huerta), 2,571; Baroyeca, 1,000; and Río Chico, 1,400. Hastings thus concludes that the Indian uprisings' and Apache raids' "deterrent effect[s]" on the fundamental processes of colonial growth [have] probably been overstated." Hastings, 337-340.

Hastings' interpretation is not only at odds with contemporary sources in general, but suffers from chronological imprecision. His population figures show an increase between 1678 and 1763, not between 1740 and 1763, the period for which he draws his conclusions. Contemporary sources emphasize the mid-1760s as the period during which the hispanic population, though not declining, became concentrated and increasingly inactive economically. Moreover, Hastings extrapolates increased economic activity from the population growth without giving any evidence to refute available sources showing a decline in economic activity after 1750.

[62] Pfefferkorn, 285.

[63] Navarro García, *José de Gálvez y la Comandancia General*, 121-122.

BLOWING THE WHISTLE: DECISIVE ROYAL INTERVENTION (1767-1810)

Provincial officials and presidial officers sent a chorus of pleas for aid to Mexico City and Spain. The Crown's response was atypically prompt, for by the mid 1760s the Bourbons were committed to altering life in New Spain considerably, in some cases radically. The shock of the British occupation of Havana (1762-1763) at the end of the Seven Years War (1763) had triggered the Bourbon reform program for Spanish America. Attention was particularly focused on New Spain, whose developed wealth made it the greatest prize to be kept or lost when the next expected war with Britain erupted. To the Bourbons, New Spain was the empire's most valuable resource in strengthening the peninsula in the continuing international power struggle during the eighteenth century. As part of the Bourbons' general plan to strengthen the whole northern frontier, the Crown decided to make its presence decisively felt in the Northwest and to lay the foundations there for permanent stability and continuous expansion of economic activities.[64]

For the first half of the eighteenth century, the Crown had supported and promoted the generalized concept of an expanding frontier in the region, prompted by the growing fear of foreign aggrandizement. In the 1760s that threat seemed quite real indeed. At the same time, the past two decades had seen a general breakdown in order and stability. The existing pacification and settlement framework no longer functioned even passably. Royal intervention, in the form of detailed, comprehensive policies, backed by a firm royal presence, was deemed necessary for the construction of a stable frontier society, one that could then serve as a base for extension of Spanish control many hundreds of miles north and west.[65] Thus, when official reports came from Sonora about the sharp decline in mining revenues, the widespread impoverishment of settlers, and the prevailing unruliness of the tribal Indians, officials in Mexico City moved promptly to implement the general frontier program in the area.

The viceroyal officials were also prompted by the secret order for the immediate implementation of another general Bourbon reform: the expulsion of the Jesuits. The Crown had come to consider the order a stubborn, threatening exception to its absolute rule. The regions of Spanish America dominated by the order seemed in the Bourbons' eyes to have become nearly autonomous, unmindful of royal authority. The hasty, callous removal of the Jesuits in late 1767 profoundly altered the balance of power among the

---

[64] Stagg, *First Bishop of Sonora,* 8. See David A. Brading, *Miners and Merchants in Bourbon Mexico, 1763-1810* (Cambridge, 1971) and John Lynch, *The Spanish-American Revolutions, 1808-1826* (New York, 1973) for a general discussion of Bourbon reforms.

[65] Navarro García, *José de Gálvez y la Comandancia General,* 157.

competing subsocieties in Sonora and Sinaloa. The Crown quickly brought in a reduced number of Franciscans as substitutes in the northern part of the province.[66] However, because of royal determination to intervene decisively on the side of the settlers in order to foment a firmly rooted, expanding, hispanic community, the missionaries were consigned to a marginal role. Henceforth, the padres were to be merely adjuncts, helping to order and prepare the outer fringes of the frontier for such a society.

A military expedition was sent from Mexico City in early 1768 to restore order and to introduce reforms to resolve the anticipated problems arising from the Jesuits' departure. It was organized and eventually led by José de Gálvez, the visitador general sent to New Spain in 1765 to implement preliminary reforms and make a general inspection as the basis for a more thorough reform program. By 1771, through the twin tactics of constant pressure of armed force and lenient peace terms, Gálvez succeeded in pacifying Sonora and northern Sinaloa.[67]

With the rebellious tribes in submission, royal attention turned to bolstering the frontier defenses against the Apaches. The presidial companies, which had been expanded in number over the previous three decades, were beefed up and made considerably more efficient through strict regulations, and an additional garrison was established at Bavispe (1779).[68] In 1785, a new policy was instituted which finally brought relative peace to the Sonora frontier. It combined strong military pressure to force the Apaches to agree to peace (including the reinstitution of the deportation of captured hostiles to

---

[66]Stagg, *First Bishop of Sonora,* 9-12. The Jesuits in Sonora and northern Sinaloa were hurriedly sent under armed guard to the landing at Guaymas, where they were confined in miserable quarters for nine months. Most boarded the ship for San Blas in ill-health, which was aggravated severely by a voyage that took three months instead of the normal six days, due to storms and inexperienced navigators. The immediate departure overland for Guadalajara resulted in the death of twenty of the fifty-one missionaries along the way. From that city, they were taken to Veracruz, from where they sailed for Europe in March, 1769.

See Herbert I. Priestly, *José de Gálvez, Visitador-General of New Spain, 1765-1771* (Berkeley, 1916), and Alberto Francisco Pradeau, *La Expulsión de los Jesuitas de las Provincias de Sonora, Ostimuri y Sinaloa en 1767* (México, 1959) for a detailed discussion of the expulsion.

[67]Bancroft, *North Mexican States,* 565, 567, 660-667; Kessell, 75; see also Priestly, *José de Gálvez – Visitador General.*

[68]Shull, 35-42, 85, 93-95; Sidney B. Brinckerhoff, "The Last Years of Spanish Arizona, 1786-1821," *Arizona and the West,* 9 (Spring, 1967), 7-8. The presidios established between 1741 and 1765 had been unable to contain either the growing unrest among the mission tribes or the Apache-Seri incursions. The soldiers were inexperienced and poorly equipped; most were recruited locally, and not a few were consigned criminals. The commanders (and often the provincial governor) were busy as merchants for the troops and made a substantial profit on the provisions and goods they supplied for their soldiers. Surplus supplies were frequently requested from the viceroyal capital to carry on a trade with the settlers as well.

Mexico City, and after 1788 to Cuba) with a rationing program that made their raids unnecessary.[69]

To complement these reforms in external defense, the Crown, acting on recommendations from Gálvez, strengthened civil and ecclesiastical administration. The province of Sonora and Sinaloa was placed under the jurisdiction of the newly created Provincias Internas in 1776 and became the Intendancy of Arizpe a decade later. In 1781 the bishopric of Sonora was created, comprising that intendancy and both Californias.[70] From 1774 to 1781, under Gálvez's initiative, an extensive undertaking was organized to create a settled route to California which would connect it with New Mexico.[71] The route was opened in 1774 and the chain of California missions began, but the link was severed in western Arizona by the Yuma disaster (1781) was a major setback to Gálvez's frontier design, disillusioning the Franciscans and dampening the efforts of those endeavoring to connect Sonora and New Mexico permanently.[72]

Through the stern subjugation of the rebellious tribes and the pacification of the frontier, the Bourbons had thwarted the Indian alternative for colonial society. Simultaneously, it had set in motion the disintegration of the mission subsociety. Missions from the Yaqui valley south were secularized. Those to the north were entrusted to the Franciscans (largely because the secularization-minded Gálvez and his reforming subordinates realized that few secular priests were either available or particularly inspired). Both priest and friar found that little remained of either the once-prosperous resources or the discipline of the missions, and the Crown, in its general inattention to the pleas of the clergy for assistance, indicated its disinterest in arresting the decline.[73]

Following the Jesuits' expulsion, royal authorities had confiscated mission property, regarding it as belonging to the Jesuits rather than to the Indians. The royal trustees temporarily entrusted with the custody of the property wasted or embezzled the wealth of most, if not all, of the missions.[74]

---

[69]Brinckerhoff, 8-13; Shull, 98-102; Max L. Moorhead, "Spanish Deportation of Hostile Apaches—The Policy and Practice," *Arizona and the West*, 17 (Fall, 1975), 206-207, 210, 219. Most of the Apaches accepted the diplomatic bribe of food, liquor, and trinkets in the new frontier policy after 1785. Expeditions were continually sent out against the diminishing numbers who refused to submit.

[70]Stevens, ii; Bancroft, *North Mexican States*, 678; Villicana, 61. All three sources detail the extensive geopolitical and administrative alterations in the Provincias Internas between 1776 and 1810. Stagg, *First Bishop of Sonora*, fixes the date of diocesan establishment at 1780. The Californias were made into a separate bishopric in 1836.

[71]Kessell, 96-97; Marc Simmons, "Spanish Attempts to Open a New Mexico-Sonora Road," *Arizona and the West*, 17 (Spring, 1975), 12-19.

[72]Kessell, 140-145.

[73]Bancroft, *North Mexican States*, 670-672; Kessell, 14, 19-25.

[74]Bancroft, *North Mexican States*, 670; Stagg, *First Bishop of Sonora*, 14-16.

According to one of the Franciscans, the royal trustees,

> . . . taking advantage of that specious title, issued orders to the village magistrates as if they were their superiors, and forced the Indians to work without pay, or at most, for only their rations. Some of these low-born trustees, who only shortly before were hungry and ill-clad, assumed so much power that they punished the magistrates, whipped the Indians, ordered the women to provide them with abundant food and clothing, and finally disposed arbitrarily of these assets according to the dictates of their cupidity and personal interests.[75]

To add to the obstacles facing the new missionaries and secular priests, the Indians regarded them as religious functionaries only, who were neither to restrict their economic activities in any way nor coerce their spiritual participation. The governor, Lieutenant Colonel Juan Claudio de Pineda, reinforced this attitude upon entrusting the missions to the Franciscans by specifying that the Indians were not to be compelled to attend religious services.[76] The friars soon began writing their superiors that their mission villagers often did not comply with their annual tribute, avoided working for the missions' benefit while pursuing their own private interests, went to work in the mines whenever they chose and without permission from the missionaries, broke social customs of morality and respect, and failed to assemble for daily mass. Some had begun breaking into the friars' quarters and stealing items from the church. When the missionaries tried to discipline them, the local Indian officials told them they were free to do as they pleased and excused them.[77] One of the Franciscans concluded that though the Indians had previously had only a few vices, now ". . . they are so debauched, insolent, and filled with the concept of liberty that they find themselves involved in drunkenness, stupidity, gambling, and in thievery outside and sacrilege inside the church."[78]

The secular priests soon began to invent excuses for leaving their materially unattractive posts, since the spiritual rewards were apparently insufficient. By 1784 only five remained in the pueblos. The friars saw their missions gradually reduced to skeleton communities as Indian families left their charge to work for the colonists, who were developing mines, farms, and *haciendas* around or on mission lands.[79]

---

[75] De los Reyes, "Sonora Manifiesto," *in* Stagg, *First Bishop of Sonora*, 36.

[76] Stagg, *First Bishop of Sonora*, 13; Kessell, 16-19.

[77] Kessell, 27-63; Charles R. Carlisle and Bernard L. Fontana, "Sonora in 1773–Reports of Five Jaliscan Friars," *Arizona and the West*, 9 (Spring-Summer, 1969), 45, 182, 187-189.

[78] Carlisle and Fontana, 187.

[79] Stagg, *First Bishop of Sonora*, 91; Ocaranza, 197-237.

Some arrive as farmers, choosing and usurping the best of the village land, claiming that it belongs to the king, and they as Spaniards have prior right; others turn loose their livestock to fatten in the cultivated fields and orchards. When the Indians complain to the magistrate about the damage caused, they are heard with scorn. If by chance an Indian gets impatient at seeing all his work lost and beats or ill-treats the animals belonging to the Spaniards, he is severely punished.[80]

The colonists were also settling in the mission villages in growing numbers, which greatly accelerated miscegenation. By 1784 non-Indians living in mission pueblos were the rule rather than the exception, and in many villages the Indians were outnumbered. By 1799 in 13 mission and 12 visita pueblos, there were 3,466 Indians and 2,809 non-Indians.[81] Only the missions of northern Pimería Alta, where fewer colonists penetrated, seemed to experience any degree of success. Yet even there the hispanic and mission communities interacted increasingly, the friars served both, and de facto secularization spread apace.[82].

By the end of the century, the Jesuit mission world was in a shambles, surviving only on the edge of the northern frontier. The way was then clear for the permanent establishment of an enterprising, urban-centered society in Sonora and Sinaloa wholly hispanic and secular. The insecurities of the frontier had been quelled. Adequate labor was assured. The economic competition of the missions had been eliminated. A strong, royal, administrative and ecclesiastical structure had been erected to provide institutional support. Gálvez's grand design in the late eighteenth century to establish population centers in order to consolidate Spanish dominion over the area also included an extensive array of economic measures, for he was bent on a thorough realization of progress. He calculated that the mining potential of Sonora alone

---

[80]de los Reyes, "Sonora Manifiesto," *in* Stagg, *First Bishop of Sonora,* 38.

[81]Ocaranza, 181, 197-237; Thomas B. Hinton, *A Survey of Indian Assimilation in Eastern Sonora,* Anthropological Papers of the University of Arizona, No. 4 (Tucson, 1959), 30. Colonist influx and miscegenation was particularly prevalent among Pimas and Opatas, who increasingly lost their numerical superiority and found themselves becoming marginal inhabitants scattered on the outskirts of their villages. In the 1790s many of the missions in Pimería Baja (central Sonora) were secularized, and in the remaining Pima and Opata pueblos of that region the colonists often outnumbered the Indians.

In Arizpe, by 1778 the presidial garrison occupied all of the old mission buildings but the church, and thirteen Spanish families occupied most of the remaining dwellings in the center of the former pueblo. The cultural effects of miscegenation were also being felt: "If one marries a Spanish woman, he no longer wishes to be treated as an Indian; he disdains the occupations and *ministerios* [offices] of his relatives; and the same follows with women when they marry Spanish men. Both affect [Spanish] dress and manners, and they are very desirous of learning the language . . . ." Morfi, 14, 18.

[82]Kessell, 100, 172-196.

would be able to restore viceroyal commerce and mining to the opulence of former times. His plans included a variety of stimulants to mining (including the introduction of machinery); the creation of a port, construction of ships, and establishment of a navigation school; and the creation of free commerce along the whole northwestern Pacific coast.[83]

The royal treasury in the late eighteenth century was incapable of financing most of these proposals. However, several of those designed to promote the rapid expansion of the mining industry, the prime mover of the region's economy, were instituted. *Cajas Reales* (royal treasury offices) were established at Rosario in Sinaloa and Alamos in Sonora, the two largest mining and population centers in the province. The new offices made the costly and risky round-trip journey to Guadalajara (four months from Alamos) unnecessary. Gálvez regularized the sale of quicksilver, so that miners could buy it at a modest price, and reduced the price of salt. Both were essential to the refining process.[84]

These measures greatly stimulated all the other mining districts in the province, though Alamos and Rosario were the chief beneficiaries. Gold placers were discovered in northwest Sonora; new silver mines were opened in northeast Sonora in the Opata country and in the Ostimuri district (the east and south); and the already extensive mining operations around Alamos once more were expanding. Mining activities were enlarged in the existing *reales* in southern Sinaloa, while new mining districts were opened in the foothills of the Sierra Madre in central Sinaloa.[85]

Livestock-raising experienced a prodigious increase after 1770. Hacendados and ranchers soon numbered their herds in the thousands. Especially in northern Sonora, where previous settlers had been few, there was a rush at the turn of the century to acquire titles to lands for stock ranches.[86] In northern and central Sinaloa intense rural colonization accelerated for agriculture and stock-raising.[87] The proliferation of stock in the region was so great that the price of cattle per head dropped from ten pesos to three pesos between 1797 and 1802. The region's mines and the settlement of Upper California provided growing markets for hides, tallow, and fresh and salted beef. The same

---

[83]Navarro García, *José de Gálvez y la Comandancia General,* 153-157.

[84]Alberto, Francisco Pradeau, *Sonora y sus casas de moneda* (México, 1959), 15-17; Antonio Nakayama, *Documentos de Rosario,* 7.

[85]Bancroft, *North Mexican States,* 686-691; José Francisco Velasco, *Sonora,* translated by William F. Nye (San Francisco, 1861), 105-124, 132. The latter work is an abridged translation of Velasco's *Noticias estadísticas del Estado de Sonora* (México, 1850).

The principal mining districts were: Cienguilla, San Francisco, and Santa Rosa (northwest Sonora); Sinoquipe, Cananea, Babiacanora (northeast Sonora); San Antonio de la Huerta, Mulatos, San Javier, Alamos, and Baroyeca (southeastern Sonora); Cosalá and Badiraguato (central Sinaloa); Rosario, Pánuco, and Copala (southern Sinaloa).

[86]Kessell, 206-208; Brinckerhoff, 16.

[87]Navarro García, *José de Gálvez y la Comandancia General,* 120.

markets consumed the wheat and other crops of the developing farms and haciendas as well. Through the landing at Guaymas, which Gálvez had established as a base for his military expedition, wheat was also sent south on small schooners and sloops to the tropical ports of San Blas, Acapulco, Realejo, and Chiametla. This last port, in southern Sinaloa, was additionally the center of a fishing trade that supplied the interior east of the Sierra.[88] The merchants, free of their former Jesuit competitors, expanded commerce in step with the other economic sectors. Small caravans of traders even began to traverse the difficult route to New Mexico with some regularity.[89] Economic resurgence was particularly strong and widespread after the turn of the century.

URBAN NOTABLES LAY CLAIM (1770-1810)

The Northwest's newly found peace and promising economic opportunities attracted a large influx of white immigrants after 1770.[90] The most numerous and influential segment of them were settlers whose vision of society was more stable, urbane, and refined than that of their predecessors. They came directly from Spain, built up prosperous farms and haciendas, established commercial trades, and developed on-going mining operations.[91] Equally important they came with a sense of permanence and a desire to sink their roots into the region and make it their own. They brought with them a vigorous urban tradition to do so.

The large majority of these Spanish immigrants were from small towns and cities of northern and eastern Spain, which had arisen in the early and middle phases of the Reconquest from the tenth through the thirteenth centuries. Such towns and cities had emerged generally as imitations or replacements of the highly urbanized and commercialized population centers of Moslem Spain, their development reinforced by the pilgrimage route to the shrine of Saint James at Compostela and by the general revival of cities and trade in the northern Mediterranean. The residents of these urban centers had early been set apart juridically from the seignorial dominaton of the countryside, acquiring local privileges and prerogatives, and becoming constituted as a corporate body (the municipio). Merchants and artisans had spearheaded this movement, and their special burguesia status in time had been conferred on all the urban residents. These commercial groups, however, had not come to domi-

---

[88]Luis Navarro García, *Las Provincias Internas en el Siglo XIX* (Sevilla, 1965), 11; Kessell, 203-205.

[89]Simmons, 19-20.

[90]Stevens, 227. Although the population figures Stevens lists should be used with caution, as he himself acknowledges, they indicate a significant rise in the non-Indian population of the Intendancy of Arizpe, which reached nearly 75,000 in 1810.

[91]Velasco, 107; *Informaciones Matrimoniales, 1799-1894,* compiled from the Archivo Histórico de la Catedral de Hermosillo, by the Biblioteca y Museo de Sonora, n.p., passim.

nate the towns. Instead control was in the hands of an urban patriciate, whose members had acquired their fortunes in a variety of activities. They had generally begun in commerce and then had consolidated and expanded their wealth by investments in finance, urban real estate, and rural properties in the surrounding countryside. Well-to-do, some even rich, their social position was the urban equivalent of the English gentry, the upper end of the middle strata, with pretentions to nobility. In time they had come to refer to themselves as "notables," a term which meant the prominent families of a community who predominated in its economic activities, directed its public affairs, and maintained its tone of refined taste in style and manners.

The influence of these urban patricians had grown steadily in the late Middle Ages, expanding beyond the municipal environs to the particular Spanish kingdoms of which they were a part through their participation in the cortes. Then, beginning in the late fifteenth and early sixteenth century, their position had gradually been undermined. From above, the absolutist-minded Catholic Kings and their Hapsburg successors not only stripped away their power beyond the municipal level, but began encroaching on their local domain. From below, artisans and other middling groups pressed, at times violently, for a share of municipal power. The Communero Revolt of 1521-22, in which all three elements were involved in varying combinations, had resolved the conflict: patrician control of municipal affairs was confirmed (most notably through the expansion of the permanent sale of offices to prominent families), but royal authority was to be unchallenged.

The commitment of the new Bourbon dynasty in the eighteenth century to the economic ideas of the Enlightenment had brought a revitalization of the Spanish economy after more than a century of stagnation. The cities and towns of the north and east of the peninsula profited most from this renewed emphasis on enterprise and commercialization. Municipal life was reanimated, and the urban notables led the reawakening. Furthermore, the Bourbons' reforms in the Indies had not only greatly amplified opportunities there, but extended them to Spaniards from the north and east on more than a tightly restricted basis for the first time. And they came to the New World in growing numbers, including many urban notables.[92]

Among them was the first bishop of the Northwest, a Franciscan friar, Antonio de los Reyes, from the town of Aspe in southern Valencia. (Aspe had been taken from the Moors in 1265, and the Reyes family had been

---

[92] For discussions on the development of Spanish urban centers and the urban patriciate who dominated them in the medieval and early modern periods, see Jaime Vicens Vives, *Approaches to the History of Spain* (Berkeley, 1970); *idem, Manual de historia económica de España* (Barcelona, 1965); *idem, Historia social y económica de España y America,* vols. 3 and 4 (Barcelona, 1957 and 1959); J.M. Font Rius, *Instituciones medievales españoles* (Barcelona, 1949); Richard Herr, *The Eighteenth Century Revolution in Spain* (Princeton, 1958).

prominent in the town for many generations. Well-to-do, they owned irrigated farmland, a vineyard, several olive groves, and a three-story house on
one of the main plazas.) The bishop was accompanied by two nephews, José
and Antonio Almada. (The bishop's sister had married into a more recent but
even more notable family of the town—the Almadas, descended from a Por-
tugese count who had presided over a small town near Lisbon in the fifteenth
century. The Almadas had been figures of some importance in that nation's
history, and the boys' great-grandfather had come to Aspe in the early eighteenth century through family relations with the titled nobility of the district, the Osorio Moscosos, the grandees of Elche. The Almadas were recognized as hidalgos.) José, the eldest, had followed in his uncle's footsteps in
the clergy. Antonio had studied mining at a school established by Charles III
at Cartagena to promote the revival of that industry in the peninsula. Neither
was unaware of the opportunities then emerging in northwestern New Spain.
Their uncle and mother had been preparing the youths for them for a number
of years.[93]

Reyes had been one of the Franciscan missionaries sent out to replace the
Jesuits in 1768. He was a most vocal critic of the existing conditions in the
province and of the policies that maintained them. He courted high officials,
advocating a series of reforms. In his "Sonora Manifiesto" to Viceroy Frey
Antonio María Bucareli in 1772, he detailed his criticisms of the extant
situation and his visions for the Northwest's future. Though a missionary
himself, he relegated what remained of Jesuit mission society to the far
northern frontier, those areas bordering the unconverted tribes. Neither did
he want the continuance of the settler society as it existed in the remaining
mission villages, presidial communities, and mining camps. He disdained what
he considered the transient, tasteless character of the hispanic settlements.[94]

What Reyes desired were reforms that would encourage the refined and
educated to come to the Northwest, permanently settle, and found towns
which would become directing centers for the society. Such urban communities were to be stimulated to engage in a variety of agricultural, mineral,
commercial, and industrial pursuits and to found educational institutions
where succeeding generations could be schooled in the liberal arts.[95] He
envisioned his nephews as being an important part of such a society and
wrote their mother about it periodically. He also intended to play an important role in it himself. Through the relationship cultivated with José de Gálvez, who became Minister of the Indies in 1776, he lobbied hard for the

---

[93] Stagg, *First Bishop of Sonora*, 2-5, 44-45. A third nephew decided to remain
behind in Spain with his parents.

[94] Kessell, 75-76; de los Reyes, "Sonora Manifiesto," *in* Stagg, *First Bishop of
Sonora*, 34-40.

[95] De los Reyes, "Sonora Manifiesto," *in* Stagg, *First Bishop of Sonora*, 41-43.

creation of a separate bishopric for the Northwest, and obtained a royal audience upon his return to the peninsula in 1778. When the see was created two years later, his appointment was a forgone conclusion.[96] At a simultaneous homecoming and leavetaking in his home town of Aspe, the bishop shared his vision for the Northwest. He told about the recent past there, the risks, the dangers (at one point even letting forth with an imitation of an Apache war whoop). But he spoke more of the future. Such a fine old church as that in which he was speaking could only be found in cities in New Spain. But with the help of God and the Crown, he expected one day to see such examples of urbanity and refinement on the northwestern frontier of the viceroyalty.[97]

The newcomers to Sonora and Sinaloa in the late eighteenth century like Bishop de los Reyes and the Almada brothers carried with them an urban tradition that dated back to at least the eleventh century. They were accustomed to such a lifestyle and sought to continue to live in similar environs; such a life was now possible, owing to the conditions of stability, expanding economic opportunities, and an enlarged administrative apparatus. For them, the town was the focal point of civilized society: the center of business, of learning, and of whatever level of culture society had achieved. Urban life was what they knew, what they wanted, and what they intended to recreate in the Northwest. As a consequence, towns began to emerge, fed by the growing non-Indian population—newcomers, veteran colonist families, and offspring of the growing miscegenation. The Crown encouraged this urban settlement on the frontier through a settlement law in 1791, which set aside generous amounts of land surrounding each presidio for assignment to permanent settlers.[98]

At least five population centers in Sonora and Sinaloa merited the label of towns by the end of the eighteenth century. (There had been small clusters of colonists previously, usually grouped around presidial garrisons and mining camps, but they had lacked the permanence, size, and level of economic and social complexity of the new centers of the late eighteenth century. There had been little commitment to fixed residence among the prior colonists, who had not really proceeded beyond frontier transience.)[99]

---

[96]Stagg, *First Bishop of Sonora,* 14, 45-60; Kessell, 149-153.

[97]Stagg, *First Bishop of Sonora,* 61-63.

[98]Brinckerhoff, 15. The settlement law set aside four square leagues (7,022.44 hectares) at each presidio for assignment to the settlers by the local commander, with the hope that the presidio would develop into a town. The receiver of the grant had to make full use of the land as a condition of ownership.

[99]This development clearly seems to be the case for Sonora and northern Sinaloa. For central and southern Sinaloa, however, it is not clear when the first towns emerged, since the available sources are too few and general to hazard more than a tentative conclusion. This region, like that to the north, experienced its first substantial economic expansion in the latter half of the seventeenth century with the growth of mining centers

The town of San Miguel de Horcasitas had grown up around the presidio of the same name. Clusters of settlers sprang up around and within the protective walls, joined by Indians from the surrounding area who left the mission pueblos to work for them. In time, San Miguel became the prosperous marketing center of a growing agricultural district.[100] Arizpe, a former mission village, had germinated as the first administrative center of the Provincias Internas (1776) and then of the Intendancy of Sonora and Sinaloa (1786). There were also numerous productive mines and developing farms and haciendas nearby.[101] Rosario, meanwhile, had become Sinaloa's most prosperous population center. Besides the stimulation from the mining boom in the surrounding district, the town monopolized the commerce of southern Sinaloa and what is now northern Nayarit.[102] In the old conquistador settlement of Culiacán a merchant community had emerged by the late eighteenth century. At the crossroads of commerce proceeding from Mexico City destined for Sonora and the Californias, the community dealt in merchandise from Spain, China, and the interior of New Spain. Development of its own agricultural district and of mines at Badiraguato and Cosalá in the neighboring foothills of the Sierra Madre further stimulated its commerce. The permanent

---

and agricultural districts to supply them. However, it did not experience the deep unrest and disorder of the mid-eighteenth century as did the areas to the north. Navarro García (*José de Gálves y la Comandancia General,* 120-121) briefly notes that mining in Sinaloa had lagged considerably through most of the eighteenth century. But an agricultural and stock-raising population of some importance had continued.

Nonetheless, the best hypothesis, given available evidence, is that the southern districts experienced a prolonged stagnation, from which they revived in the latter half of the eighteenth century with the influx of immigrants and the expansion of economic activities to the north. Nakayama's work on the history of the Rosario seems to support this interpretation. Another possibility is that the mining developments of the latter half of the seventeenth century were sustained through the whole of the eighteenth century. The demographic question correlates with the economic one—whether the southern region's population rose steadily after 1700, or whether it remained generally static until after 1770, as in the northern areas.

[100] Shull, 16, 25-27. Shortly after the presidio was moved to San Miguel in 1758 from its former site at Pitic, the residence of the governor was relocated there. The administrative capital was transferred to Arizpe in 1776, but by then the town's function as a marketing center had been firmly established.

Many of the farms and haciendas in the surrounding agricultural district were developed by Spanish immigrants. For example, Víctor Aguilar and his younger brother Dionisio, from a small town near Burgos, settled near San Miguel. Víctor married Ana María Escobosa, daughter of one of the town's principal families, and built up a prosperous hacienda. *Informaciones matrimoniales,* San Miguel, 1799, José Vélez Escalante to María Josefa Iñigo; Lieutenant R.W. Hardy, *Travels in the Interior of Mexico, 1825-1828* (London, 1829), 110. Hardy's work has been reprinted by Río Grande Press, 1977.

[101] Bancroft, *North Mexican States,* 688.

[102] Nakayama, *Documentos del Rosario,* 7.

location of the episcopal see there in 1799 made it the Northwest's ecclesiastical center. [103]

The most well-developed urban center in the Northwest was Alamos. The vigorous intervention of the Crown in the development of the region after 1767 had initiated a prolonged period of prosperity for Sonora's principal mining district. By the 1780s the town's population had grown to nearly five thousand inhabitants. Another three thousand were employed in the mining camps of Promontorios and Aduana; those in the other outlying settlements numbered about two thousand. The result was a thriving commerce which attracted enterprising merchants from Sinaloa and representatives of Mexico City and Guadalajara merchant houses, as well as immigrants from other areas of New Spain.

Large fortunes were made by the miners and merchants, who added to their holdings by building up large haciendas. The taste for luxury soon asserted itself: handsome, flat-roofed, porticoed residences were situated wall-to-wall along clean, cobblestone streets leading off the main plaza, which was attractively laid out in flower beds and palms. There was a broad alameda fashioned according to José de Gálvez's design, lined with spired poplars (*alamos*) from which the town took its name.[104] All bespoke the general air of growing wealth and refinement, of what such urban notables called progress.

One of the most prominent of the *alamense* gentry was Bartolomé Salido y Exodar, a peninsular who came to Alamos around 1770. He was soon named contador of the recently established treasury office, rising to the post of treasurer, which he held for many years. He was also the custodian of the Crown-owned mercury that was dispensed to the miners. As such, Salido's influence in the community was enhanced even further. Later, with the creation of the intendancy, he was appointed *subdelegado real* (royal deputy to the intendant) for the district. Salido married into the rich and influential Elias González family, most of whom moved to Arizpe, the capital of the new intendancy, where they became that town's most prominent and politically powerful family. The Salido residence in Alamos occupied a whole block. The colonnaded front patio, colorfully shaded by a variety of flowering shrubs, gave way to several high-ceilinged salons with red tile floors, carved wooden

---

[103] Navarro García, *Sonora y Sinaloa,* 38, 40-42, 51, 55, 67; Francisco R. Almada, *Diccionario de historia, geografía, y biografía sonorenses* (Chihuahua, 1952), 225, 452, 687, 701-702. Culiacán was located at the junction of one of the branches of the road from Durango to the east and the coastal road coming from Guadalajara that led north into Sonora.

The see of the newly created bishopric was never established in Arizpe as officially mandated (1783). The first bishop decided to reside in Alamos. His successor changed his residence to Culiacán, the third bishop moved the see to Rosario, and his successor returned it to Culiacán in 1799.

[104] Miles, 3-10; Stagg, *First Bishop of Sonora,* 74-75.

doors, and whitewashed walls and ceilings interrupted by dark beams and crystal chandeliers. Silverware, hand-painted porcelain, and crystal adorned the dining table.[105]

It was Salido who welcomed Bishop de los Reyes and his nephews on their approach to Alamos in 1783, inviting them to spend the night at the hacienda of his niece and ward, Luz de Alvarado y Elías González. De los Reyes was quite taken with the Salidos and their town, which he came to know well while delayed for several months in his journey to Arizpe (waiting for a military escort and for the rainy season to pass). Indeed, he decided to make his permanent residence there, rather than in the administrative capital. Raised in the urban tradition of the peninsula and a principal representative of the Crown's promotion of an enterprising, urban society, the region's first bishop not surprisingly fixed his ecclesiastical office in the population center that most epitomized the society then emerging in the Northwest. De los Reyes was influenced in this decision by the offer of the Alvarado family mansion, made by Luz de Alvarado and her uncle, to serve as his episcopal residence. The house, inherited by Salido's other niece (María Guadalupe), had been vacant since her husband had been transferred to the royal treasury office in Guadalajara. The bishop gave the absence of such a suitable residence in Arizpe as the reason for his request to approve the transfer, along with the more central location of Alamos in the diocese.[106]

Bishop de los Reyes did find Alamos deficient in one important regard: though recently erected, the modest, brick, parish church he judged to be unbefitting the impressive character of the rest of the town. The bishop shamed and cajoled the town's notables at every opportunity to promote the construction of a large stone church—a basilica—like that of his native Aspe. Once again, it was Bartolomé Salido who came to the bishop's assistance, proposing the appointment of a committee to raise funds. The persuasiveness of Salido's argument with fellow notables on behalf of a new church was rooted not only in spiritual and cultural pride, but as well in material concerns. Such an impressive ecclesiastical establishment might well tempt royal administrators to make Alamos the provincial capital, with an accompanying growth in population. Financial pledges were soon forthcoming. There being no professional architect as yet in Sonora, de los Reyes insisted that plans be secured from Spain. Two years later (1786) the plans for the basilica arrived: a baroque-styled edifice with twin towers. (The bishop supervised the construction with scrutiny until his death from pneumonia the following year.) De los Reyes also considered education a prerequisite of urbane society. He introduced the first formal schooling, setting up a primary school and a cátedra of

---

[105] Stagg, *First Bishop of Sonora,* 73-74, 76.
[106] *Ibid.,* 76-77, 81, 85.

Castillian and Latin grammar. This chair was filled by his nephew, Padre José Almada, who assumed the role of parish priest not long after.[107]

Meanwhile, the bishop's other nephew, Antonio, was becoming one of the wealthiest and most prominent men of Alamos. Upon learning of Almada's training in mining and metallurgy at their first meeting, Bartolomé Salido offered him the job of managing two mines in Promontorios inherited by his nieces. Within a year, Almada and Luz de Alvarado were married and he assumed direct control over the mines and her prosperous hacienda, Tapizuelas. Using his wife's inheritance as a base, the young Almada built his fortune in mines and land. He bought out his sister-in-law's share of the Peñasco mine in Promontorios, acquired the richest mine in Aduana (La Balbanera), and purchased the mines of El Trinidad (*real* of Yécora) in the foothills of the Sierra Madre bordering the upper Mayo Valley.[108] The Salidos and Elias González in-laws served as godparents for his four sons and one daughter, who each married into the principal families of the town.[109]

By the first decade of the nineteenth century the prolonged competition among the subsocieties in colonial Sonora and Sinaloa had ended. The two-hundred-fifty-year contention among the transient settler frontier, the Jesuit mission commonwealth, and the autonomous Indian tribal communities had given way to the permanent implantation of a Society more intensely enterprising and urban than in the Spanish colonial world in general. The Crown, under the Bourbons, had played a significant part in this transformation, having abandoned its traditional role of arbiter for that of advocate. The timing and intensity of that royal intervention had led to the development of this society along rather unique lines.

During almost the entirety of the colonial period, the province of Sonora and Sinaloa had been largely isolated from the rest of New Spain. In that relative isolation, the Jesuits' hold on the Indian tribes and the continuing security problem in the countryside had discouraged the formation of the

---

[107] *Ibid., 76, 85-86, 93; Almada, 687-688.* The basilica was completed in 1804, but with only a single tower.

[108] Albert Stagg, *The Almadas and Alamos, 1783-1867* (Tucson, 1978), 12-16. With the death of Colonel Francisco Julian de Alvarado and his wife, the couple's only two children, Luz and María Guadalupe, became wards of their mother's sister (Barbara Elías González de Zayas) and her husband, Bartolomé Salido. In addition to being a miner and hacendado, Alvarado was royal treasurer in Alamos, most likely Salido's immediate predecessor. Stagg, *First Bishop of Sonora*, 74.

[109] Stagg, *First Bishop of Sonora*, 92, 95; *idem, Almadas and Alamos*, 22-25. Ignacio wed one of Salido's daughters, while his elder brother José de Jesús married an Elías González. Almada's other two sons wed daughters of the Zavala and Quiros families. His lone daughter died in infancy.

Salido's children, like those of Almada, married into the emerging prominent families of the town: Palomares, Gil, Cevallos, and Ortiz. Almada, 639, 710-711.

more mixed, semi-feudal, and proportionately more rural society that generally predominated elsewhere in the viceroyalty. Consequently, the immigrants arriving after the mid-eighteenth century faced only a minimal resistance to forming the kind of society they had known back in the towns of northern and eastern Spain. The mission commonwealth had been broken and was disintegrating. The autonomous tribes had been brought into submission and the frontier secured. Sustained economic growth was finally being attained in the region under the stimulation of royal assistance. The result was the formation of a society of numerous small, genuinely urban population centers dominated by interlocking networks of interrelated, prominent families—like the Almadas of Alamos—who possessed entrepreneurial inclinations, a taste for refined living, and a strong sense of their hispanic origins. These enterprising people, drawn to the Northwest by its promise, transformed its potential into their own personal fortunes and left in the families they founded a societal legacy to the future states of Sonora and Sinaloa after independence.

2

Borrowed Time
(1810-1831)

Independence had paradoxical implications for Northwest New Spain. In its outward aspect, in the limited confines of the war for independence, it touched the Northwest less than any other region of the viceroyalty. Yet in its deeper sense, in the broadened framework created by the introduction of new historical forces and possibilities, it affected no other region of the new republic of Mexico more, with the possible exception of the Yucatán. The reason for this paradox lies in the late germination of an enduring hispanic society in the Northwest, nurtured by the reform policies of the Bourbon Crown.

The colonial experience in the province of Sonora and Sinaloa was at odds with the general pattern in New Spain. At the beginning of the nineteenth century the church was weak, particularly in regard to the lower clergy, from whose ranks came considerable support for the insurgent cause. The pattern of powerful haciendas, worked by resentful peones and opposed by independent villagers trying to retain their lands in the face of encroachment, had not yet become firmly entrenched. The Indians were still predominantly tribal, not having been fragmented into a decentralized, localized pattern of separated villages. They had been accorded special status and protection by the Crown, though the pressures of white encroachment had accelerated after the expulsion of the Jesuits. Therefore, they were not inclined, as were the Indians of central and southern Mexico, toward affiliating with the popular Creole-*casta* movement, led by Father Miguel Hidalgo and then by Father José María Morelos, which initiated the decade-long struggle for independence. Peninsulares and first generation Creole migrants made up a much larger percentage of the population in Sonora and Sinaloa than in other regions. Their support of the Crown was solid, since they were the chief beneficiaries of its policies. The *casta* element had not had time to develop a self-conscious and long-standing sense of grievance. The military presence, manifest in the presidial garrisons and in the frequent holding of royal offices by career officers, was formidable. Moreover, the bulk of the military establishment was, thus, composed of regulars, who were more loyal to the Crown than the Creole militia, which composed the bulk of the royal military force generally in the viceroyalty.

In the Northwest, then, Bourbon policies had successfully molded a new colonial society. Elsewhere in the viceroyalty, those same policies had falteringly striven to reform an existing, traditional colonial society.[1] Northwest New Spain was the Bourbons' own offspring, not a stepchild. Consequently, the ties between them were stronger than elsewhere in the face of emancipation pressures. The reality of separation, which had a strong effect on the economy and resulting politics of Sonora and Sinaloa, was likewise felt more profoundly.

The notables of the Northwest, and the populace in general, were living on borrowed time in the wake of independence. They were orphaned to a republican, externally oriented future for which they were little prepared, but which temptingly held great promise. The post-independence present was not of their making. Yet they had to come to terms with it if they were to make passage successfully to such a future. They could rely on their Bourbon past, which had so strongly nurtured them, but this temporal inheritance was limited; it was borrowed.

INDEPENDENCE AND THE FUTURE: ECONOMICS

No movement for emancipation was generated from within the Northwest, and only one real, direct intrusion came from without. In the winter of 1810-1811, an insurgent expedition led by José María González Hermosillo was sent by Father Hidalgo to win the Intendancy of Arizpe to the patriot cause. The expedition met with initial success in southern Sinaloa, the district most connected with the traditional Hapsburg colonial society and least characteristic of the new Bourbon colonial society in the Northwest. The rich mining town of Rosario was captured, the small royalist force defending it overwhelmed. San Sebastián fell uncontested. However, Intendant Alejo García Conde hurriedly marched south from Arizpe with reinforcements (including contingents of Opata Indians), rallied royalist forces, and turned the insurgent commander's uncoordinated frontal assault at San Ignacio into a rout. Hermosillo fled southward, his expedition in a shambles beyond repair. García Conde returned north, nipping the few rebel buds that had sprouted in northern Sinaloa in response to the Hermosillo expedition.[2]

---

[1] Two recent works illustrate the relation between existing regional societies and the course of the war for independence: Brading's *Miners and Merchants in Bourbon Mexico, 1763-1810* and Brian Hamnett's *Politics and Trade in Southern Mexico, 1750-1821* (Cambridge, 1971). Though it does not extend in coverage to the Independence War, James Lockhart and Ida Altman's *Early Provinces of Mexico* (Los Angeles, 1977), through a collection of regional studies, illustrates the varied pattern of traditional colonial society in other parts of New Spain.

[2] Stevens, viii-xiii, 52-53; Miguel Domínguez, *La Guerra de Independencia en las provincias Sonora y Sinaloa* (Hermosillo, 1949), 14-28. Hermosillo was a campesino

The Northwest remained quiet thereafter, firmly in royalist control. Morelos, who carried on and expanded the insurgent movement into southern Mexico following Hidalgo's capture and execution in the summer of 1811, made no second attempt to ignite the emancipation cause in the region. When the *casta* priest met a fate similar to that of his predecessor in 1815, the independence movement broke down into pockets of guerrilla resistance. In 1821 Agustín Iturbide, a Creole royalist commander, succeeded in uniting diverse groups behind a second independence movement, which proclaimed in its Plan de Iguala an independent, Catholic nation, one in which Spaniards and Mexicans would be equal and caste distinctions abolished. Only then, with the bulk of the royalist army coming under Iturbide's banner, did royalist officials in the Northwest one by one recognize the viceroyalty's independence by adhering to the Plan de Iguala.[3] In the wake of independence, and after three years of indecision about separation or union, Sonora and Sinaloa (since 1786 the Intendancy of Arizpe) were left joined in the new state of Occidente.[4]

While the social and political turmoil of the Independence War had penetrated the Northwest minimally, its economic dislocation had temporarily curtailed Sonora and Sinaloa's rapid economic expansion. Economic ties of the intendancy with the interior had begun to break down. Mining was particularly vulnerable. The price of quicksilver trebled and immediate payment was demanded. As tools and other supplies grew increasingly scarce and mine workers were laid off, production had dropped. Farmers and stock raisers, already hampered in finding markets, had been hit with special royal taxes imposed to support the war effort elsewhere. Merchants had found themselves cut off from the principal source of their trade (the interior) and their markets in the mining districts dwindling.[5]

---

from Jalisco, and his inexperience and lack of military savvy contributed to his failure. The small insurgent bands in northern Sinaloa, lacking arms and war supplies, waited in vain for the arrival of Hermosillo's liberating forces. Those not defeated by the intendant's return northward fled into the neighboring Sierra; protected by the rugged mountains, they remained in arms for several years.

An uprising at Charay, a pueblo in northern Sinaloa, was entirely indigenous. These tribal Indians were protesting the abuses of the whites (as other tribes had done a half century earlier), rather than supporting the insurgent cause.

[3] Interpretative studies on the independence struggle in Mexico include: Hugh M. Hamill, Jr., *The Hidalgo Revolt: Prelude to Mexican Independence* (Gainesville, 1966); Wilbert H. Timmons, *Morelos of Mexico: Priest, Soldier, Statesman* (El Paso, 1963); Romeo Flores Caballero, *La contra-revolución en la independencia: los españoles en la vida política, social y económica de México, 1804-1838* (México, 1969); Nettie Lee Benson, ed., *Mexico and the Spanish Cortes, 1810-1822* (Austin, 1966); W. S. Robertson, *Iturbide of Mexico* (Durham, N.C., 1952); and Doris M. Ladd, *The Mexican Nobility at Independence, 1780-1826* (Austin, 1976).

[4] Stevens, 54-66.

[5] Navarro García, *José de Gálvez y la Comandancia General*, 10, 86-90.

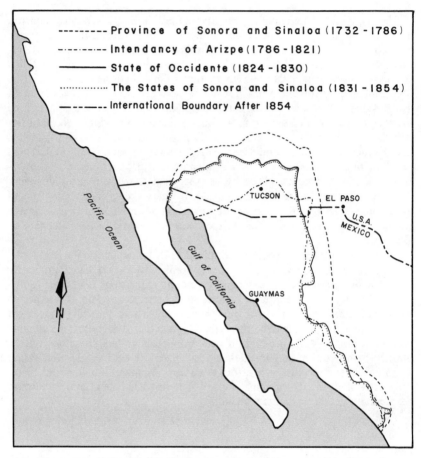

POLITICAL COMPOSITION OF THE REGION OF SONORA AND SINALOA. For two years following independence the Intendancy of Arizpe continued (governed by the intendant and a provincial deputation elected in February, 1822). In July, 1823, the constituent Congress of the new republic authorized the separation of Sonora and Sinaloa in response to petitions from a number of their leading citizens, especially those from Sonora. However, the federal constitution (promulgated the following February) recombined Sonora and Sinaloa to form the State of Occidente. Stevens, 54-66.

The Independence War had also begun to break down the region's economic isolation from the world beyond. That was far more enduring in its impact than the temporary economic dislocations resulting from the armed struggle. Foreign trade had been officially authorized for several years and increasingly carried on illegally during the course of the war.[6] After independence, the economy of Sonora and Sinaloa renewed its previous expansion, stimulated by the termination of Spanish market restrictions and the consequent growing foreign commercial contacts.[7] Within a decade, British commercial interests were calling for the permanent stationing of a British warship in that coastal region to provide security for foreign trade. Eustace Barron (at Tepic), the closest vice-consul to Sonora and Sinaloa, reported that the volume of precious metals—coined and uncoined—shipped from northwestern ports was sufficient to request such naval support. These same sentiments were voiced more strongly by Richard Yeoward, manager of a British import-export firm in Guaymas (Duff & Company). Noting that nothing tended to stimulate industry and enterprise so much as security, Yeoward suggested that instead of one British man-of-war, two should visit the western coast of Mexico every year. Well-to-do nationals and British businesspeople in the region would be spurred in their activities, he added, if such vessels were available as a kind of bank to safekeep funds, which by the late 1820s were quite considerable. United States commercial interests secured the establish- ment of a consulate in the Northwest in 1826 (at Mazatlán).[8]

The bulk of the expanding commerce after independence was with North American and European merchants involved in the India and China trade,

---

[6]*Ibid.*, 12.

[7]Stevens, 45-46. Guaymas was opened to foreign trade from 1811 to 1814 and again in 1820 (while the constitutionalists were in power in Spain). Moreover, Intendant García Conde and his subordinates frequently seemed inclined to permit foreign ships (predominantly North American during these years) to unload their goods. When they were not so inclined, or their permission was overruled by superiors, it was difficult to prevent the unloading, due to the weak defense of the coasts.

[8]*Ibid.*, 104-106. Though North American ships carried the majority of the trade during the war years, Stevens concludes that few North American ships at first dropped anchor in Mazatlán because of the hostility toward North Americans, reported by the first consuls there: local authorities did not permit the raising of the United States flag over the consulate for several years, and customs house officials were usually hostile. On at least one occasion a North American ship was attacked, and the consul fled the port for a time, fearing for his life. In time this hostility died away and North American ships traded in the port as frequently as European vessels.

This hostility seems to have derived from a general ill-will growing in Mexico during the 1820s and 1830s. The cautious, tardy granting of recognition following independence was followed by a further delay in the sending of an ambassador. And the United States' first envoy, Joel Poinsett, aroused considerable resentment by his zealous proselytization of United States political structure and his pronounced interference in internal Mexican politics, which climaxed in a public outcry for his removal in 1829. An even more important source for anti-United States feeling was the growing awareness and fear of that nation's territorial ambitions. Washington's representatives continually were instructed to seek out boundary adjustments that would have entailed the surrender of all or most of Texas; sometimes they even bluntly suggested that Mexico had proven unable to settle the northern frontier and that North Americans had every intention of doing so. Karl M. Schmitt, *Mexico and the United States: Conflict and Coexistence* (New York, 1974), 33-42.

now freed from the Veracruz-Mexico City-Acapulco monopoly. Silks, paper goods, refined sugar, cacao, coffee, tea, brandy, European and American manufactures, and whale oil were exchanged for silver bars, gold dust, minted coin, and to a far lesser extent wheat, hides, brazilwood, and pearl shells.[9] In New Mexico, Sonoran merchants encountered enterprising traders from Missouri, who were eager to exchange dry goods for mules and silver.[10] Inter-regional markets were also prospering. A steady trade in wheat, salt, hides, tallow, soap, and *panocha* (unrefined dark sugar) developed between northern and central Sonora and Baja California (by sea) and Chihuahua and New Mexico (by trains of pack mules). The merchants of central and southern Sinaloa cultivated an active trade in salt, seafood, and *panocha* with Durango, Jalisco, Chihuahua, and Zacatecas.[11]

Though specie and bullion predominated among the exports in this growing commerce, it did not signify that mining's recovery from the Independence War years was rapid or complete. Most of the mines previously worked had filled up with water and many of the shafts had caved in. The shortage of quicksilver, though not as severe as during the war, continued to keep prices high. The laborers who had drifted away the decade before were difficult to re-obtain. Many had become tied to the haciendas and farms through debt servitude, and those who were mobile required higher wages to return to the mines.[12] The lack of a casa de moneda forced the miners to exchange their *pastas* (bullion) for the minted currency received from other states at a discount. The alternative—shipping the metal to the closest mints (Durango and Guadalajara)—was just as expensive and had the added risk of much longer shipments.[13]

Under these conditions, mining failures were frequent. Those with little capital were forced to hunt and peck through abandoned mines, hoping to find an exposed vein or an outcropping, or to pan for gold and silver. Such was the case of three men who, in clearing away the rubbish at one end of the

---

[9] Henry G. Ward, *Mexico*, II (México, 1829), 313; Hardy, 458-459. Though Ward traveled through many parts of Mexico, he never reached Sonora or Sinaloa. His information concerning them is a summary of "Notes on the State of Sonora and Cinaloa [sic]," by Colonel Bourne, a fellow Englishman who traveled through the region in 1826. Ward included Bourne's account in the appendix to Volume II, pages 440-464; Ward's summary is found on pages 311-327.

[10] Hardy, 458-459.

[11] Stevens, 45, 47; Ward, II. 313.

[12] Ward, II, 449-455; José María Gaxiola, *Exposición sobre el estado actual de la administración pública del Estado de Occidente* (Guadalajara, 1829), 6, in microfilm collection of the Instituto Nacional de Antropología y Historia, Museo de Historia y Antropología (Mexico City), Sonora, Reel 23. Hereafter, this microfilm collection is abbreviated as MAHm.

[13] Juan M. Riesgo and Antonio J. Valdéz, *Memoria estadística del Estado de Occidente* (Guadalajara, 1828), n.p., MAHm, Sonora, Reel 2.

shaft of an old mine near Nacosari, found a pillar left from supporting previous workings, from which they extracted ore worth 70,000 pesos. Yet failing immediately to find the principal vein, the three split the money and quit the venture.[14] Such strokes of luck brought only ephemeral returns, never permanent fortunes. They paid off for those who, like the three gamblers above, were smart enough to quit the game early. For those for whom the temptation was too great, the mines proved a bottomless pit into which they poured their money. The commander general of the state of Occidente, General José Figueroa, and an old peninsular, Carlos Lavandera, were among the tempted. Despite an expensive outlay, the silver mine Figueroa worked near Babiácora (which had formerly produced a great deal of ore) yielded him little. Lavandera sank enormous sums into the Antonio de la Huerta mine to drain its shafts but gained next to nothing in return.[15] What was required were large amounts of capital that could clear away flooded shafts, repair their supports, and then sustain extensive operations until the veins began to pay. The only places where such funds were concentrated were the wealthy pre-independence mining centers—Rosario, Cosalá, and Alamos.

Though the owners of the principal mine in Rosario were unable to drain its main shafts completely, they succeeded in keeping the upper portion of the shafts clear of water and extracted silver from them with some profit. The miners of Cosalá were more successful, and not a few—most notably Francisco Iriarte—derived lucrative returns. Iriarte's celebrated Nuestra Señora de Guadalupe mine contained a vein of gold of considerable breadth and was free of water. He declined numerous offers to buy the mine, one by a group of foreign investors for a reported one million pesos.[16] The mines around Alamos were worked extensively and regularly; they belonged to many different proprietors, most of whom owned small shares. The princes of this mineral domain were the four Almada brothers. Using the capital accumulated by their father,[17] they amassed considerable wealth—each was said to possess at least a half million pesos.[18] The principal base for their fortune

---

[14] Ward, II, 455.

[15] Hardy, 126-127.

[16] Ward, II. 451. According to Colonel Bourne, Iriarte reportedly stashed a million pesos in gold and silver in his house, though he himself seems to have led a rather Spartan life. Perhaps his lifestyle explains his response to the various offers for his mine: Bourne reported that Iriarte, a relative of President Guadalupe Victoria, told prospective buyers that he did not want the money, and that even if he did, "he could take out of his mine double the amount of anything that they could give, in less time than they would themselves require to raise the money." (From independence until after the Intervention, one peso approximately equaled a dollar.)

[17] Ward, II, 457.

[18] Hardy, 176.

was the Balbanera mine in the *real* of Promontorios, reportedly yielding as much as 60,000 pesos monthly.[19]

All of these successful miners found the most profitable outlet for their refined ore through connections with foreign merchants and shippers, and they frequently circumvented customs duties. An example of this arrangement is seen in the copper mines worked by Francisco Escobosa and Ignacio Loaiza about twenty-five miles east of San Miguel de Horcasitas. Loaiza, a merchant of Pitic, owned a hacienda on which the mines were located. Excobosa, whose family also lived in Pitic, was then administrator of the *aduana* (customs house) in the port of Guaymas. These particulars made for a profitable partnership, given the extensive contraband then going on in the port and along the coasts of the Northwest. The valuable commodity was not the copper ore, but the portion of gold contained in it. The art of separating the two metals was well developed in China, and the Chinese ships that occasionally put into Guaymas paid a high price for the copper ore. Mules from Loaiza's hacienda were used to haul the ore to the port and returned laden with merchandise with which he stocked his commercial operation in Pitic.[20]

Such a pattern suggests that the connection between mining and foreign interests was limited to commerce in the Northwest during these first years after independence. In other parts of Mexico during the 1820s, foreign merchants in Sonora and Sinaloa, however, restricted their dealings to providing markets for the refined ore of mines worked by nationals. This trade was more profitable than what the miners had been able to obtain during the colonial period.

Markets for agriculture were also now more profitable and extensive, and, unlike mining, agriculture's recovery was easier and more thorough. The Altar, Magdalena, San Miguel, Sonora, Oposura, and Bavispe river valleys of northern and central Sonora became the breadbasket of the Northwest. The haciendas and farms there—both those established in the late colonial period and new ones—sent wheat down the Pacific coast as far south as Panama, across the gulf to Baja California, and around the Sierra Madre to Chihuahua and New Mexico. Some livestock on the hoof was driven to these latter areas, but most caravans and vessels were sent to these markets laden with livestock by-products: hides, tallow, salted beef, finished leather goods, candles, and soap. Foreign merchants handled most of this trade along the coast, and with the profits derived from it, many hacendados and farmers made improvements to increase production. New lands were cultivated, small irrigation works were constructed, and water-powered mills erected. Stock raisers expanded their operations to the broad basin grasslands to the north of these

---

[19] Stagg, *Almadas and Alamos*, 18-22, 65-67.
[20] Ward, II, 447; Hardy, 93, 411.

river valleys. In southern Sonora expansion of commercial agriculture was considerably less.[21] There, Yaqui and Mayo tribal autonomy was strong and the villagers' stubborn resistance prevented significant access to the fertile bottom lands of the Yaqui and Mayo valleys. Prospective landowners nibbled away at the fringes of these tribal lands with minimal success and considerable risk.

The principal laborers of these haciendas and farms, as well as in the mines, were the Opatas, Pimas, Yaquis, and Mayos. The Indian laborers received three reales (then 37½ cents) a day and weekly rations. In addition they were usually the carpenters, masons, shoemakers, tanners, weavers, etc., whether in the towns or on the haciendas. The Opatas largely confined themselves to northeast Sonora, while the Pimas stayed in the central districts, but they were both increasingly assimilated into the growing mestizo and white population. Though many members of their tribes were scattered over other parts of Sonora, the Yaquis and Mayos maintained a strong tribal identity and organization, especially the Yaquis. No matter where they were, they considered themselves residents of the pueblos of the two valleys, periodically returning to them for annual fiestas and to aid relatives.[22]

One of Sonora's principal hacendados was Joaquín A. Astiazarán, whose hacienda (La Labor) lay in the fertile San Miguel de Horcasítas valley between the town of the same name and Pitic. Astiazarán had come to the Northwest from Spain in the last years of the colonial era and married into San Miguel's wealthiest family, the Iñigos.[23] In the early 1820s he acquired the hacienda from his father-in-law, through his wife's inheritance.[24] His brother-in-law, Manuel Iñigo Ruiz, owned a large hacienda in the same district and a merchant house in town.[25] With such family support, Astiazarán soon made his lands very productive. Fifteen thousand pesos were expended in 1825 to cut a canal from the river, "by which means he could irrigate so

---

[21] Stevens, 29-30, 45; Ward, II, 444-452. Numerous examples of land acquisitions and the creation of large stock ranches by notables in the post-independence years are given in Ray H. Mattison, "Early Spanish and Mexican Settlements in Arizona," *New Mexico Historical Review,* 21 (October, 1946), 285-325. Among the most prominent were several branches of the Elías González family.

In addition to the grants of land made by the Crown, and later by the republican governments, lands could be acquired by payment of the price of the original grant plus the cost of the survey. Another (and probably more frequent) method employed was simply to occupy unused lands of the Indian pueblos and then—through a bribe, manufactured legal documents, personal influence, or a combination of these methods—legalize the occupation in the courts.

[22] Ward, II, 449, 458.

[23] Almada, 90.

[24] Fernando A. Galaz, *Dejaron huella en el Hermosillo de ayer y hoy* (Hermosillo, 1971), 100.

[25] Almada, 405.

considerable a quantity of land that he expected to realize the sum annually."
In his orchard trees were grafted to improve the quality and yield of the fruit,
and his library contained a variety of treatises on agriculture.[26] Two British
travelers who lodged there felt at home. They noted in their journals that
Don Joaquín had the appearance of an English country squire,[27] that the
new, red-bricked main house "strongly resembled the very large comfortable
farms in some parts of England," and that the extensive grounds and gardens
surrounding the house were laid out "in the English style."[28] Their host
served them dinner on silver plate, offering them "the best of wines," old
Catalonian brandy, and choice liquors. "Everything was of a piece in this
comfortable establishment, for the beds with which they provided us were
most luxurious."[29]

Though there were farms and haciendas in each of the Sinaloan river valleys (which ran from the Sierra Madre to the Pacific coast at regular inter-
vals), commercial agriculture beyond the local level generally was not significant, and where it was, markets were confined to neighboring regions. The
agricultural district surrounding the town of Culiacán, at the confluence of
the Humaya and Tamazola rivers (which join to become the Río de Culiacán),
was favored by extensive, fertile bottomland.[30] Its main markets were the
reviving mining districts to the east and south, in western Durango as well as
Sinaloa, especially that of Cosalá. The Chametla region south of Rosario had
an abundance of livestock, which supplied the mining centers around Rosario
and Concordia (formerly San Sebastian). The district also satisfied the demand for salt and seafood not only of neighboring districts but of many areas
in Jalisco, Chihuahua, Zacatecas, and Durango as well.[31] In the north (the
only part of Sinaloa settled by missions) the villagers of the various tribes still
held most of the good agricultural lands, in particular the Mayos in the Fuerte
valley.

The urban demographic pattern reflected the resurgence of economic activity in this first decade after independence. The growing foreign and coastal
trades were funneled through the infant ports of Mazatlán and Guaymas.
Both had been little more than landings before 1820, but by 1826 Mazatlán

---

[26]Ward, II, 446; Hardy, 109. Hardy, a commissioner of the General Pearl and Coral
Company (based in England) was sent in 1825 to superintend the company's pearl
fishing operations in the Gulf of California. By 1827 Hardy had decided that it was a
waste of money and time to continue such activities after two unsuccessful cruises, and
he left for Mexico City via Chihuahua.

[27]Hardy, 109.

[28]Ward, II, 446.

[29]*Ibid.*

[30]*Ibid.*, 460.

[31]Riesgo and Valdés, n.p.

was the leading Mexican port of the Pacific coast, with Guaymas fourth behind San Blas and Acapulco.[32]

Guaymas was physically the more developed of the two during this period. It possessed the best natural harbor on the Mexican Pacific coast, sheltered from all winds by the elevated hills surrounding the bay and by an island lying at the entrance, which left a narrow channel of deep water as the only outlet to the gulf. A customs house was erected there in 1823. Mazatlán fared poorly by comparison: its harbor possessed many dangerous shoals and islands at its entrance and was particularly unsafe when strong winds arose. Moreover, though it was opened to commerce in 1820, an *aduana* was not located there until 1828.[33] Nevertheless, the long-term advantage lay with Mazatlán. Guaymas was located well up the coast of the Gulf of California, which meant foreign ships had to backtrack to clear the Baja peninsula in order to resume their shipping routes. Increasingly, foreign shippers preferred to unload their cargoes at Mazatlán, situated near the mouth of the gulf, and then ship them in smaller coastal vessels to Guaymas.[34] This geographic reality was soon reflected in trade volume figures.[35]

European and North American merchants began establishing themselves in the two ports with the termination of colonial restrictions on commerce, marrying daughters of prominent families of the interior urban centers. A Mr. Short, an English merchant, married the daughter of Francisco Iriarte, the wealthy Cosalá miner, and settled in Mazatlán.[36] Another Englishman, Thomas Spence, set up a commercial house in Guaymas and married Carmen García. His wife's father, a *peninsular*, had only recently settled in the port himself.[37] In the 1820s, his move was the exception for members of prominent families in the important interior towns.

---

[32] *Balanza general del comercio marítimo por los puertos de la República Mexicana, 1825-1826 (México, 1827, 1828)*, 138, 182. In 1826, the value of foreign trade received in the four leading Pacific ports was: Mazatlán, 689,922 pesos; San Blas, 503,669 pesos; Acapulco, 340,481 pesos; and Guaymas, 290,180 pesos.

[33] Ward, II, 442-443; Estaquio Buelna, *Compendio histórico, geográfico, estadístico del Estado de Sinaloa* (México, 1877), 75. The customs house was first established in Rosario, then moved to the Presidio of Mazatlán (about 40 kilometers inland from the port), and finally located in the port itself in 1828.

[34] Ward, II, 442-443.

[35] *Balanza general del comercio*, 138, 182.

[36] Hardy, 80.

[37] *Ibid.*, 90; Archivo General de Gobierno del Estado de Sonora, Justicia Civil, Actos de Matrimoniales, Libro 3 (Guaymas, 1873), 61. Selections from the latter source have been compiled by the Biblioteca y Museo de Sonora in Hermosillo.

There are numerous examples of foreign merchants who settled in Mazatlán and Guaymas in the above works and in Ward.

A few foreign merchants settled in the interior towns, among them John Johnson. A Kentuckian, Johnson had come to the Southwest in 1827 by way of Missouri and the Santa Fe trail as a member of a wagon train. He engaged in yearly trading trips between

Foreign merchants such as Short and Spence recognized the future of such commercial centers. It was easy for them to do so; they had no roots or past to persuade them otherwise. But for the notables of the inland towns the shifting trade patterns were not all clear and definite, the hold of their own origins on them yet too firm. Their parents, or they themselves, had implanted urban, hispanic society in the Northwest. They had sunk more into the towns they had founded than their capital. Their roots were firmly imbedded there. Family connections had become increasingly interwoven. These towns had become focal points of refinement, education, social position, and political power. It was not easy for the most prominent citizens of these centers of society to pick up and move elsewhere unless intense pressures (either as incentives or threats) forcefully indicated the logic of such an action. Consequently, by the end of the first decade after independence, both ports were still little more than receiving and shipping points for the real commercial centers, which lay inland—Pitic, Rosario, Culiacán, and Alamos. It was in these inland towns that merchants (almost always Mexican) maintained or established their commercial houses. By 1830 each of the four urban centers had a population variously estimated at 5,000 to 7,000.[38]

Pitic experienced a meteoric rise after independence. Hardy labeled it "the chief residence of the most opulent merchants of Upper Sonora."[39] In the early 1770s, the Crown had directed the construction of the first formal irrigation works in Sonora for the settlers of the former presidio, which was revived for a time after 1779. The town had remained basically a community center for a growing agricultural district through the late colonial period.[40] But with the opening of Guaymas to foreign commerce, Pitic, situated near the important junction of the Horcasitas and Sonora rivers, rapidly became the depot of commerce for the whole of central and northern Sonora, where

---

Sonora and New Mexico through 1831, making the former mission town of Oposura in northeast Sonora (renamed Moctezuma in 1825) the center of his business interests. By 1836 Johnson had been joined by half a dozen North American traders. Johnson married Delfina Gutiérrez, the daughter of a local notable, and began turning his attention to the acquisition of mining properties at San Marcial in the center of the state. Rex Strickland, "The Birth and Death of a Legend—The Johnson 'Massacre' of 1837," *Arizona and the West*, 18 (Autumn, 1976), 265-269.

[38]Ward, vol. 2, 320, 440-464, *passim;* Hardy, 78-430, *passim;* Riesgo and Valdés, n.p., *passim.* Estimating the population of these urban centers is tenuous, and by all means inexact. Riesgo and Valdés, natives of the region, estimated the population of the four leading towns at 5,000 to 7,000. Ward's source, Colonel Bourne, seems to have estimated too high (Pitic, 8,000 and Culiacán, 11,000), most likely because he included the population of the surrounding district. Alamos, which was situated in more broken terrain, was given a population of 6,000, which would seem to verify the estimates of Riesgo and Valdés for the four leading towns. Hardy also agrees with this figure of 6,000 for Alamos.

[39]Hardy, 95.

[40]Calvo Berber, 113; Almada, 344.

all imported goods were exchanged for the products of the interior. A good part of the latter came from the prosperous and well-cultivated agricultural district surrounding the town.[41]

The town's swift ascent to prominence left it somewhat helter-skelter: the streets were irregular, the houses scattered in all directions, "with as little attempt at order as if they had blown together in a storm."[42] In the eye of the storm was the traditional Spanish town center—a plaza with a church on one side and some commodious residences on the others in which the town's wealthy merchants and hacendados lived. The family of mining entrepreneur and customs official Francisco Escobosa lived in one of the best of these homes,[43] next to that of Francisco Monteverde, one of the richest merchants in Pitic. Monteverde's stylish residence was adorned with a great number of paintings and prints as well as fine furnishings. Radiating out from the town center were the irregular streets, lined with one-story adobe buildings, giving way farther on to shacks and shanties, usually inhabited by the Indians who worked in and around town. In 1828, the state legislature renamed the town Hermosillo, in honor of the Northwest's sole (though unsuccessful) independence hero.[44]

What Hermosillo was to Guaymas, Rosario was to Mazatlán. A prosperous mining and commercial center in the late colonial period, the opening of Mazatlán to foreign commerce made Rosario the trade center for merchandise which entered through the port. Merchants from Durango and Jalisco, as well as those from Sinaloa, came to the town to purchase their stocks. There were numerous merchant houses in the town and many artisan shops, among them gold- and silversmiths. Rosario was also the chief federal administrative center of the state of Occidente (Sonora and Sinaloa), including the location of the *aduana* until 1826. Though the configuration of the city was somewhat irregular, there were houses built of stone, a plateresque parish church with a splendid altarpiece, three chapels, and not a few cobbled streets.[45]

---

[41] Hardy, 95; Ward, II, 446.

[42] Ward, II, 445.

[43] Hardy, 99. Another side of the plaza was usually occupied by the casa municipal. Hermosillo, however, was too recently elevated to the rank of municipio to have erected such a permanent edifice.

Monteverde, a native of Italy, had come to New Spain as part of the retinue of Viceroy Branciforte in the mid-1790s. Falling out of the viceroy's favor, he had migrated to Sonora, where he made a large fortune in mining. With this capital Monteverde had first dabbled in pearl fishing in the gulf and then settled down in Hermosillo to pursue commerce. Eduardo W. Villa, *Galería de sonorenses ilustres* (Hermosillo, 1948), 111.

[44] Almada, 344.

[45] Ward, II, 441; Nakayama, *Documentos del Rosario,* 8, 52. Located in the town were the *juzgado de distrito* (federal district court), the *comisario general de hacienda* (the office of the federal treasury), and an assaying office, in addition to the *aduana.*

Culiacán, without fanfare, had over the previous thirty years gradually raised itself to a position where it was now able to rival Rosario as the leading town in Sinaloa. It shared in the expansion of commerce created by the opening of the region to foreign trade. The town's surrounding agricultural district and neighboring mining *reales* provided products for export and markets for import. There was additionally untroubled access to the coast (level terrain and a distance of only 62 kilometers). Contraband was thus relatively easy and quite profitable. And even those who abided by the law found the cost of coastal shipping up from Mazatlán inexpensive compared to overland freight charges from the port to the interior markets of central Sinaloa. Looking to the future, Culiacán's more central location gave it a stronger claim than Rosario to being the capital of whatever political entities were established as a result of independence. By the late 1820s a number of merchants were in the town and commerce had made "visible progress."[46]

The town had grown slowly in an orderly fashion, with a grid network of amply wide streets extending out from the central plaza, which was surrounded "by the fine houses of the principal inhabitants." The old and "capacious" church contained "some respectable paintings." The leading families, as did those in the other urban centers of the Northwest, though not to quite the same degree, prided themselves on the purity of their ancestral blood. Dating from the 1530s, Culiacán had been the first hispanic settlement in Sinaloa, though its transformation into a valid urban center did not occur until the eighteenth century. Caution was duly exercised before admitting others to this privileged circle. The Martínez and Vega families apparently preferred to take no risk. Four of the Martínez daughters married four Vega brothers, "and the youngest daughter [was] waiting for another Vega, who [was] too young to marry."[47]

Despite these challenges Alamos remained the most eminent town in Occidente. Its relatively rich mines and extensive local commerce had spawned a significant number of wealthy families. The bulk of their wealth came from the numerous silver *reales* near the town and to the east into the border area of neighboring Chihuahua. Commercial profits lay not in the geographic extension of markets, but in the intensive markets deriving from the mining development nearby and the large amount of money possessed by the town's notables. The principal miners recovered some of their expenses by operating company stores, selling merchandise to their laborers, and filling the mule trains for their trip back home to the mine. They bought up a good part of the imported merchandise brought from Guaymas, alcoholic beverages, and a variety of other articles produced in the agricultural districts of the nearby

---

[46]Riesgo and Valdés, n.p.
[47]Ward, II, 460.

Yaqui and Mayo valleys for sale to the workers. Often, a good portion of that local produce came from their own haciendas.[48]

The appearance of the town mirrored the opulence of its leading inhabitants and the luxury in which many of them lived.[49] Its elegant stone church was the finest in the Northwest. Complementing it were the sumptuous residences of the principal miners, merchants, and hacendados (not infrequently the three in combination), which surrounded the central plaza on the other three sides. These houses, built of stone or brick and stuccoed white, were constructed on a uniform plan, each fronted by a portal of connected arches. There were a goodly number of cobbled streets, the cleanliness of which was seen in few of the Mexican towns of that day. At one end of the town was the alameda, a promenade formed of connecting lanes, lined with poplars and interspersed with stone benches.[50] On Sunday afternoons and on feast days, it became the stage for an ostentatious show of wealth. The town's prominent families went out in mule-drawn carriages "exquisitely dressed; and after driving round and round . . . till the poor mules became both tired and giddy, they return, enter their houses while a fresh pair of mules are put to the coach, and then go back and tire these also in the same way."[51]

In addition to these principal urban centers, a number of small towns had sprung up as market centers for the newly expanding agricultural districts: Oposura, Ures, Altar, and Sahuaripa in Sonora; Fuerte, Mocorito, Sinaloa, and San Ignacio in Sinaloa. There were also the mining centers of Cosalá, Baroyeca, and San Sebastian (renamed Concordia in 1828). The formerly important population centers of San Miguel de Horcasitas and Arizpe declined to this status. From the somewhat contradictory estimates available, the populations of the larger of these urban centers (Arizpe, Horcasitas, Oposura, Cosalá, Concordia, Fuerte, and Guaymas) in the late 1820s were 2,000 to 3,000; while those of the smaller ones (Mazatlán, Sahuaripa, Baroyeca, Mocorito, Sinaloa, Ures, San Ignacio, and Altar) were between 1,000 and 2,000.[52]

---

[48]*Ibid.*, 458; Hardy, 171, 176-178. The interconnection of economic activities can be seen in the arrangements worked out by the Almada family in Stagg, *Almadas and Alamos,* 21-24.

[49]Hardy, 171-172; Stagg, *Almadas and Alamos,* 32-33, 44-45, 49-50.

[50]Stagg, *Almadas and Alamos,* 25-28; Ward, II, 457-458.

[51]Hardy, 173-174. Hardy characterized the *alamenses* as haughty and provincial in their display of wealth: "There is in the appearance and manners of the inhabitants of Alamos a degree of repulsive stiffness and formality, which can only result from a super abundance of wealth . . . and a supercilious contempt for every one who is supposed to be poor. They attempt all the awkward courtesies which are peculiar to the unpolished . . . ."

[52]*Ibid.*, 74-430, *passim;* Ward, vol. 2, 440-464, *passim;* Riesgo and Valdés, n.p., *passim.* The same type of overestimate of the population of the large urban centers by Bourne (in Ward) occurs in regard to these smaller ones, while Hardy, in the few he provides, gives much lower figures. The estimates of Riesgo and Valdés again seem the most reliable.

INDEPENDENCE AND THE PAST: PROBLEMS OF SECURITY

The opening of Sonora and Sinaloa to foreign commerce was the prime stimulus for economic expansion after independence and the resulting spread and deepening of urban life. The future ran strong through the historical current then at work shaping the course of the Northwest's history. Yet the urban demographic pattern, which reflected that economic resurgence, also revealed that this new force—the erosion of the region's isolation from the world beyond—had so far not been more than marginal in its impact. The points of external contact remained limited and almost wholly economic, centered in the embryonic ports of Guaymas and Mazatlán. Foreign contact brought a return to expanding opportunity and growing prosperity, but the second generation of urban notables were essentially building upon the pattern of life instituted by their parents. They seem to have been ready to place their expectations in such a future, but not yet their reliance on it. As a consequence, the past had a heavier bearing on the region's post-independence present.

The underlying foundations for the extension and prosperity of this enterprising, urban-centered society remained the peace and order established by the Spanish Crown in the late colonial period. Its leaders, the notables, would discover this only too soon. When the frontier had been secured, when the tribal Indians had been subdued and quieted, when the clerical establishment had been reoriented toward the promotion of such a society and supported accordingly, only then had that society crystallized and prospered. It was within that underlying framework that the stimulus of direct contact with the world beyond was presently rejuvenating the society's economy and indirectly accelerating its growth as a whole.

Royal administration, however, was now gone. Through indifference and ignorance, the new national government was unwilling to fulfill that crucial support role. The world beyond, in the form of external markets and in the person of foreign merchants, was narrowly concerned with profits. Most of these merchants could not see past their ledgerbooks to the underlying basis of the society's well-being. The few that could lacked the necessary broad commitment to the region. As passersby they merely commented on the situation and came forth with occasional speculative warnings. The foundation was beginning to crack.

The expansion of agriculture and stock raising in northern Sonora and the concurrent emergence of district market towns were animated by the appearance of enlarged and more profitable markets. Nonetheless, what made these developments possible was a frontier free of raids by hostile Apaches further north—a condition previously obtained and preserved through a strong, well-organized presidial system.

The presidial system, however, had begun to erode during the war years. Troop discipline had relaxed, the punctual payment of wages had been interrupted, and the shortage of minted coins had led to the use of *pagares* (paper notes) and effects as substitutes. Presidial officers had made fat profits obtaining provisions on credit and then selling them to the soldiers at exorbitant prices or by discounting the *pagares*.[53] With independence, the support of the presidios was left by default to the states, whose resources were meager in comparison to the level of expenditures the Crown had been able to provide. The soldiers were underfed, underclothed, poorly equipped, and were owed large amounts in back pay. What wages they did receive were almost always in *pagares* and effects. Corruption worsened, morale plummeted, soldiers began abandoning their presidial companies, and the caliber of the men declined.[54] Criminals were sentenced to service in the presidios and many officers were sent to the Sonoran frontier out of fear of their personal popularity and ambitions.[55] The lag between the disintegration of the presidial defense structure and the perception of the Apaches that they could once again raid successfully allowed economic expansion to take place during the 1820s. It did not, however, guarantee its continuance.

The church had been an important element in the maintenance of peace among the converted tribes of Sonora and northern Sinaloa living under Spanish rule. After the Jesuits' expulsion, it had served as a cementing force between the tribal Indians and non-Indians. But by 1827, only eighteen Franciscan friars remained in the missions of Pimería Alta, which were a supporting arm of the presidios on the northern frontier. The federal expulsion of the peninsulares that year reduced the number even further.[56] The accelerating influx of settlers reached the point that containment of encroachment on mission property was becoming next to impossible. There was no longer any legal mandate for governmental assistance, for Occidente's constitution made no mention of the missions. The state's politicos were unable to decide what to do with them—whether to tolerate them as buffers or suppress them and inherit their land and neophyte labor.[57]

---

[53] Ignacio Zúñiga, *Rápida ojeada al Estado de Sonora, Territorios de California y Arizona, 1835* (México, 1948), 51-55. Zúñiga's work was originally published in 1835 in Mexico City, and is also available in facsimile in Daniel J. Weber, ed., *Northern Mexico on the Eve of the United States Invasion: Rare Imprints* (Arno, 1976).

[54] Carlos Espinosa de los Monteros, *Exposición sobre las Provincias de Sonora y Arizona* (México, 1823), n.p., MAHm, Sonora, Reel 2; Stevens, 129. In 1821, Iturbide gave orders to continue the presidios on the same basis as before, but the imperial government failed to provide for their needs. Sonoran complaints to the succeeding federal government resulted only in the realignment of authority in 1826. By default, the maintenance of the presidios was left to the state.

[55] Hardy, 101-102. Criminals from the interior of Mexico were sentenced to serve in the presidios besides those committing crimes in Sonora and Sinaloa, where there was no state prison to confine them on a permanent basis.

[56] Stevens, 110.

[57] Kessell, 259-260, 263-277.

The secular parishes in the rest of Sonora and Sinaloa fared no better. By the mid 1820s the properties left by the Jesuits were almost completely gone and support from the government was sparse. As a result, except for those who lived in the main urban centers under the affluent care of the notables, most of the parish priests barely had enough to live on.[58] In the main towns, sons of prominent families such as Juan Elías González in Arizpe, Manuel María Encinas in Ures, Juan Francisco Escalante in Hermosillo, and José de Jesús Salido in Alamos staffed the parish churches.[59] Elsewhere, vacancies were extremely difficult to fill. When recruits could be found, they were very often those who had earned bad reputations elsewhere in the country: ". . . it was as common in Mexico to banish a friar to a Yaqui ecclesiastical establishment, as any other culprit to the frontier presidios."[60]

Far more important than the presidios and the church in the preservation of order among the converted tribes of Sonora and northern Sinaloa by the end of the colonial period had been the special status accorded the tribes by the viceroyal government. They had not been subject on the local level to control by whites and mestizos; rather, they had had a direct, separate relationship with the viceroyal authority. Their pueblos had elected their own local officials, including a captain-general, who exercised an undefined authority as head of the tribe, but in practice was responsible to the intendant. The payment of the *tributo* had not been collected, and in their pueblos the Indians had been generally free of other royal taxes. Moreover, though often fighting a losing battle, the Crown at least had made a concrete commitment to maintain the pueblos' communal lands.

The new Republic of Mexico, however, saw the Indians in a different light. Their separate, generally downtrodden status as wards of the Crown was a striking reminder of the colonial past. They did not fit into the new republican society with their restricted dress and residence, their assigned tributes, the prohibition from their entering the priesthood, and other restrictions. They were now declared to be equal citizens with whites and mestizos. But as equal citizens, the Indians were to be part of the same local government (subject directly to local and state officials) and to pay the same taxes. The new republican regime expressed much less concern about protecting the Indians' lands. In fact, it desired to break up their communal lands and make them individual farmers. In the new federal system such questions were left to the states, whose governments were in the hands of those who at best believed such communal ownership unproductive, and at worst desired to obtain such lands for their own use. Mexico City not only was unsympathetic

---

[58] Hardy, 444; Riesgo and Valdés, n.p. A priest's duties were hardly enviable, especially in Sonora, where some parishes reached 90 to 120 miles in extent.

[59] Almada, 241-712, *passim*.

[60] Hardy, 439.

to the maintenance of the Indians' communal lands, but also abdicated its responsibility in the matter.[61] It did not take the tribal Indians in the region long to realize the implications of this new republican order—that they were being given the short end of the stick.

Of all the tribes, the Yaquis and Mayos had enjoyed the widest latitude of self-government under the viceroyalty. Now, with independence, they watched their special autonomy chipped away. They were not allowed to elect deputies from among themselves to participate in either the national Congress or the state legislature.[62] Tribal government was being replaced by geographical government, with local officials under the thumb of the state's department (district) functionary. Non-Indians (whom the two tribes called *yoris*) had begun moving into the Yaqui and Mayo valleys. Some were settling in the pueblos themselves, but most were establishing farms and haciendas on the edges of the villages' lands, gradually nibbling away at them.[63] A tax was levied on trade between the pueblos.[64] In 1825, assessors appeared in the villages to measure land and value property for tax purposes (the tithe principally). The tribes in response sent a delegation to the state authorities to appeal this action, citing their traditional exemption from such taxes. When the state government answered their protests by sending troops to enforce the assessment and arrest those leaders who had opposed the taxation, the two tribes had had enough.[65]

Led by Juan Ignacio Jusacamea, commonly called Juan Banderas, the Yaquis attacked the farms, haciendas, and mining camps of southern and central Sonora in the fall of 1825. Livestock, gold, silver, merchandise, and other booty were sent back to enrich the pueblos. With this inducement and his own eloquence, Banderas secured the active support of the Mayos the following spring. Some of the Opata chiefs to the north were sympathetic but remained neutral. As the two tribes carried their destructive raids southwards towards Fuerte, the legislature, in an unnecessary panic, moved the capital

---

[61] The state legislatures generally passed laws denying Indians special communal ownership rights, a position the federal government supported. Some states, such as Jalisco and Zacatecas, began passing laws to break up village lands. Chihuahua permitted colonies to be established on unused or questionably titled communal lands. By the late 1820s, even legislatures in the central and southern states with large Indian populations had begun passing land-division laws. In practice, the laws could be enforced only to some degree in the densely settled states, and even then, only in the face of stubborn village resistance. Charles A. Hale, *Mexican Liberalism in the Age of Mora* (New Haven, 1968), 215-234.

[62] Hardy, 439; Zúñiga, 92.

[63] Zúñiga, 94.

[64] Hardy, 439.

[65] Stevens, 68; Hubert H. Bancroft, *The History of the North Mexican States and Texas, 1801-1889* (San Francisco, 1889), 639.

from that town to Cosalá, over the strong objections of the governor, Simón Elías González.

To secure the Yaqui demands, Banderas employed the traditional political modes for dealing with such crises. Circumventing local officials, he sent a delegation to Mexico City, presenting the tribes' demands to state officials in Cosalá in transit. At the same time he made extensive preparations for expanding the rebellion on an even wider scale to put increased pressure on the state authorities, and through them on the federal government. By the spring of 1827 the legislature was more than ready to grant concessions, while Banderas, with the arrival of strong military reinforcements from Chihuahua, was eager to arrange a peace. The Congress responded with a law granting federal amnesty, though its application was left to the state. Under such favorable conditions a settlement was concluded. The legislature exempted the Indians of Occidente from the alcabala on the sale of produce, livestock, and articles of personal manufacture, and from the property tax. They were allowed to keep the booty they had captured, their autonomy was to be tolerated in practice, and Banderas was recognized as the alcalde mayor of the Yaqui valley.[66]

INDEPENDENCE AND THE PRESENT: POLITICS

The Yaqui-Mayo uprising was a warning signal to the urban notables who had inherited the state of Occidente that they must come to grips promptly with the problem of relating the republican future to the colonial past, or face increasing turmoil. The federal system had pared external support to a pittance. Consequently, the colonial institutions which had maintained peace and order were now falling to pieces. The new government of Occidente had either to repair them or replace them. To repair them implied a reaffirmation of colonial society and fostered the preservation of traditional relations among the various social groups. It also required heavy funding. To replace such institutions, though possibly less expensive and promoting republican structures and attitudes, contained the risk of tumultuous reaction. The Yaqui-Mayo uprising was quite illustrative of that hazard. The representatives of the urban gentry who occupied the various state offices soon responded to the political implications of the relation between colonial and republican society. The social and economic implications they had neither the requisite understanding nor will to resolve successfully.

The state had only been created in 1824, following three years of indecision and wrangling over whether Sonora and Sinaloa should be separated or not. In the first constitution promulgated on October 31, 1825, the promi-

---

[66]Stevens, 68-75, 77; Bancroft, *North Mexican States and Texas,* 639-643. Stagg, *Almadas and Alamos,* 35-40, details the uprising's impact on the Almadas and Alamos.

nent urban families created a republican political structure that protected and fostered their interests. The government was headed by a governor (and vice-governor) elected to four-year terms. However, executive power was circumscribed by the prohibition of immediate reelection and a council of government, which, besides its consultative function, either nominated or approved all important executive and judicial offices. Political initiative, then, lay in the eleven-member, unicameral legislature (six from Sinaloa, five from Sonora). Its diputados were almost always drawn from the interlocking network of prominent families in the various important urban centers, which dominated the surrounding electoral districts. Though every male citizen over twenty-one was entitled to vote, a filtering process was achieved through indirect elections for state offices, including the requirement that electors be literate.[67]

The two-year tribal uprising forced the representatives of the urban notables in office to divert their concern from political structures to the immediate, pressing, social and economic realities. Property had been seized or destroyed, lives lost, and social tensions between Indians and whites aggravated to the point of violence. Sobered by such realities, the legislature passed a land reform act (1828), which returned to the Indians all lands illegally taken from them. But there was a catch. Leaving aside a portion for the local public estate (or community holdings), title to the remaining lands was to be issued to individual Indians. More importantly, all lands returned that were not then cultivated by the Indians were subject to seizure by the state for resale as vacant lands.[68] The Indians had claimed in traditional terms that the land was theirs because it had always been thus, whether they used it or not. The notables, and other whites and mestizos in general, saw such idle resources as impediments to the state's (and their own) advancement. The Indians had been declared equal, responsible citizens in the new republican order, and if they would not or could not make such lands productive, then

---

[67]Stevens, 54-66; Elsa Banderas Rebling, *Semblanza histórica crítica de las constituciones políticas del Estado de Sonora* (Hermosillo, 1964), 9-23. Occidente's constitution also provided for a nine-member supreme court and courts of the first instance (state district courts); the judges were to be nominated by the council of government and appointed by the governor. Positions for a secretary of government to assist the governor and a treasurer general to manage state finances were also created. The council of government consisted of the vice-governor, the treasurer general, the *fiscal* (solicitor general) of the supreme court, and two members elected indirectly. The state was divided into five departments (Arizpe, Horcasítas, Fuerte, Culiacán, and San Sebastian), which, in turn, were subdivided into *partidos* (districts). Each department was headed by a person, appointed by the governor with the approval of the council, who functioned as the intermediary between the executive and the local authorities. Populations of at least 3,000 formed municipios, governed by an ayuntamiento; those with less than 3,000 were headed by an *alcalde de policía* (local executive), and a *síndico procurador* (local attorney). All these local officials, elected directly each year, were in almost complete dependence on the department officials.

[68]*Ley para el reparto de tierras a los pueblos indígenas a propiedad particular, in* Almada, 48-50; Stevens, 75-76.

others should have the right to do so. Such entrepreneurial standards, however, were not applied to idle hacienda lands.

The pattern of temporary appeasement, but fundamental underlying alterations was repeated in the other legislation pertaining to the tribal Indians.
They were exempted from the sales tax on the goods they produced. Yaquis
and Mayos were further relieved of paying the tithe, but only for six years,
and all others who settled in the three valleys they inhabited were exempted
as well, which only encouraged further encroachment. Tribal military leaders
were to draw a government salary for life, but their offices were declared
suspended. The villagers were to receive a Spanish education whether
they desired it or not. Separate tribal military organizations were to be
abolished.[69]

The representatives of the prominent urban families apparently understood
the risks entailed in the use qualification to the land reform law and the
provisions undermining the Indians' separate status. Besides voting to support
the continuance of the presidial system, the legislature created a state militia
to guard against any future uprisings; at the same time tribal military organizations were declared suppressed. And, as "equal citizens," Indians were obligated to serve in the new militia. All males between the ages of eighteen and
fifty were to be enrolled, and the governor was authorized to call them up
when he deemed necessary. To supplement these pacification efforts, the
legislature committed the state to aid actively ecclesiastical officials in Sonora
in reestablishing and maintaining missions and parish churches.[70]

All of the legislative efforts—the presidios, the militia, the missions and the
parishes—depended on the state treasury, and it was usually empty. For the
period November 1, 1824, to December 31, 1825, revenues totaled 127,000
pesos, while expenditures reached 158,813 pesos. The resulting deficit was
actually greater since some of the revenues listed were collected.[71] By the
end of 1827, the state owed the federal government 69,000 pesos for federal
taxes which Occidente officials had collected but not remitted, trying to
cover the mounting debt. The annual deficits continued to mount, so that by
1830 the government had mortgaged the income from some of its revenue
offices (among them Guaymas, one of the state treasury's main sources of
income).[72] The fiscal records not only chronicle the state's chronic penury,
but also reveal the urban gentry's predilection for the rewards and advantages

[69]Paul H. Ezell, "Indians Under the Law—Mexico, 1821-1847," *America Indígena*,
15 (July, 1955), 205-212.

[70]Stevens, 75, 78.

[71]Antonio Almada and José de Espinosa de los Monteros, *Manifiesto del comisión de
Occidente sobre su división en dos estados* (México, 1829), 45-46, MAHm, Sonora, Reel
2.

[72]Calvo Berber, 142; Stevens, 80-81.

of political office and the corresponding halfheartedness, or naiveté, of the legislative efforts of their representatives.

Occidente had been unduly burdened by the cost of combatting the Yaqui-Mayo uprising. Contraband was rife, the existing tax system was inefficient, and many of the revenue officials were indolent, poorly paid, and corrupt. But this was not the whole story. The salaries of the public officials were all out of proportion to the revenues obtainable at the time and to the pressing social and economic problems confronting the state.[73] In the fourteen month period ending December 31, 1825, a third of the 158,813 pesos spent went to pay the salaries of the state and federal diputados, the governor, secretary of the government, treasurer general, and the bishop and his staff (*curia*).[74] In the budget drawn up by the treasurer general in May, 1827, 1,000 pesos were annually earmarked to support the missions, while legislative salaries totaled nearly three times that amount.[75]

At issue was the notables' conception of what were the purpose and priorities of the new state of Occidente and its government. Under the Crown, the direction and financing of royal government in the Northwest had been broad and inclusive. Its goal, which was part of the larger purpose of permanently settling and securing the entire northern frontier, had been the overall harmony and progress of the region. Thus, the Crown had been cognizant of and attuned to the larger forces at work here from within and without. The royal government had, therefore, worked to achieve several important objectives: submission of the Apaches to secure the frontier, concessions of local autonomy to the tribal Indians to insure internal order, sustenance of the missions and parishes to provide a common denominator and cultural center for the various social groups, and policies to stimulate the economy and facilitate expansion.

In contrast, the notables' political conceptions were quite parochial. In 1826 an English observer pungently noted those matters most on the minds of Occidente's leaders—and they were not the pressing problems facing the state.

> Unfortunately every man here acts as though he were himself governor. The members of congress [the state legislature] . . . suffer their passions and jealousies to derange the transactions of the [legislature] ; and, instead of attending to the affairs of the province, for which duty they

---

[73] Hardy, 435-436.

[74] Stevens, 81; Almada and Espinosa de los Monteros, 45-46. The governor's budgeted salary was 4,000 pesos (though in 1825, more than 6,000 pesos were actually expended), that of the secretary of the government and diputados 3,000 pesos, and that of each judge of the supreme court 2,000 pesos.

[75] Stevens, 81.

received 3,000 pesos annually, occupy their time in dealing in personalities and indulging in the bitterest invective against each other.

The [legislature] sits every day; and what with the heat of the weather, and pugnacious ejaculation of its members, the deputies are under the necessity of retiring from business about one o'clock, having met at ten, the whole of which time is taken up in firing off angry sarcasms at their adversaries and in praising their own disinterested patriotism . . . . How is it possible that a state can prosper, when its representatives, instead of devoting themselves zealously to the welfare of their constituents (if not from patriotic feeling, at least from a sense of delicacy in the discharge of duties, for the performance of which they are paid so handsomely by the inhabitants who confide in their integrity), seem to be so actuated by other motives . . . ?[76]

For most notables the government seems, then, to have been more a prize to be won than a responsibility to be fulfilled, more a battleground on which to triumph over one's opponents than a forum for solving the new state's pressing problems. To some the prize was the power and financial rewards of office; to others it was control over the location of the state capital and the rewards that it would bring to their town; to still others, it was the division of Occidente or its continuation. In most cases, all three motives seem interwoven in the minds of the state's leaders, and between 1825 and 1830 the issue that preoccupied them was a parochial struggle over the determination of geopolitical boundaries, to the benefit of particular urban centers and districts.

The town gentry of northern and central Sonora initially viewed the newly created state of Occidente with suspicion. They complained of the unequal representation in the legislature, even though Sinaloa clearly had the larger population. What disturbed them most was the location of the capital at Fuerte. Since far back in colonial times, the seat of government for the region had always been in the northern half of Sonora, in recognition of the paramount importance of maintaining peace on the frontier. They did not believe that the situation had changed, considering the predicament the presidios and missions were in after the withdrawal of the Crown's financial support. However, the Yaqui-Mayo uprising temporarily dampened their separatist sentiments as they realized that Sinaloa's financial strength was needed.

The prominent families of the towns of central and southern Sinaloa were dead set against the union of the two entities throughout Occidente's brief existence. They claimed they were having to foot the bill to meet problems (the missions, the presidios, the Yaqui-Mayo uprising) that did not affect

---

[76] Hardy, 182-183. Lieutenant Hardy attended several legislative sessions and talked with a number of the diputados and other officials while in Fuerte in the late spring of 1826.

their security one bit. Besides, the habitual northerly location of the seat of government for too long had reinforced and symbolized the shunting of their interests.

Only the notables of the center of Occidente (northern Sinaloa and southern Sonora—principally the towns of Fuerte and Alamos) were committed to union. From colonial times they had been close neighbors, usually under the same political jurisdiction. They felt the insecurity of being islands in a sea of latently hostile, potentially volatile, Indian tribes. With Sinaloa and Sonora united, the capital would be close at hand, providing greater security and more attention to their interests.[77]

The five years (1824 to 1829) of wrangling over the division of Occidente and the transfer of the capital from Fuerte, to Cosalá, and then to Alamos reveals the parochial political conceptions of those who inherited political power in the region. In the maneuverings of the representatives of the various urban family networks can be seen the provinciality of their concerns.

No sooner had Occidente's first legislature convened (1826) in accordance with the new constitution than the issue of division of the state was formally introduced. The sponsors, diputados Ignacio Verdugo and Luis Martínez de Vea, were members of the leading families of Culiacán; their origins dated back to the Conquest in the 1530s, and they had commercial interests as well as urban and rural real estate holdings there. They knew full well that with its central location and current economic and ecclesiastical importance, their town would in all probability be the capital of the new state of Sinaloa resulting from such a division of Occidente. The southern push of the Yaquis and Mayos towards Fuerte later that year, which caused the relocation of the capital to Cosalá, temporarily tabled the division question. But by January, 1827, the two diputados from Culiacán had succeeded in pushing through a petition for division to the national Congress. It was a brief triumph, however. Bound by the prohibition against modification of the federal constitution for six years (until 1830), the Congress declined to consider the petition. Verdugo and Martínez de Vea's ambitions were not quelled by the decision. Unable to secure the seat of government for Culiacán by division of the state, they determinedly sought to obtain it through transfer of the capital of Occidente to Culiacán.[78]

The Sonorans, with the support of the diputado from Fuerte (Jesús Gaxiola), quickly moved to head off the transfer. They had lost the upper

---

[77]Stevens, 67-98; Bancroft, *North Mexican States and Texas*, 645-646. Stevens gives a detailed account of the political infighting over the question of division of Occidente and the location of the capital between 1825 and 1830.

[78]Stevens, 84-85, 89, 102; Almada, 526. A special legislative commission reported favorably on the proposal for division, as did two-thirds of the ayuntamientos of the state, whose opinion had been sought by the legislature.

hand during these months because only two of their representatives had been present in Cosalá. The two diputados, Tomás Escalante (Arizpe) and Jose Manuel Estrella (Hermosillo), joined by Gaxiola, claimed that events had proven the move to Cosalá unnecessary, that the government should thus return to Fuerte, and that in any case the proposed transfer to Culiacán would sacrifice Sonora's interests to those of Sinaloa. The three diputados realized their numbers were too small to defeat the transfer, so they employed a tactic that would be resorted to frequently in the succeeding legislative history of the region. They simply walked out, leaving the legislature without a quorum, unable to act. With the arrival of the three absent Sonoran deputies in the fall of 1827, the unionists regained control. The capital was returned to the center of the state of Occidente, to Alamos, whose defenses were much stronger than those of Fuerte and whose greater proximity was more to the Sonorans' liking.[79]

The transfer, however, was not achieved without a struggle. The acting governor, Vice-Governor Francisco Iriarte, the rich miner of Cosalá, had been instrumental in securing the transfer of the capital to that town. He was determined to keep it there, and vetoed the legislature's decree. An armed mob of townspeople was recruited to insure enforcement of his decision. Fortunately for the unionists, the state's military commander, Colonel Mariano Paredes y Arrillaga, intervened on the legislature's behalf, forcing Iriarte and his supporters to acquiesce in the transfer of the government to Alamos.[80]

The unionists sought to consolidate their position during the next two years (1828-1829). Spearheading the efforts were the representatives and allies of the notables of southern Sonora and northern Sinaloa, centered in Alamos and Fuerte.[81] José María Almada was named vice-governor by the legislature and served as acting governor during leaves of absence. His brother Antonio, along with José de Jesús Espinosa de los Monteros, wrote the report of a special legislative committee to the Congress (*Manifiesto de la comisión de Occidente sobre su división en dos estados*), which opposed the division of Occidente. Espinosa de los Montero's brother Carlos, a priest, used his position as one of Occidente's diputados to the national Congress to lobby for the state's preservation in that body. The Espinosa de los Monteros family, though natives of Culiacán, appear to have identified with the new seat of government, as many of them later established themselves in Alamos and Guaymas.[82] The Gaxiola family followed a similar pattern: natives of Cosalá,

---

[79] Stevens, 90-91, 201; Almada, 247, 526.
[80] Stevens, 91-92. Iriarte had become acting governor with the resignation the previous year of Governor Simon Elías González of Arizpe.
[81] Bancroft, *North Mexican States and Texas,* 645-646.
[82] Almada, 45, 48-50, 253.

the three brothers lived in the several capitals of Occidente, finally taking root in Alamos. Nicolás María had held the office of treasurer general of Occidente since its inception. Manuel María, a lawyer, had been serving on the state supreme court since 1826. It was José María Gaxiola, nonetheless, who played the most decisive role in the unionist cause.[83]

Perhaps from fear, probably in retaliation for his use of militant force to resist the capital's move, the legislature had removed Iriarte from office in November, 1827, accusing him of various violations of the constitution and had replaced him with Gaxiola, an avowed unionist. Iriarte had appealed his removal to the Congress.[84] This appeal put added pressure on Gaxiola to consolidate the unionists' position as quickly as possible. Unfortunately, the new governor's recent past did not inspire solid confidence among lukewarm unionists and neutrals. In 1823, while serving as collector of the tithes in Rosario, he had been accused of embezzling 20,000 pesos but the charges had been dropped when he made full restitution.[85] Neither did his first official acts assure any but the most fervent followers. The most vocal divisionists were persecuted; some were even jailed. The governor illegally ordered an increase in taxes and a military draft to beef up the state militia, attempting by these measures to have sufficient funds and troops to sustain his adminis-tration in the face of divisionist pressures and maneuverings.[86]

Gaxiola's motive aroused growing suspicion among the prominent families of the towns of northern and central Sonora, those who had held the balance of power in the division question. The prior taint of corruption raised the possibility that the governor was using the new taxes to line his own pockets and those of his family. That one brother controlled state finances and the other served on the supreme court only left Gaxiola under even greater sus-picion—and not only as to personal greed. With familial support in such key offices, the governor's arbitary jailings and illegal raising of additional militia took on a more menacing tone. Moreover, with peace restored in the Yaqui and Mayo valleys, the advantage of union had lost much of its appeal to most Sonorans north of Alamos. When in early 1829, Gaxiola disobeyed an order from Congress reinstating Iriarte as governor, and the state legislature, after heated debate, decided to support his defiance, the urban gentry of northern and central Sonora swung over to the divisionists.

---

[83] Miles, 187; Almada, 306-307. Nicolas María Gaxiola had served as provisional vice-governor of the new state, and, as acting head of the government in the fall of 1825, had published the state's constitution. He was acting governor again from August through November, 1826. As treasurer general (1824-1831), Gaxiola was a permanent member of the council of government.

[84] Stevens, 92.

[85] Almada, 306.

[86] Stevens, 93-94.

Hoping that a show of force would coerce Governor Gaxiola into resignation, the divisionists began recruiting armed volunteers in Cosalá, Culiacán, Guaymas, Hermosillo, Horcasitas, and Oposura. Gaxiola refused to back down, relying on the support of the state militia. The militia's commander, however, was no longer the governor's ally, Colonel Paredes. His replacement, General José Figuera, who owned mines near Arizpe, in late August, 1829, made an emotional appeal to the legislature to reverse itself on the grounds that public opinion was now clearly on the side of the divisionists and that to attempt to oppose it would be ruinous. Two days later, the legislature abandoned Gaxiola, reinstated Iriarte, issued a general amnesty, and agreed to take up again the division question. Stripped of all official support, Gaxiola had no choice but to resign.[87]

The division of Occidente was now inevitable. The notables of southern and central Sinaloa had always advocated it, and the removal of the capital to Alamos and the deposing of Iriarte had only made them more determined. Their counterparts in northern and central Sonora also had become convinced that the normal conditions on which their prosperity depended could never be realized as long as Sonora and Sinaloa remained united. Their representatives in the new legislature (installed in April, 1830) allied to petition Congress again to terminate the union. Free of the six-year prohibition against modifying the federal constitution, the Congress in October decreed the division of Occidente into the states of Sonora and Sinaloa, to take effect the following March. The division line fell between Fuerte and Alamos. Hermosillo and Culiacán were designated as the capitals of the new state.[88]

The representatives of the region's notables had wrangled for five years about the geopolitical boundaries of their society, each seeking the advantage for his town's family network. They had also devoted considerable attention to the generous endowment of official salaries. The Yaqui-Mayo uprising and

---

[87]*Ibid.*, 95-98; Bancroft, *North Mexican States and Texas*, 645-646.

[88]Stevens, 98. The departments of San Sebastián (southern Sinaloa), Culiacán (central Sinaloa), and Fuerte (northern Sinaloa and southern Sonora) were to constitute Sinaloa; those of Horcasitas (central Sonora), and Arizpe (northern Sonora) were to make up Sonora. A month before the decree of division, the Occidente legislature had separated the partido of Alamos from the department of Fuerte and annexed it to that of Horcasitas, at the request of the ayuntamiento of Alamos. The *alamenses* preferred union, but if Occidente were divided, they wanted to be a part of Sonora, as they had previously stated in 1827 in their response to the poll of ayuntamientos on the question of division. In 1831 the constituent legislature of Sinaloa tried to extend its jurisdiction to the partido of Alamos by declaring void the action of September, 1830. The ayuntamiento of Alamos resisted, supported by Sonora's constituent legislature. In January, 1832, the Congress ruled against Sinaloa's claims and Alamos remained part of Sonora. Almada, 528-529.

In the elections of April, 1830, Sonoran divisionists won the top executive offices, reflecting the shift in sentiment of the previous two years. Francisco Escobosa (Hermosillo) was elected governor and Leonardo Escalante (also from Hermosillo) vicegovernor. Almada, 246-248.

the steady deterioration of the presidios and missions were portents of a present whose days were numbered. Yet local politicians conducted business as if these post-independence years were unencumbered by such historical imperatives. It was as if the present for them had a comfortable extension into the future. In point of fact, they were not the future's creditor, but the past's debtor. Their present was borrowed and a decade had already gone by. In the following decade, their time would run out.

3

Visions on the Periphery
(1831-1837)

The first decade after independence in Mexico had been a time of definition, a time for designing the nature and direction of the new nation. But by 1830 it was clear that the new national leadership, centered in Mexico City and the surrounding core region, agreed only on the broad designs: that the nation was a reality, or soon would be, and thus could be taken for granted; that it had great potential to become a world power; that habits of the colonial experience were deeply ingrained; that a commitment to a republic had been established, at least among the active citizenry; that as people of the enlightenment, the nation's leaders would employ reason to solve politics as a riddle rather than force to resolve it as a struggle. Yet a growing split among this national leadership was emerging as the process of filling in the details of those broad designs began in earnest. There was no unified vision of what Mexico should be. By 1830 two separate visions had begun to form about what character the nation should assume and in what direction it should move. During the succeeding decade, each vision—one federalist, the other centralist—tried to assert itself, to impose its will on the nation, and failed.

Most of the country became enmeshed in this political and ideological struggle, but not necessarily in the same terms, or to the same degree, as the national leadership and the active citizenry of the country's central core which it predominantly represented.[1] The centralist and federalist visions,

---

[1] Russell E. Chase, Jr., in a paper presented to the Northern Great Plains Historical Conference (Winnipeg, October 21, 1972), "Mexico, 1821-1867: The Apocalyptic Vision," challenges the traditional view of this period found in standard texts on Mexican history. Rather than a condition of chronic political disorder creating economic stagnation, Chase contends that economic and social structures have a "life of their own," best measured by long duration cycles. He suggests that, "because of definite structural weaknesses, the economy of Mexico may well have reached a crisis stage and become stagnant in the decades after 1810 quite apart from the independence movement or the political upheavals of the post-independence period, which may, however, have accentuated this stagnation." Chase further argues that regional studies which exist

though alone in national scope, were not the only ones emerging in the new nation. There were other visionaries who had a sense of what they, people like them, and the locales they lived in should be and could become. Out on the periphery of Mexico, new conditions were present with the opening of direct contact with the international economy and the termination of royal sustenance and mediation. Consequently, new possibilities were emerging, but there were unexpected liabilities as well. These were the concerns of which regional visions were made: how to respond to direct contact with the outside world, and how to step into the vacuum of economic support and social arbitration created by the crown's exit. The focal issues of the centralist-federalist ideological conflict—the roles of the church and the army, the legal privileges enjoyed by both, the degree of centralization of political power—entered into these visions only when and as they affected these concerns.[2]

Whether hacendados or mine owners, seeking order and access to develop land and other resources; merchants, fighting over markets and growing commercial contacts; or capitalists, with projects for shipping, infrastructure, or manufacturing, the urban notables of the Northwest shared a common vision of progress for their own locales during these years. The essential elements of

---

suggest great diversity in the regional economies of Mexico. The available evidence suggests that in many regional economies (Chase goes on to suggest the pattern applies to all), contact with the international economy through foreign merchants and their capital created a dynamic situation in which new economic structures were challenging and gradually replacing existing ones, with resultant political stresses and strains.

The framework provided by Chase corresponds more accurately to the evidence available for this study of the Northwest. The visions emerging on the periphery of Mexico grew more from this challenge to, and gradual replacement of, the existing economic system and the resulting political tensions than from the federalist-centralist visions emanating from the Mexican heartland.

[2] Studies by Howard F. Cline and Nelson Reed suggest the emergence of at least two visions in the Yucatán. Creoles envisioned an expanding, enterprising economy based on the exploitation of new products for direct sale to international and Mexican markets. Political conflicts arose between the Yucatán and Mexico City, and within the Yucatán itself, over restrictions and access to these markets. The Mayans, in reaction to the changes in land tenure and labor relations ensuing from these new economic structures, launched the Caste War to create an autonomous Mayan society—the People of the Cross—that endured for half a century. Howard F. Cline, "The 'Aurora Yucateca' and the Spirit of Enterprise in Yucatán," *Hispanic American Historical Review* 27 (1947), 30-60; *idem,* "The Sugar Episode in Yucatán, 1825-1850," *Inter-American Economic Affairs* 1 (1948), 30-51; Nelson Reed, *The Caste War of Yucatán* (Stanford, 1964).

The creoles in the frontier region of the North (whose pattern of of economic life was substantially different from that of the Northwest), stimulated by direct trade with the United States, hindered in that trade by Mexico City and yet largely unaided by the latter in combatting devastating Apache and Comanche Indian raids, tempted and yet at the same time threatened by the example of Texas secession, in the late 1830s proposed a confederation of the northern states. In one sense, the Texas affair can be seen as the triumph of a vision on the periphery born of new economic and social structures and threatened by the establishment of a centralist government, which would not tolerate the realization of such a vision. Robert Lister and Florence Lister, *Chihuahua: Storehouse of Storms* (Albuquerque, 1966); Charles Harris, *The Sánchez Navarros: A Socio-Economic Study of a Coahuilan Latifundio, 1846-1853* (Chicago, 1964).

their vision were twofold: how to relate most advantageously to direct contact with the international economy, and how to establish firm, permanent domination over those who hindered or protested against the changes in society necessitated by such relations. The visions were formed and acted upon far less on the basis of abstract principles or traditional custom than on that of pragmatically working out those external relations and the means of internal control they necessitated.

SONORA: HOW TO SUSTAIN PROGRESS

The underlying reality confronting the prominent families of the urban centers of the newly created state of Sonora was such that vision formation and vision realization were imperative. There was no more time to borrow with regard to the internal security vacuum left in the wake of independence. In their midst was a large Indian minority, whose patience had almost worn out. At their gates to the north were the increasingly bold Apaches, from whom it was impossible to conceal the deterioration of the presidial defenses and the missions. And they were now left to face such problems without the financial and military support of their counterpart in Sinaloa. The security vacuum had to be filled immediately if progress and its accompanying prosperity for the urban notables were to be sustained. Profitable relations with the international economy would be minimal at best unless new means of internal control were found. Though the English Lieutenant R.W.H. Hardy was speculating on Occidente's destiny in 1826, in fact, he was accurately describing the ominous prospects for a future that Sonora would soon face.

> Were it possible to restore all, or even a portion of the mines of this state to their pristine splendor, Sonora would indeed be an exceedingly rich province; but as this appears to be improbable, and [since] their revenues [are] being drawn from no other existing sources except that of commerce, which is trifling, . . . I am quite at a loss to conjecture how, without funds, industry or enterprise, it is possible that they should long be able to exist as a free and independent state.[3]

Despite such critical problems facing the new state, its leaders, drawn from the principal urban centers, were initially absorbed in the comparatively petty problem of which town was going to be the state capital. The preoccupations of Occidente's politics ran on unabated.

The federal decree of separation had designated Hermosillo, and the constituent legislature had confirmed that selection; but the residents of Arizpe and its neighboring pueblos would not concede. They petitioned the new constitutional legislature (April, 1832) to transfer the capital to that town. It

---

[3]Hardy, 436-437.

had been for many, many years the traditional seat of authority in Sonora, they said, and was still the military headquarters of the federal commander for the Northwest, being the center of the defense against the Apaches.[4] The provisional governor, long a resident of Hermosillo, opposed the move. Compared to Hermosillo's commercial rise, Leonardo Escalante argued, Arizpe was economically backward with the exception of a few mining operations. Furthermore, located on the upper reaches of the Río Sonora valley, it was geographically removed from three-quarters of the state's population. The state treasury would suffer, since the most productive revenue offices were in Guaymas, Hermosillo, and Alamos. Besides, Escalante warned, the problem of the Yaquis and Mayos merited more attention at present than that of the Apaches. The revolt of 1825-1827 was still fresh in the minds of those in the central and southern portions of the state.

The legislature, nevertheless, disregarded Escalante's vigorous objections and at the end of the month decreed the transfer of the government to Arizpe with an armed guard, under orders of Colonel Simon Elías González, commander general of the Northwest and a resident of Arizpe. As their counterparts at Cosalá had done five years before, the diputados took precautions in case the provisional governor might try to obstruct them.[5]

The paramount concern with the location of the state capital emphasizes the extent to which the urban gentry in Sonora were bound by the Occidente legacy of inter-urban rivalry and factional politics. The prominent families of Hermosillo and Arizpe, who had joined forces in Occidente politics, were now at odds over the same concerns reduced in scope and rendered more local. Yet both sides in the dispute couched their claims in the framework of the problems of internal security. Escalante and his supporters in Hermosillo added the prospects for economic expansion in the future. Thus, the quarreling over the location of the capital reveals the evolution of the politics of the previous decade into a new framework constructed around the concerns of progress and the internal security that was a requisite for such economic growth. That evolution proceeded rapidly as the problems of internal control quickly became critical.

The 1828 agrarian law had not curbed the encroachment on Indian lands. It had actually intensified it by arming the *yoris* with new legal subterfuges to hide their seizures and by beginning the process of breaking up communal lands into private holdings, which made such land much easier for them to purchase.[6] The Yaquis and Mayos were additionally aggrieved because their

---

[4] Stevens, 101. Leonardo Escalante, elected vice-governor of the state of Occidente for the term from 1830 to 1834, was named provisional governor of the new state of Sonora by its constituent legislature. He entrusted the government to the first constitutionally elected governor, Manuel Escalante y Arvizu, in May, 1832. Almada, 246.

[5] Villa, 184-187.

[6] Zúñiga, *Rapida ojeada*, 118-119.

autonomous status was again being threatened. In October, 1830, the federal government had suppressed the office of captain-general held by Juan Banderas and ended official recognition of the tribes' self-government. The constituent legislature had confirmed this new circumscription a year later by placing the Indians' pueblos within the jurisdiction of the partidos of Buenavista and Alamos and, therefore, under the authority of the prefects who governed those districts. The tribes were to have no special status, and the Indians knew this arrangement meant only one thing—the *yoris* would have the full power of the state behind their settlement on tribal lands and would gradually try to reduce them to complete submission. The tribes' suspicions were soon confirmed. The government began trying to collect taxes in their villages.[7]

In the previous uprising, Banderas had been content with securing local autonomy. Now he resolved to unite the various Sonoran tribes into an Indian Confederation, led by himself as chief, to drive the *yoris* out of the state once and for all. Deprived of the protective hand of royal arbitration, faced with the accelerating pressures for economic expansion by the *yoris* stimulated by direct foreign contact, Banderas and his supporters were compelled to conceive a vision of their own. Unwilling to accept the changes accruing from the new economic structures and the socio-political control sought by the *yoris*, they had little alternative but to envision a society void of such aggrandizing elements. It was the same vision grasped by the Mayans at the other end of the country a little more than a decade later.

For two years, Banderas had sent messengers to the other tribes in the state, especially the numerous Opatas, to secure their support. Acquiring guns for the first time, he had also been collecting arms and munitions. His plan was to march on Arizpe, the new capital and military headquarters of the state and to unite with Opata and Pima forces on the way. Satisfied with the promises of support received from them, he set out in August, 1832, with a thousand-man force. The state's new constitutional governor, Manuel Escalante y Arvizu, divided the hastily recruited militia to quell the uprising. The governor led the main body of state forces to strike at the Yaqui and Mayo villages, and sent the remainder under the command of Leonardo Escalante to cut off the Yaqui-Mayo army. Escalante's force, numbering four hundred, found Banderas' army at Soyopa, a small village on the lower Moctezuma River southeast of Ures, waiting for their Opata allies. Only a few came, however, led by Dolores Gutiérrez.

Though the other Opatas were very much in sympathy with Banderas's point of view, the approach of Escalante's militia force apparently convinced them that neutrality was the wiser choice. The Opatas had always been ambivalent in their feelings toward the Spanish, and now the Mexicans. For all the

---

[7]Stevens, 113; Almada, 334.

oppression they had suffered, about which they complained loudly, they could not in the end challenge in arms those who had brought them the hispanic culture they had so readily adopted, who had intermarried with them and had extolled them as the finest of their race in the Northwest. With this unexpected turn of events, Banderas's vision of a united Indian Confederation died. In the ensuing battle the Yaquis and Mayos suffered heavy losses. Banderas and Gutiérrez were captured, taken to Arizpe, and executed. The two tribes carried on the struggle for nine months, under a new leader, Insa Cameca, and aided by the Seris to the northwest. But state forces gradually wore them down, forcing the tribes to accept peace and submit to state authorities—at least for the time being.[8]

The Yaqui-Mayo revolt was a cue for the Apaches. They had been watching the deterioration of the colonial frontier defenses since independence—the erosion of the presidial system, the decline in the numbers of missionaries in the Pimería Alta, the weakness of the Occidente government in the face of the previous Yaqui-Mayo uprising. In 1831 they had begun cautiously to renew their raids against the frontier settlements of Sonora and Chihuahua. Swift military response by the federal military commanders of the two states had forced them temporarily to agree to peace. The commanders, nevertheless, had made a fatal mistake. They had made no mention in the peace treaty of continuing the rations that had been given the Apaches for more than fifty years. The state governments accordingly had ended them, smugly informing the Apaches that they must now work for their subsistence.[9]

The Apaches' different interpretation of the word *work* would soon come back to plague state officials. Permanent acceptance of peace by the Apaches could only be purchased; it could not be forced upon them by pretentious Mexicans, whose military might fared poorly in comparison with that of the Spanish. The Apaches understood the rations to be the price of peace. Deprived of what they had come to consider rightfully theirs, they had determined to acquire the equivalent and more in renewed raiding, retiring to their homelands to wait for the opportune moment.

In early 1833, in the midst of the Yaqui-Mayo uprising, Apache raiders struck the Sonora-Chihuahua frontier with a fury. Making good use of mountain cover to disperse along several trails, the Apaches divided into small bands; striking with lightening quickness, they burned and looted buildings, killed the men, took captive as many women and children as they could carry, and rounded up all the livestock that was readily available. The war parties rendezvoused as they headed back northward, dropping off various

---

[8]Bancroft, *North Mexican States and Texas,* 652-653; Stevens, 114-115.
[9]Stevens, 122-123; Almada, 73.

bands to serve as decoys or to lay ambushes for any soldiers or volunteers pursuing them.[10]

In New Mexico the Apache raiders found North American traders eager to buy up the booty and stolen livestock. The North Americans primarily purchased mules and hard silver currency, both in great demand in the rapidly developing state of Missouri, the lower South, and the new Indian territory of Oklahoma. For their efforts the Apaches received cloth, paints, knives, iron for making arrows and lancepoints, and—most importantly—rifles, guns, powder, and lead, with which to expand their raiding activities. Mexican officials complained of this commerce with the North Americans, but many Mexicans in Texas and New Mexico trafficked in the stolen goods themselves. The Apaches even sold the captives they did not want or could not use themselves to Río Grande gentry and small North American and Mexican traders.[11]

The presidios were no longer capable of defending the frontier against the Apaches. Having already dwindled to less than half their former effective strength, they were now more a motley collection of poorly fed, underclothed, badly organized hangers-on than a disciplined fighting force. Usually indebted to wily merchants and ambitious officers out to make an easy peso, and abandoned by a national government too preoccupied with political turmoil in the interior states and Texas to provide any real assistance, the presidial troops had little will to fight. The only assistance sent from Mexico City was in the form of a commander general for the Northwest and a few aides, who absorbed Sonora's meager revenues and usually failed to understand the nature of frontier fighting. Increasingly destitute and demoralized, the presidial troops deserted in growing numbers. In a few years, the presidios existed in name only.[12]

The state government, thus, was left almost completely alone to contend with the Apache incursions, and it was firmly in the hands of the prominent families of Sonora's principal towns. The constitution of 1831 reflected the determination of these families to establish firm control at both the state and local levels. Their representatives, who had composed the constituent legislature which drew up the constitution, had centralized most power at the

---

[10] Ralph A. Smith, "Indians in Mexican-American Relations Before the War of 1846," *Hispanic American Historical Review* 43 (February, 1963), 39-40. The principal trail followed by Apaches raiding in Sonora split into three prongs at the present international boundary. The one to the west led to the mines, farms, and haciendas of the Magdalena and upper San Miguel valleys. The one to the east passed into the Moctezuma valley. The central prong continued due south down the Sonora valley. Another trail wound down the Sierra Madre. The Apaches thus had their choice of striking the foothill settlements of Sonora to the west or those of Chihuahua to the east.

[11] *Ibid.,* 41-42.

[12] Stevens, 130.

state level, as the Occidente constitution had done. All state elections were to be indirect, with literacy required of all electors. Circumscription of municipal prerogatives was considerable. All local elections were subject to the approval of the executive power in accordance with the laws, as were leaves of absence requested by local authorities. The governor was also given ultimate oversight over municipal finances. He was empowered to name the municipal treasurer from nominations submitted by the ayuntamiento, while the local treasurer was dependent on the state executive to the same degree as the officials of the state treasury. Additionally, all complaints against municipal authorities on economic grounds were to be resolved by the governor. Though local elections were direct, urban notables were given the advantage through requirements of literacy and property or profession for holding municipal office.[13] Consequently, it was the representatives of the urban gentry in the executive, legislative, and municipal offices who were now directly responsible for facing the deteriorating situation on the frontier. It was to them that the mounting, desperate cries to do something were directed as the Apache incursions increased.

The legislature authorized the governor to aid the commander general in April, 1834, empowering him to raise a volunteer force and to negotiate a loan of 30,000 pesos to maintain them. In a second decree (July) the volunteers were allowed to keep whatever they captured from the enemy as an added incentive. Within a year, however, these forces proved inadequate to contain the Apaches.[14] The legislature then turned to a declaration of war (September, 1835), employing patriotic fervor and the citizens' obligations to defend the state where appeals for volunteers and economic incentives had failed:

---

[13] Manuel Corbalá Acuña, *Sonora y sus constituciones* (Hermosillo, 1972), 29-59, 250. As in the Occidente constitution, there was a consejo de gobierno to advise and to present nominations for judicial offices to the governor.

The state was divided into eight *partidos* for administrative purposes: Arizpe, Moctezuma, (formerly called Oposura), Hermosillo, Horcasítas, Buenavista, Baroyeca, Alamos, and Figueroa. A legislative decree on June 1, 1834, created two additional *partidos*: Ostimuri, with its *cabecera* (district seat) at Sahuaripa; and San Ignacio, with its *cabecera* at the pueblo of the same name. Buenavista was renamed Salvación. Each district was headed by a prefect, named by and directly responsible to the governor. MAHm, Sonora, Reel 24.

[14] Decrees of the Legislature on April 14 and July 3, 1834, MAHm, Sonora, Reels 17 and 18. Contributing to the failure of the state's defense efforts was the rebellion of the presidial troops in early July against the commander general, Colonel Francisco Javier Arregui. The soldiers charged him and state authorities with engrossing the funds intended for defense and thus depriving them of adequate pay, rations, and clothing that were due them. The replacement of Arregui with local frontier veteran Lieutenant Colonel José María Elías González restored order in the presidios, but not morale, as the underlying grievances remained. Villa, *Historia de Sonora*, 187-188.

Considering that neither the continued campaigns of the Commander General, nor the repeated measures taken by the legislature and the government to punish them, have been adequate to contain their [the Apaches'] furor; that, in order to remove the apathy which is found in some pueblos and authorities in defense of their homes, it is necessary to remind them of the fulfillment of their debts; and ultimately desiring to prevent the possible extermination of the State which it represents, the legislature decrees the following [measures] . . . .[15]

Since the Apaches were declared the common enemies of the state, all towns and villages were empowered and required to combat them, with each citizen assuming the obligations imposed by the constitution. The government was to entrust to the ayuntamiento of each *cabecera de partido* (district seat) a deposit of munitions, which it was then to maintain. The authorities of every organized locality were to raise and keep a deposit of supplies through donations from those who could afford it, to provision those who could not and were, thus, obliged to alternate in military service every fifteen days. The governor was to name military commanders for each district who would organize and direct all military operations, with local authorities assisting them in whatever they required. To enhance the zeal of those engaged in the campaigns, the governor was instructed to pay a bounty of 100 pesos for the scalp of every Apache warrior fourteen years or older. To help meet these financial obligations, the government was to use the money accruing from the reduction in salaries of all state officials decreed the previous November.[16]

The legislature's declaration of war produced a determined campaign, but it lasted only a few months, as the government could not make good its financial commitments.[17] From the outset, Sonora had been in fiscal straits, as the customs receipts from Guaymas (one of the state's main sources of income) had been mortgaged to pay Occidente's debts. The new government had been so penniless it had had to borrow money to print the state's constitution. Conditions had only barely improved. Contraband was rampant, especially through Guaymas. Many revenue officials were dishonest and most performed poorly, for their salaries were meager and they had little, if any, training. The *contratistas* (those collecting revenues on contract) knew how

---

[15] Decree of the Legislature, September 5, 1835, MAHm, Sonora, Reel 17.

[16] *Ibid.*

[17] Bancroft, *North Mexican States and Texas,* 654. The Apaches agreed to peace terms in August, 1836, but the peace was only temporary. The ardor of the recruits cooled with the cessation of hostilities, and no doubt even more with the inability of the government to make good its payment of bounties and supply of munitions. The Apaches soon felt strong enough to resume their incursions.

to take advantage of the situation for personal benefit. There were revenues available, the state just never received a very large share of them. As a result, the government frequently turned to willing merchants for loans at high interest rates.[18] A mint was established in Hermosillo as a way to help pay state bills, but it ceased to function after 1835 for lack of funds to operate it.[19]

The official creation of a scalp market, meanwhile, had only made things worse on the frontier. The Apaches rightly viewed it as a war of extermination when their women and children were scalped too. No official could exactly tell the difference—or rarely bothered to make such distinctions—between the scalp of a woman or man, or that of a teenager or child. The intensity of what had become a vicious war was exemplified in the 1837 Johnson "massacre," popularly celebrated in a *corrido* (folk ballad).

John Johnson was a North American merchant, recently settled in the district town of Moctezuma (formerly Oposura) in the northeast corner of the state. Prompted by a devastating Apache raid on the nearby village of Noria in late March, he and seventeen other North American traders and trappers—some residents like himself, most passing through—set out with five Mexican mule drivers with official permission to recover as many of the livestock driven off, and any other booty, as they could. Finding the Apache band in southwest New Mexico, they employed the ruse that as North Americans they had been expelled from Sonora because of the Texas War and proposed to sell flour, sugar, and gunpowder. Informed by a young captive that the Apaches intended to ambush the party once the goods had been purchased, Johnson laid a deadly ambush of his own. While the Apaches were examining presents spread out on the ground, Johnson touched his cigar to the fuse of a concealed swivel gun loaded with scrap metal. The shrapnel ripped through men, women, and children. In all, the Apaches lost nineteen (including three women), with another twenty wounded in the succeeding two-hour fight. Before retreating, Johnson took several scalps as evidence to Mexican authorities of his successful enterprise. Whether the 1834 bounty law was still in force is unclear. The presidial commander urged the governor to reward Johnson with 100 pesos.[20]

In the face of such atrocities, the Apaches' fury knew no bounds, and the towns and villages of the frontier districts were now left almost solely on their own. Some managed to maintain a regular body of militia to pursue the

---

[18] José Agustín de Escudero, *Noticias Estadísticas de Sonora y Sinaloa* (México, 1849), 53; Calvo Berber, 142.

[19] Pradeau, *Sonora y sus casas de moneda*, 41-44.

[20] Strickland, 257, 270-275. Strickland's reappraisal challenges the traditional account of the incident, which is based on the exaggerated stories and descriptions of North American traders.

Apaches. Most, however, came to resemble medieval fortresses resisting periodic attacks, whose on-again, off-again, armorless knights sallied forth to
discourage—temporarily—the marauders and bring a brief respite to the slowly
depopulating countryside, which the Apaches now raided almost at will.[21]

The failure of the war against the Apaches revealed the growing inability of
the government to handle the state's problems. Though the urban notables
had centralized power, their representatives were proving themselves unable
to wield it effectively. The frontier was becoming a nightmare; production
was in actual decline. The fertile lands of the Yaqui and Mayo river valleys
were no closer to being exploited. The peace terms concluding the uprising in
1833 had only secured the tacit submission of the tribes. It had returned
them peacefully to their villages; it had not opened the doors to their lands.
The Apache incursions had made the latter prospect even more remote.
Agents of foreign commerce hung near the coast, venturing only infrequently
out of the port of Guaymas in such precipitous conditions.

By default, the prominent families in the various urban centers were increasingly left to deal with such obstructions to their vision of progress at the
local level through their ayuntamientos. Yet even here the lack of habits of
collective, impersonal policy-making and the unavailability of sufficient funds
owing to antiquated tax methods, restricted taxing powers, economic dislocations, and the frequent preference for private gain at the public's expense
combined to thwart their efforts through the ayuntamientos, as they had
those of their representatives in state offices. Public impotence led many
among the notables to private action. Their response to the need for public
instruction illustrates these tendencies.

The notables of Sonora's urban centers shared the belief held commonly
among the ruling elements in post-Independence Mexico that education was
essential for the refinement of their children. Its diffusion among the popular
classes was also important to make the transition to representative government an orderly one.[22] Moreover, they came from a tradition in which education was considered an integral part of town life. With the assistance of the
church, schools had been established when the first urban centers began to
form in the late eighteenth century. The Occidente legislatures had passed at
least two plans to establish primary schools in the towns and pueblos, one
calling for state financial assistance; but neither plan had materialized.[23] The
constituent legislature in 1831 authorized the provisional governor to find the
necessary means to establish a secondary school in Hermosillo, but the plan
never came to fruition. The same fate befell the legislature's request three
years later that the governor make a study of the resources needed to set up

[21] Bancroft, *North Mexican States and Taexas,* 654.

[22] Riesgo and Valdés, n.p.

[23] Alfredo Ibarra, *Sinaloa en la cultura de México* (México, 1944), 30; Almada, 226.

primary schools and literary institutes (secondary schools).[24] In 1835 the diputados again fixed their attention on the dearth of public instruction in the state. They decreed the establishment of primary schools in all population centers with 500 or more persons. The municipios were to solicit teachers, pay their salaries through tuition from parents (the state agreeing to pay half in all but the largest towns), require all parents to send their children to school, conduct weekly inspections, and supervise quarterly examinations. Another decree provided for the establishment of a literary institute for secondary instruction, under the supervision of the government and with scholarships provided to potentially talented boys from poor but upstanding families, four of whom were to be Indians.[25]

There were no funds to realize such programs—for the reasons noted previously—and the burden of providing public instruction fell completely upon the municipios, more specifically upon the urban gentry, the only ones who had the political power and money to attempt to tackle this pressing need. In a few towns, working through the ayuntamientos they controlled, they were able to set up and sustain rudimentary primary schools.[26] Arizpe's city council even endeavored to found a secondary school. In March, 1835, it asked Richard Jones, then an instructor at the Instituto de Guadalajara, to come to the state and organize a *colegio.* "There is not a single educational establishment in the state," the town fathers informed him; only "a few very bad primary schools," in which a few children received the first rudiments of an education. Though the ayuntamiento left the choice of the school's site to Jones, as might be expected it recommended Arizpe for its location, noting that the town was the state capital, "the concurrence of functionaries of influence and respect, who without doubt will be friends of the school which [Jones would] establish." The municipal authorities promised a tuition of eight pesos a month and a hundred students.[27] But there were not enough

---

[24] Almada, 226.

[25] Decrees of the Legislature, May 5 and July 14, 1835, MAHm, Sonora Reel 2. Instruction in the primary schools was to include the three "Rs," the *doctrina* (Roman Catholic catechism), and *nociones del catecismo político* (civics). Weekly inspections were to be made by the municipal judges, and the quarterly examinations on the catechism and civics were to be conducted by the parish priest and a citizen chosen by the town officials, respectively. Alamos, Hermosillo, Moctezuma, Sahuaripa, and San Ignacio were to provide a monthly salary of 30 pesos, Horcasitas 20 pesos. In the other towns and villages, which received subsidies from the government, the monthly salary ranged from 8 to 16 pesos, depending upon the size of the community.

A state scholarship to the literary institute was to be provided for each *partido*. The ayuntamiento of the *cabecera* of each district was to make the selection based upon the criteria stated in the decree.

[26] Almada, 47, 226, 586.

[27] Letter from the Ayuntamiento of Arizpe to Richard Jones, March 7, 1835, MAHm, Sonora, Reel 2.

families with that kind of money to spare in Arizpe or any other town in the state alone. Jones remained in Guadalajara, where there were.

The church, which had done so much to foster public instruction during the late colonial period, was no more effective than the government (state or local) in serving as a vehicle for the promotion of education. It was impoverished and in decline. The dwindling number of priests (found almost solely in the principal towns) barely had the time and the resources to attend to administering the sacraments.[28]

In most towns, therefore, the notables turned to private action when public efforts failed or their prospects were poor. Some cooperated to support private schools. As often as not, however, they preferred not to bother and sent their children outside the state, where secondary and professional education could be obtained along with primary schooling (and a far better primary education at that). This was especially true for the peninsulares, who had come to Sonora at the end of the colonial period, amassed considerable fortunes, and retained a more cosmopolitan outlook. Victores de Aguilar sent his sons José and Dionisio to the national capital to study law.[29] Most of the sons of Francisco Monteverde, a wealthy merchant and hacendado of Hermosillo, also were educated in Mexico City. Manuel and Florencio pursued the careers of mining engineer and assayer; Pedro and José studied law.[30] Ignacio Pesqueira was taken to Seville for schooling at the age of eight by his uncle and godfather, Francisco López, and completed his education in Paris.[31] Antonio Almada sent his son Gregorio to study in Belgium and France.[32]

SINALOA: HOW TO CORNER PROGRESS

In contrast to the increasingly frustrated Sonoran notables, unable to realize their vision of progress, conditions during the same decade favored their counterparts in Sinaloa. Internal security there was not a problem. There was no frontier to be periodically scourged by the Apaches, no accompanying drain of the public coffers entailed by its defense. Though potentially rebellious Indians were settled in pueblos throughout the northern part of the state, they were fragmented into a number of small tribes, each with its own language. Extremely parochial in outlook, they had no formal, traditional structure to bind them together as had the Opatas, Yaquis, and Mayos to the north. Besides, Sinaloa was already a largely mestizo society; the tribal Indians of the northern districts made up only a small percentage of the state's population.

---

[28] Escudero, 40.
[29] Almada, 21; Hardy, 110.
[30] Almada, 483-484.
[31] *Ibid.*, 574.
[32] Stagg, *Almadas and Alamos*, 67.

Sinaloa's geography favored the expansion of contacts with the international economy, in particular that of markets for foreign commerce. It did not have Sonora's communications problems. Most of its population was strung out along a succession of river valleys that intersected the coastal plain, tied together by the old camino real and expeditious, inexpensive coastal navigation. The mining centers set back in the foothills of the Sierra Madre were readily accessible, as the coastal plain narrowed from an extension of only seventy miles in the north down to twenty miles in the south. Though separated from central Mexico by the rugged Sierra Madre, the central core of the country did not seem nearly so far off to a Sinaloan in Mazatlán as it did to a Sonoran in Arizpe. It was as far for a *vecino* (permanent resident) of Mazatlán to travel to the Sonoran capital as to the capital of the nation. The important commercial center of Guadalajara was closer than Alamos.[33]

Political conditions on balance also favored foreign contact. Sinaloa's constitution, not merely a carbon copy of that of Occidente, contained several liberal provisions which loosened existing economic and social structures. It was the first state to abolish *la mano muerta* (mortmain); among the first to order the division of communally held lands; and the only state to prohibit completely the clergy and those in active military or militia service from holding public office.[34] In addition, Sinaloa was more directly involved in national politics than Sonora. Besides its greater geographical proximity to the capital, especially through its ties with Jalisco, there was a constant national presence in the state from an early date—the garrison of the national government in the burgeoning port of Mazatlán.

There was less inducement to urban life in Sinaloa than in Sonora. Fertile river valleys were numerous and the coastal plain provided ample arable land. There were neither Apache incursions to drive people to seek shelter in safe urban surroundings nor periodic eruptions of Indian violence to discourage them from setting down roots in the countryside. There was little geographical isolation within the state to create the need for a large number of urban centers to service self-contained sections in the rural areas. Nevertheless, the control centers of Sinaloan society were to be found in the state's towns, as had been the case since their emergence in the late colonial period, and the inter-urban rivalries spawned during the ill-fated state of Occidente remained as a pivot around which political life in the new state revolved.

Those rivalries were less extensive, but more intense than in Sonora. In the decades following separation, the conditions which made urban life less compelling in Sinaloa at the same time nurtured a concentration of urbanization that profoundly affected the state's history. In particular, these

---

[33]*Departamento de la Estadística Nacional: Sonora, Sinaloa, Nayarit* (México, 1928), 292-305.
[34]Ibarra, 95, 157-158.

conditions—and those aiding foreign contact and internal security—meant that realization of the urban notables' visions of progress was more likely and that, in turn, the competition for dominance over that progress would be keener and more consequential.

Fortunately for the urban gentry of Culiacán, which had been made the new state's capital (largely because of its central location), the fortunes of their competitors were declining. Fuerte, once the orb of Occidente geography and now at the extremities of the new political entity, became a small regional market town, dependent almost wholly on local agriculture. Cosalá, Concordia, and Rosario, whose fortunes had risen since the end of the previous century with the number of pack mules carrying in precious metals from the surrounding mining camps, felt the effects of the general decline in mining throughout the country. Capital formation could not keep pace with rising costs, particularly those of quicksilver and machinery required to extract lower-grade ores at deeper levels. The Iriarte family, owners of the lucrative Guadalupe de los Reyes mines, found their operations gradually sinking into debt. By 1838, they were foreclosed by their creditors.[35] The shifting lines of commerce from the interior to the coast also hurt these towns. Rosario, the most prominent of the three, had suffered an additional setback when the *aduana maritima* and the other federal offices of the state aligned with it were transferred to the expanding port of Mazatlán.[36] Mining never completely played out in these towns, and that small production kept them a slight cut above the other regional market centers: Mocorito, Sinaloa, and San Ignacio.

In marked contrast, Culiacán—with commerce at the core of its economy, located near mining districts, and in the heart of a fertile and the most developed agricultural district in the state—grew steadily. Its notables, mostly hacendados and merchants, were at a marked advantage in contesting with those of other urban centers for economic and political predominance in the state. Securing the state capital had only whetted their appetite. They did not wait long to assert their political hegemony over the rest of the state and, with that control, to move to favor the advancement of their own locale.

In February, 1834, the military commander of the federal forces stationed in Culiacán, Colonel Carlos Cruz de Echeverría, supported by the recently arrived Colonel José Urrea and a clique that had been formed from some of the prominent families of the capital, staged a successful coup. State forces were defeated and the head of the government, Vice-Governor Manuel María Bandera, arrested. A provisional government was set up and elections for a new legislature were held, since the existing diputados had fled the capital,

---

[35] Buelna, *Compendio*, 41, 84.
[36] *Ibid.*, 67.

refusing to cooperate. Bandera soon escaped and reunited the legislature in Cosalá. The conflict seems to have been foremost a struggle between prominent families of Culiacán and Cosalá for political control of the state. The` notables of both towns had been principal contestants in Occidente politics and had generally cooperated to further central and southern Sinaloa interests. However, now that the political arena was considerably narrowed, they found themselves the only potent contenders.

The first elected governor of the state was Antonio Iriarte, most probably of the Iriarte family of Cosalá. The ties of Bandera, acting in his stead, are not revealed in the sources available, but the fact that he sought Cosalá as a refuge and the seat of his deposed government is indicative. Rebellious eruptions against the provisional government in Culiacán occurred through the rest of the year, principally centered around Cosalá. Bandera and the loyal legislators tried to carry on the deposed government, but their forces were inadequate to enforce their will outside the district. In contrast, the provisional government in the capital soon had the tacit support of the national government, most likely because of Colonel Urrea's close ties with Santa Anna, who seized power in April in alliance with the centralists. The Santa Anna government intervened discreetly, acting on the premise of trying to mediate the conflict. Unable to secure compliance from the rest of the state, and faced with mounting pressure from Mexico City, Bandera formally resigned in January, 1835, thus giving legitimacy to the new governor, Manuel de la Vega, who had replaced the provisional government.[37]

In the long run, Echeverría and Urrea had only played a supporting role. The real masterminds of the coup had been the Vega family, who headed a clique among the capital's notables that dominated Culiacán's rise to political predominance in the state. The first Vega, Baltazar de la Vega Colon y Portugal, had come to Culiacán with his wife in the mid-eighteenth century, after first having sought his fortune in San Miguel de Horcasitas. Vega had prospered in commerce and their children had married the sons and daughters of the most prominent families of the community, thus establishing themselves as permanent fixtures among Culiacán's gentry. The family had extended itself through the northern part of the state, but its principal branch remained in Culiacán. One of Don Baltazar's grandsons, Jose María de la Vega, had married Isidora Rabago of the Condes de Rabago, and their five sons formed the nucleus of the political clique that had seized control of the government.[38]

---

[37]José Mena Castillo, *Historia compendiada del Estado de Sinaloa* (México, 1942), I, 194-195; Eustaquio Buelna, *Apuntes para la historia de Sinaloa* (México, 1924), 16-18; Almada, 806-807.

[38]Antonio Nakayama, *Documentos ineditos e interesantes para la historia de Culiacán* (Culiacán, 1952), 125.

After a decent interval of time, the eldest son, Manuel, became governor, supplanting the triumvirate and two succeeding provisional governors. The dominant figure and brain of the Vega family, however, was Rafael. Educated in Europe, talented, and clearly the most distinguished of the five brothers, Rafael had first appeared in state politics as a diputado in the constituent legislature. In these early years, Rafael deferred to his older brother in heading the government, directing the clique from the background. Younger brothers Francisco, Joaquín, and Ignacio played subordinate roles.[39]

The principal object of the Vegas in controlling public administration (as was true for most notables) was to foster progress. In particular they wished to further their own commercial interests, those of their supporters, and, to a lesser extent, those of the capital as a whole. A few months after the coup, Culiacán's nearby port of Altata was opened to coastal trade, encouraging a greater flow of commerce through the capital to the interior.[40] The Vegas and other members of the clique imported large shipments of contraband goods under the friendly eyes of the state treasury officials. With such control over the possibilities for illegal trade, they acquired a numerous clientele, whom they permitted to share in the profits of such speculations.[41]

By the late 1830s Culiacán notables—and most of all the Vegas and the clique they headed—had conclusively dispensed with their post-independence rivals. Control of the state and of its advancement to their benefit now seemed assured. But on a bay along the southern shores of the state had sprouted a thriving port which, unlike Altata, was beholden to no interior town. Commerce was Mazatlán's sole claim to importance; but at a time when agriculture was backward, mining in a slump, and industry virtually nonexistent, a town's future centered on commerce—as the Culiacán gentry knew only too well.

From its founding in 1806 until the conclusion of the independence war, Mazatlán had been a simple landing with a makeshift wharf and a posted lookout. Merchants from towns and mining centers in the region deposited their goods on its beaches (largely precious metals) to trade with whatever

---

[39]Amado Gonaález Dávila, *Diccionario geográfico, histórico, y estadístico del Estado de Sinaloa* Culiacán, 1959), 645-646, 650-651. The triumvirate was composed of José Palao, Manuel de la Herran, and Augustin Martinez de Castro. Martinez de Castro became an important figure in the Vega clique and frequently served as interim or provisional governor.

[40]Buelna, *Compendio,* 32. Altata was situated 37 miles southwest of Culiacán at the mouth of the Río Culiacán, which emptied into a very wide and scenic bay. Largely controlled by interests in the capital, it served as the port of entry for Culiacán's commerce.

[41]*El Sinaloense* (Culiacán), November 5, 1847, MAHm, Sinaloa, Reel 4. In addition to their commercial interests, the Vegas established in Culiacán the first cotton textile mill in the state, the Fábrica de Coloso.

ocean or coastal ships that might perchance weigh anchor. Formally opened to trade in 1822, Mazatlán had grown so quickly that in 1828 the federal *aduana* and its complementary office were moved to the port.[42] Within the space of the next decade, Mazatlán had become the major distribution center for goods arriving on the Pacific coast by sailing ships from China, the Isles of Sandwich (Hawaii), Europe, and the eastern United States.[43] The port's navigational assets left a lot to be desired. However, it lay strategically at the entrance to the Gulf of California and was centrally located on Mexico's Pacific coast, with ready access to the Sierra Madre and the interior, and these advantages overshadowed its nautical deficiencies.[44] From the port long mule trains bore rich silks and lace from China, aromatic spices from the East Indies, and fine linens, cloths, wines, and tableware from Europe for sale in Sonora, Durango, Chihuahua, and western Jalisco (today Nayarit), in addition to Sinaloa. The rapidity and extensiveness of this commercial development had caused alarm in the interior of the country, especially in Guadalajara, whose merchants had previously had the trade of northwestern Mexico largely to themselves. In 1837, a pamphlet appeared in that city bitterly attacking the growing encroachment of Mazatlán commerce on its merchants' trade territory and asking the closure of that port to foreign commerce.[45]

A group of Mazatlán's *vecinos* had organized to combat the implications of the Guadalajara pamphlet, and from their meetings was born the idea of asking for authorization to form an ayuntamiento to counter any such future threats with greater muscle. The petition was granted and the ayuntamiento was installed later that year. Mazatlán immediately began to take on a greater appearance of regularity. The first school was established that year by the municipal authorities and work on the Church of San Jose was begun (it was completed five years later). A post office and capitanía del puerto were also installed in 1837. The department (the state being now under the centralist regime) lent a helping hand by authorizing three hundred pesos to build a jetty to prevent the conversion of the port's northern peninsula into an island during high water.[46]

---

[42]González Dávila, 361. Because the bay of Mazatlán was shallow, the larger and heavier ships were forced to weigh anchor outside the harbor. Rocky hills to the north and craggy islands to the south sheltered the harbor, but there was no protection to the west and southwest, where the harbor opened to the broad Pacific and its frequently gale-force winds. John Russell Bartlett, *Personal Narrative of Explorations and Incidents in Texas, New Mexico, California, Sonora, and Chihuahua* (London, 1854), 486.

[43]Albert Gilliam, *Travels in Mexico* (Aberdeen, 1847), as printed in *Secretaría de Obras Públicas*, ed., *Viajes en México—crónicas extranjeras, 1821-1855* (México, 1964), 375.

[44]Buelna, *Compendio*, 31.

[45]Luis Zúñiga Sánchez, *Apuntes para la historia de Mazatlán* (Mazatlán, n.d.), 20-21.

[46]*Ibid.*

The municipal authorities were Sinaloans, but the rich purses of the foreign merchants dominated the port. The merchants' connections with important overseas manufacturers, mercantile houses, and shipping firms obtained for them a wide clientele among the port's citizenry and interior merchants. They tended to set the style of life—cosmopolitan and mobile. Initially, the foreign colony was composed largely of Spanish and English people, such as John Kelly, one of the most extensive wholesalers in the city. By mid-century they would be joined by an influx of Germans.[47] Contraband was the paramount concern of these foreign merchants. They cared little who occupied the seats of government as long as the politicians left alone the lucrative illegal traffic through Mazatlán.

NATIONAL CONNECTIONS: ALIGNING REALITIES WITH VISIONS

By the late 1830s, urban notables in Sonora and Sinaloa, having previously been spectators in the political struggles going on in central Mexico, had begun to be drawn into the centralist-federalist conflict. Their visions had begun to operate in realities that were proving unexpected, unwanted, or inadequate. This made them increasingly open to an outside force that might alter those realities to begin to favor (in the case of Sonora), or favor more (in the case of Sinaloa), the realization of their visions of local progress. At the same time, after nearly a decade of contention, the focal issues which delineated the centralist and federalist visions had been brought into the open, amplified, and clarified. The urban gentry were now beginning to perceive their applicability to the visions and realities at work in the Northwest. The extent to which those focal issues were pertinent to their concerns—progress, and the internal control and foreign contact that made it possible—would determine the degree to which the Northwest became involved in the centralist-federalist political and ideological struggle.

The role of the church in society and its traditional power and privilege was not very relevant to the Northwest. Since the expulsion of the Jesuits seventy years before, the church's position had been declining. It was now impoverished and weak, especially in Sonora. It had few, if any, lucrative real estate holdings and little accumulated capital wealth, as in most of the rest of the country. Except for the lucky handful in the principal towns, the curates

---

[47] Josiah Gregg, *The Diary and Letters of Josiah Gregg: Excursions in Mexico and California, 1847-1850,* edited by Maurice Garland Fulton (Norman, 1944), 327. Enrique and Jorge Melchers, together with Celso Fuhrken, in 1846 formed Melchers Brothers and Company, which quickly became one of the leading commercial houses of Mazatlán. González Dávila, 367.

hardly had enough to live on. Their adobe chapels were wearing away, as was their influence over their congregations. To at least one observer it seemed that religion was "almost coming to be unknown in the states of Sonora and Sinaloa."[48] There were not enough secular clergy in Sonora to serve a majority of the twenty-seven parishes in that state. Of the eighteen priests residing there in 1834, six were either too old or too sick to actively serve their parishes, leaving twelve to minister to the scattered populations of the second largest state (in area) in the country. Though the bishop of the diocese resided in Culiacán, the church exerted little more influence in Sinaloa. The parish churches there were also extremely poor and the clergy few in number.[49]

The only instance in which the church became an important concern in the politics of Sonora and Sinaloa during the decade was the decree of the federalist Congress, initiated by the Gómez Farías government, secularizing all the missions in the Republic. The Sonoran legislature formally petitioned Congress to exempt from the decree the missions of the Pimería Alta on the northern frontier. The diputados' plea was not argued on clericalist principle. Though they cited the effect on meeting the already critical spiritual needs of those who resided in the state's towns and villages caused by the draining of parish priests to serve the mission communities, their main concern was wholly secular—the effect it would have on the increasing insecurity on the frontier:

> ... there would be such an inconstancy among those crude beings [the mission Indians] with that sudden change that, leaving them abandoned, would bring them to the ultimate prostitution. The work of so many years would be lost, and this dislocation would end in producing in those tribes a disorder that would compound those [insecurities] which today the State already suffers, uniting them with the barbarous and obstinate Apaches and filling all the northern frontier with domestic enemies. The total ruin of that part of the state [the Pimería Alta] would follow, a district that today maintains the greatest tranquility, respect, and submission to the supreme authorities of the Federation and the State.[50]

---

[48]Escudero, 40. A separate bishopric was established for the Californias in 1836.

[49]Initiative of the Legislature of Sonora to the General Congress Concerning the Secularization of the Missions of the Pimería Alta, May 27, 1834, MAHm, Sonora, Reel 21.

[50]*Ibid.* Though the secularization order was revoked shortly afterwards by the succeeding centralist government, by 1842 the remaining missions in northern Sonora were near expiration. Funds from the church synods dried up, the Franciscans stopped sending replacements, and there were no secular clergy available to minister to these former missions. Kessell. 294-311.

The role and privileges of the military were also of interest to the urban notables. In general, the military's presence was minimal, and where it did occur, the troops were concentrated in a specific place or district for a special task. The presidial troops that remained in Sonora were maintained by the state. The military commander and aides assigned by Mexico City exercised a loose command over them. State officials worked with the federal commander and tried to coordinate the operations of the militia with those of the presidios to strengthen frontier defenses. The concern of the urban gentry in Sonora was not the legal, constitutional status of the military, but the degree of their assistance in combatting the Apaches on the frontier.[51] Federal troops in Sinaloa became generally confined to the port of Mazatlán. The garrison was not large, and its principal function seems to have been to defend the northwestern coast in the event of an external attack (Mazatlán had become the expected prime target of such an aggression because of its increasing commercial importance). Federal commanders did play an important role in the coup of 1834 directed by the Vegas, and the garrison in Mazatlán would intervene in politics increasingly after 1840. However, the concern of the Sinaloan notables was not the constitutional relation of the military to the states. Rather, it was the impact they might have on the balance of political power in the state and on the flow of commerce.

The one issue of the centralist-federalist conflict which significantly affected the vision of the urban notables in Sonora and Sinaloa was that of the geographical location of political power and the degree of its centralization. The federalist system basically left them on their own, for better or worse. In contrast, under the centralist system the governor was at best theoretically an agent of the government in Mexico City, appointed by it and subject completely to its will. The state judiciary and treasury were similarly controlled. The legislative function was put in the hands of a popularly elected departmental assembly, subject to the superior authority of the centralist government and its agent, the governor.[52] This issue of the degree of centralization of power coincided with, and animated further, a division that had begun to emerge within the urban gentry of both Sonora and Sinaloa by the late 1830s. The division in Sonora stemmed from the questions of what were the most effective means to realize the vision of progress, who was to benefit

---

[51] Zúñiga, *Rápida ojeada,* 26, 34.

[52] Decree of the General Congress Establishing the Centralist Government, October 23, 1835, MAHm, Sonora, Reel 24. In Sonora, the departmental assembly consolidated the ten *partidos* into four prefecturas. The ayuntamientos were reduced to two, Hermosillo and Arizpe, with the prefect and sub-prefects having ultimate direct control over all local government. Decrees of the Departmental Assembly, March 20 and April 11, 1837, MAHm, Sonora, Reels 2 and 10.

from that progress and to what degree, and what should be the specific characteristics of the society that would result from that progress. In Sinaloa, where internal security problems were absent, where economic expansion (at least in the commercial sector) was happening, and where the population was more culturally homogeneous, the division was over the distribution of benefits from the progress then occurring.

The concentration of urbanization at work in Sinaloa by 1840 had narrowed the division among urban notables into essentially two emerging factions: the Vega-led clique and their clients among the prominent families of Culiacán and the other district towns of northern and central Sinaloa, who had come increasingly to depend on the clique's commerce; and the foreign merchants in Mazatlán and their clients among the *porteño* notables and those in towns in the southern part of the state. As commerce steadily expanded, each faction sought to corner a larger and larger share of the benefits accruing from that mercantile development. Each was finding that the room for growth without encroaching on the other's markets was rapidly disappearing. Both were learning that the agencies of government were a critical factor in pursuing those markets. It was in this context that the issue of the degree of centralization of power became important for each.

Control of state government for the Vegas and their clients had become vital to insure the unimpeded flow of contraband. The Vega clique had begun using official machinery to try to exclude competitors from the benefits of illegal trade (then rampant on the Pacific coast) by vigorously enforcing revenue laws on them. The Vega faction's commercial rivals would, thus, be put at a commercial disadvantage. The judicial branch was similarly being employed. Since almost all business was then based on credit, the Vegas used the courts to enforce repayment from their debtors and elude sums owed to their creditors, especially when illegal trade was involved. The courts also were becoming a useful tool to shield their cronies and persecute their enemies.[53]

State officials had no say in matters governing the introduction of foreign merchandise, but once those goods entered the state, the *alcabalas* and other state taxes levied on commerce were important in determining the flow of trade through the interior. State officials and state courts then had jurisdiction. Under the federalist system, the states possessed a considerable degree of sovereignty, and, accordingly, their officials had extensive leeway in determining and executing policies, with little interference except in matters relating to foreign relations. Moreover, control over the official machinery was almost wholly determined by factors within the state. Under such

---

[53] *El Sinaloense,* November 5, 1847, MAHm, Sinaloa, Reel 4.

conditions, the Vega clique had the advantage in the competition for control over the development of commerce. Their willingness to ally with federalists nationally was, thus, understandable.

In contrast, federalism then offered no advantage to the foreign merchants of Mazatlán and their clients. Left to their political resources, they were no match for the Vega clique in controlling state government. It was only with the intrusion of the centralist regime in 1837[54] that their rivals fell from power, that their petition for the creation of an ayuntamiento for the port was granted, and that aid was forthcoming to construct the jetty to impede flooding.[55] Ironically, for the Mazatlán faction centralism had come additionally to mean no government, not more government. Under federalism, though the power of the national government was weaker, the state administration directed by the Vega clique was actively working against their interests. Under centralism, Mexico City's power was theoretically much stronger. But the foreign merchants and their clients were finding that, in fact, the national government, whether centralist or federalist, had little direct power over their interests. The Mexican government was still in its infancy, torn by political strife and distracted by covetous nations in Texas and Veracruz. Added to this was the remoteness of the Northwest coast, given existing transportation facilities. The centralist system, in the peripheral areas of the country at least, stripped away the powers of the states but was largely inattentive to their effective governance. As a result, contraband was much easier for the Mazatlán faction, since there was far less chance of being burdened with the onerous taxes and competitive disadvantages levied and enforced by a state regime beholden to the Vega-led clique and its allies. Moreover, through their consuls' contacts with Mexico City, the foreign merchants in particular had greater influence on state agents of a centralist regime than on state officials under a federalist system. Consequently, when in the following years the foreign merchants and their clients chose sides, they leaned pragmatically toward the centralist—and later conservative—axis.

The division among the prominent families of Sonora's urban centers was more complex. The developing split was not as focused as in Sinaloa. It was between coalitions of urban notables rather than between cliques concentrated in two towns (and their clients there and in neighboring districts). More importantly, the simpler, more specific question of who was to benefit—and to what extent—from progress was overshadowed by the problems of how to renew progress in the face of deteriorating internal security conditions and how to relate the large tribal Indian minority to such a pro-

[54]Buelna, *Historia de Sinaloa,* 18-19.
[55]Zúñiga Sánchez, 20-21.

gressing society. Both coalitions were becoming persuaded that the degree to which power was centralized vis-a-vis Mexico City had a direct bearing on the solutions to these problems. Those allying with federalism in particular were finding that issue critical.

Rafael Elías González, the interim governor of the department of Sonora during the summer of 1837, articulated the perceptions of those among the urban gentry in sympathy with federalism on that issue as it pertained to the Apache problem. The governor informed the citizenry in a circular that the department government had been unable to find a single means to impede these incursions within the powers conceded it under the centralist system. Nor, he said, could the central government lend aid because of its own lack of resources exhausted by the war in Texas and the great difficulties in communication between the capital and the northwestern frontier.[56] Recent experience had convinced Elías González that the centralist system could not remove the obstacles to Sonora's progress.

Sympathies with the federalist cause were strongest among the urban notables in areas feeling most acutely the effects of the deterioration of internal security. Elías González was a member of one of the most prominent families of military men on the frontier, whose principal center was Arizpe. These men, or their fathers, had spent their entire lives keeping the Apaches at bay to foment the settlement of the frontier and, when necessary, had assisted in subduing rebellious tribes in other parts of the state. They had established stock-raising haciendas and had dabbled in mining—usually unsuccessfully, though occasionally striking a brief bonanza. But the foundations of their family holdings were stock-raising haciendas that had been established on the northern frontier from the Santa Cruz valley east to Fronteras, especially since 1820.[57]

Three of the Elías González brothers had made their careers in the presidial companies, as had their father and grandfather, the family patriarch. All three were presently at the top of the military heap in the region. José María, a colonel, had been commander general (of Sonora and Sinaloa) from 1834 to 1837, when he was replaced by the centralist government. His brother Ignacio, a lieutenant colonel, was his second-in-command. José María had also been a diputado in both the Occidente and Sonoran legislatures. Simon, the eldest and also a colonel, had been the first governor of Occidente, the commander general of both Sonora-Sinaloa and Chihuahua-New Mexico, and in 1837 was appointed governor of Chihuahua, having been nominated for

---

[56]Circular from the Interim Governor of the Department of Sonora to Its Inhabitants, August 8, 1837, MAHm, Sonora, Reel 10.

[57]For numerous examples of the Elías González family's land acquisitions and ranching activities, see the works listed in the bibliography by Mattison, and Galáz.

the same post in Sonora as well. Rafael's public role had been solely political; his service included several municipal, judicial, and executive offices and culminated in his term as interim governor.[58] In addition, he managed the family's extensive hacienda holdings.[59] A fifth brother, Juan, was the parish priest of Arizpe. He had been a diputado to the state's first legislature and a member of the provisional departmental junta that oversaw the transition to the centralist syatem.[60]

It was to the military families (such as that of Elías González) that Sonora principally had owed its progress during the late colonial period. After Independence, they had been called upon to preserve that continuing economic growth in the face of mounting pressure from the Apaches and growing hostility among the christianized tribes. They and their town, Arizpe, had been at the center of power in Sonora for decades. Now they felt their position and their vision of progress being undermined by officials hundreds of miles away.

Their allies were the urban gentry of Alamos. The titular head of federalist sympathizers there was José María Almada, the youngest of the Almada brothers, but the most ambitious and successful of the four. Almada had increased the wealth inherited from his father by acquiring the little-developed Quintera mine in 1830, which he had then turned into a richly productive operation. In addition, he had acquired a number of large haciendas in southern Sonora and the neighboring district in Sinaloa.[61] He had also been intimately involved in the post-independence politics of the Northwest. He had served as prefect of Alamos and twice as acting governor of Occidente. As governor, he had promulgated the 1828 argarian law. During the Yaqui-Mayo revolt of 1832-1833, Almada had obtained the rank of colonel in the militia and directed the operations to subdue the Mayos; afterwards he had served as prefect of the *partido* of Salvacion, which included the Yaqui valley.[62] Almada's lucrative mining and hacienda enterprises—like those of the other merchants, miners, and hacendados of Alamos—depended upon access to Yaqui-Mayo land and labor. Only the permanent subjection of the two tribes could assure the continued growth of their economic interests.

The prominent families of the towns on the frontier and in the southern section of the state shared a vision of the nature of progress for Sonora, of

---

[58] Almada, 239-243.

[59] Zúñiga, *Rápida ojeada,* 31.

[60] Almada, 239.

[61] Miles, 13, 184; Stagg, *Almadas and Alamos,* 56, 65-67.

[62] Almada, 48-49. The Elías González family was related to the Almadas through the Almadas' grandmother, who was the Elías González brothers' aunt. Almada, 239; *Informaciones Matrimoniales,* Arizpe, 1830, Joaquín Elías to JesúsElías.

the means for its realization, and of the relation of the tribal minorities to the society it would foment. For these families, Sonora was a potentially prosperous land for whites and mestizos to develop. The Apaches were to be beaten into submission, since they were savages incapable of being civilized. They had no place in Sonora's future. The christianized tribes within the state, however, did—if, that is, they accepted the role that was offered them: assimilated, mexicanized peones and laborers. For these federalists, Sonora was a land to subdue and transform into a cultured, literate society, with growing cities and towns as its base.

The principal theorist of this federalist coalition was Ignacio Zúñiga, a veteran presidial officer, a diputado and senator for Occidente in the Congress, and since 1831 the *interventor* (auditor) of the customs house in Guaymas.[63] Zúñiga from long experience knew the intricate set of conditions upon which the internal security of the state depended. He also had been planning several enterprises to foster exploitation of the resources of the southern part of the state. In 1835, he had joined that experience and those plans into a treatise addressed to the national government, *Rápida ojeada al Estado de Sonora.* Zúñiga described in detail the predicament in which Sonora found itself, explained why internal security had so deteriorated in the state, and proposed measures to turn the situation around and resume sustained economic growth. His proposals for specific enterprises to develop the southern part of the state were made in more detail in a *memoria* (an official account or record) to the Congress six years later when he was a diputado to that body.[64] In a larger sense, in these writings Zúñiga expressed the vision of progress shared by supporters of federalism in Sonora.

The solution to the Apache problem, in Zúñiga's view, was' to restore the colonial presidial system. With the resulting protection, the frontier would be repopulated and revived. The more settled the region became, the less the Apaches would be able to penetrate it. It was the solution of the late colonial period that only needed more time for fruition.[65]

The ex-presidial commander, however, was more concerned about the christianized tribes within the state. He understood that the primary source of their hostility arose from the loss of their lands. The Opatas and Pimas Bajos of northeast and central Sonora, where the white and mestizo population was already firmly entrenched, were particularly aggrieved. Zúñiga

---

[63]Almada, 850-851. Zúñiga had entered the military at the end of the colonial period, rising in the ranks to command the presidios of Tucson, Pitic, Horcasitas, and Bacoachi. His brother Anselmo had followed a similar career, reaching the rank of lieutenant colonel and being elected a diputado to the legislature in 1834. In 1842, both brothers were elected diputados to the Congress.

[64]Ignacio Zúñiga, *Memoria sobre el permiso de la navegación de los Ríos Fuerte y Yaqui* (México, 1841), MAHm, Sonora, Reel 2.

[65]Zúñiga, *Rápida ojeada,* 32, 43.

believed that to eliminate their antagonism the tribes' land claims should be satisfied, by the national government if necessary. Satisfaction of land claims was essential,

> . . . not only because it is the cardinal point of the questions which feed and nourish the reciprocal aversion between *vecinos de razon* [white and *mestizo* residents] and Indians, but by dividing into diverse hands the resources and means of fomenting agriculture and stock-raising, the Country will be effectively developed, and the amalgamation of the families and the . . . [Indians] obtained.[66]

However, Zúñiga's qualification that such land settlements were to be made "without injury to the *vecinos de razón* who lived in the pueblos," and his desire for miscegenation indicated the temper of his conceptions concerning the extent of justice due the Indians and their eventual fate in a progressing society.[67] His discussion of the Pimas Altos on the northwestern frontier reveals these conceptions in vivid detail.

Located along the Magdalena and Altar river valleys, the villages of the Pimas Altos were becoming rapidly dominated by non-Indians engaged in commerce, grain farming, and stock raising. More of such *vecinos de razón* should be attracted to these districts, Zúñiga said, so as to increase and mix the population: "the *vecinos* will gain because they will live contentedly and peacefully, and the pueblo because it will have these additional residents, useful as farmers, stock raisers, and taxpayers."[68] Zúñiga, in contrast, did not see the Indian villagers in such roles. He saw them as carpenters, masons, cowhands, tanners, weavers, domestic servants, and peones. Through education (moral and artisanal, that is) they would be made "useful and laborious citizens."[69] The tribal Indians were to disappear, being transformed through biological and cultural assimilation into the obedient laborers of enterprising whites (and *mestizos* to a lesser extent).

The primary focus of Zúñiga's attention was the rich potential of the Yaqui and Mayo valleys. That region contained more cultivatable land than any other part of the state, was watered by navigable rivers, and had a climate able to grow tropical cash crops. Military garrisons should be established, he said, to insure the complete submission of the tribes. Secondly the lands of the pueblos should be surveyed and all resulting unused land should be opened for cultivation. To make it flourish, the region then needed only

---

[66]*Ibid.*, 120-121.
[67]*Ibid.*
[68]*Ibid.*, 136-137.
[69]*Ibid.*, 41.

entrepreneurs and capitalists, he believed, to establish colonies and planta-
tions and to facilitate interior navigation with the opening of the Sonoran
coast to domestic shipping enterprises.[70] Zúñiga himself was one of those
eager and willing enterpreneurs.

In 1835 Zúñiga had solicited a number of concessions from the central
government to exploit the abundant resources of the Yaqui, Mayo, and
Fuerte valleys on behalf of a company he headed. The company planned to
construct dockyards, provide shipping up the rivers and along the coast, set
up a navigation school to train Yaqui and Mayo sailors, and establish agricultural and extractive colonies. Mining, in addition to commercial crops, was
then important to the success of such a shipping firm. Accordingly, Zúñiga
asked the national government to allow the export of gold and silver ores
(which had been prohibited since 1822) as the solution to the growing stagnation of the mining industry. Zúñiga's solicitations, however, became lost in
red tape, "that disagreeable business."[71]

Zúñiga was only too aware of the effects such entrepreneurial projects as
his would have on the southern part of the state and the two tribes who
inhabited its most fertile districts. That, however, was precisely the point for
this expectant entrepreneur and others of the federalist persuasion: the transformation of those valleys and their tribal inhabitants was crucial to their
vision of progress.

> Consequently, the first and most immediate benefit of my enterprise
> will be the conquest (permit me that phrase) of [these tribes] for
> civilization, the arts, commerce, and agriculture: our nationals will flow
> into their *pueblos*, intermixing with them and their daughters, familiar-
> izing them with our manners and customs, inspiring them with new
> necessities and possessions, and changing absolutely the physical and
> moral makeup of these people, as the species is disgraceful in its present
> state.[72]

---

[70] *Ibid.*, 40.

[71] Zúñiga, *Memoria*, 4, 8-13. On behalf of the company of which he was a partner,
Zúñiga asked for an exemption from taxes on the purchase of machines, tools, and
equipment and for the privilege to navigate the rivers in foreign boats for two years; at
the end of this time the company was to have constructed its own dockyards and to have
built at least two ships of its own. In those first years the foreign boats would supply the
company with machinery and equipment to set up workshops, necessities to provision
the colonies, and transportation to move the production of mining, agriculture, and
stock raising from the interior and along the coast.
The Congress sent Zúñiga's solicitation to the executive, which replied that it was
powerless to make the concessions, through Zúñiga had cited laws that said it could. He
resubmitted the proposal six years later, and it was then approved. Zúñiga died before
being able to begin the enterprises. *Ibid.*, 4; Velasco, 85.

[72] Zúñiga, *Memoria*, 6.

Not to undertake this metamorphosis of the Yaquis and Mayos would be fatal to Sonora's progress:

> These Indians will be all our good or all our evil, and they will be also for the country of my birth; because if they remain pacific, we will have carpenters, blacksmiths, sailors, peones for the colonies extracting wood, dyes, resins, for the raising of cotton and other agricultural crops. If they do not, . . . all will be lost: without them nothing can be done, because without labor nothing is practicable.[73]

To resecure and populate the frontier, to develop the Yaqui-Mayo valleys, Zúñiga said, assistance was needed from Mexico City. That aid could not be merely the token support "of a commander general removable at every turn, preoccupied solely with the attentions to the proceeds and performance of the port of Guaymas." What was needed, he declared, was a combined plan, which incorporated assistance for all the various internal security problems facing the state.[74] Instead, the national government to date had been inattentive to the state's needs.

> I have heard persons very close to the government speak with more ignorance when discussing remote Sonora than they do when speaking of Tunkin or Bidedulgerid . . . . Sonora scarcely has been considered with the attention demanded by its commercial importance and, relatedly, as a point which touches both New Mexico and Upper California and which should begin to form the line of our territory towards the North.[75]

Detrimental as this neglect had been during the prior federalist regime, under the centralist government Sonora's plight was far worse:

> . . . changed into a department, it had been divested of everything. It saw the demoralization of the agents of government; it noted the inefficiency of the supreme [central] provisions and laws; notorious to it was the impossibility of a remedy, or even of creating the desire for one among the higher powers. It felt itself losing much of the condition of freedom it had obtained through national emancipation, without by this change being better protected.[76]

---

[73] *Ibid.*
[74] Zúñiga, *Rápida ojeada,* 43.
[75] *Ibid.,* 34.
[76] Letter from Ignacio Zúñiga to Carlos María Bustamante, December 1, 1842, MAHm, Sonora, Reel 10.

The central government had usurped the former functions of the state and held veto power over the latter's officials and funds. The initiative now lay in Mexico City, Zúñiga said, and, as far as Sonora was concerned, nothing was happening there. When assistance was requested, ". . . the representations of the superior political and military officials perhaps were not even read, since many have remained unanswered."[77] Centralism had not, could not, and so—Zúñiga and many others among the urban well-to-do of Sonora now believed—*would* not solve the state's internal security problems, nor assist in its progress. At least, they said, under the federalist system the state's officials could legally try.

Those among the notables who supported the centralist regime seemed less ardently concerned with what Sonora could or should be than, more pragmatically, with what it had been and presently was. They welcomed the benefits accruing from progress, but they expressed no grand designs for the state. They seemed far more content to secure a comfortable, prosperous place for their families, believing that preservation of the state as they had grown up in it and knew it was the better way to obtain such comfort and prosperity. They looked to the central government, as their parents and grandparents had looked to the Spanish Crown, to provide protection and continuity and to hand out and confirm offices. In their view, federalism and its attendant state prerogatives had brought only "dangers and disorders which knock us down and destroy us." The state government had met only with failure after failure in meeting its responsibilities. In contrast, they looked to the centralist system as being "more stable and secure, and from which would result better guarantees of liberty and tranquility which promote the common well-being of all individuals. . . .[78]

The centers of centralist sympathy were the towns and villages along the Horcasitas, lower Sonora (centered around Ures), and lower Moctezuma valleys. This predominantly central part of the state was a region of prosperous farms and haciendas, worked by peaceful (though, as Zúñiga pointed out, often averse) Pima and Opata villagers, and one which only occasionally felt the wrath of the Apaches. Centralist-leaning families had penetrated the Indian pueblos and lands, benefitting at the latter's expense; but they had never pushed them too far, too fast. The fact that the Opatas and Pimas had been far more open to assimilation than the other tribes had merely confirmed their experience. By not demanding ultimatums of complete transformation and submission, they had been able to live peacefully among the Indian villagers and prosper.

---

[77] *Ibid.*

[78] Resolution of the Junta Convoked by the Ayuntamiento of Hermosillo to Discuss and Act upon the Pronouncements Made in Zacatecas and Orizaba Calling for the Abrogation of the Federal Constitution, July 9, 1835, MAHm, Sonora, Reel 24.

An ambitious young hacendado near Ures emerged as the leader of these centralist sympathizers—Manuel María Gándara. He embodied their experiences, articulated their views, and commanded their support through strength of personal will and political savvy to such an extent that he had no counterpart among the federalist coalition. Manuel María was the eldest of nine children of Juan Gándara, who had come to Sonora from an Andalusian village near Granada at the end of the eighteenth century and had built up a prosperous hacienda (Bamori) near the former mission pueblo of Ures. Don Manuel's own hacienda of Topahue, west of Ures on the way to Hermosillo, encompassed the village of the same name, whose Indians worked on the hacienda. Gándara cultivated hundreds of acres of fertile bottomland along the Sonora river, which he used for irrigation. He also owned large herds of livestock. In 1830 he had married the daughter of a prosperous hacendado of Horcasitas, Victores Aguilar. In addition, Gándara had expanded his interests by obtaining the contract for collecting the *diezmos* (the tithe) for the *partido* of Ures.[79]

Gándara had entered politics at the state's inception, and was named *fiscal* (solicitor general) of the supreme court, in which post he served for two years.[80] He achieved notoriety in 1833 by trying illegally to assume control of the government. The legislature in January had dissolved itself because of the continuing difficulties over the transfer of the capital to Arizpe, particularly with the acting governor, Vice-Governor Jośe Ignacio de Bustamante y Escalante. In collusion with ex-Governor Leonardo Escalante, Gándara orchestrated the naming of substitute diputados, who, in turn, designated him as governor and Escalante as vice-governor. This illicit government, installed in Hermosillo, defied the authority of the legitimate administration in Arizpe for eight months, until Gándara, faced with mounting popular disapproval, dissolved the unauthorized legislature, declared his government disbanded, and pronounced (with his followers) adhesion to the legitimate executive, Manuel Escalante y Arvizu. The latter's absence on campaign against the Yaquis and Mayos had probably made possible Gándara's attempt to seize control of the government.[81] Two years later Gándara had signed the resolution of a Hermosillo junta supporting the call for an end to the federalist system, signifying his alliance with the centralist cause.[82]

---

[79] Almada, 288; *Informaciones Matrimoniales*, Ures, 1800, Juan Gándara to María Antonia Gotari, and Hermosillo, 1830, Manuel María Gandara to Dolores Aguilar. When Gándara's parents were forced to leave the state in 1828 in compliance with the law of expulsion (of Spaniards), Manuel and his brother Francisco were allowed to remain, since they had been born in Mexico and were adults. They operated the family's hacienda in their father's absence. Two years later the law of expulsion was rescinded and the family reunited, excepting the elder Gándara, who had died.

[80] Almada, 288.

[81] Corbalá Acuña, *Sonora y sus constituciones,* 18-19.

[82] Resolution of the Hermosillo Junta, July 9, 1835, MAHm, Sonora, Reel 24.

The incident in 1833 made manifest the audacity and scope of Gándara's political ambitions. That Manuel Iñigo had become one of his principal allies tells even more about the objectives he would seek in the emerging federalist-centralist conflict in the state. Born to a prosperous hacendado family of San Miguel de Horcasitas at the end of the eighteenth century, Iñigo had initially pursued a bureaucratic career, serving as the subdelegado real of his home town in the last years of Spanish rule. In 1822, he was elected to the provincial deputation, a legislative body under the Iturbide empire. Iñigo then seems to have left office-holding for commerce, taking advantage of the accelerated flow of trade through Sonora after independence. By 1830, he had established a thriving commercial house in Guaymas: Manuel Iñigo and Company. With friendly ties to the port's customs officials, and with branches of his firm in Horcasitas and Hermosillo,[83] by the late 1830s Iñigo had come to dominate Sonora's interior commerce.[84] The bulk of his trade was with the still prosperous hacendados, farmers, and storekeepers of the central districts of the state—with people like Manuel María Gándara. As was the case for the foreign merchants in Mazatlán, Iñigo's interests were best served when administrative authority was weak and distant, when he could manipulate isolated customs officials with his purse strings. Though his family was based in Horcasitas, where centralist sympathies were strong. Iñigo's adherence to the centralist government apparently stemmed largely from the furtherance of personal interest.

That Iñigo and Gándara had gravitated toward one another by the late 1830s is not surprising. Gándara's insatiable appetite for political power, his tendency toward unprincipled methods, and his strong following among many of Iñigo's customers could serve the Guaymas merchant's interests. At the same time, Iñigo was no rival to thwart Gándara's ambitions. Though he had served as the port's municipal treasurer for several years, he had sought no other political office. Instead, his expanding capital resources could be used in fiscally sustaining an administration, insuring political loyalties, and financing a revolt—if it came to that.[85] However intense the sympathies among those allying with the centralist cause might have been, the two men who became the dominant figures in the group that brought them together seem to have been motivated for the most part by the personal opportunities offered by such an alliance. Gándara had been unable to gain control of state politics under the federalist system. Intervention in state affairs by a central

---

[83] Almada, 405. In 1839, Iñigo established at Los Angeles near Horcasitas the first cotton textile mill in the state. The mill was in operation for more than one hundred years, though with several interruptions and changes in ownership.

[84] Calvo Berber, 157.

[85] Almada, 405; Captain Guillet, "Las notas sobre Sonora del Captain Guillet, 1864-1866," translated by Ernesto de la Torre Villar, in *YAN—Ciencias Antropológicas,* no. 1 (México, 1953), 46-59.

government might weight the political scales in his favor. Iñigo's economic interests were better protected and furthered by more cooperative officials, whose policies originated from a distant authority too weak to enforce them effectively.

The infusion of the centralist-federalist conflict into the visions of progress among urban notables in Sonora and Sinaloa in the late 1830s altered the consequences of politics there significantly. Inter-urban rivalries and familial concerns remained the core of such politics. The situation now became so intense, however, that politics was no longer just a competition for public office, an opportunity kept within the bounds of toleration for the opposition, consideration for the losers and minorities, and a certain degree of decency of tactics by all. Instead, it was becoming an increasingly impassioned struggle in which the stakes were high, the room for accommodation slight, the consequences more grave.

4

Visions Gone Awry
(1837-1854)

In the late 1830s the urban notables of Sonora and Sinaloa in varying degrees were drawn into the federalist-centralist conflict that had been engrossing the rest of the nation for nearly a decade. Their own visions had been largely frustrated in the first years of statehood. The question of the location of constitutional power now seemed to them not only pertinent, but the means to surmount the realities retarding those visions. Yet in the succeeding two decades those realities remained, becoming even greater obstacles than before.

The federalist-centralist connection alleviated nothing. Instead, it led to more complications. National political interests were guided by the desire for local allegiance and support in their own struggles far more than by any commitment to render assistance to the concerns of provincial notables. The year by year debilitation of power and will in Mexico City only further divested such connections of their reciprocity. It also left increasing room for external forces and considerations. By the 1840s, these were considerable and no longer solely benign: a war with the United States, the lure of a gold rush in California, a series of filibustering expeditions, the purchase of territory.

Notables throughout the Northwest found their grip on things slipping. Visions on the nation's periphery were becoming muddled, not more clarified. The visionaries were increasingly fragmented, their visions compromised by a pessimistic pragmatism that lost sight of the larger view and counseled concession, at some points even abdication, to the *status quo*. Politics turned ever more personalist, vicious, and self-interested. Such was especially the case in Sonora.

SONORA: PROGRESS NO LONGER A PROMISE

In the late summer and fall of 1837, federalists in the southern and northern districts of Sonora, first independently and then in concert, conceived of an alternative to control of the state from Mexico City: to take control of the revenues of the department and destine them to the war against the Apaches, and to obey only those orders and laws from the central government which did not inhibit these aims. This plan in no way was to be interpreted as a proposal for independence, though some might claim it so:

> ... the necessity of a regime in which is enjoyed as much indepen-
> dence as is necessary for the economy and interior government of
> the department, and [which] is under the tutelary shadow of the
> republic, are and have been the political principles of [Sonorans],
> who ... can be condemned only by those who do not know what
> it is to be forced to have recourse at a distance of more than fif-
> teen hundred miles for aid in exterminating the Apaches.... By
> this and no other thing have the change of government and the un-
> fortunate position in which Sonora [finds] itself generalized these
> principles ...[1]

A meeting of numerous residents of Arizpe, held September 11 and attended by department authorities in the capital, drew up a petition to the central government asking that it concede to the department the special right to govern its own internal affairs. The petition was signed and presented to the ayuntamiento. A month later it appeared in the official newspaper in Mexico City. Upon learning of the petition, President Bustamante interpreted it as a revolt in Sonora engineered by General José Urrea, recently appointed commander general of Sonora and Sinaloa. But the general was at that time still in Durango. Bustamante's interpretation proved to be prophecy rather than a correct analysis of the present. Up to this point the federalists had shown moderation, petitioning for an exception to the Constitution of 1836, but Bustamante's disparagement of their motives "generalized public opinion around making effective in the department such an exceptional regime...."[2] With General Urrea's arrival soon afterward, moderation gave way to open revolt.

The return of the general is more apt phrasing, for Urrea, having followed in the footsteps of his father and great-grandfather, was a product of the Sonoran presidios. After independence, he had risen to prominence by correctly choosing General Santa Anna's coattails and had commanded detachments in various parts of the country. His distinguished service in Texas had made him a national figure.[3] Despite the plaudits

[1] Letter from Zúñiga to Bustamante, December 1, 1842, MAHm, Sonora, Reel 10.
[2] *Ibid.*
[3] Almada, 804-808. Urrea's great-grandfather, Bernardo, had founded the presidio of Altar and had fought the rebellious Pimas and Seris in the mid-eighteenth century. For three brief periods he had served as acting governor of the province. Urrea's father, Mariano, had served in the presidios of Horcasitas, Tucson (where José was born),

and his new command, Urrea was returning home with an axe to grind. He believed that he should be coming back to his native state as governor. The departmental junta had nominated him as its second choice, behind Colonel Simón Elías González (appointed governor of Chihuahua). Nevertheless, President Bustamante had passed over him in favor of Gándara, the junta's third choice. On December 26, Urrea led a barracks revolt proclaiming the reestablishment of the federalist system.[4]

The derivation of the commander general's federalist convictions is somewhat unclear. With his patron, Santa Anna, he had been on both sides of the ideological fence since 1823. Possibly the loss of Texas (where he had fought brilliantly) led him to conclude that the centralist system could not cope with the frontier states' problems and threatened to leave them to Texas's fate. Urrea was also aware of the growing federalist sentiments in the department, especially in its capital, and of the rejection of the latter's petition for local control by President Bustamante.[5] Through his mother, an Elías González, he was related to that family and to the Almadas, both among the most influential federalists in the state.[6] Family ties, an understanding of local problems and sentiment, personal ambition, and the grudge he harbored against the centralist government for passing over him combine in all probability to explain the new commander general's motives.

Urrea's plan was tempered. The Constitution of 1824 was to be reformed by an extraordinary national congress to be convoked by Presidente Bustamante, who was recognized as the provisional head of state. The states were to organize their interior governments provisionally until the reformed constitution was promulgated. Elections were to be held for constituent legislatures, that would select provisional state executives.[7] Urrea's proposals crystallized the mounting discontent among Sonoran federalists. The prospect of immediate establishment of their own state

---

Bacuachi, and Altar, which he commanded. He had supported the Plan of Casa Mata, which created the Republic, and had been appointed commander general of the Northwest. His resistance to superior orders (to entrust his command to successors) had led to his arrest in 1825. Support of the Plan of Montaño two years later had resulted in his permanent exile in Guayaquíl, Ecuador.

Young José had served under his father against the insurgents in various parts of the country and during the first years after independence. With his father's exile, his own career had appeared ended. But he had attached himself to Santa Anna in the defense of Vera Cruz against the ill-fated Spanish invasion of 1829 and had risen in the ranks in ensuing years, serving principally in Durango.

[4]*Ibid.,* 808.

[5]Letter from Zúñiga to Bustamante, December 1, 1842, MAHm, Sorora, Reel 10.

[6]Almada, 806.

[7]Junta of Departmental Officials and Notables, Arizpe, December 26, 1837, MAHm, Sonora, Reel 24.

government especially coincided with their concerns, recently voiced in meetings and petitions. Their response was enthusiastic. In the midst of such pronounced federalist sympathies, Governor Gándara had little choice but to convene that same day the departmental officials and notable residents of the capital to consider Urrea's plan. The deliberations produced a near unanimous adhesion to it. Only the head of the departmental junta, José Lucas Pico, refused to back it. The municipios of Alamos, Altar, and Hermosillo quickly declared their support.[8] Notables from these towns, the capital, and the northeastern frontier dominated the extraordinary legislature convoked in accordance with the plan. They elected Urrea governor and Leonardo Escalante vice-governor upon their installation the following March (1838).[9]

With little opposition to the new regime in evidence, and with authorization to organize whatever forces and use whatever funds he deemed necessary, Urrea marched south to secure Sinaloa's adhesion to the federalist cause. He left Escalante as acting governor and Colonel José María Elías González as commander general.[10] Most of the Alamos notables pledged financial support to finance the expedition, led by the generous donations of the four Almada brothers and the general's kinsman, Miguel Urrea, who had married one of José de Jesús Almada's daughters. Urrea had placed the Almadas in important positions: he made Antonio prefect of Álamos district and José María prefect of the neighboring Salvación district (the Yaqui Valley and Guaymas) and colonel of the local militia.[11]

In Urrea's absence, the legislature quickly moved to implement the federalist system and remove the obstacles to the state's progress. To defend against the continuing Apache incursions, it authorized the executive to negotiate with neighboring states regarding defenses and to plant military colonies along the frontier, with an offer of land pensions to those who would serve in them. Provisions were passed to stimulate concessions to entrepreneurs, to concede exclusive privileges for up to ten years to inventors, and to concede titles of property to enterprises constructing irrigation works. The legislature also enacted a system of primary education and approved Hermosillo's request to establish a literary institute.[12]

Federalist plans to promote progress and transform Sonora through the aggressive action of the state government soon came to nothing. Urrea

---

[8]Stevens, 149, 151-153, 157; Eduardo Villa, *Galería de sonorenses ilustres* (Hermosillo, 1948), 180.

[9]Corbalá Acuña, *Sonora y sus constituciones*, 238, 251-252.

[10]Villa, *Galería de sonorenses ilustres*, 181-182.

[11]Stagg, *Almadas and Alamos*, 60-61.

[12]Stevens, 153-154; Ley Orgánico, April 2, 1838, MAHm, Sonora, Reel 24.

met with initial success in northern and central Sinaloa. But his defeat near Mazatlán by General Mariano Paredes, in command of the national garrison and supported by the centralist preferences of the southern part of Sinaloa, forced him to grudgingly retreat to Sonora.[13] In the meantime, Gándara had been quietly recruiting troops in the San Miguel Valley. He had gone along with the federalist revolt out of necessity, gambling on the possibility that his public adherence might yield his continuance as governor. When that possibility had vanished, he had begun preparations for a counter-revolt. Upon hearing of Urrea's reversals in Sinaloa, from Horcasitas Gándara publicly denounced the federalist rebellion as treason against the supreme government, to which he now professed his abiding loyalty and through which he proclaimed himself Sonora's legitimate governor. Villages in the San Miguel Valley, as well as Gándara's supporters around Ures, followed suit by pronouncing their support. The ensuing civil war lasted six months and was fought on a scale and with an intensity without precedent in the state.[14]

Gándara quickly defeated federalist forces led by Vice-Governor Escalante. However, the approach of Urrea's returning troops (mostly from the northeastern frontier), buttressed by recruits from Alamos district led by José María Almada, presented a formidable challenge.[15] Nevertheless, Gándara accepted that eventuality. In preparation for the counter-revolt, he had secured an alliance with most of the tribal Indians in the state: the Opatas, Yaquis, Mayos, and Papagos.[16] This was an unprecedented break with long-standing attitudes and past actions of the urban gentry in Sonora. None among them had dared previously to turn the tribal Indians against fellow gente de razón. They had always acted in solidarity to contain any outbreaks of caste warfare and to bring the tribal Indians to complete submission when possible. To enlist the tribal Indians in political conflicts among the urban notables went against their common vision of progress. Nevertheless, Gándara's personal ambitions, the loyalty of his followers, and the greater tolerance of centralist sympathizers in general toward the tribal Indians overrode these considerations.

The support of the tribal Indians tipped the military balance in Gándara's favor. They fought with a vengeance, and with good reason. Gándara had secured the alliance with promises to uphold their land claims—including the recovery of those formerly held—and with supplies of arms

---

[13] Bancroft, *North Mexican States and Texas,* 658.
[14] Stevens, 155-156.
[15] Stagg, *Almadas and Alamos,* 62.
[16] Stevens, 159.

and munitions.[17] Moreover, in retaliation, Urrea had carried the war personally to the Yaqui-Mayo pueblos. Property was destroyed, several tribal leaders were executed, and a great number of villagers were killed without mercy.[18] Though Urrea was able to win some victories, his troops were gradually worn out by the more numerous centralist forces. Even more fatal was the arrival on the northern periphery of the central government's patriotic appeal for support against an imminent war with the French. The appeal forced Simón Elías González, military commander and governor of neighboring Chihuahua, to side with the centralists. Up to that time, he had remained neutral.[19] Coinciding with Gándara's offer of amnesty, the appeal convinced numerous federalist leaders to defect, among them Colonel José María Elías González, the commander general. Urrea was then forced to abandon the state.[20]

Alamos families paid dearly. A ransom of 50,000 pesos spared the town from plunder. The Almadas' rural holdings were not immune; some of their ranch houses were burned, their crops destroyed, and cattle stolen. José María and Antonio were removed as prefects.[21] Gándara moved to consolidate his position. Relations with the central government were once more secure, owing to his eradication of the federalist rebellion in the state. All laws passed by the extraordinary legislature were declared annulled.[22] The capital was transferred to Ures—for better attention to the diverse problems of the department, Gándara said.[23] Most likely, he did not want to repeat the situation in which he found himself the year before in Arizpe. The governor surrounded himself with loyal supporters in the new capital and assumed the military general command. In order to control the *aduana* in Guaymas, he deposed the administrator and accountant.[24] Opponents accused him of imposing forced loans and contributions and of tinkering with the public treasury to improvise a personal fortune and reward his family and friends. Before the counter-revolt, they contended, the unpretentiousness of Gándara's interests were commonly known.[25] In July, 1840, the governor purchased the hacienda

---

[17] *Ibid.;* Almada, 240, 289, 808.

[18] Fortunato Hernandez, *Las razas indígenas de Sonora y la guerra del Yaqui* (México, 1902), 115.

[19] Stevens, 156-159, 202 (fn. 80).

[20] Almada, 240, 808.

[21] Stagg, *Almadas and Alamos,* 62.

[22] Stevens, 157, 159.

[23] Calvo Berber, 152.

[24] Almada, 289.

[25] Letter from Zúñiga to Bustamante, December 1, 1842; *Informe* (report) of the Diputados of the Constitutional Junta of Sonora to the Supreme Government, Ures,

of Topahui for 14,000 pesos. The following March, he acquired the Topahue hacienda for 5,000 pesos.[26] His younger brother Juan Bautista rapidly became a prosperous merchant in Ures.[27] His chief ally in Guaymas, Manuel Iñigo, with pro-Gándara officials now manning the customs house, began converting his dominant mercantile position in the state's interior trade into a near monopoly.[28]

The centralist coalition was becoming a clique, unconcerned with ideological underpinnings, losing sight of the larger, long-run vision of progress for the state. Gándara and his circle of allies, relatives, and clients were increasingly preoccupied with advancing their own personal interests; they had little consideration for the condition of the state as a whole or for the overall framework upon which their interests and those of the other urban gentry in the state ultimately depended. The renewal of the civil war in 1842 accelerated these tendencies among centralist sympathizers and touched off a similar process among the federalists, though not nearly to the same degree.

Gándara's control depended upon the support of Mexico City. In the fall of 1841, he could no longer count on it. Santa Anna had returned to power and he did not wait long in rewarding one of his longtime followers. General Urrea returned to Sonora in May, 1842,[29] as governor

---

October 31, 1841, MAHm, Sonora, Reel 3. Opponents also claimed that Gándara's debts and business failings prior to 1838 were widely known, to the extent that he could not obtain credit anywhere in the department for more than 200 pesos. A perusal of notarial excerpts (Galaz, 122-213) does not substantiate such claims.

[26] Galaz, 225-226, 232-233. Galaz's work is predominantly a collection of printed excerpts from the archives of the notary public in Hermosillo covering the period from 1780 to 1901. Smaller sections are devoted to significant events affecting that city between 1784 and 1940 (based largely on municipal archives available after 1870) and to various institutions and facets of life that have been important since Hermosillo's inception.

[27] Almada, 287.

[28] Calvo Berber, 157.

[29] Almada, 809. Urrea had left Sonora with a small force, traveling east across the country, trying to link up wuth other centers of federalist resistance. In Tampico he assumed command of a revolt against the central government and parlayed with the French admiral blockading the Gulf coast for arms and supplies. He was defeated in May (1839), forced to capitulate a month later in Tuxpan, and imprisoned. From prison he continued conspiring. Freed by supporters, he secured the backing of various units around Mexico City and launched a revolt that succeeded in seizing the national palace, President Bustamante, and his ministers, but within two weeks he was defeated by General Gabriel Valencia. Urrea then fled to Durango, where he organized another unsuccessful revolt (January, 1841). He reached Sonora only to be driven out of the state again by the Gándara government. His seconding of the Santa Anna-Paredes-Valencia coup against Bustamante in August led to his reinstatement in the army and his appointment as governor and commander general of Sonora. Almada, 808-809; Villa, *Galería de sonorenses ilustres,* 182.

and commander general.[30] He immediately undertook a campaign against the Apaches and sent an armed expedition to the Island of Tiburón (just off the Sonoran coast) to remove the Seris from that refuge in order to provide greater safety for the trade in transit between Guaymas and Hermosillo and towns to the north and west. He expedited a regulation for the use of the waters of the state's rivers and proposed the opening of a line of maritime communications between Sonora and Baja California across the gulf. Urrea also moved to break up Manuel Iñigo's profitable contraband operations and stranglehold over interior commerce. The illegal activities of the latter's clients also came under scrutiny.[31]

Urrea's resumption of power and his aggressive policies enabled Gándara to mount a revolt within two months. Relatives, friends, and clients, whose fortunes had come to depend in great part upon his retention of office, quickly declared their support. Manuel Iñigo provided ample funding. The tribal Indians understood well Urrea's intentions and the implications of his policies for them from four years previously. His expedition against the Seris confirmed them. With little hesitation or difficulty, Gándara secured their armed assistance, again supplying them with weapons and munitions.[32] The tribal Indians' assumptions were immediately corroborated. Within a few days after the outbreak of the rebellion, Urrea issued a stern warning to them: the lands of any Indians who participated in the revolt would be confiscated. The governor's offer of pardon to the Opatas and Pimas in early August was accepted. He commuted the penalty of land confiscation in exchange for their service in the Apache campaigns. However, suspicions and hatred ran too deep among the Yaquis and Mayos to accept such overtures. Early the following year, Urrea demanded their complete subjection. He decreed that all goods and lands they had seized be returned to their legitimate owners, that they surrender their arms and be deprived of their use in the future, and that they could not leave their pueblos without permission from authorities named by the government.[33]

The war dragged on, more personalized and embittered than four years before, paralyzing the economy and causing considerable destruction of life and property. Neither side was able to decisively defeat the other. Sonora's three diputados to the national Congress—Ignacio and Anselmo

---

[30]According to one source, the general command of Sonora and Sinaloa was divided in 1842 (Almada, 16). Another report fixes the date of separation at 1835 (Stevens, 207).

[31]Calvo Berber, 157.

[32]Almada, 289, 405, 654-655.

[33]Decrees of July 12 and August 8, 1842; January 3 and February 7, 1843, MAHm, Sonora, Reel 24.

Zúñiga and Manuel María Gaxiola (the former two ardent federalists, the latter a moderate)—charged Gándara with letting loose a caste war that threatened the ruin of the state and, most certainly, their hopes for progress and the transformation of Sonora.

> The crime [of Gándara] is without doubt the gravest and most consequential for a society such as Mexico's, composed in great part of castes: it is a question of the high crime of stirring up the castes of Sonora into a general uprising, horrible and destructive movements, whose only aim is the triumph of the barbarians, the destruction of the civilized element, and the decimation of Sonora and of other Departments which would necessarily develop in its ruin. If Señor Gándara is the perpetrator of such an atrocious and barbarous crime; if he is the one who has incited the Yaquis, Mayos, Opatas and Pápagos to rebellion, he must be punished.

> The question which today is debated in Sonora is reduced to these precise terms. Must the will of the Indians be the only law ruling the destinies of Sonora? Must it be that which decides the governing of the Department? Must the Governor be the only one whom the Indians want? And if this is the case, to what would that part of society [the civilized part] be reduced? To its total annihilation.[34]

Such charges and the increasingly vindictive tone of the war neutralized growing numbers of centralist sympathizers. The more personalized Gándara's rebellion became, and the more he relied on the armed strength of the tribal Indians, the more wary these sympathizers became. It was this reaction that, in large part, prevented him from gaining the upper hand as he had in 1838. The central government, too, had become suspicious of Gándara's motives and loyalty.

No longer trusting either side, the central government attempted to end the strife in 1844 by sending a neutral outsider to take control of the department, but met with only temporary success. In late December, Urrea used the barracks revolt in Mexico City by Gómez Pedraza and the

---

[34]*El Siglo Diez y Nueve* (México), November 12, 1842, MAHm, Sonora, Reel 3. Called to Mexico City by the Secretary of War (General José María Tornel) to answer the charges, Gándara denied that he was acting solely to establish his family's domination over the state and that he had instigated a caste war to accomplish it. Tornel in his *memoria* to Congress recommended bringing formal charges, but soon afterwards, there was a change in the personnel of the national government and the case was buried in the archives. Gándara returned to Sonora and relieved his brother of command of the movement. Almada, 289-290.

The Opatas staged an uprising in 1839, the Papagos in 1841. Both were quelled by Gándara. Almada, 289.

moderados to occupy again the offices of governor and commander general. When forced to step down a few months later, he delayed leaving the state as ordered. In a few weeks (June, 1845) he led a coup to depose the new governor, José María Gaxiola, but was quickly countered by the new commander general, General Francisco Duque, who obliged Urrea to leave the state.[35] The ease with which Urrea's coup was foiled indicates the degree to which the federalist coalition had become personalized and fragmented. The general's ambition had outdistanced his representation of federalist expectations. He had responded to *gandarista* abuses in kind, intensifying persecutions, inflaming passions, and increasing the destructiveness of the war to a level which most federalist partisans and sympathizers had not intended and from which they stepped back in consternation. In addition, the fact that Urrea had not been adverse to profitting personally from the war was reminiscent of some of the accusations levelled against Gándara and Iñigo. In 1843 he had unsuccessfully sought to create a monopoly on the salt pits at the mouth of the Río Yaqui, which supplied all of the interior towns.[36]

Almost immediately, Gándara and Iñigo, seeking to profit from the political vacuum created by Urrea's departure, staged a revolt based once again in the Horcasitas Valley and around Ures. The moderate government of Governor Gaxiola, supported by Commander General Duque, resisted successfully until it lost backing from Mexico City. In concert with the pro-centralist Paredes revolt nationally (February, 1846), Colonel Fernando Cuesta, second in command, allied with Gándara to depose Gaxiola and Duque and became provisional governor and commander general.[37] Cuesta arbitrarily named a new departmental assembly, headed by Juan Gándara and dominated by his brother's followers.[38] When the barracks revolt of General Mariano Salas reestablished the federalist sys-

---

[35] Almada, 306, 656, 810. In June, just before the attempted Urrea coup (and the succeeding Gándara revolt), General Duque had brought together Urrea, Manuel Iñigo, and other prominent figures of both sides in Hermosillo to sign an act of reconciliation. Those attending had promised to employ all their influence to see that their followers abided by it, and to acknowledge as legitimate governor Gaxiola, in whose house the meeting was held. *El Conciliador,* June 30, 1845.

The Herrera government ordered Urrea to entrust the two offices to its appointees and come to Mexico City to assume the office of senator, for which he had recently been elected. The general fulfilled the order of entrustment, but intentionally delayed his departure.

[36] Velasco, 49. The salt had long been considered as belonging to the Yaquis. Urrea forced the Yaquis to sell the salt to him at half a peso per *carga* (load) and then delivered it in launches to Guaymas at four times that amount. The monopoly did not survive long, however, as it was impossible to prevent the importation of salt from the Island of Carmen in the Gulf of California, north of the port.

[37] *El Centinela,* September 26, 1845; Almada, 205, 290, 656-657.

[38] Calvo Berber, 157; Corbalá Acuña, *Sonora y sus constituciones,* 252.

tem six months later, Cuesta readily acknowledged his allegiance and convoked state elections. The pro-Gándara departmental assembly concurred.
Gándara was elected governor and his followers won a majority in the
new legislature. The following January, the legislature declared the Constitution of 1831 back in force and a year later (1848) reformed it in
accordance with the reform of the federal constitution.[39]

From Vision to Lamentation

That the *gandaristas* so readily assented to the reinstitution of federalism, that they met with such success in the state elections, and that
their triumph was accepted without any noticeable protest can be only
partly explained by the national government's preoccupation with the recent
outbreak of war with the United States and the *gandaristas'* control
of the provisional government. There was a new political mood emerging
among the prominent families of Sonora's urban centers. The intrusion of
the question concerning the degree of centralization of power in the nation had not altered the realities holding back sustained economic
growth. Instead, it had spawned increasingly malicious civil strife, which
had, in turn, compounded the problems of obtaining internal security
and greater foreign contacts. The visions of progress had turned into a
nightmare.

In the frontier districts "hundreds of families, reduced to beggary, have
been driven from their homes, after witnessing the slaughter of parents,
wives, and children by the ferocious barbarians [Apaches] ...."[40] Unable to till their fields regularly, their livestock driven off, their homes
and sheds burned, they had fled south, leaving behind "ruined [haci-
endas], ranchos, corrals, and other remains of a civilized community,
now overgrown with tall grass and shrubbery."[41] The mines and placers
reopened after independence or recently discovered were now largely deserted. Even if one dared risk losing his or her scalp, labor was very
scarce and the price of quicksilver and other supplies was skyrocketing.
Commerce had dwindled to an irregular trickle with the road to Chihuahua and New Mexico severed and those to the south generally unsafe.[42] If the countryside was untenable, the towns and villages were
only a little better off. Several had been abandoned. The residents of the

---

[39]Corbalá Acuña, *Sonora y sus constituciones,* 239-240, 253; Almada, *passim.*
Sonora's reformed constitution, promulgated on May 13, 1848, reduced the existing ten
partidos to nine, each headed by a prefect appointed by the governor. Reformed Constitution of the State, May 13, 1848, MAHm, Sonora Reel 24.
[40]Velasco, 85-86.
[41]Bartlett, 413.
[42]Velasco, 133-134, 136-146.

rest lived in constant terror, few venturing outside their communities except as part of well-armed groups.[43] In once prosperous, now nearly depopulated Bacuachi, "In such constant fear do these people live, that . . . it [is] impossible to hire two men to take out . . . mules to a meadow half a mile from the village . . ." for pasturing. In Arizpe "no one dared venture into the Alameda after dark."[44]

The extent of turmoil on the frontier as a whole can also be seen by comparison with the reversals besetting the *partido* of Altar, which comprised the northwest corner of the state and was, thus, at the western extremity of the Apache incursion routes. Most of the mining discoveries of the 1830s had occurred in that district. These discoveries had transformed the presidial village of the same name into a bustling town. The community doubled in population, reaching an estimated 4,000 inhabitants. Several retail shops were established, selling foreign and domestic goods procured in Hermosillo. Stock and grain haciendas and ranchos were prospering. Then came the Apache raids and the Papago uprising of 1841, which caused the abandonment of the mines, the crippling of agriculture and stock-raising, and the shrinkage of trade. Altar lost much of its newly found population.[45] In the districts to the east, the devastation was worse.

> All this part of Sonora, without doubt the most interesting of the Department, is being converted into a rude cemetery which announces to Sonorans, silently but energetically, extermination, ruin, and destruction . . . . Thus, we vegetate more than we live, we unfortunate *frontereños* . . . .[46]

Spared the wrath of the Apaches, southern Sonora had been scarred by the periodic ravages of the rebellious Yaquis and Mayos during the civil wars. Livestock herds had been reduced by more than half, and many farms and haciendas had been destroyed or abandoned for want of labor and theft of livestock. Most whites living in and around the Mayo pueblos had fled to more protected places.[47] Those few who remained in the good graces of the Indians did not dare make improvements on the lands they tilled, most of

---

[43] Kessell, 284-289.

[44] Bartlett, 276, 284.

[45] Velasco, 65-67, 143-144.

[46] Petition of the Ayuntamiento of Arizpe to the Sub-Prefect of the District, April 1, 1844, MAHm, Sonora, Reel 3.

[47] Acosta, *Apuntes,* 151-152; *El Centinela,* August 1, 1845, MAHm, Sonora, Reel 11. The Yaquis permitted very few whites to live among them and these were mostly traders,

which were rented from the pueblos.[48] Most mining operations had been discontinued. When not at war, the two tribes had continued to market their beans, grains, and artisanal products in Guaymas, Alamos, and other communities. Foreign and national commerce had been curtailed, however, as the land and sea connections with Guaymas had become tenuous at best and the region's purchasing power had diminished.[49]

The towns of Baroyeca and Buenavista had become villages. Alamos had suffered only a slight population drop, owning to the influx of those fleeing from the Indian pueblos and the white communities nearby. Nevertheless, the town's economic position had declined. The profits from the mines were far less than what they once had been. Commerce had accordingly slumped. Much of the property its leading families had acquired and built up in the Yaqui and Mayo valleys was in ruins. The Almadas, the Salidos, the Ceballos now largely lived off their accumulated wealth, waiting for better days to return.[50]

Central Sonora had fared much better than the northern frontier and the south in the decade of civil strife since 1837. Being at the margin of the Apache incursions and, for the most part, *gandarista* (and thus less subject to tribal Indian hostility), it had suffered only occasionally and rather minimally. It had continued as the breadbasket of the state, and, with the decline in other areas, its importance had grown. Wheat exports had steadily increased. Stock-raising, though lacking the expansive grasslands to the north, had been stimulated by the reduction of herds elsewhere in the state. The only existing wagon roads connected Guaymas, Hermosillo, and Ures and provided regular and generally safe transportation, which was sadly lacking in the rest of the state. This type of transportation was also far less expensive than by mule

---

not farmers. The Mayos were more tolerant in allowing whites to settle in their pueblos, especially those at the eastern end of the lower Mayo Valley. Velasco, 57, 61.

One of those forced to abandon his holdings was José Otero of Buenavista, who fled to Alamos leaving his three ranches at the mercy of the Yaquis, who drove off livestock from them valued at 30,000 pesos. Velasco, 83.

There were also personal losses, such as the Yaquis' killing of three Salido cousins on their way home by way of Guaymas in 1844, after a decade of study in Spain. Stagg, *Almadas and Alamos,* 70.

[48] Escudero, 115.

[49] Velasco, 83, 129-131. The mines around Buenavista and Baroyeca had been deserted on account of the civil war. José María Almada's Quintera mine and many others around Alamos had discontinued operations, as the insecurity of the roads had escalated the price of quicksilver and other mining supplies and had necessitated the use of costly, heavily armed escorts for the silver trains. In addition, Mayo labor had become much less available.

[50] *Ibid.,* 26, 82, 84. The *partido* of Baroyeca was merged with that of Alamos by the reformed constitution of 1848; that of Salvación became the district of Guaymas, the *cabecera* being moved from Buenavista to that port. Both alterations in the political divisions of the state reflected the shifts in population caused by the civil war.

train. In addition, central Sonora (especially its three principal towns—Hermosillo, Guaymas, and Ures)[51] had benefited by becoming a haven for those leaving the frontier.

Hermosillo had become the largest and most prosperous town in the state. Its role as distribution point for foreign and national goods coming into Sonora through Guaymas and as collection point for exports going out through that port had been expanding since the state's separation from Sinaloa. Twenty-five mercantile establishments and ships handled the trade. Several were large wholesale firms. There were a number of artisan shops, especially for carpentry and leather making. Three aqueducts furnished the town with water and irrigated the surrounding gardens, orchards, and croplands. Several public buildings had been erected: a municipal building, a prison, an assayer's office, a school, and the state mint (having been idle for some time, this building was now used as a barracks for troops).[52]

The growth of Guaymas had been more accelerated but less assured. In the early post-independence years, the business of the port had been dominated by foreign merchants.[53] Since then, it had become shared increasingly by Sonorans who had quit the turbulent frontier to start a new life in the more placid, more potentially prosperous confines of the Bay of Guaymas—people such as Wenceslao and José Iberri of Bacuachi, Santiago Campillo, José María Maytorena, and Francisco A. Aguilar of Horcasitas.[54] An observer at midcentury noted that "There are several families of wealth here, whose houses are handsomely furnished, and who enjoy the luxuries of a residence near the coast."[55] Yet the port's commercial development had been hampered somewhat. Several times the port had had to thwart proposals to close it to foreign trade, introduced in the Congress by deputies from Veracruz, Mexico City, and Jalisco who desired to regain their colonial control over commerce in Sonora.[56]

---

[51]*Ibid.*, 31, 38-40, 56, 95. Numerous Yaquis worked the lands of the haciendas and farms strung out along the lower Sonora and Horcasitas valleys. Some also labored in artisan shops in Guaymas and Hermosillo.

[52]*Ibid.*, 36, 40, 52; Bartlett, 466-470.

[53]Bartlett, 478-479.

[54]Almada, 131; John R. Southworth, *El Estado de Sonora—sus industrias, commerciales, mineras y manufacturas* (Nogales, Arizona, 1897), 44; Selections from the *Archivo General de Gobierno (Sonora), Justicia Civil, Actos de Matrimoniales*, Guaymas, 1871, 4. The selections were compiled by the *Biblioteca y Museo de Sonora*, hereafter cited as BMS.

[55]Bartlett, 478. Ringed by dry, stony hills, at that time Guaymas was almost wholly dependent on commerce, even in meeting its daily necessities. Food for the port came from the Yaqui and inland valleys ten to thirty miles away. Water was hauled from wells in the "suburbs" in leather bags on the backs of donkeys.

[56]Stevens, 106. The general dispositions of 1837, 1842, and 1848 confirmed Guaymas's status as a port of entry.

Ures owed its recent rise to prominence primarily to the transfer and permanent location of the capital there. Though Urrea had announced the removal of the seat of government back to Arizpe (April, 1844),[57] the transfer was never carried out. He was replaced the following month by General Duque, who remained in Ures. Three years later the state legislature declared Ures to be the official, permanent capital of the state.[58] The influx of frontier emigrants had also aided the town's growth. Among them was Antonio Carrillo, a native of Bacuachi, who moved to Ures in 1842 and engaged in commerce. At mid-century the town possessed a sugar mill supplied by the neighboring haciendas, a few commercial firms, several retail shops, a jail, a substantial church, a school, and the weekly official newspaper, *El Sonorense.*[59]

By 1847 Sonorans in general and most urban notables in particular, including those in the three towns that had retained a measure of prosperity, cared little about the merits of political ideologies or personalities. They wanted an end to the civil strife that had been tearing their state apart and compounding the already serious internal security problems.

> Sonora is at present the victim of disunion, and Sonora after . . . years of war . . . begins to know the results of its division, begins to understand that no society can be permanent when its members are in opposition . . . . The War in Sonora has been purely of personalities: the desire to get ahead, to aspire to another position from that which one holds, to destroy one's rivals . . . .[60]

A port newspaper claimed that the nation's policy had also hindered Guaymas's growth. Given the fact that it was the Mexican port farthest from European and eastern United States markets, the paper said, the continually rising tariffs had made its position even less competitive with other ports. All pleas to alleviate this disadvantage by lowering customs duties to balance the higher transportation costs had fallen on deaf ears. Such tariffs may have curtailed expansion of the port's trade to regions on the eastern side of the Sierra Madre, but did not restrict the flow of commerce through Guaymas to Sonora. The merchants of Veracruz, Tampico, Mexico City and Jalisco could have demonstrated that with their ledger books. What the tariffs did do was insure the proliferation of contraband, which hurt those individual merchants who could not or did not choose to benefit from it. *El Conciliador*, April 14, 1845.

In 1836, the first port works to improve maritime movement had been initiated. Governor Manuel Escalante y Arvizu authorized the construction of the first wharf, to be paid for with donations and the imposition of a modest quota on imports and exports. The contract was awarded to the port's wealthiest merchant, Manuel Iñigo, who began construction in November. Almada, 325.

[57]Circular of Governor and Commander General Urrea of the Department of Sonora to Its Inhabitants, April 16, 1844, MAHm, Sonora, Reel 3.

[58]Decree of the Legislature, February 15, 1847, MAHm, Sonora, Reel 3.

[59]*Informaciones Matrimoniales*, Ures, 1862, Gabriel Corella to Dolores Carrillo; Velasco, 32-33.

[60]*El Conciliador*, April 14, 1845.

In such a prevailing political climate, Gándara's relinquishment of the government in 1849 to his elected successor, José de Aguilar, was not surprising. Though his brother-in-law, Aguilar had been a neutral in the previous civil war. Gándara had indicated his political flexibility four years previously in a petition to the national government for reinstatement as governor: ". . . I declare that I neither abhor nor love the federal system or centralism; that, as a private citizen and as public funtionary, I will adhere to one or the other system as soon as one of them is adopted by the Nation . . . ."[61] Gándara had correctly read which way the political winds were blowing.

The agony of the civil war years was now over. The prominent families of the state's urban centers had once again established bounds for their political divisions. Nonetheless, their visions of progress were no closer to realization. The Sonorans' woes had not ended. During the war with the United States, a year-and-a-half blockade of Guaymas beginning in October, 1846 (with outright occupation of the port the last six months),[62] paralyzed business throughout most of the state.[63] Moreover, peace brought little comfort for the northern frontier. Though the United States, by the Treaty of Guadalupe Hidalgo, assumed responsibility for the Indian tribes living north of the new boundary (the Gila River), its Congress, embroiled in the slavery question and bent on economy, provided far too inadequate funds to even begin to cope with the Apache incursions into Mexico. The U.S. War Department, unfamiliar with the nature of fighting in the West, manned its forts almost entirely with immobile infantry.[64] Worse still, these small garrisons and arriving settlers began making arrangements with the Apaches. The latter offered not to molest the North Americans if they in turn would not interfere with the Apaches' activities in Mexico.[65] The tempo and scope of Apache incursions into Sonora accelerated. One raid alone (January, 1849), which extended south to the environs of Ures, resulted in the death of eighty-six persons.[66] Local officials in Cumpas reported that with the depopulation of the presidial community of Fronteras and the lack of any of its own funds, their village

---

[61] Almada, 289. Having studied law in Mexico City, Aguilar up to the late 1840s had pursued a judicial career: judge of the federal district of Sonora and the Californias, judge of the first instance (state district court), and finally a justice of the state supreme tribunal (he became president of this tribunal in 1848). *Ibid.,* 21.

[62] Bancroft, *North Mexican States and Texas,* 665-669.

[63] *Memoria* of Governor Manuel María Gándara, January 27, 1849, MAHm, Sonora, Reel 3.

[64] J. Fred Rippy, "The Indians of the Southwest in the Diplomacy of the United States and Mexico, 1848-1853," *Hispanic American Historical Review,* 2 (August, 1919), 363, 378, 388, 395.

[65] Kessell, 303-305, 309-310; Charles D. Poston, "Building a State in Apache Land," II, *Overland Monthly,* 24 (August, 1894), 205.

[66] Rippy, 388.

was now defenseless in the face of the Apache incursions. Other nearby communities were being depopulated and Cumpas was now threatened in the same manner. In the previous month, forty persons had been killed, sixteen of them from their village.[67]

At the same time, the lure of the gold rush in California was beginning to drain population from the entire state. The already depopulating frontier lost many of its remaining defenders. Throughout the state wages and prices were forced up because labor was scarce and production stopped.[68] An estimated ten thousand persons left the state between 1848 and 1850; many of these shortly returned, some with sizable amounts of gold, most with little, if any. The gold succeeded only in bidding up prices and shortly vanished from the state as payments for imports.[69]

Those returning from California unfortunately came back with more than gold. In November, 1850, a boat carrying passengers from San Francisco brought a cholera epidemic to Guaymas. With the rudimentary health facilities and practices then existing in the area, it quickly spread to most of the towns and villages in the state.[70] The port and Alamos lost an estimated one-third of their populations; the parish of Altar lost 1,116 people.[71] Though the poorer classes bore the brunt of the epidemic, it claimed among its victims such notables as Ignacio Almada (then prefect of Alamos), ex-governor José María Gaxiola, and Juan B. Gándara, recently a diputado and substitute governor.[72]

Little wonder then that Governor José de Aguilar's *Memorias* of 1850 and 1851 read like lamentations from the Old Testament. Public security, the governor told the legislature, was weak. The federal military colonies authorized in 1848 had not yet been established, nor had the promised federal subsidy been received to maintain the four companies of the newly created national guard (1848), which itself still existed largely on paper. The California emigrations and the cholera epidemic deprived the guard of much of its

---

[67]Representation from the Authorities of Cumpas in the Name of Its Citizenry Concerning the Apaches, February 26, 1849, MAHm, Sonora, Reel 24.

[68]Kessell, 309; Bancroft, *North Mexican States and Texas,* 670.

[69]Governor José de Aguilar, *Memoria del Estado de Sonora* (Ures, 1851), 30-31. Governor Aguilar estimated that the amount of gold brought back from California totaled more than 500,000 pesos.

[70]Almada, 162. Francisco Velasco poignantly described the primitive state of health care then existing in the state: "There is not a hospital in the State, nor a drug store worthy of the name; the only one, in Hermosillo, is poorly supplied with drugs of inferior quality, and without any practical chemist or apothecary. Neither are there any established physicians of accredited skill and experience; the few who are found in the State are foreigners, who are only sought out in cases of urgent necessity. The inhabitants, in case of sickness, are generally left to the tender mercies of quacks and old women." Velasco, 23.

[71]Bartlett, 480; Stagg, *Almadas and Alamos,* 74-75.

[72]Stagg, *Almadas and Alamos,* 72-73; Almada, 287, 306.

manpower and played havoc with its registration rolls.[73] The indigence of the state treasury left those forces that had been organized, however irregularly, generally without arms, clothing, or officers to train them. Banditry had become commonplace. The civil war years had made it attractive and less risky; jails were few in number, easy to escape from, and frequently without funds to feed prisoners or maintain men to guard them. The state and municipal treasuries were impoverished from the United States' blockade, emigration, the cholera epidemic, and the expanded Apache raids.[74]

At least the state government was functioning, an accomplishment which could not be claimed by many of the municipios. In the smaller communities, there was no on-going treasury, no jail, no police, no public improvements of any kind, no parish priest. In some the lack of residents forced the suspension of annual elections of town councilors, leaving the justices of the peace and municipal attorney alone to govern them. Many of the local judges could not even sign their own names. The towns were only a little better off, scraping up enough revenues to support rudimentary schools, jails, and municipal buildings. Guaymas was the best off, having recently established gas street lights and a regular police force.[75] Only the notables of that port, Hermosillo, Alamos, and Ures could lay claim to being the enterprising, urban society their parents and grandparents had implanted in and envisioned for Sonora. And even they were going through lean times.

> . . . Our painful situation and the misfortunes which surround us . . . are the fruits of the different epochs and prolonged dissensions through which the State has had to pass, in which demoralization has been generalized and virtue lost, enervating, thus, the action of the government and the development of the infinite resources with which nature has privileged our soil . . . .[76]

Governor Aguilar's lament expressed the self-doubt and despair that was now seeping into the minds of Sonora's urban gentry. There was a growing lack of confidence in their ability to manage existing conditions, let alone transform

---

[73] Governor José de Aguilar, *Memoria del Estado de Sonora* (Ures, 1850), 4-5, 12-13; *idem, Memoria* (1851), 17, 40. The organization of the national guard in the states of the Republic was authorized by the federal law of July 14, 1848.

[74] Aguilar, *Memoria* (1850), 5, 8-13.

[75] *Ibid.,* 10, 14; *idem, Memoria* (1851), 25-26. Of the state's total expenditures of 72,072 pesos in 1849, only 314 pesos went to support primary instruction. In 1851, there were twenty-four primary schools in the state; the government assisted eleven of them, and five were financed privately. *Idem, Memoria* (1851), 15-17; *idem, Memoria* (1850), *Números* 3 and 6.

There was some secondary instruction provided at one school—that founded and directed by Gregorio Almada in Alamos. Almada, 226.

[76] Aguilar, *Memoria* (1850), 3.

them. During the late colonial period the Crown had been a reliable surrogate when their parents and grandparents had found themselves unable to cope with the situation alone. The national government now apparently was less able to deal with the realities confronting the state than they themselves. Worse still, Mexico City did not truly seem to care. The enterprising urban society that their forebears had implanted was in disarray. The prominent families of Sonora's urban centers felt the failure not only of realizing the progress envisioned in the post-independence years, but also of maintaining what their parents and grandparents had achieved. Nowhere was this state of affairs better mirrored than in the fate of the once-proud administrative and military center of the state—Arizpe.

> In the time of its prosperity, it is said to have contained a population of 5,000; but the civil discords and the encroachments of the Indians have reduced it to less than 1,500 .... There are many [buildings] of stone ... capped with a projection of brick, besides having a variety of architectural ornaments sufficient to impress one with the former wealth of the place and taste of its people. It is indeed melancholy to walk through its deserted streets, and see its dilapidated tenements, neglected courts, and closed stores.[77]

External Panaceas

For two decades Sonoran notables had been preoccupied with the internal security side of their equation of progress. Foreign contact had been taken for granted as a positive force that would follow once the containment of the Apaches and the subjection of the tribal Indians gained a degree of permanence. The consequences of the War with the United States, however, were raising a serious question about whether the effect of foreign contact was necessarily salutary. The United States was giving only lip service to its pledge of responsibility regarding the Apaches; it had even begun to appease them. More threatening ultimately was the tone and scope of expectation expressed by many North Americans heading west. Josiah Gregg, veteran of the Santa Fe trade and the War with Mexico, boldly stated the destiny of his compatriots in his diary while in the port of Mazatlán.

> I have long been of the opinion that the Anglo-Saxon race is destined to govern the entire American continent, at no very distant period— especially North America. And now do I believe that this California "gold fever" will serve directly to accelerate the matter .... When the precious metal begins to fail, the "thousands and tens of thousands" of adventurous spirits who have flocked there, will begin to look about for

---

[77]Bartlett, 282-283.

something else to do, commensurate with their inclinations . . . . They
must then commence scattering out among their neighbors—whether in
a friendly or hostile manner—whether in search of gold or other fortune. In this way do I believe that all the Pacific coast will soon be
occupied as far South as this place, and ultimately farther . . . . And the
intelligent classes of citizens in all parts, seem sensible of the near
approach of their political dissolution. But what can they do? They are
without means to prevent it.[78]

At mid-century, Gregg's expectations were no|pipe dreams. Nor were the
fears arising among Sonorans that their state might fall into the hands of
North Americans mere paranoia. Emigrants from the eastern United States,
bound for California by way of Santa Fé and across northern Sonora, frequently turned their livestock loose into unfenced grain fields, or entered
houses, pistols in hand, forcing the inhabitants to hand over whatever suited
their whim of necessity, and committed "other outrages which make one who
has any national pride blush to hear recited."[79] These were merely scattered
bands of adventurers passing through. In early 1851, only insufficient funds
prevented an invasion of the state led by the quartermaster general of California, Joseph C. Moorehead, who planned to annex Sonora (and Baja California) to the United States.[80] Reports also surfaced that the state was up for
sale. The state's official newspaper reprinted an article from the *New York
Herald,* which claimed that it learned from "an agent of the Mexican government" that its officials were finding themselves increasingly compelled to
consider selling Sonora, Chihuahua, and Baja California to find funds to keep
the government operating. And besides, it was impotent to protect these
lands from Indian incursions. The *Herald* urged the United States government
to take advantage of the opportunity.[81]

With their vision of progress blurred, with the underpinnings of their enterprising urban society eroding, and with aggressive, covetous North Americans

---

[78]Gregg, 324-325.

[79]Bartlett, 423-424.

[80]J. Fred Rippy, "Anglo-American Filibusters and the Gadsden Treaty," *Hispanic
American Historical Review,* 5 (May, 1922), 156, 159; Rufus K. Wyllys, *The French in
Sonora, 1850-1854* (Berkeley, 1932), 52-55.

[81]*La Voz del Pueblo* (Ures), October 9, 1851, in *Mexican Newspaper Miscellany*
(from the Bancroft Library, University of California at Berkeley), Microfilm 828, University of Arizona Library, Reel 3. The University of Arizona Library newspaper collection will hereafter be cited as UAm.
   For a more detailed study of these purchase negotiations, see James M. Hill,
"America Looks Southward, 1830-1860" (M.A. thesis, University of Missouri, 1950),
58-60, 75-77, 152-158. Hill's thesis discusses in detail the efforts of the United States to
acquire various combinations of Mexico's northern states and territories by offering to
assume the claims of its citizens against Mexico as payment; the negotiations and motives
behind the Gadsden Purchase are also discussed in this source.

on their borders, Sonora's urban gentry began to question what precisely was the nature of their ties with Mexico, and whether at present any such ties existed in truth. Spain had nurtured their society in its infancy. Within the new Republic of Mexico, they had failed to sustain its growth and had even lost ground, while the nation had proven itself unable and seemingly uncaring enough to reverse the deteriorating situation. The temptation was to seek an outside force, yielding to its domination in exchange for preservation of their way of life.

> Sonora in its actual state of abandonment, of misery, of insecurity, lack of protection, of guarantees and of liberty, is found exasperated; [it] has lost all hope of life, and the time is not far off when the delirium of its sufferings will cause it to throw itself into the hands of a neighbor who offers it protection, aid, and, in sum, an enchanting and pleasantly surprising life, such as today is enjoyed in upper California, from which many Sonorans return delighted . . . .[82]

Some among the urban gentry yielded to the temptation, concluding that annexation by the United States was inevitable and the only viable choice open to them. But there was an emerging consensus among most influential Sonorans that the only way to ward off this growing threat from the north was through colonization of the northern frontier. Those previously of the federalist persuasion were discouraged by the state government's inefficacious record of resolving internal security problems. Those of centralist sympathies were not attracted to the authoritarian ideologies of dictatorship or monarchy emanating from the new conservatives in the interior of the country. They had either become *gandaristas,* their politics personalized, or they had become part of a growing group of moderates such as José de Aguilar, who sought to be non-ideological, pragmatic.[83]

Those of all three political persuasions now agreed that colonization was the only viable alternative left to preserve their independence within the larger Mexican configuration, while at the same time salvage their vision of progress.[84] The frontier could not be colonized with Mexicans because it was too difficult and slow.[85] But in California there was a growing collection of

---

[82]Mariano Paredes, *Proyectos de leyes sobre colonización y comercio en el estado de Sonora* (México, 1850), 4. Paredes's colonization plan has been translated by Odie Faulk in the *New Mexico Historical Review* (October, 1964). See also Patricia Herring, "A Plan for Colonization of Sonora's Northern Frontier—The Paredes *Proyectos* of 1850," *Journal of Arizona History,* 10 (Summer, 1969), 103-104.

[83]Aguilar, *Memoria* (1850), 3.

[84]*El Sonorense,* June 25, 1852.

[85]Report of the Commission Named by a Junta of Notables Meeting in Ures, February 12, 1852, MAHm, Sonora, Reel 11.

discontented foreigners (non-Anglo-Saxons), particularly the French, disgusted and abused by Yankee discrimination and arrogance. If the government would concede them lands and other privileges in order to draw them to the largely depopulated frontier, reasoned this consensus among most urban gentry, they would form a barrier against the dreaded Apaches—and the now as-much-feared North Americans.[86] The existing surplus of Sonoran women, due to the long years of civil war and Apache campaigns, would ensure that the colonization was permanent and assimilated. "That barrier today is of civilized foreigners," some prominent Hermosillo residents noted, "but inside of half a century their children will be as Mexican as we are and as civilized as they."[87] Confidence in the biological process apparently remained among the notables, if in little else.

The Sonoran legislature passed a colonization law in 1850, with generous concessions of land and ten-year exemptions from state and municipal taxes in return for the colonists' obligation to contribute both their persons and possessions to the defense of the state.[88] But the following year, the Congress declared the law unconstitutional, claiming that it alone had the power to legislate the bases for colonization.[89] The efforts of Sonora's federal diputados to secure passage of bills promoting colonization in the state also came to naught.[90] Nevertheless, the Congress did adjust the national colonization laws to make them more favorable to foreigners, and the federal government began to promote immigration abroad, especially among the French in Cali-

---

[86]Letter from Some Citizens of Hermosillo to the Interim Governor of the State, January 8, 1852, MAHm, Sonora, Reel 11. The abuses endured by foreigners in California after annexation by the United States are detailed in Wyllys, chapter two.

[87]Letter from Some Citizens of Hermosillo, January 8, 1852. The letter contained the signatures of almost all those with political and economic influence in the town, including the Monteverde, Escalante, Noriega, Morales, Uruchurtu, Rodriguez, and Loaiza families, among others.

[88]Decree of the Legislature, May 6, 1850, MAHm, Sonora, Reel 24. The state law provided that Mexican entrepreneurs be given preference over their foreign counterparts in securing concessions. Each colonist was to receive a generous grant of land (which could not be resold for six years) and an exemption for ten years from all state direct and indirect contributions, from all taxes on imported supplies and tools—as well as those on the goods they produced, and from the tax on the assaying of any gold or silver mined.

[89]Herring, 106.

[90]Paredes, 6-24. Diputado Paredes submitted two bills to Congress in 1850 to promote colonization in Sonora. The first authorized generous land grants and twenty-five-year exemptions from various personal and indirect taxes in return for the obligation of the foreign colonists to become Mexican citizens and to defend the frontier. The second was designed to ensure colonization by declaring all foreign goods passing through Guaymas free of customs duties for twenty-five years. This latter measure, he maintained, would promote immigration and furnish badly needed capital to develop Sonora's abundant, but as yet largely untapped, resources. Given the previous opposition in the central core of the country to commercial expansion in the Northwest, the provisions of the second bill most likely were the main reason for the rejection of the whole project in the Congress.

fornia through its consuls there. Citizens of the "most preeminent Latin nation," smarting from their treatment by the Yankees, they were considered the most eligible and predisposed Europeans to serve as an impediment to Manifest Destiny.[91]

The response to these overtures was not long in coming. During 1851-1852, three expeditions of French colonists from California came to Sonora. These colonization efforts revealed the French adventurers' narrow objective of finding quick fortunes, their irresoluteness when the latter did not materialize, the growing suspicions and fickleness among the notables, and the extreme, violent measures such foreign adventurers would turn to when hindered in pursuing the bonanzas that had eluded them through years of failure.[92] The last expedition, led by Gaston Raousset, the prodigal son of a French noble family, was the most ambitious.

Raousset was in partnership with the *Compañía Restauradora,* whose principal stockholder was the wealthy banking firm of Jecker de la Torre & Company. The company had just received a federal concession to exploit the fabled mines of Arizona, located on the present northern border of Sonora, west of Nogales.[93] Raousset's party was to explore the district, locate and

---

[91]Wyllys, 16, 57-58.

[92]*Ibid.,* 58-65. Charles Pindray, for example, having come to California in 1850, had been forced to settle for the livelihood of a hunter supplying San Francisco with game. Hearing of the opportunities opening up for foreign colonists in Sonora from the new Mexican vice-consul in that port, he had recruited a party of ninety or so of his compatriots. A popular subscription was raised for them in Guaymas upon their arrival (late November, 1851)—provisions, implements, horses, and nearly 1,800 pesos. The state government conceded them the abandoned lands of an old mission pueblo (Cocóspera on the upper San Miguel River) and promised them additional horses, mules, and supplies. There, the honeymoon ended. Apache raids carried off many of their stock and the promised provisions failed to materialize. The state treasury had no funds to spare, and word of Pindray's unsavory reputation reached the new commander general, General Miguel Blanco, by way of the French ambassador in Mexico City, who was a stockholder of the *Compañía Restauradora,* which sought to expolit the same area. A desperate attempt to demand the fulfillment of the government's promises in Ures only antagonized state officials. Upon his return from the capital, Pindray was found dead, shot through the forehead by unknown assailants. Most of his followers, already discouraged, gave up and headed for San Francisco. The remainder chose a successor among them and tried to hang on.

At the same time, another party of French adventurers had obtained a concession to work the abandoned mines of the Gila Valley to the north from the Mexican consul in San Francisco. They reached Guaymas in early April, 1852, accepted Mexican citizenship as required, and settled in the Santa Cruz Valley south of Tucson. Their illusions of finding abundant gold placers were shortly dispelled and they quit the venture, splitting up into small groups to find their way back to San Francisco.

[93]Almada, 79-81, 390-392; Manifesto of Governor José de Aguilar to the Sonoran Public, September 28, 1852, MAHm, Sonora, Reel 11. The then legendary mines of Arizona were first discovered about 1736 north of the old mission of Saric. The glowing accounts of the first finds had prompted the Crown to claim them for itself, but they were abandoned shortly afterwards because of the growing Apache incursions. Expeditions had been organized in 1817 and 1834 to try to renew work in the mining district, but the Apaches had cut the efforts short.

denounce the mines, and take possession of the surrounding countryside in accordance with the concession. The members of the armed contingent, almost wholly French, found their reception in Guaymas (June, 1852) somewhat disconcerting. While the local authorities and citizenry were friendly enough, there was a distinct coolness on the part of state officials. The truculent manner of Raousset's predecessors had antagonized them and set them wondering about the French colonists' real intentions in coming. But the chilly welcome had another source as well. The unfriendliness of the principal figures in the government was also the product of economic motives. The financial magnates of Mexico's Pacific coast (Barron, Forbes & Company), unsettled by the *Compañía Restauradora's* invasion of its territory, had put together a subsidiary corporation (Forbes-Ocegura Company) to reach and claim the coveted mines first. They had just succeeded in wooing to their side Governor Aguilar (then on a leave of absence), Interim Governor Fernando Cubillas, and Commander General Miguel Blanco, as well as several influential political figures, such as Manuel María Gándara. Some, most notably Aguilar, had been involved in the rival venture.[94]

Raousset ignored the regulations regarding the arrival of armed and organized immigrants, which state officials now decided to enforce strictly.[95] He refused to renounce his nationality or to appear personally before the commander general in the capital to obtain permission for his party of two hundred men to travel armed through the state. The *Compañía Restauradora* then broke the contract and stopped all supplies. Convinced of the complicity of General Blanco and other state officials with the Forbes-Ocegura Company (who were preparing a punitive expedition against him), Raousset sounded out leading men in the frontier villages about the prospects for a general uprising of the frontier population and, if their grievances and compensation were rejected for the French, a possible proclamation of the independence of Sonora. A number of prominent citizens in several villages promised their support or indicated interest. Raousset and his men then marched south, taking Hermosillo and calling on Sonorans to join them. Those with influence in the frontier villages sat on their hands. General Blanco organized a large state force, which cut the French off before they could reach Guaymas and forced them to leave the state, surrendering all their arms.[96].

---

[94]Wyllys, 68-85, 103; Almada, 39. Gándara was also busy on the frontier with his own enterprises, centering on the Santa Cruz Valley that led north to Tucson. In partnership with a group of European expatriates, he planned to stock a large sheep operation, while the Europeans were to manage it (Kessell, 313). The large acreage was formerly part of the mission of Tumacácori, which had been purchased by Gándara's brother-in-law, Governor Aguilar, in 1842. Though he retained title, Aguilar evidently purchased the lands for Gándara's use. Mattison, 293-294.

[95]Manifesto of Governor Aguilar, September 28, 1852.

[96]Wyllys, 83-132.

Undaunted, Raousset returned two years later (July, 1854), under the cover of President Santa Anna's invitation of small groups of foreigners (other than North Americans) to serve in the army on the frontier against the Apaches. There was no friendly reception in the port this time, however. William Walker's unsuccessful filibustering expedition to Baja California the previous winter, the independence of that territory and Sonora, had stirred the already growing xenophobic feelings in Sonora. On July 13, Raousset's expedition of four hundred men was soundly defeated in Guaymas by the national guard of the port under the new commander general, General José María Yáñez. Raousset was executed, and all but a few of his men were deported.[97]

After these experiences with the French colonizing expeditions, the prominent families of Sonora's towns were left with the conclusion that the future they sought rested on themselves alone. All prospective outside forces had proven to be a menace, not a benefactor. They had quickly learned what the Yankees were up to. The California French, whom they had figured could be employed to stave off the rapacious advance of their new northern neighbors, had deceivingly proved no better. Their own national government, which had rarely lent a friendly hand, was now giving them cause for serious doubts as to whether it was not an enemy as well.

Part of their state (what is today southern Arizona) had been ransomed for the maintenance of Santa Anna's dictatorship through the Gadsden Purchase in 1854. General Yáñez, who had paid considerable attention to the Apache problem and had just ended for good the designs of the French filibusters, was soon replaced for failure to punish the latter as rebels.[98] His successor, General Domingo Ramírez de Arellano, fixed his residence in Guaymas, was indifferent to the Apache incursions, and winked at the steadily growing contraband being introduced underneath his nose. As a result, he was dismissed and the port was temporarily closed. The new governor and commander general, General Pedro Espejo, kept most of his troops stationed in Guaymas and Hermosillo.[99] There was, thus, no one for the urban notables

---

[97]*Ibid.*, 133-225. For another account of the Raousset expeditions, see Margo Glantz, *Un folletín realizado: la aventura del Conde Raousset-Boulbon en Sonora* (México, 1973).

[98] Wyllys, 185-189, 214-218, 224; Almada, 836-841. The dismissal of Yáñez provides an example of Mexico City's continuing lack of understanding of the situation on the country's periphery. Santa Anna removed the commander general because of the latter's leniency toward the prisoners. Yet from Yáñez's prospective, his needy military command did not have the funds to support so many prisoners until the supreme government had decided their fate. Secondly, the national guard unit in Guaymas wished to return to their civilian occupations; he would then be left with a dangerously small force with which to guard the French filibusters. Finally, Yáñez did not want to provoke any retaliation by the French government.

[99]*El Nacional* (Ures), September 7 and October 5, 1855, MAHm, Sonora, Reel 11.

of Sonora to rely on but themselves to maintain and expand the enterprising, urban society they had inherited. And their own record in the previous two decades did not inspire confidence.

STATE OF SONORA, 1854. Location of major physical and political characteristics of the area. Boundaries and *cabeceras* shown are from 1854. Earlier place names are given in parentheses.

SINALOA: THE RIVALRY OF TWO CITIES

The prominent families of Sinaloa's towns did not seem to face such glum prospects for the realization of their progress. North Americans in their wildest expansionary expectations reached down the Pacific coast beyond Mazatlán, yet no concrete filibustering expeditions or plans had materialized to actually threaten parts of the state (though the annexation of Baja California and Sonora would have put Sinaloa on the front lines of Manifest Destiny). The tribal Indians in the northern part of the state remained fragmented and unresponsive to the unrest of their counterparts in Sonora. Internal security was, thus, of only minimal consequence. Foreign contact had steadily increased, though it had continued almost solely in the form of foreign merchants and commercial markets. The despair and doubt that was now prevalent among Sonora's urban gentry had not arisen in the state.

The lack of such feelings, however, did not mean Sinaloa's notables had not been frustrated in their desires for sustained economic growth. Frustration had not given way to despondency and uncertainty, but it had become more intense and tinged with intolerance and even malice. The concentration of urban growth and economic opportunity had accelerated. Culiacán and Mazatlán had continued to corner an ever-increasing share of commercial markets and of the stimulants that fostered their expansion. The prominent families in the other urban centers of the state had been left in the backwaters of these mercantile currents. Beyond the clientele connections obtained with the trade through Culiacán and Mazatlán, there was little to spur the growth of their towns and their surrounding agricultural or mining districts. Such conditions, however, had not mitigated the frustrations of the notables of the capital and the port. The rivalry between them had become acute, the perceived stakes non-negotiable. The expansion and centralization of commercial markets had failed to satisfy their desires for sustained economic growth. They had, instead, heightened the expectations of their visions of progress and encouraged the notion of "all-or-nothing" in the realization of their visions. In Sonora, the intrusion of the federalist-centralist conflict had sparked a bitter civil war and had then given way to a certain forbearance among urban notables. In Sinaloa, though far less ideological in tone, involvement in the national political struggle had deepened steadily.

The plans of the Vega clique to dominate Sinaloa had suffered a setback with the introduction of centralism. No longer in control of the executive branch, they lost the 1837 elections for the departmental junta. At the same time, as noted previously, Mazatlán was given municipal status and aid to improve its port works. Hoping to regain control with the return of federalism, the clique and its clients supported the unsuccessful Urrea expedition of 1837. Four years later they made another unsuccessful bid to return to power. When the existing departmental assembly, being in recess, failed to declare for or against the federalist revolt which broke out in several parts of

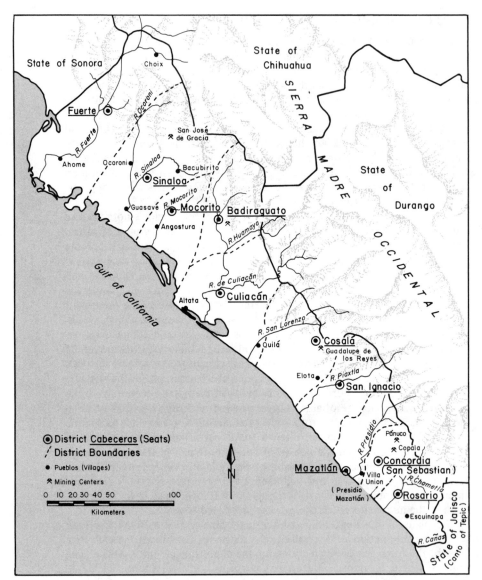

STATE OF SINALOA, 1854. Location of major physical and political characteristics of the area. Boundaries and *cabeceras* shown are from 1854. Earlier place names are given in parentheses.

the country, the Vegas and their partisans temporarily supplanted it with another assembly beholden to them. However, Santa Anna's successful coup later that year established a military dictatorship, and his appointee was made governor and military commander of the state. The executive established residence in Mazatlán. The departmental junta, nevertheless, remained in Culiacán under the watchful and waiting eyes of the Vegas. Their chance came with Santa Anna's fall at the end of 1844. Rafael de la Vega was acknowledged as provisional governor by the new moderado government in Mexico City and two years later was elected constitutional governor with the restoration of the federalist system. Prohibited from seeking reelection the following year, Don Rafael deftly arranged for a stand-in to win the election, who then moved aside for one of his protégés, Pomposo Verdugo, to serve as acting governor.[100]

The Vegas moved quickly to tighten their political domination of the state to prevent another fall from power. They filled public offices with their relatives and cronies. Elections were tightly controlled, frequently held throughout the state in the houses of their agents and clients, and often took place without the knowledge of the general citizenry.[101] Swift retribution fell on those trying to cross them. When the ayuntamiento of Cosalá refused to reinstate an employee tried and convicted for the embezzlement of a large sum and for operating a clandestine tobacco manufactory, Governor Rafael de la Vega suspended the town's authorities and dispatched a force of fifty men who arrested them and took them back to the capital as prisoners.[102]

For the Vega clique and its clients, the primary purpose for such extensive governmental control was the mercantile benefits it made possible. By the late 1840s, so intense had the rivalry between the capital and the port become that political domination was now perceived as necessary not only for the expansion of commercial markets, but for their preservation as well. The Vegas and their clients, themselves deeply enmeshed in contraband activities, had watched with alarm the growing extension of Mazatlán's commerce into their accustomed markets. Centralism had provided *porteño* merchants with protection, but little regulation. Under such conditions, the port's initial and natural advantages had been permitted to operate with few impediments. Now once again in control of the state government and buttressed by the return of the federalist system, the Vega clique immediately used the political apparatus to diminish those favorable circumstances. In 1847 they secured through the federal government the opening of Altata to overseas commerce.[103] Mazatlán's monopoly on the introduction of foreign goods was

---

[100] Buelna, *Apuntes*, 18-35.
[101] *Ibid.*, 31.
[102] *El Sinaloense*, November 5, 1847.
[103] Buelna, *Compendio*, 32.

thereby terminated, and wider contraband opportunities for themselves were now possible through the manipulation of the customs officials in their satellite port. The Vega clique also enacted new state tariffs and other taxes on commerce. By employing its control over public administration to avoid paying such taxes on its own trade and vigorously enforcing their collection on Mazatlán's commerce, it began to turn the port's former competitive advantage to its own favor.[104]

Though above all motivated by their own avarice, the Vegas also looked after Culiacán's interests, and capital notables in general prospered. The opening of Altata to foreign commerce benefited even those not connected with the Vega circle by enabling them to skirt the intermediaries in Mazatlán, though not nearly as extensively as the Vegas and their clients, who garnered the profits of contraband as well. In 1846, the Vega government put the state mint into operation. Authorized sixteen years before, the construction of the building to house the mint had been delayed by civil disorders.[105] The mint added impulse to Culiacán's commerce by attracting the flow of precious metals through the capital rather than the port and by putting more hard currency in circulation. The children of the town's prominent families attended the first secondary school in the Northwest, the Seminario Tridentino, founded by Bishop Lázaro Garza y Ballesteros in 1838. It had been temporarily housed in the residence of Rafael de la Vega while its own building was being constructed. In 1842, the same year construction of the school was completed, work was begun on a cathedral for the town under the direction of Bishop de la Garza.[106] The price of such prosperity for the Culiacán gentry in general, however, was increasing political subservience and the growing risk of fallout from the retaliatory depradations inflicted by the Vega clique's enemies.

As the Vegas' grip on the state government tightened, the foreign merchants in Mazatlán and their clients found their profits being squeezed and their markets threatened. The traditional device of buying off venal customs officials had already become more difficult. As their numbers and their trade had grown, Mazatlán's foreign merchants had become a growing source of irritation not only for commercial interests in Culiacán, but also for officials in Mexico City, who saw desperately needed revenues escaping from them, and for commercial competitors in the interior, whose markets were being poached upon through the unfavorable price competition created by the contraband. The foreign merchants had begun to purchase the support of the

---

[104] *El Sinaloense,* November 5, 1847.

[105] Ramón Beltran Martínez, "Apuntes para la historia de la casa de moneda en Culiacán," Congreso Mexicano de Historia, Estudios Históricos de Sinaloa (México, 1960), 231.

[106] González Dávila, 561-562.

federal garrison and the port's hangers-on to alleviate these increasing official restraints. The latter were employed, for example, in early 1849 to "welcome" the new collector of customs sent from Mexico City: they greeted him as he approached town with menacing jeers and even stones. The new functionary was unable to take possession of his office and kept a respectful distance from the port. Such methods, as well as that of encouraging the federal troops to engage in a barracks revolt, were timed to coincide with the arrival in the port of large commercial expeditions from Europe or the Orient, during which time the ships were unloaded with little or no customs duties collected.[107] The soldiers preferred to dance to the pecuniary melody of the foreign pipers rather than to the air of obedience emanating from the far-off governments in Mexico City.

Frequently, these barracks revolts coincided with rebellions on the national scene, such as the Paredes' rebellion to oust the Santa Anna dictatorship, the Paredes' coup to dump the Herrera government, and the Santa Anna revolt to re-establish the federalist system. The Mazatlán garrison was at an ideological loss as it waffled back and forth among centralist, moderate, and federalist governments in Mexico City. But the objectives of the port's foreign merchants and their clients became more sharply focused. Seven of the eight barracks revolts they funded between late 1844 and early 1849 followed the Vega clique's return to power. Their purpose became as much to end the Vegas' renewed hold on state politics as to utilize national political conflicts to continue and expand their contraband activities.[108]

Seemingly, the foreign merchants and their clients found a willing ally to accomplish this imperative task in the person of Colonel Rafael Tellez, an ambitious and venal career soldier. Tellez arrived in Mazatlán in April, 1846, in transit with a section of troops sent by the Paredes government to Upper California to defend that territory against an invasion by the United States. But the opportunities for personal gain in the port soon overshadowed any sense of patriotic duty. Tellez, with his forces and the garrison, pronounced against Paredes and for the restoration of the federalist system under Santa Anna (whom he personally followed) and took command of the port, surrounding himself with devotees. He helped himself to the customs revenues, on the pretext of maintaining his troops, and cooperated with the foreign merchants in their contraband activities. He ignored the War Ministry's order to see that all North Americans leave the port and that their consulate be suspended. When Tellez was relieved of his command in January, 1847, he refused to comply with the orders and retained command over the port

---

[107]Gregg, 236; Buelna, *Apuntes,* 22-33.

[108] Buelna, *Apuntes,* 22-33. The revolts were in November, 1844; January, 1846; March, 1846; May, 1846; January, 1847; and January, 1849.

independently of the government. That summer he attempted to seize control of the state government by sending troops north to remove Governor de la Vega. The force succeeded in occupying Culiacán on September 17. They sacked the commercial houses of the Vegas and their friends and found large quantities of smuggled merchandise that had been introduced through Altata and other points along the coast under the protection of authorities beholden to them.

The following January the federal government, disgusted with Tellez's intransigence and his ill-preparedness and retreat in the face of the United States' occupation of Mazatlán, intervened on behalf of Governor de la Vega. The imminent conclusion of the war against the United States freed federal troops to force Tellez to submit and leave the state. With such backing from Mexico City, the Vega government was thereafter in firm control of the state. Two barracks revolts staged in Mazatlán within the following year (July, 1848, and January, 1849) failed to accomplish more than to provide accelerated contraband activity.[109]

The teeter-totter nature of the rivalry between the Culiacán and Mazatlán merchant communities, however, had not ended. The Vega regime received a severe setback a few months after Tellez's departure with the premature death of its able director, Don Rafael. His younger brother Francisco, who succeeded him and was elected governor in late 1851, was far less diplomatic and more inclined to rigid implementation of the regime's interests.[110] These liabilities soon played into the hands of Mazatlán's foreign merchants, who had been waiting for another opportunity. The Vega clique's control of the state also depended upon the support of, or at least tolerance by, the national government. By 1852 a blustery conservative movement, which had replaced the now-defunct centralist party, coalesced around the aging Lucas Alamán, and the moderado government was in serious trouble.

In early May, at the initiative of the diputado for the district of Mazatlán, the legislature passed a decree abolishing the state *alcabala* and replacing it with a direct contribution on commerce and industry. The Vega government wholeheartedly concurred, anticipating a rise in revenues. But the Mazatlán merchants had supported the measure with other ideas in mind. They were now free of the cumbersome *alcabalas* and immediately set out to undermine

---

[109] Mena Castillo, I, 211-234. With the series of victories scored by the United States forces in the Valley of Mexico and with the occupation of the capital in the late summer of 1847, the fighting diminished considerably. Guerrilla activities carried out against the occupation army in various states, and supported by the *puros* (radical federalists), inflicted considerable losses. But the moderados secured a majority in Congress and, determined to secure a peace, suspended the hostile activities of most federal contingents to improve the chances of successful negotiations. In March, 1848, the Treaty of Guadalupe Hidalgo was signed, ending all hostilities.

[110] González Dávila, 650-651.

the new contribution. In this, as in other efforts to gain influence in the government, they utilized their clients, the Mexican merchants and other prominent nationals of the port. With such a community of interests, the local assessment board lowered their quotas in wholesale fashion.

Just as quickly, Governor de la Vega retaliated. With no attempt to negotiate the dispute, he disqualified the local board's assessments and then doubled them to arrive at the contributions to be levied. The foreign merchants staged one of their now-customary demonstrations in reply. Throngs of the port's less consequential citizenry gathered in front of the residence of the municipal president, protesting vigorously, newly-acquired silver pesos in their pockets. Intimidated by the vehemence of the crowd, he agreed to petition the government to repeal its new contribution assessments and promised they would not be collected until the petition was acted upon by the government. For good measure, the foreign consuls in the port filed a complaint before the commander general, Ramón Morales, contending the onerous contributions injured their respective compatriots.

Don Francisco refused to budge an inch. He ignored the port's petition, suspended the municipal president for his irresolute behavior, and ordered the competent authorities in Mazatlán to collect the contributions. When the judge of the first instance and the district prefect appeared before the commercial houses to enforce the collections (late May), however, they were refused admittance and a hastily recruited mob drove them away, throwing stones and shouting viva to commerce and muera to the government. To put an end to such intransigence, the governor entered the port in mid-June with a section of the national guard. The foreign merchants, now desperate, resorted to their trump card. With a number of ships lying in the port ready to unload their cargoes, Captain Pedro Valdés on July 11 led a majority of the federal garrison in revolt, surprising and capturing the commander general, Governor de la Vega, and his national guard troops. To obtain their release, Don Francisco agreed to abandon the port, with his forces disarmed, and to return all the contributions that had been collected to date.

The same afternoon a meeting, well-attended by foreigners, was convoked by the leaders of the revolt. A resolution was approved calling upon the federal government to convert the district of Mazatlán into a territory, separating it from the rest of Sinaloa. Given the federalist system then operative, it was the only way to elude the competitive disadvantages officially (and often illegally) imposed by the Vega government from Culiacán, short of outright independence, which the foreign merchants and their clients knew Mexico City would never tolerate.[111] In September another option became available to the port's commercial interests with the conservative revolt

---

[111] Mena Castillo, I, 245-249.

against President Arista. The proposal for separation was dropped. Captain Valdés seconded the revolt, proclaiming himself governor and commander general. Valdés's troops marched on Culiacán, taking the capital in October and sacking it with a vengeance. Governor de la Vega tried to organize an effective resistance, but with Arista's fall (January, 1853) the national government could no longer be counted upon for assistance as it had been five years before. By the following March, having been decisively defeated in the district of Fuerte, his last outpost, he abandoned the effort.[112]

The Vega regime had been toppled finally. While the venal Santa Anna government again ruled the country from Mexico City, supported by the conservatives, the foreign merchants and their clients, in partnership with Governor and Commander General Valdés and his successors, controlled Sinaloa. Once again a department, the capital was formally transferred from Culiacán to Mazatlán, and the port of Altata was closed to overseas trade.[113] The foreign merchants, their clients, and allies were at last ascendant.

And what good times these were for the port! The recently developed California trade blossomed. With increasing frequency steamers plied between Mazatlán and San Francisco bringing quicksilver, machinery, and reshipped European goods, in exchange for precious metals, hardwoods, hides, and *panocha*. Sailing ships arriving from Europe and the Orient continued to increase in numbers. The Europeans in the port dominated the trade in the face of the pretensions of Yankee merchants by regularly receiving from the customs officials remittances of a large portion of duties levied on their goods.[114] Contraband flourished: one of the most notorious of the illegal importations was that by Melchers Brothers and Company in July, 1854, in collusion with the administrator of the *aduana* and the head of the federal treasury office in the port.[115]

Mazatlán now reached a population estimated at from ten to twelve thousand. Along its patterned, though narrow, streets were large, handsomely built homes, wholly in the old Castilian style with short columns, moorish capitals, and ornaments. There were many well-stocked commercial houses and shops, vying with the fashionable stores of New York in the quality of their merchandise in the opinion of one visitor from the United States.[116] Two hun-

---

[112] *Ibid.*, 254-259.

[113] Buelna, *Compendio*, 32, 92-93. Captain Valdés decreed the transfer of the capital to Mazatlán after capturing Culiacán in October; the move was later confirmed by the new conservative government. Altata was closed to foreign commerce in February, 1853.

[114] United States Department of State, *Report of the Commercial Relations of the United States with All Foreign Nations* (Washington, 1857), Mazatlán, Vice-Consul Charles B. Smith, 419.

[115] Buelna, *Apuntes*, 41.

[116] Bartlett, 486.

dred fifty children were receiving primary education in two private and two public schools.[117] The port in the mid-1850s was considerably in advance of any city or town in the Northwest. Indeed, only San Francisco surpassed it on the entire Pacific coast north of Panama.[118]

After nearly a generation of conflict, the commercial interests of Mazatlán had apparently supplanted the Culiacán gentry's predominance. Through the years, the stakes in their mercantile rivalry had escalated to such a point that being the loser meant being the victim. Political reversals had become translated into severe impairments to the potential for future progress, as well as serious damage to economic interests in the present. The embittered contention between the notables of the two towns had not ended. By 1854 there was too much at stake in the internal logic of the conflict for that. Yet envelopment by a new and broader struggle would alter the composition of that urban rivalry and eventually create the possibilities for different political and economic configurations in Sinaloa. The same broadened struggle would also permeate Sonora, with similar consequences. Through that experience, the urban notables of the entire Northwest would come to feel themselves truly part of a larger whole, a national entity.

---

[117] *Departamento de la Estadística Nacional: Sinaloa, Sonora, Nayarit,* 80.
[118] Bartlett, 486.

5

Somos Mexicanos

(1854-1866)

Late one night in early April, 1857, John Coleman Reid and eighteen companions came upon an irrigation ditch a few hundred paces from the village of Caborca, thirty miles down-river from the town of Altar. Dead tired, they had just fled from an ambush by a party of four hundred armed Sonorans, in which they had lost four men and had had to abandon their horses. The men quenched their parched throats, pausing to rest and consider their next move. Ahead of them the unceasing drone of hundreds of Mexican voices made it evident that General Henry Crabb "did not have the quiet possession of the village," as two villagers from neighboring Pitiquito had told them earlier that day. The constant discharge of arms fire and the periodic roar of a cannon convinced Reid and the others that Crabb and his advance party of about seventy were besieged and that "a further attempt to join our country-men would be the extremest folly." There was no alternative but to try to make their way back to the community of Calabasas across the border in the Gadsden Purchase territory.[1]

The retreat was hard to accept, the culmination of failure. Reid, a native of Marian, had left with a party of fellow Alabamans the previous fall. Under the protection of a garrison at Calabasas were others who had come to the Gadsden territory to seek their fortunes. But, as Reid rather stiffly put it, "Here we found that our conceptions did not warrant our deductions therefrom." The Apaches made panning for gold dangerous and risky considering the few returns thus far obtained. In addition, large-scale mining of the abundant copper, lead, and iron ores discovered required expensive machinery and greatly improved transportation to turn a profit. The prospect of Apache depredations also made stock-raising risky. Furthermore, practically all of the

---

[1] John C. Reid, *Reid's Tramp; or, A Journal of the Incidents of Ten Months of Travel Through Texas, New Mexico, Arizona, Sonora, and California* (Selma, Alabama, 1858), 209-215.

lands worth tilling had already been taken by the first immigrants. Consequently, Reid and his companions had been preparing to return home when Crabb's emissaries arrived from California (by way of Fort Yuma) with the tempting offer of 160 acres of the best public lands in Sonora to each who joined his colonizing expedition there. Crabb had also promised a bonus to each of $50 a month until the Mexican government acknowledged the new Sonoran administration of Ignacio Pesqueira. They had been told that Crabb had the assurances of concurrence in the project from many of the state's most influential people. For those like Reid, without any gainful prospects in sight, Crabb's emissaries were "as deliverers to a people in a desolate country . . . ."[2]

What then had gone wrong, Reid and his companions surely wondered, as they made the arduous and uncertain trek on foot back to Calabasas. They had encountered only hostility from the Sonorans, first passive, then violent. The government with whom Crabb had dealt had now turned against him. Reid had thought the Mexicans ignorant, deceitful, yellow, and thus unable to develop their land. He had believed the importation of Anglo-Americans to be the panacea for the ailings of the state and considered those like himself the rightful heirs to its undeveloped wealth.[3] Reid and his compatriots were unaware, however, that xenophobia had been building among Sonorans since the first filibustering expedition after mid-century. External forces had proven to be a threat to them, not the assistance they had first expected. The notables had become suspicious of the motives of foreigners purporting to assist in the promotion of security and economic activity in the state. The general populace, bearing the brunt of foreign depredations, had become hostile to such intruders.

In one sense the fate of Reid, his companions, and the Crabb expedition was a culmination. It would be the last such filibustering enterprise. Those north of the border came to understand that the use of such proposals of assistance as ploys for annexation or political domination would no longer be tolerated. Such external contacts would have to be established on Sonorans' terms or on conditions acceptable to them. After a generation the urban gentry, who still controlled the politics of the state, had come to the realization that no matter how unsuccessful the fulfillment of their visions of progress had been, the price of external support had proven too high. Their interests ultimately could be secured and advanced only through their own initiative and direction.

---

[2]*Ibid.*, 194-197.
[3]*Ibid.*, 220. Reid, after making it back to Calabasas, returned home to Alabama, along with many of his original party, by way of San Francisco, Panama, and New Orleans.

In another sense, however, the Crabb incident marked a beginning. Neither Reid, nor his fellow North Americans, nor even the notables of Sonora or their counterparts in Sinaloa, were aware of the full implications of the new era into which the Mexican nation was then drifting. Within a decade, the nature of the republic would begin to be redefined and the emerging redefinition severely tested. In the process, the urban gentry of the Northwest, and to a lesser extent the general populace there, would become intensely involved in national politics. They would come to identify fully their fortunes with those of the country as a whole. They would come to feel themselves truly at home in the nation.

NEW NATIONAL VISIONARIES

A new regime was in the process of consolidating power in Mexico City, one markedly different from its predecessors. Because of that difference, it would come in time to earn the respect and loyalty of the large majority of notables and of the general populace in the Northwest. The difference lay more in possibility than actuality. For the first time since the mid-1830s there was a government in the national capital that had a fresh vision of what Mexico was and what it could become. That vision was boldly proclaimed in the just-promulgated constitution (February 5, 1857). In theory, it made the politics of the preceding two decades petty and knavish by comparison. Yet the change was far more of heart and mind than of habit and practicality. The will was more than ample, but it was guided by an intention that was private as well as public.

The liberals who had formed that vision were for the most part young professionals, generally from notable families, or tied to them through marriage or clientage. They were joined by regional and local bosses (*caudillos* and *caciques*) and their clientele. Not infrequently there was overlap. Their response to the conditions existing at mid-century, their decision to act, was based on the post-independence events. None had known the viceroyalty as adults; many not even as children. The young professionals in particular had little in common with the colonial past. Many had been educated in Europe. Most of the rest had attended the new schools established during the republic. Education, usually with a liberal bent, was one of their two decisive common experiences. The other was the turmoil and directionlessness of the country since the mid-1830s in which their personal aspirations for advancement in political influence, wealth, and social position had been generally frustrated.[4] They blamed the persistent vestiges of the colonial order for such

---

[4]The careers of these young liberals had constituted a sort of shuttle between the states and Mexico City. Though the large majority of them had entered politics at the state level, many had been schooled in the national capital, and by the late 1840s some had reached the national level as diputados and government ministers.

unmet expectations, as well as for the state of disorganization and humiliation into which the nation had sunk.

And for them, Mexico was a nation. They took it almost as a given. It was not a collection of varied cultures and peoples that necessitated an authoritarian force to be held together and made workable. The mistake of the post-independence years had not been nationhood, but the increasingly tyrannical resistance to its fulfillment by the vested interests of the colonial order. There had been little freedom or opportunity for the nation to grow and for individuals, especially those like themselves, to advance. As far as this political conception meant the right to prerogative, vis-à-vis centralized authority, the local and regional bosses concurred. Those with strong entrepreneurial inclinations, but as yet modest holdings, were also attracted to the young professional's view of the cause and solution to the country's malaise.

Guided primarily by the conceptions of these young professionals, the liberals sought a more rational, regularized political structure, one which kept arbitrariness to a minimum and placed a premium on the freedom to maneuver, be it economically, politically, socially, or in combination. Theirs was a social liberalism that went beyond the enlightened, legal liberalism of their federalist predecessors. They understood the legal privilege and economic underpinnings upon which the vested interests of the colonial period depended, especially those of the church. They differed, however, on the degree to which and the speed with which those privileges and underpinnings should be abolished or curtailed.

The new liberal regime was the product of a national movement created during the Ayutla Revolt of 1854-1855, which had been initiated to remove Santa Anna and his cronies. The fighting had ceased to be between different sections of the army or between the army and state militias. The opposition ranks had become filled with large forces recruited from among local people, in general mobilized by local liberal *caudillos* and *caciques* on a clientele basis. These forces were "popular" not in the sense that commoners had any significant input in the movement's direction, but in that they became caught up in the struggle. In addition, the armed struggle between such popular forces (often guerrillas) and the army had been long and hard, not merely a matter of maneuvers, words, and deals as it had been previously. Furthermore, the scope of the conflict was far more extensive than ever before. The fighting had gone on continually over most of the country.

The liberal movement had continued to gather strength after the armed struggle had ended, centered around a national program embodied in the Constitution of 1857. The movement's core was the common social background of the young professionals who had come to lead it. Initially it was national in large part because of their ability to come together and communicate common aspirations, transcending regional preoccupations. At the same time, the national scope of the movement had been reinforced by the extensive regional support it received, centered around local bosses and their clientele. In response, conservatives had begun to form a mass movement of their own. Previously relying on the army, as had been customary in post-independence politics, they had begun seeking to mobilize common people to resist the liberals' attempt to reorder Mexican society.[5]

Given the emergence of such large, popular political movements that were national in scope, the Northwest would have found it very difficult to avoid involvement, even had the region's inhabitants desired it. In fact, increasing numbers did not seek isolation. Many among the new generation of notables responded to the liberals' vision. Most were professionals or aspiring entrepreneurs or, as was increasingly the case, both. The old colonial order based in the central core had left them hanging on the periphery while it maneuvered for hegemony, rendering no assistance yet frustrating their efforts to expand opportunity. The liberals seemed to be saying that they considered the Northwest and other peripheral regions integral parts of the nation. Their interests and their participation in the nation were not to be determined by the calculations of the powers in the center of the country, deliberating about and for them. Unlike the federalists, for whom there persisted a relational gap between the national government and the states, the new liberals clearly defined a national sovereignty in which the integrity of the states was preserved. The pinnacle of power was lodged in a national Congress, composed of representatives from the various states, that counteracted excessive local power and arbitrary presidential rule. Many notables in the Northwest were drawn to such a resolution of the prior federalist/centralist dichotomy, which had failed to mesh with the realities existing in their region.

A number of those attracted to the liberal movement, while studying in Mexico City, Guadalajara, or abroad, had been exposed to the liberal ideas then current in academic circles. The liberals' program enlarged constituencies and opened up avenues for gaining state and national influence, particularly for local professionals who shared their views. The constitutional provisions to break up corporate holdings mirrored the prior futile efforts to end the tribal Indians' control of the best lands in the region. The liberals' emphasis on nationalism struck a chord among those faced since their youth with the continuing threat of foreign domination. It also attracted the general populace, which had developed a deepening hostility toward such foreign interlopers.

---

[5]This interpretation of the liberal movement is drawn from varied and differing sources, most notably: lectures at Harvard University by John Womack; Richard Sinkin, "The Mexican Constitutional Congress, 1856-1857—A Statistical Analysis," *Hispanic American Historical Review*, 53 (February, 1973), 1-26; Justo Sierra, *The Political Evolution of the Mexican People* (Austin, 1969), originally published in 1901-1902; Walter V. Scholes, *Mexican Politics During the Juárez Regime, 1855-1872* (Columbia, Missouri, 1957).

In contrast, the recruitment of conservative support was handicapped considerably. The core of the conservative movement was the defense of traditional prerogatives and institutional structures, in particular those of the church. As noted previously, such traditional elements of colonial society were not strong in the Northwest. Clericalism and the defense of corporate privilege therefore aroused few impassioned feelings there. Only the tribal Indians and the small clerical establishment in the region could find a strong ideological basis for support of the conservative cause. Others allied with it for solely practical reasons.

The initial response to the liberal and conservative movements in the Northwest was one of discretion and a touch of indifference. The liberals nationally had no formal authority, no established constituencies. They only declared their authority through a process culminating in the Constitution of 1857, proposing a program they thought would secure them widespread support. Those in the Northwest (as elsewhere in the country) were then faced with the decision of whether to endorse the liberals' program and recognize the authority of the constitutional structure it had created, or to side with the conservatives in opposing it. It took most several years, many over a decade to make that decision firmly. The transition from the existing political alignments to new ones, based on association with the opposing sides of the national conflict, was meandering. Firm connections were slow and uneven in coming, solid commitments hesitant in being tendered. And even then, the bases of those alignments were never simple, since they wove together ideological, material, and familial concerns.

ADJUSTMENT TO THE AYUTLA AFTERMATH

The triumph of the Ayutla Revolt in the late summer of 1855 had been generally welcomed in Sonora, though far more out of relief over Santa Anna's fall from power than enthusiasm for the new regime. Sonorans' accumulated suspicions of whatever kind of national government ruled from Mexico City would have to be proven unwarranted before they would embrace any new regime. Guaymas citizens fired off a stern admonition to the new supreme powers, protesting the recent sale of *La Mesilla* (the Gadsden Purchase) by Santa Anna and warning that they would not "consent to or tolerate at any time, whatever the pretext, cause, or circumstances, the alienation of a single inch of Sonoran territory, to any foreign power . . . ." Nor would they tolerate any armed or pacific intervention on Sonoran soil. They were prepared, they said, to resist any such attempt.[6] Similar protests were sent by citizens of Ures and Arizpe.[7]

---

[6] *La Voz de Sonora,* December 14, 1855.
[7] *El Nacionel,* December 31, 1855, and January 25, 1856.

At the same time, the political vacuum created by the national revolt had ignited another bitter struggle for control over the state. The previous decade of political toleration had rapidly ended. In seconding the Ayutla Revolt, the state's towns and villages had agreed on Manuel María Gándara as provisional governor and commander general.[8] The ever expedient Gándara had supported the barracks revolt against President Arista (1853) and had been rewarded by Santa Anna with the office of commander general. The arrival of General Yáñez in April, 1854, however, had reduced him to second in command, stationed on the frontier, and he soon had resigned. The following year, he abandoned his former benefactors to second the Ayutla Revolt. Again, his rewards of office were brief. The following March (1856) President Comonfort appointed José de Aguilar provisional governor and Colonel Pedro Espejo commander general, perhaps having gotten wind of Gándara's centralist past and preferring to rely on Aguilar, a moderado like himself. Gandára relinquished control over the government, but he refused to give up the military command to Espejo, whom he had just forced out of office in alliance with the Ayutla Revolt. He obliged Aguilar, through a show of force, to acquiesce in his retention of the office of commander general.[9]

Knowing from prior experience that his brother-in-law would most likely not be content with that position alone, the governor had then sought new allies. The provisional council of government was composed of a cousin, Francisco J. Aguilar, the veteran federalist José María Escalante y Moreno, and three younger, soon-to-be liberals, Ignacio Pesqueira, Manuel Monteverde, and Antonio Morales.[10] Escalante y Moreno had entered politics at an early age as a diputado in Sonora's first two legislatures. He had supported Urrea and had served the general most ably as administrator of the customs house in Guaymas in the early 1840s. After several years of service in the federal treasury office, he had been elected again to the legislature in 1851. Monteverde, a young mining engineer just returned from studying in Mexico City, had been selected as *suplente* (alternate) in the first and second departmental assemblies in the mid-1840s, both pro-Gándara. He also had been elected to the legislature in 1851.[11] Pesqueira had been schooled in Spain and France. After his return to the state in 1839, he had divided his time between manag-

---

[8]*Ibid.,* September 7, 14, and 21, 1855. The citizens of Ures, in seconding the Plan of Ayutla, had added the proviso that General Yáñez, then a hero in the state for his defeat of Raousset, be named acting governor and commander general. When he declined, a commission from Ures offered the position to Colonel Gándara on the grounds that he had been second in command to Yáñez and was, though then inactive, the highest ranking military officer in the state. The other towns and villages concurred in this selection.

[9]Almada, 291, 875.

[10]Calvo Berber, 188-189.

[11]Almada, 248, 484.

ing a hacienda he was developing near Banámichi and campaigning against the Apaches, commanding the local forces of that village and neighboring pueblos in Arizpe district. He had risen to prominence in January, 1851, having led a vigorous, though unsuccessful, attack on a band of marauding Apaches and having been elected an alternate to the legislature shortly thereafter. He had then returned to the national guard, rising to the rank of major in 1854 and being appointed prefect of Ures district by the governor and military commander sent to the state by Santa Anna. Nevertheless, Pesqueira had seconded the Plan of Ayutla.[12]

In selecting these members to the council Governor Aguilar had made clear his determination to resist any efforts Gándara might make to seize control of the government. Pesqueira, whom Aguilar named president of the council and inspector of the national guard, had just been dismissed by Gándara as inspector of the federal military colonies. The young commander had at first refused to recognize Gándara's retention of the general command.[13] This was not Pesqueira's first run-in with the Gándaras. Through the summer and early fall of 1851, they had publicly charged Pesqueira, Monteverde, Escalante y Moreno, and Morales with a conflict of interest in questions over the state's tobacco monopoly. The four diputados had led the majority, and the minority, directed by Jesús Gándara, had tried to undermine their legislative control through orchestrated attacks in the official newspaper.[14] Aguilar had chosen people he could rely on to oppose Gándara.

The prospects for a constitutional return to power, thus, had not looked promising for the aging Gándara in the early summer of 1856. He had been

---

[12] *Ibid.*, 574-575; Rodolfo F. Acuña, *Sonoran Strongman: Ignacio Pesqueira and His Times* (Tucson, 1974), 14-16.

[13] Acuña, 21. On August 1, 1855, the then governor and commander general, General Pedro Espejo, had named Pesqueira inspector of the military colonies on the frontier. Santa Anna's Secretary of War, however, did not approve the appointment because Pesqueira did not belong to the permanent army and ordered the young commander replaced. Nevertheless, he remained in his post and when various towns began seconding the Ayutla Revolt a few weeks later, he joined them (Almada, 575). Though schooled in liberal ideas, his prior endorsement of and service in the Santa Anna government indicates that the denial of promotion in Mexico City most probably played a significant role in his decision to support the Ayutla Revolt.

[14] *La Voz de Sonora*, July 23, 30; August 13; October 1, 1851, Reel 3. Monteverde at that time was the administrator of the state tobacco monopoly, Escalante y Moreno and Morales were his subordinates, and Pesqueira was a contractor in the planting of tobacco. Gándara and his fellow diputados accused their four colleagues of not remitting the full ten per cent of sales due the state, of blocking attempts by the minority to investigate in the matter, and of protecting their tobacco interests further by removing the state's consumption tax on tobacco and the municipalities' *derecho de piso* (a local tax on storage of merchandise). The four legislators denied they were withholding any taxes from the state, claimed the removal of the state and municipal taxes was proper in accordance with the terms of the contract for the tobacco monopoly, and denied any personal interest in the matter. No further sources could be found to determine the veracity of these accusations. Legal action was not brought against them.

dumped from office by the liberals in Mexico City. His successor had linked up with his enemies, whose rapid rise to political and military prominence was a serious threat to his own ambitions. They would be controlling the government in the state elections soon to be held. In July, Gándara engineered a revolt. A subordinate took Governor Aguilar and other state officials captive in Ures. The frontier troops, whom Gándara had just moved to Hermosillo and Guaymas, seconded this action, as did most of the villages in Ures district and the Opatas. In a meeting in the capital, municipal authorities and the public endorsed the proposal returning Gándara's previous council of government to office and naming its president, Ramón Encinas, as acting governor. Pesqueira immediately rallied those loyal to the government. As president of the council and, therefore, successor in the governor's absence, he declared himself substitute governor, and, as commander of the national guard, ordered state forces to resist the revolt. By the end of August, Gándara capitulated and left for Mexico City once again to plead his case. Though his brother Jesús succeeded in fostering an uprising among the Yaquis and Mayos, it was extinguished by the following January.[15]

The *gandarista* party had still counted strong components in its ranks, and yet Pesqueira had defeated them handily in a little more than a month. The Yaqui-Mayo uprising had been contained and terminated within a few months. Gándara had relied on the same elements he had united twenty years before: his devoted relatives, friends, and followers in Ures district and the tribal Indians. The troops from the frontier colonies had responded to military command far more than political affinity. New political circumstances were taking shape and the aging Gándara had not perceived them. Economic and demographic growth was shifting to the western districts of the state: Guaymas, Hermosillo, Altar, and Magdalena. There, the *gandarista* party was weaker than in the previous decade. At the same time, through the defeated uprisings, economic encroachment, and miscegenation, the numbers and strength of Gándara's Indian allies in the northern part of the state had declined noticeably.

Initially, Pesqueira too had employed outworn, discredited tactics and support. He had undertaken negotiations with a filibustering party from California for their assistance in putting down the Gándara revolt. Henry Crabb, through his marriage to the daughter of Agustín Ainza, a native of Hermosillo and then a prominent merchant in Los Angeles, had learned of Sonora's economic promise and its current political strife. While on a visit to the state in June, 1856, Crabb had approached Governor Aguilar with a plan to colonize the frontier with five hundred Sonoran émigrés, who were tired of the

---

[15]*La Integridad Nacional,* July 18, 1856; Bartolomé Almada, *Exposición . . . al Supremo Gobierno,* October 7, 1856, MAHm, Sonora, Reel 11. Almada's exposition is an account of the Gándara revolt, the steps leading up to it, and a defense of Pesqueira's actions in opposing it. See also Almada, 658.

discriminatory life increasingly imposed upon them in California. The wary Aguilar declined the overture.[16] The schemes of the likes of Walker and Raousset were apparently still very fresh in his mind. Nevertheless, his communications with Crabb were used by the *gandaristas* for their revolt a few weeks later: they charged that he was about to sell the state to filibusters.[17] With Gándara soon holding the upper hand, Pesqueira had been more receptive to Crabb's offer and the two men had reached an understanding. Crabb and his colonists would receive land grants and mining concessions along the frontier in return for their military services against the *gandaristas*.[18] The latter had been defeated, however, before Crabb's expedition had been fully organized.

In addition to such dealings with North American filibusters, Pesqueira had also begun to respond to the new political context that was emerging in Sonora. A generation younger than Gándara, he had succeeded in joining new elements to the old federalist coalition. The leading families of Alamos had been quick to back Pesqueira. Staunch federalists, their opposition to Gándara was long-standing and bitter. With their financial aid, a force of four hundred had been raised to resist the revolt, and a scion of the Almada family (Bartolomé) had been sent to Mexico City to defend Pesqueira's action before the Comonfort government against Gándara's claims.[19]

Pesqueira also counted a new generation of military officers among his supporters. Some, such as the Corella brothers, Angel and Joaquín, and Pesqueira's brother-in-law, Jesús García Morales, like himself had risen in the ranks of the local frontier forces. Others, somewhat younger, such as Crispin S. de Palomares (Alamos), José T. Otero (Baroyeca), and Próspero Salazar Bustamante (Guaymas), had become officers in the national guard. They deplored Gándara's long-standing alliance with the tribal Indians and his recent resort to pulling troops from the frontier to serve his political machinations. These men were now Pesqueira's loyal subordinates, commanding the units of the national guard in behalf of his government.

To these groups Pesqueira had added a third—the leading commercial interests of the central part of the state. Some were established firms: the Monteverdes (Hermosillo) and the Aguilars (José in Hermosillo, his brother Francisco A. in Guaymas, and their cousin Francisco J. in Ures). Others, like Cirilo Ramírez (Hermosillo), Wenceslao and José Iberri (Guaymas), and Torcuato de la Huerta (Guaymas), were new people in commerce. Pesqeuira also

---

[16] Acuña, 31-35.

[17] *La Voz de Sonora,* February 27, 1857, Reel 24.

[18] Robert H. Forbes, *Crabb's Filibustering Expedition into Sonora, 1857* (Tucson, 1952), foreword; Reid, 194-196. According to Reid, an emissary from Gándara reached Crabb shortly after the latter's negotiations were concluded with Pesqueira.

[19] Stagg, *Almadas and Alamos,* 83-90.

had the support of most foreign merchants: John A. Robinson and Thomas Spence (Guaymas); the Spaniards José and Celedonio Ortiz, and French immigrants Juan Pedro, Francisco, Pascual, Pedro Andres, and José Camou (Hermosillo). These merchant capitalists had been expanding their investments into land and mining, building up sizable holdings.[20] They were looking for a politician of similar entrepreneurial inclinations, with military experience, who could bring stability to the state and foster the exploitation of its resources. In Pesqueira, educated in Europe, a veteran of the Apache wars, a commercially minded hacendado, they felt they had found such a person.

Scarcely had Pesqueira begun to consolidate his government, than reports abounded (January, 1857) that Crabb had left California with an armed party of one hundred, headed overland by way of Arizona, with more than a thousand to join them later at Altar by sea. The project for settling Sonoran émigrés on the frontier had been only a cover. A loser in the struggle for political power in California, Crabb had seen in Sonora a way to recover his future. With the help of others who had risked and lost in the gold placers, in business ventures, and in politics, Crabb planned to seize at least the northern part of Sonora (whose inhabitants he believed would be sympathetic), declare its independence, and annex it to the United States.[21]

By the winter of 1857, however, Pesqueira no longer had had any possible need of Crabb. The new political alignment in Sonora was solidly in his favor. President Comonfort had rejected Gándara's claims and had bestowed his blessing on the Pesqueira government. Such connections with Crabb then could have proven a dangerous embarrassment. To admit any armed body of Anglo-Americans—and the reports reaching the governor described them as just that, not Sonoran émigrés—would have endangered his political position. There would have been certain hostility among Sonorans in general and members of the liberal government in Mexico City, whose nearly completed constitution was decidedly nationalistic in tone.[22] To solidify his standing with both, Pesqueira had launched a vigorous crusade against the "foreign invaders" through the official newspaper and circulars to the people. For good measure, Gándara was implicated through the accusation that he had been dealing with the filibusters to regain control over the state.[23]

Pesqueira had perceived well the change in how Sonorans felt about themselves over the previous seven years, most particularly the prominent families of the state's urban centers, whose political support was critical. The defeat of the Walker and French filibustering expeditions had converted the prior

---

[20] Almada, 31-692, *passim*; Guillet, 56-58. (Captain Guillet served in the French expeditionary force in Sonora during the Intervention.)

[21] Forbes, foreword, 7-8.

[22] *Ibid.*, 13.

[23] *La Voz de Sonora*, February 20, 27; August 7, 1857, Reel 24.

feeling of despair and helplessness in the face of an aggressive neighbor into a growing sense of outrage and a desire for vengeance. The Gadsden Purchase and rumors of other territorial sales had only intensified their hostility and strengthened their will to resist. Among Sonorans was emerging the sense that their larger identity was as Mexicans: "(The) filibusters are trying to strip us not only of our properties, our wives, and our children, but also of that which is today most dear to us—the name of Mexicans which we carry and will carry always with pride . . . ."[24]

Into this contagion of chauvinism and xenophobia had walked Crabb and his fellow adventurers. They had believed as Raousset and Walker before them that the people of Sonora, especially those in the frontier districts, were weak, that they had lost confidence that they could ever restore order in the state, and that they would welcome those intent on bringing them under the protective wing of the United States. At Caborca, Crabb's party was entrapped by national guard units swarming in from neighboring communities and districts. Crabb and every man of his party were executed. Only a sixteen-year-old boy was allowed to go free.[25] John Reid and his fellow Alabaman adventurers had been fortunate to have made their way back to Arizona free and alive. Crabb's was the last filibustering expedition to Sonora. There would be no more illusions about enfeebled Sonorans who had lost confidence they could restore stability and progress to the state and would thus welcome annexation.

> Sonorans have given ample proof of the displeasure with which we have viewed the pretensions of our neighbors; we admire their institutions, we acclaim their progress, but we prefer above all our nationality, because our race cannot be amalgamated with theirs and because we have faith in the future and we believe that Mexico will be called within a very short time to figure among the first nations of the American continent. The government in Washington ought not delude itself by professing the ideas of its journalists: that in order to become masters of Sonora it must do so by conquest.[26]

Pesqueira had chosen his nationalistic policy wisely. Crabb's humiliation firmly cemented his relations with the federal government. In Sonora, his political stock soared, as evidenced by his landslide victory in the state elections that summer.[27] The governor added to his prestige in the fall when

---

[24] *Ibid.*, February 27, 1856.
[25] Acuña, 36-38. Crabb's support expedition of a thousand men never materialized. California authorities opposed its organization and Crabb's partner, General John Cosby, failed to carry out his part of the bargain to enlist the promised volunteers. Forbes, 7-8.
[26] *La Voz de Sonora*, February 27, 1856, Reel 24.
[27] Ramón Corral, *Obras históricas* (Hermosillo, 1959), 29.

news reached the state that the federal government, pressed by its critical financial situation, was being pressured by the United States to sell another part of the national territory, which included Sonora. Pesqueira immediately called on the legislature (which complied whole-heartedly) to protest to the Congress that such negotiations should cease and that Sonora would never consent to its sale or mortgage against its will.[28] Sonora's will was not tested, however, as Comonfort declined the offer.[29]

In a little more than a year, Pesqueira had presided over the transformation of a loosely knit coalition of those opposing Gándara's return to power into a solid majority, whose core was the notables of the important towns of the state. These urban gentry were now determined to resist any attempt to sell or seize their state, receptive to the principles of the new federal constitution, and expectant about finally getting down to the task of fomenting progress in their state.

As in Sonora, the response to the Ayutla Revolt in neighboring Sinaloa initially had seemed to follow the political pattern that had evolved in the previous two decades: another swing of the pendulum in the struggle between the notables of the state's two principal urban centers. Mazatlán's ascendancy had been cut short. Faced with the *fait accompli* of the abandonment of the country by Santa Anna in August of 1855, the leading foreign and national

---

[28]*La Voz de Sonora,* October 16 and November 13, 1857. Rumors and reports of such purchase efforts by the United States had appeared in Sonoran newpapers for at least six months. *Idem,* May 1 and 15, 1857.

The reports circulating in the Mexican and California press were well founded. The new president of the United States, James Buchanan, had instructed his government's minister to Mexico, John Forsyth, to offer the Mexican government twelve to fifteeen million dollars for the purchase of Baja California, nearly all of Sonora, and northern Chihuahua. The transaction was to include a mutual claims settlement and perpetual transit rights over any line of communications that joined the Atlantic and the Pacific across Mexico. Hill, 160-161.

The previous February, acting on his own, Forsyth had attempted to obtain territorial cessions indirectly. Up to then unable to purchase such acquisitions, he offered Mexico a loan in the form of a floating mortgage on lands which, according to Forsyth's calculations of the fiscal bankruptcy of the Mexican government, would eventually fall into the hands of the United States through the rights of foreclosure. President Comonfort initially accepted a series of agreements by which the United States was to lend Mexico fifteen million dollars. Seven million of that sum was to be applied to the repayment of outstanding U.S. claims and the liquidation of the English debt convention, with thirteen percent of Mexico's customs revenues obligated to cover this sum borrowed from the United States. The remainder of the loan was to be used by Mexico City at its discretion, and, in lieu of repayment, Mexico was to reduce its tariffs by twenty percent for American merchants and shippers. However, these agreements were not acceptable to the out-going Pierce administration. In Mexico, they were vigorously attacked for what they were—a scheme by which the United States could acquire more Mexican territory. Such domestic pressure forced President Comonfort to withdraw his tentative acceptance of the agreements. Hill, 79-81.

[29]Hill, 161.

figures in the port, in agreement with Governor and Commander General Miguel Blanco, had declared their neutrality. They also had taken the opportunity to modify the tariff regulations regarding the collection of import duties. Culiacán, meanwhile, had not delayed in seconding the Ayutla Revolt. Observing Mazatlán's neutrality, the new liberal government in Mexico City had ordered severed all trade in foreign goods between it and all other ports and states adhering to the Plan of Ayutla. By then, that meant most of the country. The citizenry and garrison of Mazatlán had quickly tried to redeem themselves by declaring their adhesion to the new national government, but they had been too late. President Alvarez had taken note of the glaring discrepancy between Culiacán's consistent loyalty and Mazatlán's frequent infidelity to the federalist cause in the past. He had named Pomposo Verdugo provisional governor and the capital had been returned to Culiacán.[30]

Very quickly, however, the new political context broached by the liberal-conservative conflict had begun to surface. The selection of Verdugo had aggravated and brought into the open an emerging split in the apparent unity of the Culiacán notables. Verdugo was a product of the Vegas. He had married into the family and entered public life under the tutelage and protection of Rafael de la Vega. The latter had elevated him to provisional governor in 1846 and again from 1848 to 1850. Once more in control of the state executive, he had chosen Augustín Martínez de Castro, an old *veguista* ally, as head of his council of government.[31] There was a growing segment of the Culiacán gentry who believed that the Vega regime should remain part of Sinaloa's past and feared its resurrection. The naming of Verdugo as provisional governor had done nothing to allay their apprehension. Some were simply those who had been left out of the Vega clique. Others were former clients who had been weighing the growing cost of their support arising from the reprisals levied periodically by forces from Mazatlán. But there were still others who believed that the liberalism that had triumphed with the Ayutla Revolution was ushering in a new era for Sinaloa and the nation. In such a dawning political climate, the Vegas' patrimonial clique was for them ideologically unacceptable.

The young professionals then coming into prominence (particulary in Culiacán) held such ideological convictions. Educated at the local Seminario Tridentino and/or in Mexico City and Guadalajara,[32] introduced to the liberal

---

[30] Buelna, *Apuntes*, 41-43.

[31] Francisco Javier Gaxiola, *Revista histórica del Estado de Sinaloa, 1856-1865* (México, 1894), 130, 136. The central figure in this work is General Antonio Rosales, who came to the state in the mid-1850s and died in 1865, fighting for the republican cause.

[32] Villa, *Galerá de sonorenses ilustres*, 170.

ideas then present in intellectual circles, trained in law, medicine, engineering and letters, this first truly Sinaloan generation among the capital's prominent families had come of age. Liberalism in their eyes meant politics open to the many and led by the educated, who merited public office on account of their talents, not their particular family's interests. This is not to say that such young professionals from the urban gentry were ready to relinquish their ascendancy in Sinaloan society to those they considered beneath them. It simply meant that politics was no longer to be the contested patrimony of a particular family and their relatives, clients, and friends. It was to be open to the educated and talented of all prominent families—not only those from Culiacán, but as well those from other towns who took up residence in the capital. Also included were young men of lesser means who acquired the necessary academic credentials and became assimilated into the Culiacán establishment. Such a young liberal was Eustaquio Buelna. Born in Mocorito to a prestigious family, Buelna had attended the Seminario Tridentino and then gone on to law school in Guadalajara. Upon his return to Culiacán in 1855, he had immediately thrust himself on the political scene, being named prefect of the district when the *vecinos* declared for the Plan of Ayutla.[33]

Another well-educated, young liberal was Antonio Rosales. From a small village in Zacatecas state, Rosales had been schooled at the *Seminario de Guadalajara*. After enlisting in the national guard to resist the United States' invasion (serving near Monterrey), he had returned to Guadalajara where he wrote poetry and established several newspapers ardently espousing liberal principles.[34] His bold opposition first to the moderado government and then to the Santa Anna regime had led twice to his arrest. He had then moved to Mazatlán. But once his liberal convictions had become widely known, General Blanco had ordered him to the district of Choix in the far northeast corner of the state.[35] Rosales had there joined the Ayutla Revolt. His talents had been brought to the attention of Governor Verdugo and he had been appointed first the governor's private secretary and then, soon afterwards, the secretary of government.[36] As editor of the official newspaper, he promoted liberal ideas and reforms and widened its scope by introducing items of literary interest.[37]

This new liberal element had soon made its influence felt. Rosales, in addition to disseminating liberalism through the official press, had organized

---

[33] González Dávila, 64-65. Other young men of letters and law emerging in the state were Francisco Javier del Castillo Negrete, Carlos Galán, Jesús María Gaxiola, Luis del Castillo Negrete, Francisco Gómez Flores, Francisco C. Alcalde, Luis Alverez León, José C. Valadés, and Dario Elenes Gaxiola. Ibarra, 81.

[34] Almada, 698.

[35] Gaxiola, F.J., 14-16.

[36] González Dávila, 534.

[37] Gaxiola, F. J., 34.

public administration. He and others, both in and out of public office, had worked strenuously to snuff out various conservative counter-revolts before they could become established, especially in the neighboring district of Cosalá.[38] At the same time, Verdugo had begun running into trouble.

In the fall of 1856 a number of the capital's notables, in a petition to President Comonfort, had accused Verdugo of wrong-doing. They charged that he was governing as the Vegas had, concentrating power and using the government to further his own private interests. Though the charges were exaggerated, and dismissed by Comonfort, they were not without foundation. The response of the governor and other Vega holdovers cast doubt on their loyalty and intensified the liberal opposition. The following spring, Verdugo took a leave of absence just as it came time for the recently sanctioned federal constitution to be published and sworn to by all the officials in the state. His close ally, Martínez de Castro, who as president of the executive council was next in line, declined to head the government, alleging ill health. There was considerable opposition to the new constitution from the bishop, Pedro Lozo, and some—including a number of liberal sympathizers—would not swear allegiance to it, fearing the church's threat of excommunication. However, when the heat had passed and state elections were imminent, Verdugo, Martínez de Castro, and other associates took the oath and returned to office. The capital press censured strongly their vacillating conduct. Rosales, who had not hesitated to swear to uphold the constitution, left the government.[39]

In the state elections of June, 1857, the provisional government appears to have tried to influence the results to assure the victory of the Vega clique. The clique had fallen out of favor with the Culiacán notables, their counterparts in the northern districts, and public opinion in general, while the reformist doctrines of the liberals had begun to permeate such circles. The office of governor was not in dispute. General Yáñez, popular in the Northwest for his resistance to the Yankee filibusters, triumphed in all eleven electoral districts. The contest was for vice-governor and control of the legislature. No one expected General Yáñez to serve very long in office, if at all, owing to his military obligations. The vice-governor would in all probability manage the executive. The *veguista* candidate was the youngest of the five

---

[38]*Ibid.*, 34, 120-121.

[39]*Ibid.*, 130, 160-162, 169-170. Whether Verdugo took the leave of absence for the express purpose of avoiding swearing oath to the constitution and the controversy brewing around it is disputed. Mena says it cannot be substantiated. But Gaxiola and Buelna conclude that circumstantial evidence is too strong. Gaxiola notes that in March, 1858, after the conservative Tacubaya Revolt had succeeded in Sinaloa, Verdugo publicly retracted his oath to the federal constitution, manifesting that, though his government had been identified with the liberal cause, he inwardly shared the ideas of the Mexican clergy and that he had never abandoned his religious beliefs. Verdugo never again returned to figure in Sinaloan politics. Buelna, *Apuntes,* 44-45; Mena, I, 267-269.

de la Vega brothers, Joaquín. The opposition candidate, Rafael Esquerro, won one more district than Vega, but he did not have an absolute majority of the total electoral votes. As a compromise, Leonardo Ibarra was elected by the legislature.

The legislature itself was narrowly split: six diputados were determined to eliminate the Vegas and their followers from public office; five desired the full reestablishment of *veguista* control over state politics. The minority was a sizable one, and the Vegas' partisans in the legislature were able to obstruct the majority when they wished. They concurred in the passage of badly needed laws pertaining to the operation of government, for example. But knowing they would lose in the drafting of a new state constitution and organic statutes implementing it, they boycotted sessions, leaving the legislature without a quorum and suspended by early December, 1857.[40]

With President Comonfort's switch to the conservative cause late that same month in proclaiming the Plan of Tacubaya, the politics of Sinaloa and Sonora once again became intertwined, as the liberal adherents in both states moved to support one another. In part their drawing together was the result of geography. Southern Sonora and the northern half of Sinaloa were strongly liberal. Being adjacent, liberal forces could move back and forth across the states' common boundary quickly and with little opposition. Of equal importance were the political cohesion fostered by a common ideology, the crystallization of ties with the national liberal movement, and the relative homogeneity of the core of liberal sympathizers in the Northwest—the prominent families of the towns of northern and central Sinaloa and almost all of Sonora.

The federal garrison in Mazatlán, under the now-familiar General Pedro Espejo, pronounced for the conservative Plan of Tacubaya on January 1, 1858. It recognized the existing state constitutional executives, General José María Yáñez and Vice-Governor Leonardo Ibarra (then acting governor in the general's absence). Though elected governor the previous summer, Yáñez had decided to remain as commander of the Division of the West, based in Mazatlán. His closest supporters were the heart of the reactionary party in Sinaloa, but his popularity in the state, the enlarged force he commanded in Mazatlán, the immediate submission of the national guard and state and federal officials in the port, and the recognition of Ibarra as substitute governor led the legislature in Culiacán to capitulate feebly. Officials in the other districts soon followed its lead. The capital was again transferred to Mazatlán.[41]

---

[40] Gaxiola, F.J., 171-182. The anti-*veguista* liberal faction in Culiacán defeated the provisional government's candidates.

[41] *Ibid.*, 189-192, 206-208. By order of President Comonfort (September 14, 1857), the general military commands were suppressed and replaced by the assignment of a chief of arms in each state, subordinate to regional divisional commanders. Almada, 169.

In control of their state government, Sonoran liberals immediately took the initiative. Governor Pesqueira unswervingly committed his administration and the political majority that supported him to the cause of Benito Juárez and the Constitution of 1857. His resolution was not dampened by the fact that another *gandarista* revolt had just broken out (its principal support being among the tribal Indians), which soon cast its lot with the Plan of Tacubaya. Gándara took personal direction of the revolt, but by April (1858) his disparate forces had been defeated, his brother Jesús had been killed, and he had been forced to take refuge outside the state. The new conservative President Felix Zuloaga named him governor and military commander of Sonora. There was no other prominent figure in the state who had mobilized any significant support in favor of the new regime in Mexico City. In wait for the opportune time to return to the state, Gándara attached himself to the successful revolt in Sinaloa.[42] But there he soon found the conservative cause a besieged camp rather than an aggressive base for the spread of the counter-revolution to Sonora.

The over-dependence of the conservatives in Sinaloa on General Yáñez's prestige and the size of his forces was proving their undoing. The general was shortly needed elsewhere by the Zuloaga government in Mexico City, as were a good portion of his troops. Encouraged by liberal successes in neighboring states, Sinaloan liberals began to revive, agitate, and coalesce. In August a group in the northern border district of Fuerte, led by Plácido Vega, declared openly in support of the Juárez government. The following day liberals in Culiacán similarly pronounced under Lieutenant Colonel Ignacio Martínez Valenzuela, in command of the local garrison. The young lawyer Buelna was sent to Vega with a proposal to fuse the two movements—presumably under Culiacán's leadership, since Vega refused. Martínez Valenzuela lacked funds to raise popular forces and would not resort to forced loans to secure them, in all probability because much of those loans would have had to be taken from prominent families in the capital. Vega, through his relations with the nearby *alamense* gentry, had secured the support of Sonoran Governor Pesqueira—first in the form of arms and later in troops, largely financed by the leading families of Alamos.[43] That winter, Pesqueira personally led an expedition of Sonoran recruits to rally Sinaloan liberals and to bring about the recovery of the state to the liberal camp. The Culiacán liberals had little choice but to fall in behind the Vega-Pesqueira expedition. The combined

---

[42]Corral, 29-31; Almada, 291, 330. Corral's book is actually a composite of three works written by him in 1885-1886 and first published in 1886 in *La Constitucion,* the official newspaper at that time: "Reseña Histórica del Estado de Sonora, 1856-1877," "Biografía de José María Leyva Cajeme," and "Las Razas Indígenas de Sonora."

[43]Buelna, *Apuntes,* 49-54; Gaxiola, F.J., 209-222, 246. Liberals in Mazatlán, led by Pedro Sánchez and Fortino León, had begun organizing forces, which operated in the countryside of the southern part of the state. Gaxiola, F.J., 210.

forces swept down the state with little difficulty until they reached the outskirts of Mazatlán. They unsuccessfully besieged the port until the arrival of a contingent from Chihuahua (in answer to a previous appeal from Vega for aid) and of liberal forces from Jalisco that had been operating on the Tepic border to the south.[44] Pesqueira had declared himself provisional governor of Sinaloa previously in Alamos. After the decisive taking of Mazatlán on April 3, 1859, the various elements in the state recognized him in that office. Pesqueira spent two months consolidating the liberals' hold on the state and then, entrusting the government to his chief ally, Plácido Vega, he returned to Sonora.[45]

The jubilant reception Governor Pesqueira received was marred by the fact that his return had been hastened by a renewed threat from the *gandaristas*. Driven out of Mazatlán along with the other conservatives, Gándara had taken refuge in Arizona where he could agitate his partisans more directly. The Opata chief Juan Tanori in June led his followers in revolt, calling for Gándara's return to power. The Yaquis and Mayos returned to the fray that fall in reaction to Pesqueira's initiation of a formal campaign to pacify them. A final effort was organized by Remigio Rivera a year later. All these attempts to restore the *gandarista* regime failed to last more than a couple of months. These sputterings of an antiquated and obsolete coalition revealed the ideological bankruptcy and political frailty of the conservative cause in Sonora. By November, 1860, Pesqueira felt in firm enough control to reconvene the legislature, which, after having voted the governor extraordinary powers to conduct the war, had been in hiatus for two and a half years. The following February a new state constitution was formulated, patterned after its federal counterpart, and a general amnesty was granted to all but the *gandarista* ringleaders.[46]

SONORA: AN OVERTURE TO PROGRESS

Even before the end of the Reform War, Governor Pesqueira had begun to address himself to the economic and social improvement of Sonora. In imple-

---

[44]Corral, 33-34; Almada, 330-331.

[45]Almada, 576; Gaxiola, F.J., 246.

[46]Corral, 35-36, 38-41; Almada, 331-332, 577. There was one more challenge to Pesqueira's liberal government. In August, 1861, a federal garrison in Fuerte under the command of Colonel Antonio Esteves pronounced in favor of the Plan of Tacubaya, marched north, and defeated a small force in Alamos. Esteves won over a number of young hotheads from some of the leading *alamense* families—including two sons of José María Almada—who charged Pesqueira with arbitrary rule and the imposition of unjust forced loans in prosecuting the war. Esteves also received the support of the Mayos and the Yaquis, who feared Pesqueira's announced plans to develop their valleys. The march on Hermosillo, however, was quickly intercepted by several national guard contingents, who routed Esteves and tracked down most of those who retreated toward Chihuahua. The Yaquis and Mayos soon agreed to peace. Almada, 658-660.

menting his policies, Pesqueira was quick to appropriate any federal powers which the Juárez government permitted him to take or was powerless to prevent him from taking. This tactic was generally endorsed for several years by the urban notables, who preferred local management of the state's resources and wealth, given the national government's prior record. In particular, they were resentful and suspicious of Mexico City's dealings with foreigners concerning their state. The first option on Sonora's resources was theirs. They had applauded first his obstruction and then rude expulsion (May, 1859) of a San Francisco-based land surveying commission, which had bought into the federal concession rights obtained by the Jecker Company a few years earlier.[47]

In July, 1859, upon his return to Hermosillo from Sinaloa, Pesqueira had expedited a series of dispositions which invaded the jurisdiction of the federal government. He decreed that the federal prohibitions against real estate activities by, or on behalf of, foreign interests in the border zones delineated by the Constitution of 1857 were to be strictly enforced—by the state government if necessary. The governor also assumed direction of the federal customs offices on the border and in the port of Guaymas, as well as of the military colonies on the frontier. Regulations were decreed for the customs and commercial agents, and the free passage of goods through Sonora to the Arizona Territory was authorized. In assuming such prerogatives, Pesqueira had cited the existing state of war and the lack of communications with the Juárez government in Veracruz. However, even with the war's end, the governor continued to exercise these jurisdictional powers, yielding only under strong pressure from Mexico City to desist. With the commencement of the French Intervention in 1862, Pesqueira began to engross these areas of federal jurisdiction once again.[48]

There was every reason to assume these powers from Pesqueira's perspective. Besides the enhancement of his own personal political power, such prerogatives greatly assisted the implementation of his commitment to put Sonora firmly on the road to progress. For forty years Mexico City had been unable, sometimes unwilling, to foster security and economic growth in the state. Political and diplomatic obedience to the federal government Pesqueira did not question. But if Mexico City could not or would nor help him in promoting the economic and social improvement of the state, then, he believed, it at least should allow him the freedom to try to do it alone. Pesqueira and his followers were only reiterating the declarations of the Sonoran federalists a generation before. In their enunciation of the difficulties to be surmounted they did so as well. Their solutions, however, in several respects broke new ground.

---

[47] Acuña, 53-61.
[48] Almada, 576-577.

The frontier problem was as chronic as ever. Pesqueira's long range goal—to resurrect the presidial system, combining a line of forts to protect resettlement and rationing to lure the Apaches off the warpath—required large-scale funding on a sustained basis that was not yet feasible.[49] In the meantime, as a stopgap measure, Pesqueira instructed his prefects and national guard officers in the frontier districts to pursue Apache raiders persistently.[50]

The Pesqueira administration also viewed the problem of the intransigence of the Yaquis and Mayos as the federalists had a generation earlier. The two tribes were sitting on top of the most fertile lands of the state, squandering them by cultivating only a small portion (enough to provide a copious subsistence and small sales of produce to the port of Guaymas). The remainder of their lands should go to those who wanted to bring progress to the region, to develop its resources and make the region commercially productive. Pesqueira and liberals in general believed that to accomplish this end the two tribes would have to be subjugated by force (since they would not submit peacefully) and then assimilated into "civilized society" through education and contact with those who would settle in the region. Moreover, the taxes accruing from the commercial exploitation of the region would help lift the government out of its fiscal morass.[51] In short, the state would finally have peace, Sonorans would have access to more lands, the government would pocket badly needed revenues, and the Yaquis and Mayos . . . well, they would receive "civilization" and the opportunity to work full-time for their new neighbors.

The governor had the full support of the liberal-dominated legislature, which authorized him to establish a garrison in each valley to contain Yaqui-Mayo unrest, and, with the tribes so pacified, to survey and redistribute the tribal lands. Those necessary for their subsistence were to be adjudicated to the Indians; the rest were to be awarded to those interested in investing and/or settling in the region.[52] To implement this legislative decree, the government set up a colony in each valley. The Mayo valley colony was under the direct supervision of the government;[53] that in the Yaqui valley was

---

[49]*La Estrella de Occidente,* May 18, 1860, Reel 4.

[50]Corral, 31.

[51]*La Estrella de Occidente,* July 6 and 27, 1860, Reel 4.

[52]Decree of March 24, 1858, MAHm, Sonora, Reel 11.

[53]Decree of August 4, 1859, MAHm, Sonora, Reel 4. The government-established colony on the Río Mayo received a grant of 500 hectares (about 1,250 acres) for the community and 10,000 hectares for individual cultivation. Each colonist was to receive from 12½ to 50 hectares, the precise amount depending upon the size of the individual's household. The price was three pesos per hectare, which could be paid on credit at five per cent interest annually. The colonists were to reside in the colony for at least three years and were not to sell their land during this period. They were to construct whatever irrigation works they deemed necessary, financed through their own funds and those of the colony as a community.

entrusted to General Jesús García Morales, the governor's brother-in-law and closest subordinate, and Lieutenant Colonel Crispin S. de Palomares, one of the important young officers in the national guard. The government assisted the latter colony by floating a loan to build a canal to irrigate its lands.[54] Both colonies were composed largely of Sonoran émigrés returning from California. Foreigners were welcome, but were required to become Mexican citizens.[55]

Governor Pesqueira was interested in providing not only security to develop the state's resources, but also improved transportation to move them to market. In his approach to this concern, he was more aggressive and expansive than his federalist predecessors. When General Angel Trías, representing the Compañía Americana y Mexicana, arrived in Ures in mid-1860 to solicit from the legislature the right to build the Sonoran portion of a railroad from El Paso to Guaymas,[56] the governor and the official newspaper vigorously promoted the project: "The century asks for it; civilization demands it; interest, honor, and glory irresistibly impel our people to go marching on with a firm and sure step, along the road to civilization."[57] A letter to the editor from "various *sonorenses*" stressed the nationalistic necessity of the proposed railroad: "Mexico needs to get out of the apathy in which her political misfortunes have placed her and overcome her petty local interests, entering into the way of progress and reforms in order to place herself at the level of the

---

[54] *La Estrella de Occidente,* October 21, 1859, Reel 4.

[55] Claudio Dabdoub, *Historia del Valle del Yaqui* (México, 1964), 113.

[56] *La Estrella de Occidente,* July 20, 1860, Reel 12, and November 30, 1860, Reel 4. In El Paso, the proposed railroad was to join with another that was to connect that city with New Orleans, and from there with the large cities of the eastern part of the United States.

The idea for a railroad from El Paso to Guaymas had been in existence for at least a decade. A Frenchman, Hipólito Pasqueir de Doumartin, had received a concession from the Chihuahuan legislature for a colonization project in the northwest part of that state, which included the right to construct such a railroad. But the federal government ruled it unconstitutional. An 1854 concession by Santa Anna to Alejandro José de Atoche to build the railroad was terminated by President Comonfort two years later on the grounds of failure to fulfill the terms of the contract. In 1858, the right to build a similar railroad was again granted by the Chihuahuan legislature, to an Anglo-American company. However, the Juárez government the following year declared that the legislature had overstepped its bounds in ceding national public lands and exempting from payment taxes due the federal treasury. Almada, 269-273.

With such prior failures in mind, General Trias, in presenting his solicitation to the Sonoran legislature, argued that the two states involved had the right to make the concession since the question of who owned the public lands was still up in the air. Moreover, he contended, the Reform War had led to the suspension of the Congress and, thus, sovereignty had reverted back to the states in such matters. The general's position on the questions of state versus federal powers was similar to that of Pesqueira, and apparently to that of the members of the legislature, who approved the concession. *La Estrella de Occidente,* July 20, 1860, Reel 12.

[57] *La Estrella de Occidente,* November 30, 1860, Reel 4.

other civilized nations." Mindful of the recent past, the letter urged that the legislature require the company to be solely under the jurisdiction of Mexican law; there was still a powerful party in the United States that desired to absorb Sonora, and no doors should be left open to them.[58] The following March, the legislature granted the concession. It included the ceding of alternate square leagues of public land along the railroad and the precautionary requirement that the company be solely under the jurisdiction of Mexican law.[59]

The Pesqueira administration also hoped to upgrade the state's transportation by improving and constructing wagon roads. It hired a Frenchman, Colonel Ernesto de Fleury, as the state's engineer to survey, draw up plans, and form a budget for the construction and improvement of several such roads. One of those proposed was to connect Ures directly with Guaymas at a cost of 768 pesos. Their economic importance was widely recognized in that the average wagon could carry the weight packed by twenty mules at one-third the cost.[60]

To stimulate commerce, in December, 1860, Governor Pesqueira authorized the direct transit of foreign and national goods over a single route from Guaymas to the Territory of Arizona, with a special duty of only ten percent of the regular tariff. The trade was restricted to a single route from Guaymas through Hermosillo, Santa Ana, Magdalena, San Ignacio, and Imuris, where a frontier *aduana* would be established.[61] In addition, Pesqueira contracted the establishment and leasing of mints at Alamos and Hermosillo. The latter was operational the following year; that of Alamos the year after.[62] Both stimulated commerce by adding to the supply of hard currency.

For Governor Pesqueira and his fellow liberals, education was also essential to the state's progress. "What country, in which public instruction is widespread," asked the official newspaper, "does not visibly prosper each day . . . ? "[63] They had moved beyond their federalist parents, who had combined the traditional view of education as a mark of refinement with the Enlightenment libertarian assumption, by then widely accepted, that it was a

---

[58]*Ibid.*, August 3, 1860, Reel 12.

[59]Almada, 273-274. In 1863 the company underwent a reorganization and included Pesqueira and Governor Luis Terrazas of Chihuahua among its stockholders. Calvo Berber, 218.

[60]*La Estrella de Occidente*, April 13; June 22; August 17, 1860, Reel 12.

[61]*Ibid.*, December 7, 1860, Reel 12. Decree of March 23, 1858, MAHm, Sonora, Reel 11. By 1864, owing to abuses (primarily the introduction of non-transit goods), the direct transit privilege had become restricted to United States army shipments with special permits. United States Department of State, *Report on The Commercial Relations of the United States with All Foreign Nations,* 1864, 719, Guaymas, Vice-Consul Farrelley Alden.

[62]Pradeau, *Moneda*, 69-97.

[63]*La Estrella de Occidente,* August 24, 1860, Reel 12.

necessity for the functioning of republican, representative government. By the mid-nineteenth century the material, economic role of education was becoming evident to Mexican liberals.

Sonoran liberals had direct knowledge of the importance given to education in the newly settled but rapidly progressing state of California and territory of Arizona. With the governor's firm encouragement the legislature passed laws establishing general guidelines for primary schools, founding a state school of superior instruction (with a junta directiva created to supervise it), and allocating sizable state sums to support primary schools in impoverished municipios. More than 12,000 pesos, plus twelve percent of the state tax on alcoholic beverages, were budgeted in this promotion of public instruction.[64] A decade before, the Aguilar administration had been able to support at the most only eleven schools at less than 1,000 pesos.[65]

The policies of the Pesqueira government, endorsed generally by liberals in the state, meshed with the new political and economic circumstances in which the state found itself. Sonora was now oriented toward a united, liberal, federalized Mexico. At least a satisfactory relationship with Mexico City was being worked out. But for the time being, the state was cut off economically from the rest of the country. To the east, the only feasible passage through the Sierra Madre (the wagon road from Arizpe to Chihuahua) had been abandoned for many years because of the constant Apache menace. To the south, the roads through Sinaloa were very poor (impassable during the rainy season) and, thus, very costly for transportation.

Since independence there had been an irregular, yet growing, overseas commerce with Europe, the eastern United States, and the Orient; but that commerce had wanted only gold and silver in return for its wares and had shown no inclination to invest in the state's future with its capital. However, over the last decade, to the north and west had come a dynamic society on the make, ready to buy, eager to sell, and anxious to invest. The gradual easing of the state's internal security problems under the Pesqueira administration caused further encouragement. Yet no political interference would be tolerated. Governor Pesqueira had made that abundantly clear.

----

[64]*Ibid.*, January 8 and April 29, 1864, Reel 4. In their zeal to promote education, the *diputados,* in legislation passed in December, 1863, empowered the junta directiva to direct and administer the funds not only of the state secondary school (as its predecessor had done under the previous law), but also of all primary schools in the state. Local authorities were only to carry out the junta's policies. Governor Pesqueira believed the diputados had gone too far. The following April, when the legislature suspended itself and granted him extraordinary powers in view of the impending imperialist invasion of the state (Corral, 47), the governor declared the law unconstitutional because it delegated to the junta directiva powers reserved by the constitution to the ayuntamientos. He decreed a new law which returned to the latter full control over the funds and the direction of their primary schools.

[65]Aguilar, *Memoria* (1850), *Números* 3, 6; *idem., Memoria* (1851), 15-16, *Número* 5.

The fate of the Crabb expedition had been a warning to filibusters. In early 1859 Pesqueira had publicly stood up to the specter of direct intervention by the United States government. In response to President Buchanan's proposal in his annual message to Congress (rejected by that body) to occupy northern Sonora and Chihuahua militarily as the only effective way to combat the Apaches and guarantee the redress of injuries suffered by United States citizens in Mexico, the governor called out the national guard, with orders to repel by force any such attempt.[66] Later that year (October), reacting to the expulsion from the state of a San Francisco-based surveying commission, a United States frigate had sailed into Guaymas harbor to protest, threatening occupation of the port. The governor again called out the national guard and the frigate's captain backed down.[67]

Yet by its policies, the Pesqueira government indicated to North American entrepreneurs that it would welcome genuine economic trade and investment. The latter's gradual perception of the governor's careful delineation between political interference and economic penetration is seen in the writings of Silvester Mowry, a former army officer and boundary commissioner who had begun investing in various business enterprises in Arizona. In early 1859 Mowry had advocated the acquirement of Sonora: "The natural outlet for the productions of Arizona must be through a port of the Gulf of California, and the acquisition of California necessitates the possession of Sonora."[68] The Arizona entrepreneur believed that it was through the Apaches and the contrasting characters of Mexicans and North Americans that such annexation was bound to take place.

> The Apache Indian is preparing Sonora for the rule of a higher civilization than the Mexican. In the past half century the Mexican element had disappeared from what is now called Arizona, before the devastating career of the Apache. It is every day retreating farther south, leaving to us (when it is ripe for our possession) the territory without the population.[69]

> The mines in the hands of the Spaniards yielded enormous profits to the miner; they were men of indomitable enterprise, who employed capital, science, and spared no expense to succeed in their adventures; whereas the Mexican is poor, without energy, and too lazy to trust or help himself. Formerly, Sonora the rich was a proverb; now, Sonora the poor is a stubborn fact—but not from the want of the elements of richness. These once developed, she will once more become Sonora the rich and may be great.[70]

---

[66] Hill, 162; Almada, 400-402.

[67] Acuña, 58-64.

[68] Silvester Mowry, *Arizona and Sonora* (New York, 1864), 16.

[69] *Ibid.*, 36.

[70] *Ibid.*, 45.

The Spanish race has but just touched these treasures. It remains for the American people to make good the prediction. With the organization of Arizona and the acquisition of Sonora, a new impetus will be given to the Pacific. The Mexican population will recede before the energy of American career.[71]

Despite his disdainful evaluation of the Sonorans' character (ignoring the biological and cultural ramifications of his neat dichotomy between Spanish grandparents and their Sonoran children and grandchildren), Mowry did acknowledge the emerging self-confidence among the urban gentry in the state:

Some years past the property owners looked forward to annexation to the United States as an inevitable event. The civil war [the Reform War] has put an end to these ideas, and peace having been established at home, Sonora looks to herself, with the incidental help given by foreign capital and emigration, for her regeneration and future greatness.[72]

By 1864, Mowry was writing about Sonora's awakening from its doldrums. He omitted any mention of political acquisition. Rather, he spoke glowingly of the state's progress under the Pesqueira administration.

The prospects of Sonora have much improved since 1859. The constitutional power of the state has been boldly asserted and maintained with courage and ability by Governor Pesqueira; the disturbances caused by the Yaqui Indians suppressed with a firm hand, revolutions nipped in the bud; and profound peace maintained for a long time past.[73]

Mowry also cited the opening of a new port (La Libertad) on the Gulf north of Guaymas and the liberal railroad concession granted by the legislature as proof of Sonora's recent progress. The state's abundant resources and ready supply of cheap, docile labor were given as evidence for the great potential awaiting North American investors.[74]

The dovetailing of Governor Pesqueira's policies with Yankee entrepreneurial interests brought about a flush of economic activity in Sonora, beginning in 1860. The rapidly growing settlements and increasing number of

---

[71]*Ibid.*, 53.
[72]*Ibid.*, 41.
[73]*Ibid.*, 92.
[74]*Ibid.*, 92-97.

military forts in Arizona created a demand for Sonoran provisions, and a growing number of wagons began hauling freight between Guaymas and Tucson.[75] A thriving trade quickly sprang up between Sonora and California through Guaymas. By 1862 a steamship line was making a round trip between that port and San Francisco every forty days. This growing trade in turn stimulated Sonora's traditional commercial ties with Europe, the Orient, and the Mexican ports to the south by increasing the state's purchasing power and its communications.[76]

Scores of North American capitalists (especially from San Francisco) began arriving, lured by the prospect of exploiting the rich mining potential of the state. From Guaymas, they fanned out into central and southern Sonora, generally buying up mines of proven promise, but not infrequently denouncing mines of unknown value on the basis of whatever tips and rumors were floating around. They imported the latest mining machinery and equipment from San Francisco (including that powered by steam) to work the mines on a large scale.[77] By the mid-1860s there were more than twenty North American mining companies organized in Sonora, not to mention the considerable number of individual investors and prospectors, with a total investment estimated at more than a million dollars.[78] They were soon joined by numerous Sonoran business people, most of whom were investing capital accumulated in commerce. Among the most prominent were: Manuel Monteverde, Celedonio Ortiz, Dionisio González, José de Aguilar, and the Camou brothers (from Hermosillo); John A. Robinson, Fernando Cubillas, and Matías Alzúa (Guaymas merchants); and the governor himself. The Almadas of Alamos had resumed mining operations as well.[79]

The chief beneficiaries of this economic upturn were the state's two leading commercial centers, whose predominance was further strengthened. Hermosillo, the mercantile hub of the interior of the state, had acquired another spoke—the growing trade north to Arizona, and the enlarged markets resulting from the revival of the northwest districts of Altar and Magdalena in response to Arizona's demand for foodstuffs. The California trade and the

---

[75]Poston, "Apache Land," *Overland Monthly,* 24 (August, 1895), 207-210; *idem,* 25 (September, 1895), 293.

[76]Charles P. Stone, *Notes on the State of Sonora* (Washington, 1861), 12-13; United States Department of State, *Commercial Relations,* 1864, 719, Guaymas, Vice-Consul F. Alden.

[77]*La Estrella de Occidente,* February 13, 1863, Reel 12; December 18, 1863, Reel 13; February 12, May 6, and June 3, 1864, Reel 4.

[78]United States Department of State, *Commercial Relations,* 1864, 719, Guaymas, Vice-Consul F. Alden; *idem,* 1873, 828, Guaymas, Consul Alexander Willard.

[79]Almada, 21-692, *passim*; Mowry, 96-97; Velasco, 175-181. The last source comprises an appendix to Velasco's work on mining during this period, written by William T. Robinson (of San Francisco), who had invested in mines in Alamos district.

new mint fattened Hermosillo's line of commerce through Guaymas. Long trains of wagons now moved back and forth between Sonora's first genuine city and that port, hauling the wheat so prized in California for its quality, hides, and precious metals from the newly opened mines to the southeast, brought to the city's mint for coinage and certification. A stagecoach line provided regular and rapid passenger and communications service. Hacendados and farmers in the surrounding district expanded production to supply the new markets.[80] On the Hacienda de la Alameta, fifteen miles from Hermosillo, were large fields of wheat, corn, sugarcane, and cotton. Its owner, the old *gandarista* Manuel Iñigo, possessed a flour mill, blanket manufactory, sugar mill, and wagon manufactory to convert the raw materials produced there into salable processed goods.[81]

Merchants and tradespeople from interior towns and villages, including commission agents of Hermosillo's commercial houses, converged on the city in increasing numbers to acquire stocks of European and Oriental dry goods, household wares, and luxury items, California-made agricultural and mining tools and equipment, and lumber from the Pacific Northwest for construction. They also came to buy the fabricated products brought in from nearby haciendas, such as Iñigo's *Almeta,* and even more now from the city's nascent manufacturing firms that had sprung up during the previous few years. Many of them employed up-to-date machinery acquired from San Francisco foundries. There were nine flour mills (two steam-powered), four *panocha* mills (three steam-powered), a wagon and carriage factory, a few brick and glass plants, some small distilleries, and a growing number of craft shops.[82]

Guaymas likewise bustled with activity. Besides the monthly visits of the San Francisco steamer, a growing number of sailing ships owned by the port's merchant community were employed in traffic between Guaymas and the ports of the Mexican west coast.[83] It was also the way station for North American capitalists coming to Sonora. In the cantinas rumors, hot tips, and stories were exchanged between newcomers, veterans of the mining districts, and Sonorans eager to make a sale or be cut in on a deal rumored to be a

---

[80] Stone, 8-9; Guillet, 51.

[81] Mowry, 95.

[82] *La Estrella de Occidente,* May 23, 1862, Reel 12; *idem,* June 3, 1864, Reel 4; Stone, 8-9. In 1864, a group of Hermosillo businesspeople headed by Celedonio Ortiz, the Camou brothers, and Dionisio González formed the Compañía Industria Sonorense and bought the cotton mill of Los Angeles (founded in 1836 as a small operation by Manuel Iñigo), which had been idle for some time. The mill (located between Horcasitas and Hermosillo) was to begin operations on a large scale early the next year. The company had already begun making advance cash purchases of the cotton crops of several hacendados in the vicinity. *La Estrella de Occidente,* April 8, 1864, 720, Guaymas, Vice-Consul F. Alden.

[83] Stone, 12-13.

bonanza.[84] Some Yankee business people were content to invest in Guaymas itself, buying up town lots and acquiring landed property outside the port.[85] In the midst of this flurry of economic activity, the port's merchants (both the long-established immigrants, such as John Robinson, and their generally more recently settled Sonoran counterparts, like Fernando Cubillas and Torcuato de la Huerta) lined their pockets and ventured out into new investment fields. Robinson, a merchant in the port since the 1820s and United States consul from 1848-1857, seems to have had his fingers in every pie. Besides commercial and mining interests he had acquired large tracts of land, including that around the Bay of Lobos to the northwest, which he hoped to convert into a port connected to Tucson by railroad (an enterprise never realized). In addition, he opened a hotel, complete with French restaurant, to accommodate the numerous foreigners sojourning in the port.[86]

With such strong economic currents centered in Guaymas and Hermosillo, possession of the state capital alone was not enough to enable Ures to achieve an independent, dynamic growth of its own. "Ures," as one foreigner astutely observed, "is an artificial population which would soon be converted into a village if the seat of government were changed."[87] And even though the capital, it was rather destitute of public buildings. There was only a single large edifice, originally intended to serve as a state penitentiary, but converted into a military barracks. The population, in great part Indian, was generally poor. The town's commerce was small, unable to get out from under Hermosillo's shadow.[88]

The proposed direct road to Guaymas had not yet been realized, and the farms and haciendas along the Río Sonora above and below the town continued to market their crops through Hermosillo.[89] Most importantly, Ures' natural hinterland, the northeast part of the state, was stagnating. Its hard-to-reach valleys nestled in the foothills of the Sierra Madre were particularly vulnerable to Apache raids and discouraged the construction of wagon roads; only mule trails existed. Consequently, mining on any significant scale could not yield a profit. It cost one peso per ton to mine the ore, seventy pesos to transport it by mule to Guaymas, while only eight pesos to carry it by steamer to San Francisco.[90] The principal towns and villages had less than half the population of thirty years before. Many houses were abandoned;

---

[84] *La Estrella de Occidente,* December 18, 1863, Reel 13; May 6, 1864, Reel 4.

[85] Mowry, 93.

[86] Almada, 691; Guillet, 57; *La Estrella de Occidente,* July 17, 1863, Reel 12.

[87] Guillet, 51.

[88] *Ibid.,* 52; Stone, 9-10.

[89] *La Estrella de Occidente,* June 22, 1860, Reel 12.

[90] United States Department of State, *Report on Commercial Relations,* 1864, Guaymas, Vice-Consul F. Alden, 720.

others had fallen in ruin. The churches still standing had been robbed of everything valuable they possessed.[91]

By contrast, the northwestern frontier districts had begun to recover. The rapidly growing population across the border in south central Arizona provided a ready market for the farmers and stock raisers in these districts and helped deter the Apaches. The region's terrain of rolling plains broken by occasional small mountain clusters enabled the revived frontier forces to defend it more effectively than was possible in the northeastern area of the state. The generally level terrain also meant wagon roads could be constructed and maintained more easily and at much less cost. The former village of Magdalena in a few short years had become the market center for the region's foodstuffs and livestock sent north to supply Arizona.[92]

Alamos had contributed more financially and militarily to the triumph of liberalism in Sonora than any other town, but the returns for its efforts were mixed. The influx of North American capitalists and the establishment of the mint rejuvenated its flagging mining industry and provided a lift to commerce.[93] Some *alamenses* sold their mines; others like José María Almada chose to rebuild and enlarge their previously declining or abandoned operations, acquiring machinery from San Francisco. To assist such imports and the flow of trade through the town, the government opened the Bay of Agiabampo (located next to the Sinaloan border) to coastal trade.[94] Nonetheless, the chronic obstacle to the growth of Alamos was still nowhere near being solved. The Yaqui and Mayo valleys remained unpacified, despite the government's vigorous efforts to subdue them. The colonies in each valley had made a start, with a considerable number of settlers and work begun on irrigation canals.[95] But in 1862, in answer to the renewed encroachment of their lands, the tribes staged another uprising, destroying the colonies' crops and dwellings and paralyzing *alamense* commerce. Though government forces succeeded in ending the uprising, it was, in fact, only a truce. Most of the colonists knew it and left. Those remaining lacked adequate resources to rebuild what had been lost.[96] The colonies were teetering; with another prolonged conflict they would topple. The hopes of the miners, merchants, and hacendados of Alamos for accelerated economic expansion remained

---

[91] Colonel Ernesto de Fleury, *Noticias geológicas, geográficas y estadísticas sobre Sonora y Baja California* (n.p., 1864), in MAHm, Sonora, Reel 12.

[92] *El Nacional*, October 17, 1854, Reel 4; Stone, 13-14. Magdalena had been made the *cabecera* of its district in 1854, replacing San Ignacio. More importantly, it was located at the junction of the three main roads in that part of the state—those leading west to Altar, south to Hermosillo (and north to Tucson), and southeast to Ures.

[93] *La Estrella de Occidente*, February 12, 1864, Reel 4.

[94] Mowry, 96; Velasco, 175-181.

[95] Dabdoub, 113-114; *La Estrella de Occidente*, December 23, 1859, Reel 4.

[96] *La Estrella de Occidente*, January 23, 1863, Reel 12.

frustrated. They tried to make do as best they could, seeking out the longer and more costly (but also safer) commercial route south through Mazatlán.[97]

The individual economic fortunes of Sonora's urban centers had varied considerably since mid-century. Yet as local governments they had finally come of age. The constitution of 1861 and subsequent *ley organica* (statute law) gave the municipios more power over their own affairs. The ayuntamientos were empowered to name their own secretaries and treasurers. They were given more leeway in raising and disbursing municipal funds, though still required to submit annual budgets to the legislature for approval. Of most importance to the municipios' freedom of action was the prohibition of the district prefect from attending ayuntamiento sessions or from intervening in any way in their affairs (with the single exception of a serious breakdown in public order).[98] This decentralization of political power created greater opportunity for local action, and the notables responded.

Fifteen years before, Governor Aguilar had lamented the lack of persons, especially those qualified, to direct the municipios. Now municipal offices were being permanently filled, and in the larger towns they were frequently contested in local elections. In great part this change was due to the fruits of the first real beginnings in education initiated a generation earlier. Those school children were now young adults. They were joined by the growing number of business people who had left the insecurity and stagnation of the villages to make their fortunes in the commercially active towns. The increased prerogatives of the ayuntamientos attracted them to public office; from these positions they could assist and promote their business interests, as well as satisfy a usually genuine sense of civic concern. The expansion of the economy at last gave such municipal authorities a semblance of adequate revenues with which to work, especially in the larger urban centers. Regular, permanent police forces were organized; public instruction was put on a firm footing. In Alamos and Guaymas alone, there were about five hundred and three hundred children, respectively, attending school.[99]

---

[97]*Ibid.*, November 7, 1862, Reel 12.

[98]*Constitución política del Estado de Sonora,* February 13, 1861, MAHm, Sonora, Reel 4; *Ley Orgánica para el gobierno y administración interior del Estado,* December 3, 1862, MAHm, Sonora, Reel 24.

[99]*La Estrella de Occidente,* November 7, 1862, and February 13, 1863, Reel 12; *idem,* December 18, 1863, Reel 13; Manifesto to the Citizens of the State, November 30, 1864, in Almada, 373-374. The population estimates available for the principal urban centers are: Hermosillo, 12,000-13,000 (Fleury), 15,000 (Guillet), 11,000 (Stone); Guaymas, 2,000-2,500 (Fleury), 5,000 (Guillet), 3,500 (Stone); Alamos, 6,000-7,000 (Fleury), 6,000 (Stone); Magdalena, 2,000 (Stone). Stone's figures seem the most reliable. The population figures reveal clearly the extent to which Hermosillo had become the state's most prosperous and prominent urban center, with nearly double the population of the next largest, Alamos. Fleury, 12-15; Stone, 8-14; Guillet, 51.

SINALOA: THEME AND VARIATIONS

A similar municipal resurgence was underway in Sinaloa, though it was less pronounced than in Sonora. The state's towns and villages had never experienced such hard times as those of their counterparts to the north. What internal disorder there had been was sporadic, brief, and largely confined to the rival urban centers of Mazatlán and Culiacán, though the recent Reform War had disrupted most sections of the state. Economic activity, stimulated primarily by contacts with foreign commerce, had steadily increased, though again the resulting prosperity had largely been concentrated in the two principal towns of the state. By the same token, Sinaloa was not experiencing the surge of economic activity after the Reform War that so encouraged the recovery of Sonora's economy. The limited evidence available does not reveal the significant degree of direct North American investment manifest in Sinaloa's neighbor. In the post-war years economic activity apparently was continuing at the same steady pace throughout the state, except for the extreme southern section, where a dogged fight continued with Manuel Lozada's forces for control of the Tepic border area.[100] The resurgence of the municipios, then, was only minimally the result of economic expansion; primarily it stemmed from the new political realities then emerging in the state.

The constituent legislature elected in December, 1860, produced a very liberal constitution the following April.[101] The new constitution extended direct election to all state offices (the first to do so in the nation). Secondly, a strong federalist arrangement between the state and the municipios was instituted. Both measures reflected a clear reaction to the political hegemony exercised by political cliques led by the Vegas and the Mazatlán foreign merchants since the mid-1830s and to the centralization of political power in those two urban centers. The critical constitutional factor in this regard was the relationship between the governor's agents at the local level (the prefects and their subordinates, the directores políticos) and the governing bodies of the municipios, the ayuntamientos. The constitution transposed the greater share of political power, initiative, and prerogative to the local governments.

The prefect now exercised only executive powers from the district *cabecera*, and even these powers were restricted somewhat. Elected every two years, he was prohibited from immediate re-election; this restriction made it difficult for a strong, effective link between governor and prefect to become forged. As an added check, the ayuntamiento was to verify the results of his election. In the lesser towns and villages in the district the executive was the director político, elected annually. All legislative power was reserved to the ayuntamiento, half of whose members were elected annually for two-year

---

[100] Mena, II, 55, 65, 82.
[101] Gaxiola, F.J., 296-299.

terms. The prefect or director político could make observations on the *acuerdos* (ordinances) passed by the ayuntamiento, but the latter could override this veto prerogative. Furthermore, both executive officials were to execute only dispositions of importance or of general interest. The remainder were to be administered by the commissions or agents of the ayuntamiento of the district *cabecera*. Finally, in no instance could the state government or its agents (the prefect or director político) dispose of municipal revenues.

The legislative power of the ayuntamientos was understood to be limited by the dispositions of the state legislature. However, the latter had only infrequently been the vehicle for constriction of municipal power. Much more often, it had been the far more unified, organized, and directly empowered state executive. And there was in the constitution one loophole for its local agents—the provision that either the prefect or the director político could oppose ordinances that were contrary to the laws of the state or nation, or that disrupted public order. Though final disposition in such disputes rested ultimately with the legislature, in the interim, loose interpretation of the clause gave either executive official ample room to intervene in municipal affairs when conflicts reached the crisis stage.[102] Nevertheless, overall the new constitution gave the municipios the balance of power vis-à-vis the agents of the state executive.

Plácido Vega, who had emerged as the leader of the liberal forces in the state with the aid of Sonoran Governor Pesqueira, had been elected governor in state elections in June, 1861. However, his position in the intervening years had been none too secure.[103] In part, the strengthening of local prerogative and initiative at the state executive's expense had put Vega at an immediate disadvantage in comparison to his predecessors. Armed with less constitutional power, he faced a reform-minded public opinion. In addition, Vega—unlike Pesqueira in Sonora—did not enjoy wide support among the prominent families of Sinaloa's towns. Like his predecessor, Pomposo Verdugo, Don Plácido could not escape his *veguista* past, both in his conduct in office and in the eyes of those who were not his followers. His grandfather had founded the Fuerte branch of the Vega family and his father had married the daughter of the *subdelegado* of that town at the close of the colonial period.[104] At an early age Don Plácido had dropped out of school and gone to work in Culiacán as a clerk in the commercial house of his second cousin, Francisco de la Vega. He also had served as a soldier in the latter's state forces in 1852, during the armed conflict with the Mazatlán merchants and the federal gar-

---

[102] Buelna, *Compendio*, 60-66; Ildefonso Estrada y Zenea, *Manuel de gobernadores y jefes políticos* (México, 1878), 272-278.

[103] Gaxiola, F.J., 299, 308.

[104] F.L. Quintero, "Historia panorámica de la región del Fuerte," in *Estudios Históricos de Sinaloa,* edited by Congreso Mexicano de Historia (México, 1960), 348; González Dávila, 645.

rison. Three years later he had joined those declaring for the Plan of Ayutla.[105]

Culiacán's liberals deeply mistrusted Vega. As a protégé of Pesqueira, he had cornered the leadership of the liberal cause and left them in subordination. But it was more than just an old grudge: though they acknowledged his meritorious service in the Reform War, they believed his continuance in power would only lead to a return to arbitary, personalized government in favor of a small political circle. The new constitution their representatives helped create reflected this concern. Moreover, for Culiacán notables in general, Vega had indicated distinctly that he was not a representative of their interests. The capital remained in Mazatlán, and nearby Altata, which had been opened to overseas commerce during the war, returned to its former status of a port solely for coastal trade.[106]

Despite such a commercial favor, the Mazatlán business community, especially its foreign component, had been hostile to Vega from the start. It objected to the extraordinary contributions he decreed, claiming that the ordinary contributions were sufficient to cover his administration's operating expenses. Foreign consuls reminded him that if any such revenues were to meet expenses of war, then their nationals were exempt from the contribution. Worse still, Vega cracked down hard on contraband to secure badly needed revenues. One of those injured by Governor Vega's vigorous enforcement of the customs laws was John Kelly, the British vice-consul. At Vega's initiative, District Judge Pablo María Rivera ordered the embargo of all goods in Kelly's possession, on the grounds that they were contraband, and the closure of the warehouse in which they were deposited. The foreign merchants' hostility to Vega was reinforced by that of the rapidly growing native gentry of the port. Their numbers had steadily expanded through intermarriage with foreigners and, more recently, through the return of children educated and trained in Mexico City or Guadalajara. These young people had been attracted to the tenets of liberalism, and their opposition to the governor was based on ideological grounds as well as local economic concerns. Like their counterparts in Culiacán, they did not see in Vega a person of liberal principles.[107]

Lacking the support of the notables of both Mazatlán and Culiacán would have made Vega's task of maintaining political control difficult enough in the political realities of the pre-Reform War period. Now new political elements had arisen, and the governor was opposed by them as well. The war had spawned a group of military *jefes* (chieftains), who, like

---

[105] Gaxiola, F.J., 493; Buelna, *Apuntes*, 198.
[106] Buelna, *Apuntes*, 54, 70-71.
[107] *Ibid.*, 54-56, 59.

Vega, had raised troops and gained control of the movement in their particular district. They had recognized Vega as titular head, largely because of Pesqueira's endorsement and military backing. With the Sonoran governor's departure, they increasingly bristled at being subordinated to a fellow military chieftain whom they considered no more deserving nor qualified for political office than themselves. They had become politically powerful. All enjoyed the popularity accruing from their accomplishments during the war. Most had held military command and political office jointly until the return of constitutional government. Now most commanded units of the state militia.[108] Some, like Colonel Antonio Rosales, were involved in the continuing campaigns against Lozada on the southern border. A few, most notably newly elected Vice-Governor Colonel Manuel Márquez de León, held political office.[109] The political influence of these military *jefes* quickly proved to be significant. In June, 1860, some of them—led by Colonels Remedio Meza, Mauricio Lopez, and Antonio Rosales—joined in a revolt calling for the removal of Vega as provisional governor and the immediate convocation of state elections. Though Vega managed to retain the loyalty of enough of the other *jefes* to remain in office, he agreed to hold the elections a few months later.[110]

Vega had to contend with one other new political force. The Sonoran troops had gone home after the state had been secured for the liberal cause. The Jaliscan troops, the vast majority of whom were from the neighboring canton of Tepic, had not. They had no home to which to return as long as the conservative forces of the Indian *cacique* Manual Lozada tenaciously remained in control of western Jalisco. So they had remained in southern Sinaloa, periodically exchanging incursions with Lozada. They had soon been joined by growing numbers of *tepiqueño* immigrants, many of whom had settled in

---

[108] Mena, II, 37-38.

[109] González Dávila, 497, 534, 543. Rosales had been moving back and forth between state government offices (usually that of secretary of the government) and military service (the Ayutla Revolt, the Reform War, the campaigns against Lozada in Tepic). In office, he gained a reputation for strict adherence to liberal principles, twice resigning when he determined his superiors were compromising those principles. In the various military campaigns, his service was exemplary, his rank raised accordingly. Márquez de León was also a newcomer to the state who combined careers in military service (he opposed the United States in 1847 and subsequent filibustering attempts) and public office in his native Baja California. He had come to Sinaloa to fight for the liberal cause he had long promoted in the federal territory across the Gulf of California and had achieved a notable record and growing popularity.

Lieutenant Colonel Domingo Rubí was a native of the state from a village in the southern district of Concordia. A mineworker in his youth in the nearby *real* of Pánuco, he had gained notice as an accomplished military officer during the Reform War. Another Sinaloan-born *jefe* was Colonel Fortino León, whose forces had operated around Mazatlán during that struggle. He was elected provisional vice-governor in the fall of 1860 and was instrumental in securing the return to constitutional government.

[110] Gaxiola, F.J., 271-279.

Mazatlán. The Jaliscan troops by the end of the Reform War had formally become the Tepic Brigade, responsible to the governor of Jalisco, though they were to cooperate closely with Governor Vega. The brigade and the civilian migrants formed a political interest group pressuring Vega to prosecute the campaign against Lozada more forcefully.[111] They also served as the military and political base of power for the aspirations and ambitions of the brigade's commander, Colonel Ramón Corona.

Corona was representative of the *tepiqueño* migrants. Born in 1837 in a southern Jaliscan village to a family of humble origins yet of moderate social position, Corona had secured employment in commerce at an early age. When the Reform War broke out, he was administering some mining operations in the *Real de Motaje* near the Sinaloa-Tepic border. The excesses of Lozada and the reactionaries in Jalisco led the young Corona to join others in pronouncing for the liberal cause. He soon emerged as their leader. By the end of the war, Corona had attained the rank of Colonel.[112]

Governor Vega was in serious political trouble. None of the important political elements in the state—the notables of Mazatlán and Culiacán, the military *jefes,* or the *tepiqueño* migrants—backed him. A few had even conspired against him. His prestige and popularity among the citizenry of the state in general was declining. A growing opposition accused him of tolerating no criticism in his administration and dismissing employees who raised objections, replacing them with people of his personal political circle, whom he sustained handsomely from the state treasury. The legislature, his opponents charged, had become his willing tool in the same manner. With the war's end in Sinaloa he lost his former discretionary power over the revenues of the federal *aduana.*[113] His policy of aiding other states (especially Jalisco) with funds and troops had dissipated the state treasury and necessitated the levying of extraordinary contributions and the recurrent drafting of new soldiers; this situation, in turn, bred considerable popular discontent.[114]

In such an unfavorable political climate, President Juárez's order (December, 1861) that each state raise and send a contingent to the eastern front to oppose the Intervention put Governor Vega in a bind. The order specified that the governor personally should lead the Sinaloa Brigade, composed of that state's contingent of one thousand troops and one from Sonora, which Governor Pesqueira was sending under the command of General Jesús García Morales.[115] Setting aside the problem of where to find the money to raise and maintain his state's contingent, if Vega left the state as instructed, he

[111] Buelna, *Apuntes,* 70.
[112] González Dávila, 134; Gaxiola, F.J., 500-506.
[113] Gaxiola, F.J., 306-308; Miles, 66-67.
[114] Buelna, *Apuntes,* 70.
[115] Miles, 67; Almada, 577.

rightly feared his enemies would gain control of the government. The loyalty of the other military *jefes* in the state, especially those in the Tepic Brigade, was increasingly dubious. Friction between Governor Vega and Colonel Corona and his associates over the conduct of military operations in the Tepic campaign was growing. Even worse, the *tepiqueños,* both soldiers and civilians, were rapidly developing close ties with Vega's opponents in Mazatlán.[116]

The governor desperately maneuvered to stave off what he believed would be the inevitable consequence of his departure. He stalled in sending the Sinaloan contingent, while he tried to regain his ebbing control over the state. Immediately, in the first months of 1862, he raised the contingent and personally led it in a campaign against Lozada. Upon his return in April, he illegally declared Sinaloa in a state of siege under the pretext of a threat of invasion by Intervention forces, thereby consolidating all civilian and military power in his person. The legislature meekly acquiesced. The following month Vega imposed a forced loan of 58,000 pesos, and his martial rule thereafter became increasingly arbitrary. By fall, the federal government's patience had run out, and the reports it had been receiving about the political situation in Sinaloa raised doubts about Vega's intentions. Rumors reaching Mexico City portrayed the governor as actively resisting the order to lead the Northwest's contingent to the eastern front. Accordingly, Juárez sent an emissary to Vega ordering him to bring the contingent without delay.[117]

Further stalling was out of the question. The problem became that of selecting someone to assume the governmental powers he had consolidated— someone who would be competent enough to maintain them during his absence and loyal or detached enough to relinquish them upon his return. The vice-governor, Colonel Manuel Márquez de León, had long since asked for an indefinite leave of absence (fall, 1861).[118] His replacement, Colonel Fortino León, could no longer be trusted. Vega had obtained from the legislature a year earlier permission for León to be named substitute governor to head the government while he was on campaign in Tepic.[119] But in the interim, his

---

[116] Gaxiola, F.J., 311-312.

[117] *Ibid.*, 312-322; Mena, II, 56-59. Vega declared the state of siege when conditions for such a declaration did not exist, since the threat of intervention appeared at that time only on the eastern coast of Mexico. More importantly, he did not have the power to declare such a state of siege even if the required conditions had existed. The Congress in December, 1860, had invested the President with that power. And besides, even if the state had been empowered to make such a declaration, it would have been the legislature's prerogative, not the governor's. Mena contends that the legislature initiated the declaration of the state of siege, but other sources (Buelna, *Apuntes,* 69, 71, for example) and the political context of the time indicate that Vega was the most likely instigator of the move.

[118] Mena, II, 55-56.

[119] Gaxiola, F.J., 318, 320.

increasingly arbitrary rule (in particular, his order that a relative of León's be executed without trial) had alienated León. To leave the government in the hands of Colonel Corona, a proposition long suspect, was now impossible. Corona's recent independent campaign against Lozada and sound defeat had ruptured the already strained relations between them.

The governor reverted to precedence, in the person of General Jesús García Morales. It was Pesqueira to whom Vega largely owed his rise to power during the Reform War. García Morales, a close associate of Vega's during the war and the Sonoran governor's right arm since, was a secure and immediate link to that past vehicle of success. Moreover, in practical terms the Sonoran general was a political neutral in Sinaloan politics. His commitments and interests were in the neighboring state. To skirt the legal succession of León, Governor Vega employed the unconstitutional procedure of "asking" the ayuntamientos to approve his appointment of García Morales as a means to legalize it. The municipal authorities now operating under martial law were as pliant as the legislature had been the previous April. Before finally leaving the state in February (1863), Vega decreed another forced loan of 50,000 pesos.[120]

García Morales proved to be the caretaker governor Don Plácido had intended, as Vega's subordinates and policies continued to dominate the government. The intense, growing opposition to Vega soon was transferred to his hand-picked successor.[121] The opposition was quickly aided by the Juárez government. Disgusted with Vega's deviousness, it refused to recognize the transfer of power, declared a state of siege, and named former Vice-Governor Márquez, then in Jalisco, to head the government (March 11, 1864). Márquez immediately began dismantling Vega's political clique, removing officials and employees personally loyal to him and discredited by their venality. Moreover, he initiated a reform of administrative affairs and an economizing of the budget. He also organized the districts militarily and recruited additional forces to guard against the eventuality of an invasion of the state by imperialist forces, in particular those of Lozada to the south. Márquez made one mistake, however. He incurred the displeasure of the federal government by refusing to recognize its customs officials' control over revenues of the Mazatlán *aduana*. This error, combined with Vega's direct appeal to Juárez in Mexico City (seconded by his friend and federal deputy from Alamos, Bartolomé Almada), led to the reinstatement of García Morales (April 14).[122]

Widespread discontent resumed, fanned by Vega's opponents, who claimed that García Morales would simply return to being the weak instrument of the *veguista* clique. Colonel Rosales, restored from exile by Márquez and named

---

[120] *Ibid.*, 318-319.
[121] *Ibid.*, 324, 363.
[122] *Ibid.*, 326-330; Stagg, *Almadas and Alamos,* 110, 114, 122.

military commander of the center, was the first to come out publicly against the reinstatement of García Morales. Knowing he would soon be removed from office, Rosales tried to engineer a revolt in early May from Culiacán but was unable to unify his troops sufficiently. Colonel Corona had gotten along no better with García Morales than with Vega. Decrying the continued periodic lapses in sustenance of his troops, in early summer he moved his forces to Durango, where he had assurance that he could obtain funds. This move left the southern border of the state open to raiding and the imminent threat of eventual invasion by Lozada and, thus, put added pressure on the García Morales government.[123]

THE INTERVENTION: COMMITMENTS FINALIZED

Until 1864 the French Intervention had seemed far removed to those in the Northwest. Aside from fulfillment of the order to send contingents to fight the French in the interior, the war had had little impact. The pace of economic activity in Sonora had continued to accelerate. The political wrangling in Sinaloa had steadily intensified. In the early spring of that year, however, the isolation ended. The French army pushing up from Mexico City through Jalisco reached the outskirts of Mazatlán and began besieging the port. The French Pacific squadron initiated a coastal blockade north to the United States border.[124] Reports began to circulate widely in Sonora that the emperor Maximilian and his sponsor Napoleon III had agreed secretly to make the state a French colony.[125]

---

[123]Mena, II, 79-82; Gaxiola, F.J., 331-333. García Morales devoted a large portion of his time during the remainder of 1863 to organizing the cátedras for the secondary school Vega had established in Mazatlán before his departure and to initiating construction of the project to bring running water to the port from the Río de Siqueros. Gaxiola, F.J., 334-337.

[124]Gaxiola, 372-373; Mena, II, 83.

[125] Acuña, 82; *La Estrella de Occidente,* July 31, 1863, Reel 12, and July 8, 1864, Reel 4; Poston, III, *Overland Monthly,* 296-297. The numerous reports reaching Sonora (many with solid foundation) indicated that the arrangement between Maximilian and Napoleon III, who coveted the state's renowned mining potential, was based on the premise that the new French colony would serve as a permanent reserve force in case of an invasion by the United States and as the price for seating the Austrian prince on the throne of Mexico.

French interest in Sonora had been building since the 1830s. In 1839 Louis Philippe's prime minister dispatched Jufrot de Mofras of the French legation in Madrid to Mexico with instructions to conduct a geographic survey of Northwest Mexico. His work, published in 1844, noted Sonora's reputed vast mining potential. Word coming back from French filibusters and French consuls in California a few years later served to enhance that reputation. The influx of North American mining investors in the early 1860s seemed to attest to its veracity. Ernesto de la Torres Villar, "La política Americana durante la Intervención francesa en México," 55-57. *Revista de Historia de America,* Nos. 63-64 (January-December, 1967), 55-57.

The initial reaction to the direct intrusion of the Intervention was dichotomous and paradoxical. In Sonora, the government response was one of vigorous preparation for resistance, while segments of the population decided on resignation or cooperation with the arrival of imperialist forces. In Sinaloa, almost the entire population rejected submission, while the government inexplainably dawdled. That the two governments were headed by close political associates makes the contrast even more striking.

For reasons that are unclear, Governor García Morales dallied in recruiting sufficient forces and making preparations for the defense of Sinaloa, even after the start of the coastal blockade and the arrival of French troops in the southern part of state. Given his determined efforts against imperialist forces later in Sonora, the only plausible explanation seems to be that his political insecurity preoccupied and distracted him. After troops in Mazatlán successfully halted the French advance in late March, the Juárez government sent an engineer, General Gaspar Sánchez Ochoa, to construct defense works for the port. Although they were completed in June, García Morales was lax in raising and assembling enough forces to man them. When the governor finally did act in August, his methods incensed the general public. The *leva* (draft) was considered unjust and unequal. The sudden extraordinary contribution of 100,000 pesos, in light of the fact that several other special levies in the previous two years had seemingly gone into private pockets (given the haphazard nature of military preparations until then) was thought at best another boondoggle, at worst an outrage. García Morales' days were numbered.

On September 21, 1864, the aging Francisco de la Vega pronounced against the government in Culiacán, citing its recent and by then generally odious decrees as justification. Don Francisco's real intent was to lead the state into the imperialist camp, and after a few days of only token support, he said so. The price of resistance was too high now to pay, he claimed. De la Vega was driven out of the center of the state and forced to take refuge in Durango, where French troops had secured control of the state.[126] The French occupation there a few months earlier had driven Corona and his men back into southern Sinaloa. They were now facing dispersion for want of resources, which the García Morales government had failed to send. The defense against the French south of Mazatlán had brought the various military elements active in the state together, and, though it would not be officially confirmed until December in the formation of the Army of the West, Corona (now a general) in fact was chief of all republican forces in Sinaloa and western Jalisco. Supported by the *tepiqueño* immigrants and the notables

---

[126] Gaxiola, F.J., 338-356, 370-372, 382. Francisco de la Vega was defeated and executed at the landing of Agiabampo in November by forces from Alamos under General José María Patoni. He had re-entered the state from Durango with a small force and occupied El Fuerte before being trapped on the coast just across the Sonoran border.

of Mazatlán, a revolt from this quarter was now impossible to prevent or extinguish.[127]

The revolt in October was led by two veteran Sinaloan *jefes*, Colonels Rosales and Joaquín Sanchez Román, with Corona's cooperation. Like Francisco de la Vega, they too attacked the August decrees as ruinous and cruel. But they went on to charge the García Morales administration with the incapacity to administer the state or provide for its defense. They called not for resignation to the practical and the inevitable as Vega had done. Rather, they urged the citizens of the state to resist doggedly. The citizenry had shown their support of military preparedness for some time, if not carried out in an arbitrary manner. Though Mazatlán fell to the imperialists in November through the arrival of Lozada's forces from Tepic, within two months Rosales and Corona had succeeded in transforming the state into a bulwark of effective republican resistance.[128]

The French set up elections of juntas in occupied towns which would adopt the monarchy, to serve as beachheads for conversion of the populace to the imperialist cause. They tried repeatedly through several campaigns to secure control over central and northern Sinaloa. Effective guerrilla resistance restricted their permanent control of Mazatlán and the other principal towns in the southern part of the state. Only in the port was there significant cooperation, primarily from the foreign merchants and their clients. In frustration, the French occupation forces turned to arbitrary sentencing and execution of suspected collaborators and plundering of small towns and villages; these actions only enraged the broad republican opposition and made their resolve more firm.[129]

Rosales' decisive defeat of the French-imperialist expeditionary force sent to capture Culiacán in December, 1864, won federal recognition of his government and official confirmation of Corona as chief of all Sinaloan and Jaliscan forces. Corona would have liked to have become governor himself but realized that only someone with well-established credentials in the state would be accepted. Moreover, though the principal officers of the Jaliscan-*tepiqueño*-Sinaloan forces were non-Sinaloan, a large majority of the men and lower officers were by that time Sinaloans, due to attrition during several years of fighting. Corona, thus, stepped aside in favor of Colonel Rosales,

[127] *Ibid.*, 357-362; Buelna, *Apuntes*, 76; Mena, II, 90, 108.

[128] Mena, II, 90-100; Gaxiola, F.J., 372-373, 376. By 1864, Corona had gathered around him a flock of talented subordinates, most of whom were from Jalisco, and in particular the canton of Tepic. They included Angel Martínez, Doroteo López, Jorge García Granados, Bonifacio Peña, Ascención Correa, Anacleto Correa, Francisco Tolentino, Euligio Parra, Adolfo Palacios, Bibiano Dávalos, and Donato Aucara. Gaxiola, F. J., 247-338, *passim*; Angel María Garibay D., Director, *Diccionario Porrúa de historia, biografía y geografía de México* (México, 1965, and supplement, 1966), *Passim*.

[129] Gaxiola, F.J., 374-458; Mena, II, 118-161.

known for his solid liberal credentials and very popular among Mazatlán society and throughout the southern part of the state.[130]

Nevertheless, the alliance between Corona and Rosales soon disintegrated. The prestige accruing to Rosales from his triumph the previous December and his growing tendency to be his own man made Corona uneasy—jealous, public opinion rumored. In addition, Rosales had been either unwilling or unable to provide adequate resources to sustain Corona's men in southern Sinaloa, where the brunt of the resistance to the imperialist occupation was occurring (in contrast to the relative peace in northern and central Sinaloa, where Rosales commanded republican forces). It was a familiar irritation for Corona in his recent dealings with Sinaloa's governors. Accordingly, the following May (1865) General Corona forced Governor Rosales to step down and replaced him with Colonel Domingo Rubí, the commander of one of his three brigades.[131] A native of the southern district of Concordia, Rubí managed the government honestly and faithfully through the final defeat of the Empire.[132]

In contrast to his close associate in Sinaloa (General García Morales), Governor Pesqueira had reacted promptly and vigorously to the approach of imperialist forces. Through the commander of the French Pacific Squadron, patrolling off Guaymas, Maximilian had offered to retain Pesqueira in power if he would submit to the Empire. But the governor refused to sell out.[133] He had risen to power by astutely reading the prevailing political sentiments in the state. He did not fail to do so now. His political judgement was that a strong majority of the state was committed to the republican cause. Besides,

---

[130] Gaxiola, F.J., 367, 400-401.

[131] *Ibid.*, 459-462. Corona contrived a barracks revolt through troops loyal to him in Culiacán under the command of Colonel Ascensión Correa. Corona then mediated a truce, and Rosales was forced to retire to the northern part of the state with the few soldiers who remained faithful. When Corona appointed Rubí governor, Rosales, considering the act illegal and judging the former mineworker unfit to govern, prepared to recover control. González Dávila, 534; Almada, 698.

Both Rosales and Corona sent emissaries to Juárez in Chihuahua to secure a favorable decision. With the President's decision in favor of Corona's choice and Rosales' refusal to accept it, Rubí marched on Rosales, who still had the backing of the local authorities in the northern towns. Seeing his forces outnumbered, and receiving a call for immediate assistance from Alamos, where imperialists were preparing to besiege the town, Rosales informed Rubí that he was going to relieve the Sonoran town rather than be a party to the unnecessary shedding of Republican blood. Rubí agreed to treat benevolently the towns and villages that had supported the former governor. Gaxiola, 466-470.

Rosales succeeded in driving off the advance guard of the imperialist forces, but he was then surrounded by the main body, captured, and killed on September 24. González Dávila, 534. Rosales' popularity among Sinaloans was so great that Rubí had no choice but to order public funeral rites and declare him a *benemérito del estado* (state hero). Gaxiola, F.J., 482-483.

[132] Gaxiola, F.J., 462, 507.

[133] Acuña, 80-81.

he had been sympathetic to liberal ideas since his school days in Europe, his political reputation and success rested on his adherence to the principles of the Constitution of 1857, and by now his personal commitment to a liberal, republican Mexico was firm.

With the extraordinary powers granted him by the legislature in April, 1864, he called into service six thousand national guardsmen and made extensive preparations for the expected invasion. The state's champion of the *Reforma* called on all Sonorans to join him in a holy war to preserve the Republic and the nation's independence, and most especially to avert the state's conversion into a French colony. For the emperor of France, he warned,

> [has] proposed to destroy our nationality. So that whatever be the result of the general invasion, Sonora is destined to be a French colony. Will you permit, Sonorans? Never! Count Raousset had the same idea and died on the scaffold . . . . The filibusters of Caborca, just as greedy, met the same fate in trying to conquer this coveted region.[134]

There were some who did not answer the call, however. In contrast to Sinaloa, initially there was not overwhelming support in Sonora for an unyielding resistance to the imperialist occupation. When the French expeditionary force compelled Pesqueira to evacuate Guaymas the following March (1865) and decisively routed his army at nearby La Pasión, the old *gandaristas* surfaced in various sections of the state. Summoned once again by their ever available *jefe*, who had conveniently slipped across the border from Arizona, they proclaimed their adhesion to the Empire and to Don Manuel María as rightful heir to the Sonoran government. They were soon joined by their old Indian allies—the Yaquis and Mayos (who were quite ready to support anyone who would bring down the liberal government promoting the colonization of their lands) and the Opatas. With this local support, the imperialist forces captured the main urban centers. Alamos, the bastion of liberalism in the state, was the last to fall. Their forces defeated and scattered, the liberals carried on the struggle in guerrilla bands under the direction of General García Morales, recently returned from Sinaloa. Governor Pesqueira, in ill-health and in grief over the deaths first of a son and then of his wife, withdrew to Arizona. Later, he went to California to procure more arms and munitions.[135]

Much of the Hermosillo and Guaymas business communities then concluded that Pesqueira was finished. They had backed the liberal government from

---

[134] Manifesto to the Citizens of the State, November 30, 1865, *in* Almada, 373-374.

[135] Acuña, 84-87. See also Bancroft (*North Mexican States and Texas*), Almada and Corral for detailed accounts of the Intervention War in Sonora.

its inception, but his forced loans and arbitrary tendencies had tried their patience and soured their endorsement. A large majority wished his political retirement. Some awaited a favorable opportunity for his removal. After the imperialists had won control of the principal towns, most figured that it was only a matter of time before all of the remaining republican forces were extinguished. They made their peace with the Empire, requesting permanent French garrisons to protect their towns from guerrilla attacks.[136]

Those Hermosillo and Guaymas businesspeople, however, had rushed to sell their liberal stock for imperial shares too soon. The republican forces regrouped, supplied with arms from the United States (now reunited and eager to end French influence in Mexico) and strengthened by reinforcements from Sinaloa under General Angel Martínez. During the spring and summer of 1866, they slowly regained control of the countryside. When the French troops pulled out in September, the towns fell quickly to them. The Indian tribes agreed to peace and the remaining imperialist bands were gradually hunted down or driven out of the state.[137]

The Intervention represented an ideological and economic test of nationality for all regions in Mexico, but in particular for the Northwest and the Yucatán. Their economies had become increasingly dependent upon foreign markets and stimuli. Neither region in the post-independence years had felt itself very much a part of the nation. Both had developed long-standing grievances against Mexico City that had been ignored when assistance was vitally needed, and they had been interfered with unjustly when they had struck out on their own. Annexation had been given serious consideration in both at one time or another. The Yucatán succumbed readily to the Intervention; only when the Empire was openly crumbling, and at the instigation of the Governor of Tabasco, did the region return to the republican cause.[138] Though there were various tempting offers tendered to the region's political leaders and some—for practical reasons—cooperated with the imperial occupation of parts of the region, the Northwest in general resisted the Intervention stubbornly and from the start, receiving very little assistance from outside republican forces.

For nearly fifteen years, the people of the Northwest, in particular the urban notables, had been engaged in working out an understanding of their

---

[136] Acuña, 71-74, 85, 87. Among the Hermosillo businesspeople who cooperated with the French occupation were Dionisio González; José and Juan Pedro Camou; Florencio, Pedro, and Gabriel Monteverde (Manuel, elected vice-governor in 1863, and his younger brother José remained loyal to the Pesqueira government); Juan de Dios Castro; Agustín Pesqueira (a relative of the governor); Adolfo Loustaunau; Celedonio Ortiz; and José de Águilar, the acting prefect of the department. *Periódico Oficial del Departamento de Sonora* (Ures), November 14, 1865.

[137] Acuña, 89-92.

[138] Reed, 185-198.

place in the Mexican nation and of the basis of their relations with the rest of the country. They had been tempted and challenged by proposals of annexation from the United States through purchase or filibustering expeditions. They had said no. The Reform War had forced them to make an ideological choice if they were to remain in the nation. They had said yes to the liberals. The Intervention offered them an alternative somewhere in between. They could become part of a larger political entity that was neither a foreign culture nor a nation state, but would be like the Spanish regime their parents and grandparents had known. Again they said no. The Intervention was for them a final confirmation of their decision to be part of a liberal, federalized Mexico nation.

Sonorans had once again preserved their independence in the face of foreigners coveting their state. The *gandaristas* had been finally put to rest, never again to challenge the state's now solid commitment to the Constitution of 1857 and the Mexico it promised.[139] For Sinaloans, the war had eradicated the last remnants of conservatism. Even the foreign merchants of Mazatlán, who generally cooperated with the imperialist occupation, now understood the new political realities. At an end, too, were the pretentions of the Vegas and their personal followers. Don Francisco had been hunted down and killed as an imperialist pretender. Don Plácido had been discredited, accused of embezzling funds by the Juárez government, and had fled in disgrace to Tepic, seeking refuge under Lozada's protection.[140]

Nevertheless, all of these political alterations had been achieved at a considerable price. Some towns, like Alamos and Concordia, had been cruelly sacked. Fields had been left untended or destroyed, herds of livestock depleted by and for the war, and mines abandoned. Commerce had become paralyzed. Schools and important municipal improvements had been sus-

---

[139] Almada, 293-294. Gándara accompanied the French expeditionary force, whose commander ordered the return to him of all properties embargoed by Republican authorities. Restored as a general and granted the Order of the Imperial Cross, Gándara served as a military advisor, liaison with the Indian tribes, and political confidant of the French commander. In August, 1866, he was named imperial prefect of the Department of Sonora; he never assumed office, however, since the notice arrived during the evacuation of the French army, which forced him to take refuge in Tepic with Lozada. After the war, he tried to plead before the federal government that he had been no more than a neutral during the war. Though the Sonoran government charged him with treason and the Secretary of War arrested him (May, 1868), he was released two years later and returned to Sonora, understanding that his political career was finished. He died in 1878.

[140] Buelna, *Apuntes,* 160, 198. Plácido Vega, after his arrival with the Sinaloan contingent in Mexico City, had soon been sent to San Francisco (May, 1863) to buy arms with funds received from the Mazatlán *aduana*. He returned to northern Sinaloa with some arms, but not in the amount expected. When the Juárez government called him to Chihuahua to give account of his stewardship of federal funds, he decided to seek refuge in Tepic, where until 1873 he fought with Lozada, hoping for the opportunity to regain control over the state.

pended. People had been uprooted. For Sonorans, the cost of the Intervention was particularly hard to accept. It had aborted the state's first sustained progress since independence. North American investment had gone back across the border. The proposed El Paso-Guaymas railroad, previously delayed by the Civil War in the United States, had fallen through. There was nothing left to do but try to pick up the pieces and begin again.

Sinaloans, for the first time since independence, had a taste of what their neighbors to the north had been experiencing for decades. The Intervention had caused considerable damage over much of the state, severely dislocating the pattern of steady growth in economic activity since the 1830s. Up until the Reform War political strife had been confined to the struggle between cliques based in Mazatlán and Culiacán. Other district towns had carried a large share of the burden of the resistance to the imperialist occupation and many of their leaders had quickly risen to prominence; these towns were no longer content to be pliant clients. In and around Mazatlán were the uprooted *tepiqueño* emigrants, desirous of going home, but willing to support the political ambitions of the group of military *jefes* whom the war had raised to be wielders of considerable power and influence. The potential for political instability was high, and with it came a dampening of economic prospects.

6

The Burden of Recovery
(1867-1875)

We now have peace and quiet in this State, but it is the peace and quiet that follows exhaustion and the using up of the means of making war. As the people recuperate from the prostration which was the result of their struggle against and their triumph over the imperial Mexican party in this State, we are liable at any time to have again our coast lighted by the flame of civil discord and strife . . . . An end must be made and a check placed upon all civil disturbances and revolutions that have desolated this unhappy country for years, and which still continue in some sections, rendering the laws a dead letter, life and property insecure, and, with the attendant forced loans and contributions, paralyzing all industrial pursuits.[1]

. . . until the causes of apprehensions are removed, and full confidence in the government felt and enjoyed by the people, there is little hope that this State can enter (except to a limited extent) upon a new era of progress and improvement.[2]

United States Consul Alexander Willard's assessment of the difficult circumstances facing Sonorans after the Intervention was most discerning. Sinaloans were in the same predicament. For a decade, politics in the Northwest had been excruciating, government generally desultory and frequently arbitrary, communities disrupted, and families unsettled, uprooted, and even pruned. Almost no district had been untouched or left unscarred. The price of defeat was to be left without a public future or, at best, with one suspended for a period of political penance, accompanied sometimes by private decline, even ruin. The cost of victory was to inherit a future whose promise was highly vulnerable and which offered little ease or comfort.

---

[1] United States Department of State, *Report on Commercial Relations,* 1870, Guaymas, Consul A. Willard, 647.
[2] *Ibid.,* 1871, 905.

The underlying costs of the war were more keenly felt among the urban notables than among the general populace, for the public and the private were less differentiated among the former. They claimed a greater share of the public realm and felt more responsible for it. They expected that public realm to promote their private domains. Yet progress until then had been only fleeting, especially for the notables of Sonora. Now, in the post-Intervention years, its attainment, though more anticipated, was no less uncertain, burdened by the necessity for extensive recovery. As the United States consul perceived, it was a complex, fragile, interrelated recovery. Economic recuperation required political stability, and a stable politics, as the consul stressed, had been only infrequently the norm in the Northwest.

After years of civil strife and stagnation, if not deterioration, progress on a continuing basis seemed to have commenced in Sonora in the late 1850s and early 1860s. The economy had begun to expand, leavened by the new North American markets in Arizona and California. Urban life had matured to the point where it rested on a firm footing. Local capital had sought out uncultivated lands to bring into production and had fostered the first real stirrings of industry. Foreign capital had flowed into the state to revive mining and had spilled over into the other sectors of the economy. The curtain had been raised on an era of progress. The Intervention, however, had enshrouded the state once again in a veil of prostration and recidivism.

Sinaloa had been at war almost continuously since 1858. It had not had the interlude of peace and the influx of North American capital that its neighbor had enjoyed. The state's suffering from the Reform War and the Intervention was greater also, particularly in the southern part of the state. Though meeting no resistance, the French had sacked and burned Concordia; they had set fire to numerous villages and hamlets and freely plundered. Lozada's raids from Tepic had been equally devastating. Republican troops had been generally forced to live off the land as best they could, at the expense of the countryside.[3]

Political turmoil had left the Northwest economically exhausted. If the restoration of political stability and "full confidence in the government" were prerequisites to a new era of progress, then it was also true, as Consul Willard failed to observe, that favorable economic conditions were likewise essential. They provide the climate in which confidence in government can grow, the room in which government, and politics in general, can maneuver. In times of despair, economic hardships frequently foster compromise and acquiescence, such as occurred in Sonora in the late 1840s. But expectation pervaded the post-Intervention years, expectation that was quick to be disappointed. The economic conditions left from a decade of nearly continuous war and resulting from new circumstances in the post-war years were therefore critical to the

---

[3] Buelna, *Apuntes,* 96; Mena, II, 154-156.

success of any administration and to the stability of politics in general. The economic burden facing both was considerable.

RECURRING INSECURITIES AND SHORTAGES

Though the wounds from the wars ran deeper in Sinaloa, circumstances there favored their faster healing. The state's population increased in the post-war years, unlike that of Sonora.[4] More importantly, Sinaloans could begin to pick up the pieces without fear of an Apache arrow in their backs or a Yaqui torch to their homes. By the early 1860s, Sonorans had thought that such long-standing insecurities were finally under control. By 1867, much to their dismay, those insecurities were reappearing, dampening the prospects of progress.

The tempo of Apache incursions was again increasing. Though state and local forces maintained an active and incessant persecution against them, the Apaches raided with ever more daring and abandon. They penetrated into the central districts of Hermosillo and Guaymas and made the roads of the northern half of the state generally unsafe for travel.[5] From late 1866 to 1869, an estimated 116 men, women, and children were killed; the death toll for 1870 alone was put at 123.[6] The Apaches wore down the northern countryside with hit-and-run raids against isolated farms and haciendas, like that against the large estate of José María Morales in Arizpe district in late 1869. The marauding Indians surprised the peones of the hacienda, killing three and carrying off as many pairs of oxen. The municipal authorities of Arizpe detached twenty national guardsmen, who were unsuccessful in their pursuit of the Apaches.[7] The Apaches discerned that the towns were now well defended, and so wisely avoided them.

It was soon evident to Sonorans where the source of the trouble lay. With the conclusion of the Civil War in the United States, the movement of settlers into the Arizona Territory had been renewed. With them came more cavalry detachments, whose growing number of forts and active operations increasingly restricted the Apaches in that territory. The United States Army, however, did not impinge on the flow of arms, munitions, and other goods in exchange for stolen Sonoran livestock and other valuables between the Apaches and North American merchants and traders. In 1872 it gave tacit approval to this arrangement. General Howard celebrated treaties with the two principal Apache tribes in southeastern Arizona, by which they agreed to live on reservations in exchange for food and clothing. These reservations,

---

[4] Daniel Cosío Villegas, ed., *Historia Moderna de México: La República Restaurada—la vida social* (México, 1955), 20, 32.

[5] *La Estrella de Occidente,* June 26, 1868, Reel 5.

[6] Corral, 84.

[7] *La Estrella de Occidente,* January 15, 1869.

situated along the international boundary—with no United States troops between them and the border—immediately served as a base for Apache incursions into Sonora. The Chiricahuas, led by Cochise, conveniently slipped
across the border, raided until Sonoran forces were in close pursuit, and then
returned to Arizona, secure in the knowledge that the state's national guard
could not continue to pursue them and that the United States Army would
not bother them as long as they did not molest settlers in Arizona.[8]

The permanent defeat of the conservative cause in the Intervention or-
dained that the Yaqui and Mayo valleys would become an unremitting center of
unrest. The two tribes no longer had any allies among the *yoris*. No sooner
had the Republic been restored than the Juárez government conceded to
Ignacio Gómez del Campo twenty-five *sitios* (43,900 hectares) situated along
the Yaqui and Mayo rivers.[9] A few months later, Colonel Crispin de S.
Palomares obtained a concession to survey lands between the the two rivers,
from the pueblos of Buenavista and Camoa to the Gulf of California. The
lands were to be ceded to a colonizing company. Palomares was then a federal
diputado for southern Sonora and had been one of Governor Pesqueira's most
loyal lieutenants in helping to put down the series of Yaqui-Mayo uprisings
during the previous decade.[10]

In reaction to this prospective territorial encroachment, the two tribes
went into open revolt. The garrison at Santa Cruz was annihilated, *yori* authorities and several prominent residents in Etchojoa and other pueblos were
assassinated, and livestock was carried off. Under growing pressure from state
forces waging war without quarter, the tribes agreed to end hostilities.[11] But
it was only a tenuous peace. The Yaquis and Mayos remained semiautono-
mous, as the Pesqueira government lacked the resources to bring them into
complete submission.

Insecurity also arose from the spillage of political disorders in Sinaloa over
into Sonora. In March, 1869, Colonel Adolfo Palacios pronounced in Culiacán in support of Plácido Vega, whose ambitions had not been quieted by
long years of failure. When the Fuerte garrison seconded the revolt, Pesqueira
and General García Morales mobilized state forces, fearing the revolutionaries
would invade Sonora. But the latter took note of these preparations and
moved into Chihuahua, where they were defeated shortly afterward.[12] The
following year, as part of Vega's continuing schemes to return to power in
Sinaloa, Fortino Vizcaino engineered a piratical raid on Guaymas to secure

---

[8]*Ibid.*, March 7 and July 4, 1873, Reel 6; United States Department of State, *Report
on Commercial Relations*, 1870, Guaymas, Consul A. Willard, 299; Corral, 84, 106-108.

[9]Cosío Villegas, *República Restaurada—vida social*, 74, 216-217.

[10]Almada, 552-553.

[11]*El Pueblo de Sonora*, December 17, 1867; Acuña, 99-100.

[12]Corral, 78-79.

funds and supplies. Merchandise worth more than 150,000 pesos was seized from the customs house and the port's leading merchants.[13] In 1871 Guaymas was again "held up," this time in connection with the *porfirista* revolt against President Juárez. In October, Jesús Leyva led the port garrison in declaring for the revolt's Plan of La Noria. He exacted money from wealthy citizens and then sailed south along the coast to spread the revolt to the southern part of Sonora. Governor Pesqueira moved quickly to intercept them, crushing Leyva's force in a single encounter. Meanwhile, in Sinaloa the revolt had acquired a considerable following. The state's governor, Eustaquio Buelna, had been forced to retreat to the Sonoran border. Seeing the revolt's success in Sinaloa as a serious potential threat to his own government, Pesqueira did not hesitate in answering Buelna's appeal for aid.[14]

Such spillage of disorder into Sonora tied down its government's energies and resources, despoiled some of its citizens of possessions, and heightened apprehension among the citizenry. For Sinaloa, the source of these disorders, the repercussions were much worse. In addition to the rebellions noted above, there were insurrections in January, 1868; August, 1871; and July, 1872. Nearly every district of the state was affected during most of these revolts.[15]

Disruptive and damaging in themselves, these almost year-to-year disorders created a climate in which brigandage thrived. The Reform War and the Intervention had spawned a new generation of bandits throughout the nation who had not laid down their arms along with the regular soldiers when the wars had ended.[16] Lodged in the rugged foothills of the Sierra Madre near the productive and populated communities of the coastal plain, they offered a haven and cover for unsuccessful insurgents and political refugees. In turn, the revolts provided the bandits with a camouflage of their own, to couch their activities in legitimate pretenses. The diversion of the government's resources and attention also gave them more room in which to operate.[17]

If the security necessary to promote economic activity was notably deficient in the Northwest, the capital investment required was in even scarcer supply. The policy of indefinitely deferring payment on the foreign debt, followed by presidents Juárez and Lerdo, dissuaded foreign capital from investing in the country in general.[18] The turmoil engendered by widespread banditry in the countryside and periodic revolts and political strife gave further reason for overseas investors to look elsewhere.[19] For the Northwest, there

---

[13] Acuña, 105.

[14] *Ibid.*, 109-112.

[15] Mena, II, 244-280.

[16] Cosío Villegas, *República Restaurada—vida social*, 357.

[17] *El Clamor Público*, December 7 and 14, 1872.

[18] Cosío Villegas, ed., *Historia moderna: La República Restaurada—la vida económica* (México, 1955), 481-482.

was an added problem. The United States, the most likely and largest potential source of foreign investment, as evidenced in the previous decade in
Sonora, was now caught up in developing its last frontier. Railroad capital
went into linking the rest of the country with the West, not northern Mexico.
Miners saw fortunes far more in the hills of Nevada, Colorado, and South
Dakota than in Sonora and Sinaloa. California's merchant and industrial capitalists looked increasingly east to the Rockies for markets, rather than south
to the Sierra Madre.

What North American capital there was during the post-Intervention years
in the Northwest was largely invested in Sinaloa. More than two million
dollars (approximately the amount invested in Sonora in the early 1860s) was
engaged in and around a hundred enterprises. But it was nearly all concentrated in Mazatlán and the mining centers in the foothills of the Sierra to the
east. Moreover, though United States Consul Isaac Sisson noted the favorable
returns to the several large mining operations, he was pessimistic in his overall
assessment of investment opportunities.[20]

> As for mercantile pursuits, no one can contend with the old estab-
> lished houses without a large capital. As to farming, nothing can be
> done. As to mining, it requires large capital, one experienced in mining,
> one that understands the customs and ways of the people, and has a
> thorough knowledge of the mining laws; none other can succeed. There-
> fore, to all our citizens who think of settling in Mexico, my advice to
> them for the present is, to go around it.[21]

Few North American investors ventured into Sonora. The risks from marauding Apaches and defiant Yaquis and Mayos, who disrupted nearly all
sections of Sonora at one time or another in the post-war years, were judged
far greater comparatively than those arising from the more numerous political
disorders and banditry in Sinaloa.[22] Moreover, railroads pushing west from

---

[19] United States Department of State, *Report on Commercial Relations*, 1869,
Guaymas, Consul A. Willard, 268.

[20] *Ibid.*, 1873, Mazatlán, Consul Isaac Sisson, 839-840. Sisson estimated that there
were approximately fifty North American enterprises involved in mining, ranging from
mine owners to teamsters. Another thirty ventures were being engaged in by merchants,
manufacturers, doctors, mechanics, etc., from the United States, with a combined capital
of $200,000. Twenty North American farmers, with a capital of $30,000 and owning
about 30,000 acres of land, were just making a living; there was little land for sale,
"though some of their ranches are very fine."

[21] *Ibid.*, 840.

[22] *Ibid.*, 1873, Guaymas, Consul A. Willard, 828-829. By Willard's estimates nearly
two-thirds of the total North American investment of about $800,000 was engaged in
mining, divided among six companies. There were also two North American commission
houses, with a capital of $80,000, and four ranches, with $20,000 invested. The remaining immigrants from the United States were engaged as mechanics and small traders.

Texas and east from California were redirecting Arizona commerce from its prior external links through Sonora. Even the Arizona market for Sonora's agricultural and stock production was threatened, since newly settled farmers in the Gila Valley were increasingly supplying that territory.[23]

Among local businesspeople and foreign capitalists who had remained in Sonora, confidence was low. Few were willing to risk their capital in starting new enterprises, many curtailed their businesses, and others sent their surplus funds out of the state. "[The] unsatisfactory condition of affairs," reported Consul Willard, "is relaxing the small spirit of enterprise that existed into mere conservative activity, and merchants and others in the different industrial pursuits are concentrating their ability to preserve what they possess, being consoled if, during the past twelve months, they have avoided losses."[24]

The general outlook in Sinaloa was more promising, but growth in economic activity was confined principally to the mining centers located in the southern districts (Cosalá, Mazatlán, and Rosario) and the port of Mazatlán, through which most of the trade with the mines passed. Much of the mercantile activity in the port itself did not reflect expansion of the state's economy, but rather the production of the interior regions east of the Sierra. By 1873, that interior trade was in decline.[25]

Contributing to the difficulties facing Sonoran businesspeople was a labor shortage, particularly in agriculture and mining. The laboring classes (the peones, the mineworkers, and day laborers), who made up three-fourths of the state's population, were hit hardest by the economic stagnation. "Today that proletarian class is reduced to a condition not far removed from that of a slave," professed Adolfo Almada in his bill before the legislature proposing a minimum wage of fifteen pesos a month. The diputado from Alamos told his colleagues that the existing average wage of eight pesos a month was by then simply inadequate for laborers to provide their families with the bare necessities. They lived a miserable existence. Any prolonged illness, unexpected municipal or village contribution, or loss of their meager wages through gambling or a night on the town forced them to go into debt to their employers, with the almost certain consequence of becoming entrapped in perpetual servitude.[26] Those able to ward off the latter fate still had to walk the tightrope

---

[23]*La Estrella de Occidente,* November 19, 1869, Reel 5.

[24]United States Department of State, *Report on Commercial Relations,* 1870, Guaymas, Consul A. Willard, 301-302.

[25]*Ibid.,* 1871, Mazatlán, Consul I. Sisson, 910; *idem,* 1873, 839-840.

[26]Corbalá Acuña, *Alamos,* 65-68. Almada saw the plight of the laboring classes as the prime cause for the state's political, economic, and social instability: their miserable condition, which was no better than during colonial times, made them easily susceptible to prodding into revolt, since they had little to lose.

of the draft (instituted by the Juárez government),[27] bear the brunt of the Apache raids in the countryside and the small villages, and avoid being left out of work when their employers were forced to curtail operations.[28]

Across the border in Arizona and California, jobs went begging at a dollar a day for a common laborer, two dollars a day for skilled tasks (the peso in 1873 was still worth a dollar). Women readily found employment there as cooks, laundresses, and maids, and there one could raise a family in comparative peace. Consequently, a steady stream of laboring men and women left Sonora to find relief from the Apaches, secure adequate wages to support their families, and escape from debt servitude and the draft.[29] By 1870 Governor Pesqueira estimated at least 7,500 had emigrated to Arizona and 8,500 to California in the previous decade—fourteen percent of the population. The governor added to these emigration figures an estimated 4,000 killed during the Intervention and by the Apaches to account for Sonora's considerable drop in population from 133,000 in 1861 to 108,000 only eight years later.[30] Recurrent newspaper reports indicated that the emigration continued in the 1870s, exacerbated by the growing political turmoil within the state.

There is no evidence that a similar labor shortage existed in Sinaloa. The population of that state increased slightly, from 162,298 in 1869 to 168,031 four years later.[31] An alternative opportunity for laborers was not nearly so

---

The *alamense* legislator believed that a minimum wage of 15 pesos would raise the laboring classes out of their prostrate condition and enable a large number to free themselves from debt servitude, facilitating their enlightenment, and improving their labor, which at that time was not very productive due to poor conditions and low incentives. The bill died in committee, for reasons not yet fully clear. Most likely, the prospect raised by Almada of freedom from debt servitude did not sit well with employers, who were well represented in the legislature—particularly when there was an acute labor shortage. The doubling of wages would have also impinged upon profits, already diminished in the current depressed business climate. Almada was a well-meaning notable who understood in part the long-run political implications of pitiful wages. But the overwhelming majority of the Sonoran urban gentry was neither so perceptive, nor willing to accept such a radical proposal. Sobarzo, 106.

[27]Governor Ignacio Pesqueira, *Memoria del Estado de Sonora* (Hermosillo, 1970), 23 (*Número* 14). The draft law was passed on May 28, 1869, to provide replacements for the army. Each state was required to draft its citizens at the rate of one per thousand.

[28]*Ibid.*, 31-32; *La Estrella de Occidente*, March 7, 1873, Reel 6.

[29]John Spring, *John Spring's Arizona*, edited by A. M. Gustafson (Tucson, 1966), 189-190.

[30]Pesqueira, 22-23. The population figure for 1861 was computed for the electoral law of that year; that for 1869 was derived from an official state census.

It should be noted that such state censuses were very liable to error, as state authorities often acknowledged; however, they are the best sources available upon which to base admittedly tentative demographic judgments.

[31]Governor Domingo Rubí, *Informe del Gobernador de Sinaloa al Congreso del Estado de Sinaloa* (Culiacán, 1869), 21; Buelna, *Compendio*, 59. Both Rubí and Buelna believed the actual population of the state was higher than the two censuses showed.

readily available as in Sonora, nor were there such dislocating conditions as the Apache incursions and the periodic Yaqui-Mayo depredations.

Sonora's economy was caught in a vicious circle, touched off by the dislocations and destruction of the War of Intervention. The increasing Apache incursions, added to the unrest among the Yaquis and Mayos and the political disorders imported into the state, had seriously impaired the security on which its expansion in great part depended. The insecurity discouraged investment and curtailed economic activities, keeping wages miserably low and throwing laborers out of work; these conditions fomented emigration, which, in turn, left business without sufficient labor to maintain operations. Government revenues declined since there was less economic activity to tax and since most individuals could not meet the quotas assigned to them by the law of personal contributions. New contributions would only sap what personal and capital resources remained and lower business confidence and general purchasing power even further. Yet without increased revenues, the government could not begin to eliminate the insecurities prevailing in the state and promote the various economic activities.[32]

The Sinaloan economy was also impaired by such cyclical effects, though neither so extensively nor with such complexity as in Sonora. An editorial in 1872 noted that the long series of civil disorders, including the current manifestations of the La Noria Revolt in the state, had resulted in considerable economic damage. It enumerated the government's obligations regarding the economy to alleviate such hardships.

> One ... of the principal obligations of the public power is to awaken today more than ever, by adequate means, and as circumstances permit, the spirit of association among all classes; to infuse with opportune measures a love of work; to protect industry and all the other professions; to protect affectively the working and manufacturing class, promoting in this manner the advancement of the localities; to organize schools for adults, schools of crafts and trades, and of agriculture; to establish savings banks; and to dictate other measures which would tend to improve directly the moral and material condition of our social classes.[33]

The Sinaloan government, however, was only a little better off than that of Sonora. In the first years after the war it was unable to befriend the various sectors of the economy or to promote the instruction of trade and agricultural skills. It was barely able to keep its own head above water. Already saddled with a debt of more than 33,000 pesos, the government's 1869

---

[32]Pesqueira, 3-4, 11, 31-32.
[33]*Boletín Oficial del Estado de Sinaloa,* May 30, 1872.

budget ran a deficit of nearly 44,000 pesos. Close to 36,000 pesos, one-fifth of the budget, was allotted to sustain the national guard and forces of public security then employed in combatting several revolts.[34] By 1873 the government had managed to amortize its debt, but was still having a hard time meeting operating expenses. For several months the state's judges, being unpaid, refused to preside over their courts. One-sixth of the budget still went to military and security expenses, and nothing was left for public improvements.[35] "I have been unable to find where the State has paid one cent for any improvements whatever," wrote Consul Sisson, "not a road has been opened or anything done by the government to develop the resources of the State."[36]

Included in the 1873 budget of 190,637 pesos was a proposed expenditure of 25,830 pesos for public instruction, of which 9,940 pesos was to support the newly created Liceo Rosales, a state-operated secondary school. That operating expenses were not being met that year, as indicated by Consul Sisson's report, calls into question how much of the money budgeted that year, in particular that portion for primary schools, was actually spent. For the following year, funds for public instruction were scaled down to 16,340 pesos, despite a significant rise in the overall budget and only an insignificant drop in the share allotted to the "Colegio" Rosales (9,800 pesos).[37]

The government's fiscal condition improved somewhat after 1873. The 1874 budget of 229,300 pesos was twenty percent above the previous year and included for the first time funds for public improvements (4,660 pesos). Yet expenditures for the national guard and the force of public security remained at their prior levels, while 30,000 pesos went to amortize debt; these figures confirm the financial difficulties of the previous year and indicate that the state treasury was still not healthy.[38]

---

[34] Rubí, 2-5, 17-21. The principal sources of revenue for the Sinaloan government were the *alcabalas* and the quota (*derecho de patente*) on *giros mercantiles* (commercial transactions); revenue from the latter source ranged from 25 to 300 pesos monthly for individual firms. The personal contribution on property and capital was of much less importance than in Sonora. Cosío Villegas, *República Restaurada–vida económica*, 357-358.

[35] *Boletín Oficial del Estado de Sinaloa*, February 17, 1873; United States Department of State, *Report on Commercial Relations*, 1873, Mazatlán, Consul I. Sisson, 839-840.

[36] United States Department of State, *Report on Commercial Relations*, 1873, Mazatlán, Consul I. Sisson, 840.

[37] *Boletín Oficial del Estado de Sinaloa*, February 17 and December 31, 1873.

[38] *Ibid.*, December 31, 1873.

LIMITED ECONOMIC RECOVERY

Devastated and dislocated by the Intervention, almost wholly lacking in fiscal support from the government, and with frequent lapses in its maintenance of security, the various economic sectors in the Northwest were able to make only partial, if any, recovery during the post-war years.

Mining, still the prime mover of the economy in all sections of Sonora, could not recover anywhere in the state. There was little enough capital for any kind of enterprise, and large amounts of it were most necessary in mining. Foreign investors, whose large operations had sparked mining's recovery a decade before from its post-independence doldrums, now shied away. Only six of the twenty North American companies organized by the mid-1860s had resumed operations. Two were making small profits; the rest were barely meeting expenses.[39] An English company which purchased two mines in the Promontorios mining district in 1869 introduced considerable amounts of capital and machinery. This investment gave mining and commerce around Alamos a temporary uplift. But the company remained only a pilot light in a pale of gloom, making small profits but unable to ignite the entrepreneurial spirits of other capitalists.[40]

The initial recovery of mining in Sinaloa by comparison was considerable. The United States Consul's estimate of the total foreign investment in that sector—$3,750,000 ($2,000,000 of which was North American)—was more than seven times that estimated for Sonora by his counterpart in Guaymas.[41] Rosario was by far the most productive *real*; its principal mine (El Tajo) was exploited by a North American company, which imported a large quantity of

---

[39] United States Department of State, *Report on Commercial Relations*, Guaymas, Consul A. Willard, 1868, 645, 647; 1869, 268; 1872 (Consul A. F. Carrison), 688; 1873, 828-829.

[40] Cosío Villegas, *República Restaurada–vida económica*, 127. In addition to the one English and six North American companies noted above, there were one other English firm (the combined capital of the two English companies was $400,000), two or three moderately sized German concerns, a number of Sonorans working mines on a small scale, and the usual run of scavenging prospectors. United States Department of State, *Report on Commercial Relations*, 1873, Guaymas, Consul A. Willard, 828-829.

[41] United States Department of State, *Report on Commercial Relations*, 1873, Mazatlán, Consul I. Sisson, 839; Cosío Villegas, *República Restaurada–vida econónica*, 126-127, 131-134, 138. Sisson's estimates for investment in foreign mining in Sinaloa were: North Americans, $2,000,000; the Spanish, $1,450,000; the English, $250,000; the Germans, $50,000.

Production declined at the Culiacán mint between 1868 and 1869 and between 1872 and 1873. Some of the decline—but not all—can be attributed to the permission by the federal government in 1871 to export ores. Although the production of the Culiacán mint exceeded the combined totals of those of Alamos and Hermosillo from 1867 to 1869, each of the latter surpassed the Culiacán mint in production between 1872 and 1873. The trend continued between 1873 and 1874, though Hermosillo slipped a little behind Culiacán.

steam-powered machinery. The other principal mining districts were Pánuco, Copala, and Zaragoza in the district of Concordia; San Javier in the district of Badiraguato; and Guadalupe de los Reyes in the district of Cosalá, formerly owned by the Iriarte family, now worked by a rich commercial house in Mazatlán.[42] Nonetheless, these investments were concentrated in only a small number of profitable mines, most of which were located in the southern districts that comprised the immediate hinterland of Mazatlán. They added little stimulus to the economy elsewhere. Furthermore, by the early 1870s difficulties began to plague these operations.

The establishment of a customs security force operating out of Mazatlán put constraints on contraband, which impinged on the profits of the large companies and forced many mines to shut down, particularly the smaller Mexican operations. The alternative for the mines located in the southern districts of the state—legally minting the ore at the casa de moneda in Culiacán—was costly. Roads covering the 250-mile trip were poor, when not non-existent. Freight rates were atrocious. The risks of falling prey to bandits were high, as was the risk of seizure of their ore from the mint itself during political disorders.[43] In 1868 70,000 pesos were taken by those trying to reverse the recent election results by force.[44] Sonoran miners faced the added threat of losing the sparse returns on their efforts to marauding Indians along the trails and rudimentary roads over which they sent their gold and silver. Even worse was the possibility of such Indian attacks on the mining camps themselves.[45] The federal government's high tariff policy saddled mine investors with high production costs through heavy duties on supplies from abroad (except machinery, which was duty free). Its stiff interior and export taxes on mineral production ate up their profits.[46]

Federal permission to export ores, granted in 1871 after years of pleading by the mining interests throughout the country, did eliminate some of these encumbrances. The risks and heavy freight costs of transporting ore to the mints were avoided, as well as the excessive expenses of the minting process itself. Nevertheless, the mining industry was soon beset with more vexing problems: China's unwillingness to accept Mexico's new decimal currency without a discount (whereas its former currency had been accepted at a premium); the growing preference in Europe for gold, with the resulting drop

---

[42] Buelna, *Compendio,* 39-42.

[43] Rubí, 14; United States Department of State, *Report on Commercial Relations,* 1871, Mazatlán, Consul I. Sisson, 912.

[44] Buelna, *Compendio,* 42.

[45] United States Department of State, *Report on Commercial Relations,* 1871, Guaymas, Consul A. Willard, 902.

[46] *Ibid.,* 1868, 647.

in the price of silver; and the immoderate rise in the price of quicksilver.[47] Mining prospects thus remained gloomy. Those who did not sell their mining interests cautiously awaited more favorable times to develop and work them.[48]

Industry was in far worse shape. Like mining, it required a large amount of initial capital, a very high degree of fixed costs, and, consequently, a significant degree of public security and business confidence. But unlike mining, the return on volume was low. In the prevailing atmosphere of depression and uncertainty, few had the will or the ability to either renew operations disrupted by the war or found new industrial activities. The government could spare no money to encourage industry with subsidies to overcome the unfavorable conditions. Most consumers had little left over after securing food and shelter to afford the goods produced by local industries. Those who did generally preferred to purchase foreign goods, which were at that time usually cheaper despite the high tariffs. The limited improvements in transportation in Sinaloa after 1872, largely financed by the federal government, did little to help industry there. Since most of the improvements benefitted Mazatlán's commerce, they even favored foreign competition.[49] Even more damaging to industry in the Northwest were the state and local *alcabalas*, which were frequently much greater on domestically produced goods than the customs duties on foreign merchandise.[50]

At the end of the Republica Restaurada (1876), Sinaloan industry consisted of three cotton textile factories (in Culiacán, Mazatlán, and Villa Union), which had come to supply almost all of the demand for the manufacture of coarse cotton cloth in the state; two steamdriven foundries in Mazatlán; four printing presses in that port and two in Culiacán; tanneries in Villa Union and Mazatlán; and two hat manufactories in the port.[51] Manufacturing in Sonora was even more meager: a textile factory making cheap cotton cloth; several flour mills; some second-rate looms for weaving zarapes; three or four carriage-wagon shops; and a few printing presses. Hermosillo possessed the lion's share of these limited industrial activities.[52] In both states, the usual run of artesanal activities still overwhelmingly predominated.

Agriculture in the region was largely stagnant, confined to producing for the local market. The same labor shortage that aggravated the difficulties

[47] Cosío Villegas, *República Restaurada—vida económica*, 170-175.

[48] United States Department of State, *Report on Commercial Relations*, 1873, Guaymas, Consul A. Willard, 828.

[49] Rubí, 12-14; Pesqueira, 18.

[50] Cosío Villegas, *República Restaurada—vida económica*, 295-296.

[51] Buelna, *Compendio*, 43. The Presidio de Mazatlán was renamed Villa Union in 1828.

[52] Cosío Villegas, *República Restaurada—vida económica*, 93; Pesqueira, 18.

facing miners and manufacturers in Sonora encumbered hacendados and farmers trying to put their lands back into commercial production after the war. This was particularly true in the northern half of the state, where the penetration of the Apache incursions and the proximity of the border made emigration more tempting and facile. Real and potential hostilities by the Yaquis and Mayos threatened agriculturalists in the southern part of the state. In addition, the mining depression seriously reduced the landowners' markets, while transportation restricted the sale of their crops to the immediate district.[53]

Sinaloa's agriculture, which, in contrast to Sonora's, had never been developed commercially to any significant extent, remained backward in the postwar years. Finding enough labor was not a problem, as it was in Sonora. Indeed, most of the population gain in the years following the Intervention occurred in the countryside. Nor was access to fertile lands that difficult, even in the northern part of the state, where the Indian pueblos predominated.[54] For years the villages had been gradually stripped of their lands and their inhabitants forced to work as peones on neighboring farms and haciendas, which defrauded them of their wages while the civil authorities ignored their protestations. In 1866 they had staged an uprising with the encouragement of the imperialists. General Angel Martínez succeeded in quickly pacifying the Indians, in great part because he decreed measures to remedy their grievances, ordering the civil authorities to investigate, return all lands illegally taken from them, and insure that they received fair remuneration for their labor on farms and haciendas.[55] Martínez's decree seems to have had little effect, however. Though the legislature passed a law in 1870 suspending the breaking up of communal lands into private ownership, three years later it repealed this suspension.[56] The gradual erosion of the communal lands of the Indian pueblos continued.

A deficiency of capital was the principal cause for Sinaloan agriculture's limited commercial development. The notables generally preferred to invest in commerce and mining. Even those who were hacendados confined their agricultural endeavors largely to producing corn, beans, and vegetables for the local markets and usually engaged additionally in other, more profitable

---

[53] *La Estrella de Occidente,* October 18 and November 15, 1867, MAHm, Sonora, Reel 13, and April 21, 1871, Reel 5; United States Department of State, *Commercial Relations,* Guaymas, Consul A. Willard, 1868, 646; 1870, 299.

[54] Rubí, 14.

[55] Mena, II, 191-193.

[56] *Boletín Oficial del Estado de Sinaloa,* November 17, 1873.

ventures.[57]The numerous brigands roaming the countryside stole livestock and robbed farmers of whatever cash they had on hand. And if they succeeded in getting their produce to market safely, the heavy *alcabalas* levied by the state and municipios alike devoured an average of twenty percent of the farmers' gross income. Even more taxing were the exorbitant freight charges. Trying to ship their crops to market over roads that were rudimentary (if, indeed, they existed at all) and impassable during the rainy season was perhaps the agriculturalists' biggest headache. Without improved transportation there was little inducement for Sinaloan hacendados, and notables in general, to put out what capital they had to expand commercial production,[58] yet little progress had been made by 1876.

In 1867 there was only a single road, running the length of the state, and a few crude local roadways, all constantly in need of repair. In contrast to the central and western sections of Sonora, where wagons were employed extensively, transport in Sinaloa was almost wholly by mules.[59] Two years later, despite the fact that a fund created by federal law in 1867 had accumulated 12,000 pesos, no wagon road had been opened in the state, no existing road had been improved, nor had the slightest repairs been made.[60] A rather crude, federally constructed road was opened between Durango and Mazatlán in 1873, but it primarily benefited that port's commerce and the miners in the foothills along the road. By 1876 the road running the length of the state had been upgraded to a wagon road, with a line of stagecoaches running over it, but good connecting roads to carry agricultural produce beyond local markets were still lacking. Regular, bi-monthly steamship service was established in 1872 through a federal subsidy. However, this benefited Mazatlán commerce almost exclusively, since the port was the only stop made in the state by the steamship line under contract.[61] Interior commerce in Sinaloa in particular was adversely affected by the generally poor transportation and frequent lapses of security, and even more by the stagnation of the other

---

[57]Buelna, *Compendio*, 35-37; Rubí, 14. There was some production of crops tor other-than-local markets. Cotton was grown in sufficient quantities to supply the three small textile factories in the state and the numerous hand weavers. *Panocha* was sent to Sonora and other neighboring states. Some *aguardiente* (mescal brandy) was also exported.

[58]Cosío Villegas, *República Restaurada–vida económica*, 52-54.

[59]Buelna, *Compendio*, 39, 46-47. Besides the stagecoach line running the length of the state, by 1876 there were also lines connecting Mazatlán with Concordia (near which there were several important mining districts), and Culiacán with its coastal-trade port of Altata.

[60]Rubí, 12-13.

[61]Cosío Villegas, *República Restaurada–vida económica* 549-552, 567, 576. In 1872 Sinaloa became linked with the rest of the country by telegraph through the completion of a line between Mazatlán and Durango.

economic sectors in most sections of the state. Only the commercial flow through Mazatlán recovered to pre-war levels, and that was mainly composed of the exchange of ores and minted specie for imports.

Precious metals were also Sonora's principal export item and foremost source of foreign exchange. The doldrums of the mining industry there thus constricted commerce more than in Sinaloa. The drop in mining production meant a corresponding decrease in what the state could import. Precious metals were, as well, the chief medium of circulating currency. The resulting scarcity of money created by the growing drain of gold and silver to pay for imports severely hampered the interior commerce of the state. Noticias estadísticas (periodic reports on the general state of the districts) from the prefects during the post-Intervention years unfailingly noted the decadent state of commerce due to this shortage of currency. The carry-over effect of the mining depression on agricultural markets had a further dampening effect on interior commerce, as did the risks of Apache and Yaqui-Mayo depredations in many districts of the state.[62]

These generally unfavorable circumstances and the difficulties confronting the individual economic sectors in the Northwest varied from one district to another. In Sonora, each section of the state had its own particular mix of tribulations. Apache raids were most frequent and destructive in the northeast, and the means of transportation there were the most backward and costly. The districts of Arizpe, Moctezuma, and Sahuaripa were even more dependent than elsewhere on mining to fuel the rest of the economy; thus, the mining depression was felt there the most harshly.[63] In the northwest, the districts of Magdalena and Altar were less plagued by the Apaches but faced the prospect of diminishing markets for their agriculture in Arizona. Since these districts were the least populated area of the state, local markets were small and labor shortages were a serious problem. Their proximity to the major population centers of Arizona made emigration an even more acute problem than elsewhere in the state, one they were least able to bear.[64]

In southern Sonora the stubborn resistance of the Yaquis and Mayos to white encroachment continued to stymie the economy. Even though hostilities had ceased in the two valleys after 1868, the peace was tenuous enough that those with capital to invest in agriculture lacked confidence, and

---

[62]*La Estrella de Occidente,* January 17, 1871. The noticias estadísticas from the districts, printed in the official newspaper of Sonora, recorded the problems facing the various sectors of the economy. The prefects reported on the condition of mining, agriculture, commerce, industry, public instruction, public improvements, public security, and the municipios. Much of the material that follows on the conditions in various regions of the state during this period is from these noticias estadísticas.

[63]*Ibid.,* September 17, 1869; October ? , 1870, Reel 6; November 15, 1867, Reel 13.

[64]*Ibid.,* June 26, 1868; November 19, 1969; April 21, 1871, Reel 6; September 27, 1867, Reel 13.

prospective settlers were too psychologically on the defensive after the tribes' bloody reprisals of 1867 and 1868 to return in adequate numbers for their mutual protection.[65] Furthermore, they could expect little help from the state government. With limited funds, it placed a higher priority on combatting the Apaches. The south became more isolated from the rest of the state, especially in its commercial ties. By 1875 an estimated nine-tenths of Alamos' trade was conducted through Mazatlán, even though that port was three times farther away than Guaymas.[66]

The south was further crippled by the disastrous Great Flood of 1868, both in and around Alamos and all along the Mayo River. The rampaging Río Mayo inundated croplands, drowned livestock, and left the pueblos of Navojoa, Etchojoa, Tecia, Cuirimpo, and Camoa in ruins. Losses were also heavy in the *minerales* of Aduana and Promontorios. More than half of the most important zone of the city of Alamos was completely destroyed. The neighborhood surrounding the alameda was left in almost total ruin; this area was considered the most beautiful section of the city, in which were located the residences of many of its most prominent families. A good number of these homes were severely damaged, and a few, like that of Martín Salido, almost completely demolished. In all, at least fifty persons lost their lives and more than one hundred homes were destroyed in Alamos alone.[67]

Central Sonora was better off. Its commerce and agriculture largely recovered. But the core of agricultural production—wheat for export down the Mexican Pacific coast, in particular to neighboring Sinaloa—was in trouble. The wagon roads facilitating its export were in need of repair after the Intervention, but the principal difficulty lay at the other end of the line. The settlement and development of California in the 1860s had converted that state from a buyer into a competitor. In response, central Sonora's prime customer, the port of Mazatlán, was now periodically soliciting the federal government to permit specified quantities of foreign wheat (generally from California) to enter that port free of the high protectionist duties then fixed on it.[68] The port's commercial spokesmen argued that the price of Sonoran wheat by comparison was too high. The granting of several of these requests cut into Sonora's customary export of 20,000 *cargas* (51,600 bushels). Moreover, when permission was not obtained, Sinaloan authorities frequently looked the other way as foreign wheat was introduced into Mazatlán at prices lower than those of Sonora. An even greater threat emerged in the Congress. The coastal states, led by Veracruz, made several attempts to lower the tariff

---

[65]*Ibid.,* March 10, 1871 and May 16, 1872, Reel 5.

[66]*Ibid.,* June 25, 1875, Reel 6.

[67]Corral, 76-78; Roberto Acosta, *Apuntes históricos sonorenses—la ciudad de Alamos en la epoca de las Guerras de Reforma y del Imperio* (México, 1945), 236-237.

[68]*La Estrella de Occidente,* August 9, 1867 and July 5, 1872, Reel 13.

to make foreign wheat competitive and thereby lower the price of domestic wheat nationwide. Fortunately for central Sonoran producers, all such proposals were defeated, though by narrow margins.[69]

The differentiation in Sinaloa regarding the degree of recovery and the burden of unfavorable economic circumstances was much more municipal than regional. In all sections of the state, the overwhelming majority of municipalities had been, and remained still, small district market centers, quiescent and parochial, at best only minimally affected by the larger entrepreneurial currents.[70]

In such municipios the central, and usually single, plaza was a meeting place for those who brought in their wares and produce from the surrounding countryside. A few shops surrounded the plaza, often run by agents of Culiacán or Mazatlán merchant houses. The plaza was also a gathering place for peddlars, tradespeople, and muleteers to sell livestock and other items stolen from haciendas by bandits or their own peones, small contraband, and other merchandise they had come by legally. Some passed from one little town to the next. But others operated out of a little shop or cantina near the plaza. There they attracted campesinos, day-laborers, and drifters with crude liquor, cards, and gaming. A few artisans labored at their trade in shops along the streets near the plaza—baking bread, making shoes, molding pottery. Near the plaza, standing out among the one-story adobe flats of the poor and modest of means, were the well-built homes of the few prominent families of the community, who often also owned haciendas outside of town. Located on one side of the plaza, a focal point of the town was the parish church, whose priest was usually only slightly better educated than his parishioners. If the town were fortunate, there was a municipal building on the other side of the square, most of the time looking worn and badly in need of repair. Festivities in town occurred on the day of the patron saint and in the celebration of religious and national holidays. Otherwise, the slow pace of life matched the largely static economic activity.[71]

Rosario and Cosalá were somewhat exceptions to this general picture, since they had grown up as mining centers. With the spotty resurgence of mining in the post-war years, especially in Rosario, they began to revive as more than just local market centers. Yet mining was still plagued with serious problems, held back from realizing substantial, sustained growth; so too were Rosario and Cosalá.[72]

For these small market towns to grow and become full-fledged urban centers, industry had to be established, mining developed, and agriculture

---

[69]Cosío Villegas, *República Restaurada—vida económica*, 107-108.

[70]Buelna, *Compendio*, 67-106.

[71]Cosío Villegas, *República Restaurada—vida social*, 33, 109, 331-332, 364.

[72]Buelna, *Compendio*, 67, 84.

expanded greatly and infused with modern methods and equipment. These economic sectors, however, were hobbled by insufficient capital, security, and transportation. That the previous decade of war had been hard on these district centers only further dampened prospects. They had paid the highest price for the competing armies' claims to supplies and territorial control. Concordia, in particular, had been ravaged.[73] Only commerce was very active, and it moved through existing patterns monopolized by Mazatlán and Culiacán. Thus, what market activity there was was largely concentrated in those two cities. The gap between them and the district towns and lesser municipalities had, if anything, widened since the mid-1850s. The gap between Culiacán and Mazatlán had also spread.[74]

Culiacán's population had declined from an estimated ten thousand in 1855 to a little more than six thousand in 1873.[75] The transfer of the capital to Mazatlán in 1858 was in part responsible for the decline, as was the port's ascension to the leading maritime center on the Mexican Pacific Coast. But Culiacán notables saw more than neutral circumstance in this turn of events. They had come to believe that their counterparts in Mazatlán—particularly its foreign segment—had been, and still were, deliberately trying to undermine Culiacán's interests. A petition by various Mazatlán residents to the federal government in 1872, asking for the transfer of the casa de moneda from Culiacán to that port, seemed the height of indignities to *culiacanenses.*

The port's petitioners justified the request on the grounds that revolutions frequently erupted in Culiacán and that the mint would be better situated with respect to the mining districts of the state and neighboring Durango. The only revolutions occurring in Culiacán, a paper of that city retorted, were those seconding revolts hatched in Mazatlán, whose long history of *pronunciamientos* was well known. Its customs house had been the principal lure for such revolts, and the mint would have the same fate if moved there. Though the important mining districts of Rosario and Panuco were in the southern part of the state, the paper continued, all the rest were within 60 to 120 miles of Culiacán. Furthermore, the expense of 40,000 pesos to transfer the minting operation to Mazatlán and the rendering idle of a building which cost 200,000 pesos and whose legal mortgage, along with that of the machinery, had been guaranteed with funds paid by residents of Culiacán, made no sense economically and was grossly unfair.

The petition was more than just a question of public convenience, the Culiacán paper went on to explain. It was a deliberate effort by the port "to deal Culiacán one of so many blows, draining off resources which were the

---

[73] *Ibid.,* 71.
[74] *Ibid.,* 44-46.
[75] *Ibid.,* 89-90.

result of the exclusive efforts of its citizenry." And for what reason? Because Culiacán, "so thwarted ... by that heterogeneous gathering of inhabitants from all over the Republic and the world which is called the town of Mazatlán, has not bent its knees before that port, ... has always opposed its systematic revolutions, ... [and] has not stopped being an obstacle to Mazatlecan subjugation." Were *mazatlecos* not content with the injuries caused by the periodic revolts emanating from that port? Were they not gratified by the unjustifiable removal of the capital from Culiacán and the emigration of more than 1,500 people that accompanied it? Were they not satisfied with the ever-increasing growth of their commerce, which had made their port the leading maritime center on the Mexican Pacific coast? "No, they are not content with that," said the Culiacán paper, "They look with jealous eyes on the very little that remains to Culiacán."[76]

Actually, at that very time, Mazatlán's fortunes were beginning to take an adverse turn, though it was not yet perceived. Since the transfer of the capital in 1858, the port's population had risen from 7,000 to nearly 15,000 in 1870. Its commerce had supplied Sinaloa, Durango, Baja California, large sections of Sonora and Jalisco, and parts of states bordering those mentioned, reaching into the interior as far as San Luis Potosí. Though foreign vessels sometimes had unloaded their cargo in the lesser ports of Guaymas, La Paz, and San Blas, the goods were frequently owned by Mazatlán merchants who had made better arrangements with the customs officials there than in the port itself.[77]

Central to Mazatlán's commercial growth had been the relations between the port's large commercial houses, the large majority of which were owned by foreigners, and the local merchants in the small towns and mining centers.[78] The business ties between Remigio Rocha, a Cosalá merchant, and Antonio de la Peña, the Spanish owner of one of the most important commercial firms of Mazatlán, are illustrative. Attracted by the mines of Guadalupe de los Reyes, Rocha had come to the state from Durango in the late 1850s with little money. Several years went by without any significant success. Most of the mining discoveries were falling into the hands of rich Spanish residents of Mazatlán (de la Peña among them) rather than into those of prospectors like himself. As a consequence, Rocha moved on to Cosalá, where he established himself in commerce and soon became the local representative of some of the port's important commercial houses—including that of De la Peña, with

---

[76] *El Clamor Público,* November 30, 1872.

[77] United States Department of State, *Report on Commercial Relations,* 1871, Mazatlán, Consul I. Sisson, 910-911.

[78] *Ibid.,* 910. Consul Sisson estimated the foreign mercantile capital in the port in the early 1870s as follows: Spanish, $2,500,000; German, $1,500,000; English, $750,000; French, $500,000; and North American, $50,000.

whom he had since become good friends. Through Rocha the port's commerce was distributed in the district, and, through his share of the profits, he expanded his interests into moneylending, the refining of ore, and the opening of a stagecoach line between Cosalá and Mazatlán (the stagecoach venture in partnership with de la Peña).[79]

Such business ties with the immediate interior were not the source for the adverse circumstances then beginning to affect Mazatlán commerce. The difficulties were emerging more on the periphery of the port's mercantile sphere. The just completed railroad between Mexico City and Veracruz soon promised to cut seriously into Mazatlán's trade with the interior. San Francisco had begun to absorb gradually the direct trade in Asian commerce. Ships laden with oriental goods soon ceased coming directly to Mazatlán; rather such goods came through San Francisco by the steamship lines increasingly plying the Pacific coast. The Sinaloan port was even having trouble maintaining its dominance on the northern and central Mexican Pacific coast. Growing numbers of ships were now bypassing Mazatlán as a distributor and beginning to discharge their goods directly in Manzanillo, San Blas, and Guaymas.[80]

The growing commercial competition soon took its toll. The port's population declined within three years to around 10,000 in 1873.[81] Equally important in the population loss were the transfer of the capital back to Culiacán in 1873 and the returning home of *tepiqueño* émigrés, beginning that same year with the final defeat of Lozada.[82]

THE MUNICIPIOS IN REGRESSION

Only in the early 1870s did residents of Mazatlán begin to experience the depressed economic conditions that prevailed generally in the Northwest in the post-Intervention years. Only then did they begin to feel seriously the constriction and the insecurity of their personal fortunes and livelihoods. The economic straits facing most of the poor and a number of the modest of means in the Northwest and the material constraints felt by many of the notables had collective, public repercussions as well. All levels of government

---

[79]José C. Valadés, *Mis confesiones* (México, 1966), 10-14. According to Buelna, and borne out in biographical accounts of several of the port's merchants, a large majority of foreign merchants did not take permanent root in the port. Most, after making their fortunes, left the country, leaving behind associates or relatives whom they had brought from Europe to run the business. De la Peña was one who remained until his death. Buelna, *Compendio*, 77.

[80]Buelna, *Compendio*, 44-45; United States Department of State, *Report on Commercial Relations*, 1873, Mazatlán, Consul I. Sisson, 838-840.

[81]United States Department of State, *Report on Commercial Relations*, 1873, Mazatlán, Consul I. Sisson, 840.

[82]Buelna, *Apuntes*, 161.

were critically short of adequate revenues to continue programs to improve public life. Bleakest were the prospects of local government.

Having finally come of age only a decade or so before, Sonoran municipios were now looking over their shoulders at the specter of a return to that prior age of municipal chaos. The prosperity of the late 1850s and early 1860s had provided them with the funds to at last begin to organize local government on a firm footing and to institute essential municipal services. Now these municipalities were strapped for funds. With the exceptions of Mazatlán and Culiacán, local governments in Sinaloa were impoverished. Since the transfer of greater prerogatives and powers of initiative to the municipios in the Constitution of 1861, they had been unable to systematize and stabilize local administration. The Intervention had stripped them of funds and burdened them with the reconstruction of much of what had been accomplished previously. Afterwards, it was strictly catch-as-catch-can. Primary education was generally neglected, and, when schools were established, they usually were not sustained adequately. City services such as police protection, *ornato* (beautification), and public improvements were the exception rather than the rule.[83] The ayuntamientos simply did not have the minimum revenues necessary to maintain local administration on a progressive, on-going basis.

Municipal revenues in Sinaloa were largely derived in the late 1860s and early 1870s from contributions levied on property and the *alcabalas* on commerce, and therein lay the problem. Commerce and urban property were highly concentrated in Mazatlán and Culiacán. The assessed value of urban property in 1869 totaled 1,823,401 pesos in the district of Mazatlán and 419,641 pesos in Culiacán, with the vast majority of this property located in the two cities. In no other district did assessed value exceed 100,000 pesos. The two large urban centers combined possessed nearly 75 percent of assessed urban property in the state, while their districts held only 42 percent of the total assessed rural property.[84] Most Sinaloans lived in the countryside, not in small towns. There were only 28 municipios in the whole state in 1873. The urban population was less than 15 percent using Daniel Cosío Villegas's

---

[83]Rubí, 9.

[84]*Ibid.*, 21. The district of Concordia's assessed urban property did total more than 100,000 pesos, but this figure seems questionable. The taxed portion comprises only 81,575 pesos of the total of 309,482 pesos. No other district comes anywhere near having such a proportion of exempt property in its total assessment. Rubí explains that 53,967 of the 227,907 pesos of exempt property were due to the damage caused by the Intervention; but the remaining figure is still more than double the amount of taxed property. Buelna (*Compendio,* 65) estimates the population of the town of Concordia at around 1,200 and that of El Fuerte—which had a figure comparable to Concordia's for taxed property (91,300 pesos)—at about 3,000. The figures for the other districts seem to fit in relation to their estimated populations. Only those of Concordia appear out of line and inexplainable.

definition of urban population as that in towns of more than 2,500.[85] For the small towns and villages, there was comparatively very little of the most lucrative sources of local tax revenues, and what sources there were (in particular, rural property) were ineffectually tapped because of the irregularities of administration.

Though Sonora by contrast was a far more urbanized state, the vast majority of its municipalities were no better off. In the early 1870s there were 105 municipios. Sonora's four main urban centers accounted for 27 percent of the state's population.[86] There were more urban centers of significant size and revenues than in Sinaloa. There were also many more small municipios that were pauperized. The prefect of the district of Arizpe, for example, reported in the fall of 1869 that public buildings were deteriorating for want of repairs. After local employees were paid and the bare minimum of expenditures were made, there simply were no municipal funds left over. Arizpe's public buildings, though well built, were deteriorating badly from age, which made repairs ever more pressing. The buildings of most of the pueblos of the district were in such a decrepit state that very soon they would be beyond hope of restoration. The jails could not make even a pretense of security. Two villages, Banámichi and Huépac, were able to maintain their public buildings in a decent state because of their proximity to the only serious mining operations in the district, at Bavicanora and Santa Elena (the latter worked by Governor Pesqueira). These small mining operations had generated some commerce from which the two pueblos could tap revenues. A similar report from the district three years later indicated little had changed.[87]

As the reports from Arizpe indicate, the district towns, as residences of the prefects, were more fiscally viable than the pueblos. Arizpe's public buildings were badly in need of repair, not past the point of restoration. The bare minimum of local administration was being regularly funded. Nonetheless, there was a considerable gulf between the fortunes of Arizpe and the four other frontier district towns and the much larger *cabeceras* of the center and south. Nowhere is this more evident than in the figures for the municipal income and expenditures for the fiscal years 1868-1869 and 1869-1870. The average monthly revenues of the frontier *cabeceras*—Sahuaripa, Moctezuma, Arizpe, Magdalena, and Altar—in some cases did not even exceed those of the *pueblos*; the highest was Magdalena, with an average income of 149.09 pesos

[85]Buelna, *Compendio*, 65; Cosío Villegas, *República Restaurada—vida social*, 32-33, 127.

[86]Cosío Villegas, *República Restaurada—vida social*, 127; General José Maria Perez Hernández, *Compendio de la geografía del Estado de Sonora* (México, 1872), 75-116. Perez Hernández's figures are basically taken from Pesqueira's *Memoria* of 1870, with minor changes.

[87]*La Estrella de Occidente*, September 17, 1869 and June 21, 1872, Reel 16.

a month.[88] These small towns and their districts had been economic back-waters from 1830 to the late 1850s. Their nascent progress, achieved amidst the general prosperity of the years before the Intervention, was, thus, most vulnerable to slippage in the current economic depression. They had very little to fall back on.

The four main urban centers—Hermosillo, Guaymas, Alamos, and Ures—had a little economic fat to tide them over in lean years. The average monthly revenues these large *cabeceras* had to work with were considerably larger than those of the frontier district towns and the pueblos: Guaymas, 2,027.17 pesos; Hermosillo, 1,654.06 pesos; Alamos, 961.53 pesos; and Ures, 774.63 pesos.[89] Yet even they were feeling the pinch. Alamos faced the task of rebuilding after the ruinous flood of 1868, while its mining, commerce, and agriculture continued in the doldrums. Hermosillo, Sonora's only genuine city, depended in great part on its commerce with the hinterland of the state, and that commerce was stagnant. Much of her industry was inoperative or languishing. Ures, whose well-being still rested more upon the presence of the government than on the capital's own economic activity, felt the stringencies of the times along with the state administration.[90] The Intervention had reduced Guaymas' foreign commerce to the simple consumption of the port, and the retarded economic recovery exhibited throughout the rest of the state did not allow the port's commerce to grow significantly until the mid-1870s. Even though Guaymas had more revenues than any other town in the state (because of its comparatively larger volume of taxable trade), its prefect was nonetheless reporting to the governor that its roads were in poor condition and that its jail was in great need of repair.[91]

Of all the municipios in the Northwest in the post-war years, only Mazatlán was able to make any significant headway in improving public life. It alone had the revenues to move beyond covering the essentials of what municipal services existed to upgrading and expanding them and introducing new public improvements. By 1871 the annual budget of the port had reached nearly 80,000 pesos, more than triple those of Culiacán, Hermosillo, and Guaymas. The city was lit by gas and served by streetcar. It possessed a civil and a military hospital, a spacious barracks for the garrison, a handsome customs house, and a nautical school and several primary schools sustained by the

---

[88] Pesqueira, *Número* 3.

[89] *Ibid.* These figures were for the municipal fiscal year of September 16, 1868 to September 15, 1869. Those for 1869 to 1870 were: Guaymas, 2,189.46 pesos; Hermosillo, 2,005.42; Alamos, 929.78; Ures, 814.17.

[90] Perez Hernández, 75-76, 80-81, 89-90. Perez Hernández's population figures for Sonora's four towns appear the most reliable ones available for the late 1860s: Hermosillo, 13,745; Alamos, 7,180; Ures, 5,183; Guaymas, 3,186.

[91] *La Estrella de Occidente,* December 24, 1869, and August 4, 1871, Reel 5.

ayuntamiento.[92] In 1869 municipal authorities had contracted two professional educators from Guadalajara to work in its schools. One, Davíd Antonio Urrea, was a scion of a wealthy Peruvian family; the other, Teresa Villegas, was a native of that city. Two years later, in response to numerous requests from prominent residents of the port for secondary education, Urrea established El Liceo de Niños, while Villegas founded El Colegio Independencia, which also taught telegraphy and trained teachers.[93]

The port's revenues permitted not only the maintenance of a regular elementary school system, but also the procurement of professional educators from Guadalajara to upgrade and expand it. Nevertheless, the establishment of the two secondary schools reveals more the problems surrounding public instruction than its progress during these years even in comparatively prosperous Mazatlán. The two educators resigned their positions in the municipal schools because the ayuntamiento's financial difficulties did not permit the minimum funds they deemed necessary for their work. The requests and monetary pledges of numerous port notables for a private school was far more attractive by comparison.[94] Elsewhere in the Northwest, the provision for public instruction was even more a struggle that mirrored the fiscal predicament in which the municipios found themselves.

In Sonora, the stagnation—at times near paralyzation—of the economy had left the ayuntamientos with inadequate revenues and only a scant number of citizens able to pay the special state contributions for public instruction. Some pueblos could not afford schools. Those in Moctezuma district, with difficulty, were able to scrape together enough money from the 1869 state law of personal contribution for education, from municipal funds, and from contributions from parents of school children to keep their schools open.[95] In Magdalena district, the villages were having trouble keeping their schools open on a continuous basis. Early in 1871 the schools were closed because of the paucity of funds to sustain them. Five were reopened that summer, but the prefect feared they would be forced to close again for want of funds due to the "complete paralyzation" of the economy.[96]

Even if minimum financing could be found, the task of obtaining teachers, and then holding onto them, was never ending. Those in charge of the schools in Altar, Pitiquito, Atil, and Tubutama all resigned from their posts that same year. The four ayuntamientos were in a quandary about replacing them, since there seemed to be hardly anyone around with even some semblance of qualifications who was dedicated to teaching. Pitiquito, to cover its vacancy,

---

[92] Buelna, *Compendio,* 75-76, 90.
[93] González Dávila, 639-640, 662-663.
[94] *Ibid.*
[95] *La Estrella de Occidente,* February 11, 1870.
[96] *Ibid.,* April 21 and August 21, 1871, Reel 5.

hired a poor, young boy out of the advanced primary school (recently moved from Altar to that pueblo and financed privately). The lad had not even completed his studies.[97]

Despite these revenue inadequacies and teacher shortages, by 1870 there were, according to the Sonoran government, 103 primary schools in the state, with 108 profesores, 3,737 pupils, and a monthly expenditure of 2,732 pesos. There were also two secondary schools (both in Ures) with 6 profesores, 134 students, and a monthly expenditure of 3,235 pesos. However, most of these schools were located in the pueblos, where their condition was at best rudimentary, their continuity often interrupted, and their existence usually precarious.[98]

Regularized schooling with a more or less uniform system of teaching was found only in the four large urban centers—Hermosillo, Alamos, Ures, and Guaymas. Two-thirds of the 2,942 pupils receiving instruction in 1868 attended schools in these four municipalities.[99] Only they had large enough revenues and the amenities of urban life to attract and hold trained educators (though, as seen in the case of Mazatlán, these attractions were not always enough). Such cultivated men and women could attend the spacious theater in Hermosillo, dine and dance with the well-bred notables of Alamos, or mingle with the cosmopolitan foreign community in Guaymas. In Ures was the lure of direct government support and contact with state officials and legislators. The capital received the lion's share of the more than 6,000 pesos a year the state budgeted for education, largely to support the two secondary schools there. (An average of 24.14 pesos per pupil was expended in 1869 for these two schools, as compared to an average of .73 pesos for the primary schools throughout the state.)

The state government had ambitious plans to diffuse the regularized public instruction existing in the large towns by establishing a normal school to train qualified teachers for the small towns and pueblos and by granting more funds to sustain and upgrade the schools in these areas. But there were insufficient revenues available to carry these plans to fruition. Indeed, the state treasury could barely meet its existing budget for public instruction.[100]

Sinaloa's government had no funds to spare for public instruction in 1869. The governor informed the legislature that existing primary schools far from satisfied the needs of the state and that, in most of the state, primary instruction was generally neglected by the municipios.[101] Five years later, Governor

---

[97] *La Estrella de Occidente,* August 18, 1871, Reel 5.

[98] Pesqueira, *Número* 10.

[99] *La Estrella de Occidente,* October 9, 1868. The two secondary schools in the capital were privately established but, in large part, were sustained by the state subsidy.

[100] Pesqueira, 14-16.

[101] Rubí, 15-16.

Buelna, in the middle of his term, made a concerted effort to expand education. The legislature approved his plan to formally organize public instruction in the state. Primary education was made obligatory and put in the care of the municipios, which were to be financially aided by subventions from the government.[102] The governor promoted the establishment of primary schools in the pueblos through several visits that traversed most sections of the state. In most cases, soon after his visit village authorities and residents set up schools sustained by special local contributions.[103]

By 1875 there were 215 primary schools in the state, 43 of which were sustained by the municipios; most of the remainder were supported by the local resident contribution (primarily in the villages).[104] According to government figures, there were 9,272 pupils attending school: 5,747 in public schools, 2,899 in private schools, and 326 in adult schools.[105] Only three years later, however, the government fixed the number at 4,866 children attending 176 schools.[106] The difficulties in meeting operating expenses and the scaling down of funds for primary education between 1873 and 1875 raise questions about the lasting success of Governor Buelna's efforts, particularly as regards the expansion of schooling beyond the district towns.

Buelna asserted that most schools were sustained by the local, obligatory resident contribution, which he estimated at more than 70,000 pesos, a sum, he said, the government could not have collected through taxes.[107] That amount—given the total expenditures for primary schooling in Sonora (32,784 pesos in 1869) and the expenditure of 12.18 pesos per pupil in the public schools compared to the .73 pesos spent in Sonoran small towns and villages—in itself is open to serious question.[108] The generally sluggish economic conditions and the reports of Governor Rubí and his counterpart in Sonora only a few years before of the difficulties encountered by the municipios in collecting contribution revenues place the reality of such a sum being raised and spent on education even more in doubt.[109] In view of these figures, the dramatic drop in enrollment by 1878 probably indicates that most of the village schools that Buelna promoted did not endure for very long. State aid was minimal, municipal funds almost non-existent at that level in Sinaloa, and the local resident contribution was highly unreliable. Lament-

---

[102] González Dávila, 182.
[103] Buelna, *Apuntes,* 165-166.
[104] González Dávila, 182.
[105] *Departmento de la Estadística Nacional: Sonora, Sinaloa, Nayarit,* 80-81.
[106] *El Estado de Sinaloa,* June 5, 1878.
[107] Buelna, *Apuntes,* 169.
[108] González Dávila, 571-572.
[109] Rubí, 9; Pesqueira, 15.

ing over the near absence of schooling at the village level continued through the next decade.

By 1875, after eight years, recovery from the dislocations of the wars of Reform and Intervention was spotty and transitory at best. The burden yet weighed heavily. The continuing adverse economic conditions soured and discouraged private and public exertions alike. Among urban notables especially, for whom the public and private spheres were more intertwined, and whose expectations of progress had been elevated by the triumph over the Intervention, these largely fruitless recovery efforts evoked disappointment and growing frustration. The wars of Reform and Intervention had given them, and the people of the Northwest in general, a firm sense at last of being a part of the nation, of being Mexicans. But the experience of the post-war years did not provide them with a clear definition of how, once a part of the nation, they were to relate to it institutionally and pragmatically. The result was confusion and growing conflict, which reinforced the troubled economic circumstances and which, as much as the unsettled economy, hampered recovery and the renewal of progress.

7

The Liberal-National Contradiction: Progress

(1867-1875)

The Constitution of 1857, and the movement that both fashioned it and professed to be its interpreter, had proposed a new framework for Mexican society, a new definition of its character and purpose. The Reform War had set in motion this framework and definition. The Intervention had eliminated any plausible alternative to them and had given their acceptance national scope. The popular classes were now, officially at least, part of the national context, bound together with the active citizenry of the middle and upper stratas in a common national identity. Many commoners for the first time began to think of themselves as Mexicans. The people of the peripheral states, such as Sonora and Sinaloa, also began to consider themselves a part of the national context. Urban notables had come to feel it strongly. Their states had served as sanctuaries for the republican cause and staging areas for the defeat of the Empire.

Mexico was at last a nation, and its people, with but few exceptions, functionally Mexicans. To them, the Constitution of 1857 held out the prospect, the promise, not only of full citizenship, but also of a share in what progress the nation achieved. Thus, the people of Sonora and Sinaloa finally possessed an acknowledged stake in the nation, and a claim on it. The progress they had long sought—most especially the urban notables—was now to be striven for within a national context, as part of a national effort. The idea of such participation embued them with enlarged hopes and expectations.

Effecting the liberal framework remained, however. Constitutional principles required implementation to be institutionalized. What being Mexican meant had to be spelled and fleshed out in the context of a myriad of private interests, personal loyalties, and parochial concerns. The task of the post-war years for the urban notables and the general populace of the Northwest, as for others in the reborn nation, was to find their place in that national endeavor and to secure their share of the progress anticipated by so many in the Restored Republic.

The Constitution of 1857 had espoused, and the leaders of the republican government had begun to implement, liberalism and nationalism as the twin bases for the new order and for the progress expected to accompany it. However, the economic reality of burdensome recovery and general stagnation in the post-war years seemed increasingly to place liberalism and nationalism in contradiction with one another as the foundation for progress.

Rather than a national economy, there had been only an infinite number of tiny local and regional markets, sometimes interlocking. Market patterns in the Northwest since independence had varied considerably both within the region and in its relations with the exterior. Generally, local markets had been joined into sectional economies tied to exterior commerce and demand. The decade of war had disrupted them, and their recovery thereafter was only spotty. A growing problem in the Restored Republic was the relation of these existing economic patterns, and the interests they engendered, to the national economy that was eagerly being fostered by politicians in Mexico City. The beneficiaries of such a national economy were not necessarily such local interests. Indeed, those in the Northwest found the burdens of recovery made even heavier by such emerging national patterns.

There were several corollaries to this emerging conflict between national and local economic interests, which entailed contradictions in themselves. One was the relation of the government to the economy. According to liberal theory, the creation of a national economy and the elaboration of the relations of various local and regional economies to it were functions of the actions of private individuals and groups. Yet liberal politicians at the national level were increasingly interjecting proposals for government intervention to promote and realize such national economic patterns. The effect of such intervention was to favor some through subsidies and tax exemptions and to give others an overwhelming advantage by restricting competition. Neither of these actions seemed to square with the liberal principle of the freedom of the individual to pursue economic opportunity.

In addition, the liberal tenet of free trade did not balance well with the continuing need of the federal government to maintain high tariffs in response to fiscal deficiencies and the pressures of protectionist groups. Then too, there was the matter of the free flow of capital across national boundaries. Short on capital, the existing local and regional markets and the anticipated national economy faced at best a long and dubious path to progress if they relied on domestic investment alone. Yet Mexicans in general were keenly nationalistic after the Intervention, and many national politicans were suspicious of foreign penetration—President Juárez's chief minister and successor, Sebastián Lerdo de Tejada, in particular. They were reluctant to open wide the doors of opportunity to foreigners without adequate and strict securities, for fear foreigners would gather the fruits of the country for which the people had fought so long and hard.[1]

---

[1] Cosío Villegas, *República Restaurada—vida económica,* 711.

THE RESPONSIBILITY FOR PROGRESS

Behind the contradictions regarding the relation of local and regional markets to a national economy was the larger, yet more subtle, question of who was to make economic policy and, thus, in great part determine the outcome of such contradictions. Local interests had found in the liberal cause during the war years a program they thought offered considerable leeway in local prerogative and decision-making. They had fought together because they had come to realize that they needed mutual support to establish a decentralized political framework. This framework was their understanding of the national context of which they were all now fully a part. Likewise, these local interests interpreted liberalism to mean local control, subject to the liberal principles set down in the Constitution of 1857. It was *their* responsibility and prerogative to pursue economic policies that in their judgment would foment progress. Aid from the national level was welcomed, and frequently requested, but it was to be employed as they saw fit.

However, the reality of a political economy in the post-war years led those whose interests transcended the local and regional level to an increasingly conflicting understanding of the relation of liberalism to the national context. To them, existing circumstances seemed to dictate that the creation of a national economy required initiatives and policies that were national in scope or that at least transcended local and regional concerns. That was the national context to which local interests were to adapt and, if necessary, accommodate themselves. The question for these national interests became whether initiatives and policies conformed to the liberal principles laid down in the constitution.

The emerging liberal-national contradiction had a parallel at the state level in the Northwest. There, too, disagreement began to surface over the proportional division of public responsibility for the economy. The state constitutions at the end of the Reform War had decentralized authority, giving the municipios considerably more initiative and responsibility. The legislatures also had acquired more power vis-à-vis the state executives, part of which concerned the determination of economic policy. The legislators were for the most part the representatives of the prominent families of the small district towns and larger urban centers. Economic decisions at the municipal level were made under their controlling influence. However, at the state level they had not only to compromise to reach agreement with one another, but to contend with the executive as well.

The governments of Sonora and Sinaloa during these years of fiscal strains and economic stagnation vigorously sought to absorb more and more control over public economic policy. They increasingly saw the various local economic difficulties as part of a state-wide context which only they were equipped to confront. With this justification of their initiatives, the state administrations were at times effective in fragmenting the resistance of the urban notables' representatives in the legislature, especially when the notables' particular interests were favored by such actions. The comparatively abundant evidence available for Sonora during the period illustrates the growing liberal-national contradiction both at the national and state levels.[2]

For a decade Governor Pesqueira had guided the state with considerable leeway because of the political crises created by the Reform War and then the Intervention. For much of that period, he had governed the state with extraordinary powers, since the legislature had suspended itself and the federal government had delegated its powers back to the state administrations. The governor had grown accustomed to it, and he had the brief economic boom of the early 1860s to show for it.

The post-war years following the Intervention, in his view, were another period of crisis, this time economic and social, which also called for strong executive action. In reviewing the serious exigencies occasioned by the Intervention, Governor Pesqueira told the legislature that the government "has been able to do little from the moment the extraordinary powers were retired. Deprived of this support, it has had to subject itself to a slow and difficult course, which was to be expected after such an upheaval."[3] If the governor could no longer govern the state with extraordinary powers to bring about its full recovery from the destruction and dislocations wrought by the Intervention, then he would actively run the state. He would do so by fashioning social and economic policies for the legislature's approval and by employing the full weight of executive powers, particularly through the prefects of the districts, who, in Sonora, still held office at his discretion.

A continuing complaint expressed by the governor was the inability of the municipios to administer fully and correctly the duties delegated to them by the legislature. Among these tasks were the compilation of statistical reports, the determination of tax assessments for the state contribution, the regular drafting and submission of proper local budgets for the legislature's approval, and the raising of national guard units. Pesqueira contended that close supervision of some of these duties and the assumption of others by the prefects would make their administration far more effective. His complaint was directed specifically at the small municipalities. He argued that there were many municipios that were just too small to justify their existence. Few, he said, had citizens educated enough to perform effectively in municipal offices, and

---

[2]The wide variety of sources that exist for Sonora during these years do not correspond for Sinaloa. The University of Arizona newspaper collection contains only a few papers for the state. There is scant document and official newspaper material in the microfilm collection of the Museo de Antropología y Historia in Mexico City. Local historians, such as Antonio Nakayama, indicated that there are simply no real government archives available—a fact confirmed by archival officials in the state capitol. There is no state library at work collecting and preserving sources, as exists in Sonora, and there are few geographies and travel accounts.

[3]Pesqueira, 4.

the revenues were so scarce that the ayuntamientos became an onerous burden, unable to provide any services. He proposed that the minimum population be raised from five hundred to seven hundred, thereby abolishing a number of municipios.[4]

Since independence, the municipalities in general had experienced a gradually increasing control over their own affairs and an ever widening sphere of responsibilities, especially the smaller ones. Almost all of the pueblos dated back to colonial times and possessed strong local identities, which had been reinforced and strengthened by their elevation to the rank of municipios in the early years after independence. What Governor Pesqueira was proposing was the reversal of this decentralization of power that had been going on for decades and that had been confirmed in the recent triumph of the liberal/republican movement. If the governor had his way, not a few of the pueblos would lose their municipal rights. For the towns, and particularly for the prominent families that dominated them, the governor's proposals regarding the municipios were more than a matter of a reduction in the management of their own affairs. Of greater concern were the proposals' implications for the very direction of the state government itself.

Since independence, control of the state had been almost exclusively in the hands of the notables of the towns, in various combinations, except for a brief period in the late 1830s and early 1840s. Then, Manuel María Gándara had ruled with the support of the less enterprising hacendados and rancheros of the central valleys in the bordering Ures district, and of the tribal Indians (Yaquis, Mayos, Papagos, and Opatas), who were eager to halt the growing entrepreneurial designs of the urban gentry on their lands. For the most part having been federalists, the notables had endorsed liberalism and had supported and certified Pesqueira as its head in Sonora in the office of governor, conceding to him extraordinary powers during periods of wartime emergency. Their base of power, as noted previously, was the state legislature, whose diputados represented the districts. Since the *cabeceras* (in which they lived) dominated the districts, the urban gentry almost always determined who the diputados would be. Direction of the legislature was further concentrated in the hands of prominent families of the state's four large urban centers. Their districts were given two legislators each because of their greater population. Thus, the notables of Hermosillo, Guaymas, Alamos, and Ures controlled eight of the thirteen seats in the legislature.

What was in great part at issue politically during these post-war years was the question of who was to govern and control the state in promoting its social and economic progress. Since Governor Pesqueira believed that he was

---

[4]*Ibid.*, 4-6, 11; *La Estrella de Occidente*, August 23 and November 22, 1867, Reel 13. The state constitution of 1861 delegated general areas of municipal responsibility and prerogative, which were spelled out in detail in *leyes organicas*. *La Estrella de Occidente*, October 5 and 12, and November 2 and 9, 1866.

the prime mover in bringing about both the triumph of liberalism in the state and the brief economic boom of the early 1860s, he assumed that he best could again set Sonora on the road to progress. To accomplish this goal, the governor believed, he needed strong executive powers, even at the expense of the legislature and the municipios. With the same objective but contrary logic, Pesqueira interpreted federalism to mean that all powers not specifically granted to the federal government were to be exercised by the states, in particular by their executives. Secondly, he maintained that those powers currently in dispute between the states and Mexico City, until finally resolved, should continue to exercised by his government.

The problem for Pesqueira increasingly was that neither the federal government, the urban notables acting through the legislature, nor at times the municipal authorities would agree to his credo of a political economy: that of a strong, predominant state executive. The governor went ahead anyway, stretching the limits the legislature and Mexico City tried to place on him, relying on what had worked for him before.

THE SONORAN GOVERNOR'S INITIATIVES

Internal security was one of the principal areas where Pesqueira's initiatives generated opposition, in this case from Mexico City. Using the extraordinary powers still vested in the government before constitutional authority was restored in late 1867, the governor, desiring to renew operations against the Apaches as soon as possible, reestablished the five presidial companies along the frontier under the command of his long-time associate, General García Morales. This force was supplemented by units of the national guard under the command of the prefects, as revenues permitted.[5] The following spring the Congress decreed the establishment of thirty military colonies to defend the nation's northern frontier; seven of them were to be located in Sonora.[6] A few months later the Minister of War informed the governor that, while these military colonies were being organized, the federal government would pay the state-raised forces then guarding the frontier.[7]

As the tempo of Apache incursions quickened despite its efforts, the Sonoran government began to search for a new way to attack the growing security problem in the northern districts. It was generally acknowledged within the state that the most effective force until then against the Apaches had been the national guard units from the districts. They had a direct interest in freeing their districts from Apache raids.[8] The presidial companies,

---

[5] Pesqueira, 26; Corral, 69.
[6] *La Estrella de Occidente,* May 29, 1868, Reel 5.
[7] *Ibid.,* November 20, 1868.
[8] *El Pueblo de Sonora* (Ures), December 3, 1867 and February 4, 1868.

an insignificant force of about 240 men, were composed of nonvolunteers, were poorly paid, and had little incentive to protect the neighboring districts. At best they served as advance defensive positions, obstacles for the Apaches to avoid. What was needed, the government concluded, was increased funds to maintain more national guard troops in active and constant pursuit of the Apaches. The state treasury had no more money to spare. In August, 1868, Acting Governor Manuel Monteverde (another of Pesqueira's close political associates) wrote the Treasury Secretary requesting that the federal government grant 5,000 pesos monthly to maintain the additional national guard forces.[9]

Two years went by without the advent of federal funds. Then the Sonoran legislature, coming to the support of the executive, formally petitioned the Congress for a monthly grant of 6,000 pesos over and above the amount already being expended on the presidial companies.[10] A few months later, it raised the request to 10,000 pesos a month. The state was budgeting 7,550 pesos a year, the legislature pointed out, by lowering the already miserable salaries of public officials and by suppressing other essential administrative expenditures. The citizens, soaked up to their ears in taxes as it was, could not suffer a further rise in state levies. "When the nation has its largest budget in history, . . . when Sonorans see that that money is being employed in favoring the wealthiest states with public improvements, . . . when it reaches the point that if Sonora knows that it belongs to the Mexican confederation, it is only by the taxes which it constantly has to pay," then it was time for the federal government to finally come to Sonora's aid.[11] This time it did not take long for the Congress to approve the request. Two years later, in 1872, with Apache incursions increasing in Sonora after General Howard's treaty with that tribe (which in practice permitted them to raid across the border at will as long as they remained at peace in the Arizona Territory), the Congress raised the subvention to 14,000 pesos a month.[12]

Then the partnership dissolved. Less than a year after the enlarged grant was approved, the state's official newspaper charged that the federal government was reneging on its appropriation to the state, that it was withholding part of the desperately needed funds to combat the growing menace of the Apaches.[13] The following year (1874) the subvention stopped altogether. The Lerdo government decided to return to the policy of defending the frontier solely with military colonies, claiming that the presidial companies were, in fact, such colonies. The policy reversion also included a startlingly

[9]*La Estrella de Occidente,* August 14, 1868.
[10]*Ibid.,* February 11, 1870, Reel 5.
[11]*Ibid.,* May 20, 1870.
[12]Corral, 85, 107.
[13]*La Estrella de Occidente,* January 24, 1873.

new provision for Sonoran liberals. The direction of all military operations was henceforward to be exclusively the province of Mexico City. State national guard troops involved in frontier operations were to be responsible to the federal government. Before campaigning against the Apaches, the state government now needed authorization from Mexico City.[14]

President Lerdo reversed his frontier policy because of his growing conviction that state authorities were not the best administrators of federal funds that were never as abundant as they seemed to think. An even stronger motive, in all probability, was his concern for maintaining political control over the country. With discontent against his administration steadily rising, it was not altogether unlikely that militias raised through federal subsidies by state authorities of dubious personal loyalty might one day turn against him.[15]

The reaction in Sonora was not surprising. Not only had the forces "of that which have been called military colonies," now under federal supervision, been useless in the war against the Apaches, but they were becoming a serious burden on the communities wherein they resided. The official newspaper claimed that the presidial forces near the border spent their time leaving their respective communities, proceeding through the countryside south to the mining camp of Cananea in northern Arizpe district, and then returning without ever finding a single trace of the Apaches because the Indians invaded the state by other points and raided farther into the interior. The rest of the presidial troops were occupied in traveling to and from Arizpe in search of their wages. There they spent from twelve to fifteen days each month awaiting the paymaster. This was how they spent their time, since

> ... the Executive of the Union was allowed a direct intervention in the defense of the Frontier .... They have never made a single campaign against the savages nor have they made their presence felt in any manner but that of converting into colonies pueblos organized as such by the law of the state, which are an integral part of the Sovereignty of Sonora, and whose municipalities are receiving frequent complaints in this respect.[16]

Mexico City had withdrawn from Sonoran authorities the financial support necessary to carry out their program for restoring security to the frontier and had even dared to deny them the right to deal any longer with the problem.

---

[14] *Ibid.,* October 23, 1874, Reel 6. General García Morales was named commander of all presidial forces in the state. By this time, however, he and Pesqueira had had a falling out, and García Morales had joined the opposition.

[15] Daniel Cosío Villegas, *Historia moderna de México: El Porfiriato—la vida política interior,* Vol. I (México, 1970), 205-206.

[16] *La Estrella de Occidente,* January 8, 1875.

These actions did not square with the Sonoran liberals' understanding of liberalism and its expression in a national context. Moreover, it did not make sense to them. They had lived with the problem all of their lives and thought they understood it well—at least far better than distant politicians in the federal capital.

The Apaches were not Governor Pesqueira's only concern in trying to reestablish public security in the state. In the summer of 1868, with the ruinous uprising of the Yaquis and Mayos temporarily simmering but threatening to boil over again, the Pesqueira administration sent the legislature a letter detailing its assessment that peace could only be guaranteed in the two river valleys through force and the fear it inspired. Experience had shown that the tribes' promises of submission to the law could no longer be trusted. The government's solution was the permanent establishment of forces along both rivers. Acknowledging that the state did not then possess the funds to maintain such forces, the state legislature was asked to petition Congress for funds. The plan was a near replica of that to contain the Apaches along the frontier.[17]

A few weeks later, having marshalled support from several official quarters, the Pesqueira administration directly petitioned Mexico City for financial aid. Acting Governor Manuel Monteverde wrote the Minister of War, requesting that he ask the President to dispense to the state the protection due it under the federal constitution. He cited the request of the state's military commander (General García Morales) to the federal government for authorization to establish strong military forces in the Yaqui and Mayo valleys, to be sustained by federal revenues. Monteverde also noted the legislature's recent proposal to the Congress (in response to the state executive's earlier request) to establish three military colonies there in points designated by the state government. Nevertheless, the federal government, in both the executive branch and the Congress, rejected all these requests from Sonoran officials. It agreed only to provide funds for troops when an actual Yaqui-Mayo uprising was in progress.[18] The Pesqueira government was, thus, unable to end the two tribes' relative autonomy or to establish the guarantees of complete, permanent security necessary to accomplish the large-scale settlement of non-Indians in the two valleys.

For the Pesqueira administration, bringing the railroad to Sonora was almost as important as securing lasting peace and order. Yet here, too, Mexico City thwarted the state executive's initiatives, this time joined in part by a majority of the legislature, who believed that the state was overstepping its prerogatives in the matter. At the same time, the federal government itself

---

[17]*Ibid.*, July 10, 1868.
[18]*Ibid.*, August 7, 1868.

was unwilling to bring about the construction of such a railroad in Sonora, despite the united request of both the state executive and legislature.

In 1865, by use of his extraordinary powers, Governor Pesqueira had re-negotiated the contract for a railroad from El Paso to Guaymas that he had arranged with General Trías four years before.[19] Unable to fulfill the terms of the contract, the general and the North American company he represented had lost the concession. In 1869 the Congress awarded the concession to another North American company represented by Julius Skilton, United States consul in the national capital. A similar fate befell that enterprise, which was unable to sell the necessary stock to move the project beyond the planning stages.[20]

Then, two years later, a company of North American and English capital-ists building a transcontinental railroad across the southwestern United States sent feelers out to the Pesqueira government about a line from Tucson to Guaymas, which later might be extended to Mazatlán through Alamos and Culiacán. Preparing to purchase the Skilton concession, company officials wanted to know what extent of aid the Sonoran government was willing to grant. They told the governor plainly that it would be impossible to obtain capital in the United States to build such a railroad unless the terms of the previous concessions for railroads through Sonora were significantly im-proved. The 1,700 acres of public lands per mile of track granted under the former concessions were paltry compared to the 12,000 to 17,000 acres ceded by the United States government. In addition, to ensure adequate financing there would have to be some provision for emitting bonds. In his reply, Governor Pesqueira explained to the company the problem facing his government due to the failure of the Congress to have resolved the question of whether the public lands belonged to the federation or the states. If this right of concession were removed from the states, he said, it would cripple their efforts to foment such public improvements as railroads. Nevertheless, he expressed his desire that the company send a representative to conclude a contract.[21]

Governor Pesqueira's constitutional view on the concession is not quite clear. In his letter to the company, he promised to employ his influence with the federal government to obtain what was needed in case control of public lands was definitively recognized as belonging to the federation. Yet nowhere does he question the legislature's right to authorize such a concession as contracted by the state's executive.[22] It is unclear whether he believed that a concession so authorized still needed final approval from the federal govern-ment. From Pesqueira's attitude on other constitutional questions concerning the rights of states in areas not definitely resolved, it is probable that he

---

[19] *Ibid.*, February 3, 1865, Reel 5.

[20] Corral, 95.

[21] *El Eco de Sonora*, January 30 and February 13, 1871.

[22] *Ibid.*, February 13, 1871.

believed it was the state's prerogative to grant such concessions until the federal government imposed its will to prohibit the states from doing so. Pesqueira, as noted in the case of internal security, especially felt this way in areas in which the federal government had failed to assert such powers to actively help the states. If it was not going to act, then surely, he concluded, the states had the duty—and, thus, the right—to perform such essential tasks. His understanding of liberalism in the national context was that public initiative lay with the states, subject to the distinct prohibition against such action by the Constitution of 1857. The course of action he initially pursued in the negotiations over the railroad concession was based on this understanding.

The following spring (1872) the company's representative, James Eldredge, and the acting governor, Joaquín María Astiazarán, reached agreement on a contract with the following principal modifications of the two earlier concessions: the cession of 16,000 acres of public lands for every mile of railroad constructed; permission to emit bonds of up to 50,000 pesos per mile at 10 percent annually, to be guaranteed by the state; and the obligation of the state to emit bonds of 5,000 pesos per mile, which were to be lent to the company with repayment in twenty-five years. The railroad was to serve as collateral for the bonds.[23] It was a generous concession, seeking to encourage the sale of stock through much larger grants of land and to overcome the previous difficulties of initial capital shortages through the emission of bonds backed by the state.

A majority of the legislature, however, balked when asked for approval of the concession. The committee reviewing the proposed contract (composed of Juan Antúñez and Jesús Corella) reported that the legislature did not have the power to legislate on the matter; authorization for such a concession was the sole province of the Congress. Moreover, the terms of the concession could not be accepted in order to adopt the contract as an initiative for the legislature to send to Congress.

Diputado Carlos I. Velasco led the *pesqueirista* opposition to the committee report. He admitted there were valid questions raised as to whether the state was overstepping its bounds in the matter. Nevertheless, it was not sufficient reason for the state to drop consideration of the concession altogether. This was particularly so, given Sonora's crying need for some pump primers (such as the railroads) to turn around its languishing economy:

> The progressive march of the times, the happiness of our people imperiously demand us ... to follow the path traced out by the voice of modern civilization ... Forward then, distinguished compañeros, ... not rejecting flatly the pretensions of the solicitant because we judge

---

[23] Corral, 95-96.

them onerous, but dealing with him and offering for our part that which the State can rightfully grant, without injuring its general interests.

For Velasco, the state's urgent need for recovery took precedence over the determination of the limitations on local initiative. Besides, the decision in such matters had not yet been settled definitively.

Putting aside the constitutional question, diputado Samaniego countered Velasco's assessment of the concession. Eldredge's terms were extremely liberal, he said, and yet he was not even providing a guarantee for the completion of the railroad. But it was diputado Ramón Martínez who got to the heart of the position of those supporting the committee report. The limits of state prerogative in such matters were clearly set down in the federal constitution, he noted, and the legislature must adhere to them, even if it made progress more difficult:

> . . . without vacillating, we must attend to the prescriptions of our constitution above all, though it is said we prefer the *status quo* to progress. It is true . . . that it [progress] is very important, but adherence to the law is also very important; because without this indispensible requisite, the former [progress] cannot have effect.[24]

After a protracted and ardent debate, Acting Governor Astiazarán and Eldredge became convinced that the legislature would take no action unless thorough changes were made in the contract. Accordingly, they altered it to meet the two lines of objection and reintroduced the concession for a reconsideration. The terms were made fiscally more stringent by eliminating the clauses pertaining to the emission of bonds, though the cession of public lands was raised to 22,400 acres per square mile (but no more than half the acres then existing in the state). National domain over such concessions was acceded to by reduction of the character of the concession to that of an initiative submitted to Congress for its approval.[25] Though circumscribed in his efforts, Governor Pesqueira moved vigorously to salvage the compromise. Enjoying one of his periodic leaves of absence at his hacienda, Las Delicias, he quickly returned to Ures to bring all the pressure available to bear upon the legislature. After repeated conferences between the executive and the opposing diputados, the legislature—called into extraordinary session—gave its approval to the revised concession.[26]

---

[24] *La Estrella de Occidente,* May 17, 1872. The quotes of the two representatives are taken from the official proceedings of the legislature as printed in the official newspaper.
[25] *Ibid.,* July 5, 1872.
[26] *El Golfo de Cortes* (Guaymas), July 10, 1872.

The governor, however, was unable similarly to persuade Mexico City. His justifications for the concession—the repopulation of abandoned lands, the termination of the Apache raids through such resettlement, the placing of Sonora in contact with United States markets previously unprofitable because of prohibitive freight rates, the stimulation of immigration—went unheeded. The Congress refused to give its approval.[27]

Belatedly, the federal government granted a similar concession in 1875 to a New York company represented by David B. Blair. Nonetheless, the terms contained tighter restrictions.[28] There was, thus, even less to compensate for the problem of delayed and less certain investment returns inherent in constructing a railroad across generally arid and unpopulated territory, which at that time would join populations of, at best, middling importance and not connect with any other lines.[29] Combined with the turmoil surrounding the Tuxtepec Revolt the two years following, these disincentives doomed the project. In June, 1877, a presidential decree invalidated the unfulfilled concession.[30]

On the vital matter of fiscal policy, Governor Pesqueira found himself at odds with the legislature, the federal government, and the municipios as well. At issue was who was to raise revenues and, thus, control the level and purpose of public expenditures. To provide internal security, to help construct railroads and other public improvements, to cure Sonora's ills in general, Pesqueira believed the state administration must take an active role; and that would diminish capital and, thus, depress the economy even further. But to restrict revenues to such a point that the government was able to meet only its administrative expenses would tie its hands. His administration would

---

[27]Corral, 96-97. That same year a congressional committee proposed modifications in a concession to construct a railroad from the Gulf of Mexico to the Pacific across the center of the country. The modifications included a subsidy of 10,000 pesos per kilometer for the main line and 5,000 pesos per kilometer for branches terminating in Pachuca, Querétaro, Morelia, Guanajuato, León, San Luis Potosí, Aguascalientes, Guadalajara, and Colima. The concession permitted extension of these lines to the frontier, but without such a federal subsidy.

The Sonoran official newspaper tersely commented on the apparent neglect of the state in the country's emerging railroad network: "This project manifests to us how remote are the hopes which Sonora has of being favored with the immense advantages of the railroad through the assistance of the federation. . . ." *La Estrella de Occidente,* September 20, 1872.

[28]*La Estrella de Occidente,* February 26, 1875, Reel 5. Two other groups had sought the concession. However, both asked that their subvention be paid with a part of the customs duties rather than in lands, in anticipation of the problem of generating substantial initial capital to launch the project. Since Blair sought a subsidy only in lands, the federal government granted him the concession.

[29]Cosío Villegas, *República Restaurada—vida económica,* 703.

[30]Daniel Cosío Villegas, ed., *Historia moderna de México: El Porfiriato—la vida económica* (México, 1965), 486.

be unable to open and repair roads, sustain primary schools, support hospitals and charitable institutions, or grant subventions to municipalities to encourage and enable them to realize similar public improvements.[31]

Coupled with the difficulties concerning the level of revenues was their method of being raised. The governor concurred with the prohibition of the *alcabalas* in the Constitution of 1857.[32] He shared the assumption that such indirect taxes on the various economic sectors retarded their expansion. He had relied, instead, on direct contributions levied on property, working capital, and salaried income. With the *alcabalas* drastically curtailed, if not completely eliminated, the economy would grow at a more rapid rate, resulting in increased revenues for the government through direct taxes. Pesqueira believed that this was the correct policy to bring about Sonora's recovery from the war.[33]

The legislature had other ideas. The direct contribution weighed more heavily on the towns. Urban property and capital was easier to assess than that of the countryside, particularly when security was less than certain. The location of the collection offices in the district *cabeceras* made the collection of the taxes still more facile there. The provision excluding those with property or earnings of less than 200 pesos left those of moderate income and, especially, urban notables to carry the principal burden of the direct contribution. The *alcabalas* and other indirect taxes hit everyone in the state, and spilled over to outsiders doing business there as well. Furthermore, there were important political implications. Easier to levy, less troublesome to enforce, quicker to collect, the direct contribution provided an all too tempting way, in the legislators' view, for the executive branch to enlarge itself and the scope of its activities. Accordingly, the legislature rejected shifting the tax burden more toward the direct contribution, and its decision to decentralize tax assessments actually reduced revenues from that source.[34]

Beginning in 1868, the legislature decreed that the *catastro* (the general assessment) for the personal contribution was to be made by the ayuntamientos. The immediate result was a considerable lowering of the assessed valuation of the wealth in the state, and correspondingly a drop in revenues from that source. Governor Pesqueira reacted by charging that municipal authorities were underestimating the property valuations and thus holding

---

[31] *La Estrella de Occidente,* December 20, 1867, Reel 13.

[32] *El Eco de Sonora,* December 12, 1870, and January 2, 1871.

[33] *La Estrella de Occidente,* November 22, 1867, Reel 5.

[34] Pesqueira, 7; *La Estrella de Occidente,* July 17, 1868. The law of direct contribution of 1868 levied 1/2 percent taxes on the following forms of property and income: urban and rural property; *giros mercantiles* (commercial transactions); industrial establishment gross sales; rent; and salaries from public offices, professions, or personal work. *La Estrella de Occidente,* July 17, 1868.

back on revenues. The governor not only accused some municipal presidents of trying to reduce their municipalities' share of the tax, but claimed that most of the municipios were simply unable to carry out the task with any efficiency. Most of their officials, he said, knew little of fiscal matters. In light of this, Pesqueira recommended that the *catastro* be conducted by state officials under the prefect's supervision.[35]

Whatever the degree to which the intent or the inability of the local officials was a function of the marked decline in the general tax assessment, municipal interests seem to have run counter to an increasing state reliance on the personal contribution. The municipios derived their revenues mostly from taxes on economic activities within their jurisdiction. The more depressed the economy, the more scarce their revenues. However stimulative the conversion from indirect to direct taxes might be on the economy over the long haul, in the short run such an increasing state use of the direct contribution on personal wealth increased the already heavy burden on municipal residents. Given the immediate depressed economic conditions, such direct taxes—assessed irrespective of the level of economic activity in most cases—further discouraged what activities did exist. Stagnation was, thus, prolonged and the realization of recovery made more difficult. The municipal authorities may have been protecting the personal interests of prominent local families, as the governor contended. They may have been simply inept in making the assessment. But it is highly probable they were responding to the overall and immediate effect of such direct taxes on economic activity in their localities—activity on which their municipal budgets largely depended.

The municipalities' gain from lessening the burden of the direct contribution on their residents was the state government's serious loss. It significantly curtailed the scope of the role and responsibility the state executive had assumed for itself as principal agent in the promotion of Sonora's progress. The Pesqueira administration, which had decreed the former law governing the direct contribution in 1866 and had, thus, controlled its implementation, soon complained that placing the *catastro* in the hands of local authorities had effectively left the state treasury in a growing pecuniary crisis.[36] Acting Governor Monteverde issued a stern warning to the legislature in an address to the opening of its fall session four months after passage of the 1868 law on the direct contribution. Unless the government found immediate and dependable revenues, it would be forced "to reduce administrative services to a skeleton form or use unconstitutional measures to maintain the Government of the pueblos, which is the first of its obligations." Monteverde asked the legislature to expedite a budget of income capable of assuring "the permanent

---

[35] Pesqueira, 7, 11.
[36] *La Estrella de Occidente,* October 23, 1868.

functioning of the government."[37] A few weeks later, the acting governor asked the legislators to repeal the recent law of direct contribution and to devise procedures that would ensure a much larger valuation.[38]

The legislature, however, preferred to keep a tight grip on the direct contribution and to balance the budget by cutting expenses rather than raising direct taxes. In the fiscal year 1869-1870, it reduced the direct contribution and trimmed the budget. The cuts came, in large part, from the monies assigned to the prefects—the principal administrative arm of the government—particularly in the district towns where they (and the urban gentry and legislators) resided.[39] With such legislative resistance, the Pesqueira administration began reversing its policy against the use of *alcabalas*. Beginning in 1869, it proposed, and the legislature approved, consumption taxes on nationalized foreign goods (those having already been imported through the *aduanas*), on products introduced from other states, on liquor from a similar source, and on the trade of the Guaymas merchants in particular, as well as a duty on Sonoran goods exported to other states.[40] With these additional revenues, the legislature permitted the budget to rise from 116,829 pesos in 1869-1870 to 133,792 pesos the following year, and then kept it constant through 1873.[41]

The Pesqueira administration's monetary squabbles with the legislature and the municipios were partially due to the fiscal policy of the federal government. Facing much the same fiscal crisis as the states, only on a national scale, its solution, in part, was to absorb some of the states' revenue sources. In August, 1868, Acting Governor Monteverde wrote the Secretary of the Treasury to object to the new federal revenue classification law (passed the previous May). The law had removed from the state its former half share of the *derecho de contraregistro* (an import tax) and the *alcabala* on flour (very important in a wheat-producing state like Sonora). Even with those revenues, he complained, the state had been unable to meet its expenses.[42]

---

[37]*Ibid.,* October 9, 1868.

[38]*Ibid.,* October 23, 1868.

[39]*Ibid.,* October 23 and 30, 1868, and January 22, 1869; Pesqueira, 11, *Número 7.*

[40]*La Estrella de Occidente,* October 30 and December 25, 1868, and January 1 and 22, 1869; Cosío Villegas, *República Restaurada—vida económica,* 358.

[41]*La Estrella de Occidente,* January 22, 1869; Almada, 630; Cosío Villegas, *República Restaurada—vida económica,* 358-360. The budget figure for 1867-1868 was 120,000 pesos; for 1868-1869, 119,266 pesos; and for 1869-1870, 116,829 pesos. Almada's budget figure for 1871-1872 is 141,820 pesos. He has no figures after that until 1876-1877. There were deficits until 1870 (generally caused by revenues failing to meet expectations), after which there were generally small surpluses.

It must be noted that the treasury figures for the years 1867-1876 are incomplete and, in at least one instance (1871-1872), contradictory. A more extensive study of the treasury materials during the period is needed to reach more solid conclusions concerning the exact fiscal situation.

[42]*La Estrella de Occidente,* August 14, 1868.

The central issue was the relation between revenues and action. Would the benefits be bestowed on the localities from which the revenues came? And who was best able and most desirous to see that they were? What really peeved the Pesqueira administration was that while it could not even find revenues to cover its budget of around 120,000 pesos, the federal government was collecting about 500,000 pesos annually from Sonora. Even worse, very little of that ever returned. In addition, Sonora was carrying the burden of the defense against the Apaches and the maintenance of peace among the Yaquis and Mayos. Expenses for defense and security, the Pesqueira government asserted, ought to be paid by the federation, using the income accruing from the customs house at Guaymas.[43] (During most of the Reform War and the Intervention that was just what had happened. Pesqueira had been empowered to dispose of federal revenues within the state. But with the fall of Maximilian, the Juárez government had reclaimed control over the Guaymas customs office and kept a tight rein on its income.)

In early 1872 Pesqueira took matters into his own hands when an opening appeared. With the initial success of Díaz's La Noria Revolt in Sinaloa, Pesqueira had been asked by Governor Buelna, and later by the Minister of War, to send Sonoran forces to assist in quelling the rebellion. The troops were to be sustained with federal funds. In Sinaloa and urgently in need of money, Pesqueira dispatched Buelna to Guaymas to inform the administrator of the *aduana* there, Adolfo B. Carsi, that he was to allow the unloading of a ship laden with the goods of an importing house of Mazatlán at a discount in the customs duties. Pesqueira had agreed to the discount because otherwise the ship would have unloaded at Mazatlán, where the rebels were offering merchants reductions in import duties to secure funds. Carsi and all his employees refused to comply with this order, backed by the Federal District Judge, Domingo Elías González, an ardent opponent of the governor. Under instructions from Pesqueira, Buelna then occupied the customs house by force, and the ship unloaded and paid duties in Guaymas.

Pesqueira later explained his actions to President Juárez by saying that they were necessary if his troops were to fight in Sinaloa to help preserve Juárez's government. The federal executive did not see eye to eye with the governor's reasoning. After the defeat of the La Noria Revolt, President Lerdo (Juárez's successor) ordered a federal force to Guaymas to restore in office the functionaries Pesqueira had deposed. The forces remained in the port as a permanent garrison to ensure that such an occurrence would not be repeated.[44]

---

[43]*Ibid.;* Cosío Villegas, *República Restaurada—vida económica,* 275, 360.
[44]Acuña, 113-114.

ASSESSING BLAME FOR STAGNATION IN SONORA

As in the question of control over the Guaymas custom house revenues, Governor Pesqueira's initiatives to gain the upper hand in determining economic policies were short-lived at best and usually unsuccessful. He was unable in the post-war years to establish the state executive as the public focal point for the promotion of progress. His administration was doubly trapped in the liberal-national contradiction. The same liberal justification he presented to Mexico City was turned against him by the legislature. Correspondingly, the national stance he assumed with regard to the latter was employed by the federal government as the rationale for constricting his actions. Consequently, the governor failed to repeat his performance of the previous decade. By the mid-1870s, Sonora had only partially recovered from the Intervention. The prosperous boom of the early 1860s was not being resumed. Pesqueira had staked a large part of his political position and prestige on the question of promoting progress. His popularity was due much more to his having been the overseer of economic expansion than the guardian of republicanism. How then to account for the continuing economic stagnation in the post-war years? What was holding the state back from the resumption of progress?

The governor and his followers (*pesqueiristas*) pinpointed a considerable share of the blame on Mexico City. They were quick to acknowledge the political accomplishments of the Juárez government, but alleged that the backwardness of social and economic conditions was making the political conquests sterile. The inability of the federal government to remedy the economic and social difficulties facing the country had reduced the political triumphs of the Reforma and the Intervention to the sphere of abstractions. The principle of free education had been proclaimed, but there were no funds to sustain it on more than a meager scale. Every citizen was free to exercise his or her talents, but the tariff duties and various kinds of economic restrictions absorbed the fruits of their labors. In the eyes of the federation, all states were equal, yet the frontier states, whose problems were the most demanding, merited little attention. The center of the nation received improvements; the extremities were left abandoned, as if they did not belong to the union. The country was a federation of states, yet the states were no longer sovereign in their own affairs. Mexico City absorbed all their revenues, sapping their strength and vitality, yet did little for them with the resources and prerogatives it had engrossed.[45]

The decentralized character of liberalism was being discarded by national interests, who ignored the special needs of the states and their localities. The

---

[45]*El Eco de Sonora,* February 13, 1871. This *pesqueirista* paper was edited by Javier Jofre, who had been editor of the official newspaper in the late 1860s and again filled that post in the mid-1870s.

federal government, the *pesqueiristas* contended, was centralizing revenues and authority, but Sonora was receiving little, if anything, in return. (Sonoran federalists had made the same argument on a more simplified basis thirty years before.) Federal revenues sucked out of Sonora were going to subsidize railroads, construct telegraph lines, and build roads elsewhere. The tariffs, in addition to being outrageously high, were the same in Sonora as in Veracruz, despite the great difference in transportation costs for North Atlantic trade. Mexico City, in the *pesqueiristas'* eyes, was just plainly ignorant of both the economic plight of their state and of its potential.[46] "The barriers to the free action of our state government which the negligence and the centralizing system of the national government have put up," explained *El Eco*, "are the cause of the backwardness in which we find ourselves in this state. . . ."[47]

Nowhere was this paradox of federal circumscription of state initiative and yet federal inaction more evident to the *pesqueiristas* than in the task of providing internal security. Because the Apache raids were growing worse despite the recently instituted federal subsidy, Mexico City papers and, in time, the federal government itself were concluding that the state was mismanaging the federal funds allotted it. The *pesqueiristas* countered that the annual federal subsidy of 168,000 pesos did not even begin to approach either what the Spanish Crown had given to the presidios during the colonial period or the three million pesos the United States was spending annually on its side of the border. Besides, the earlier sale of Sonoran territory by the national government under Santa Anna had placed the Apaches out of the reach of the state forces, while the United States was doing little to prevent them from crossing the border.[48]

From time to time small federal detachments had been sent to Sonora, but they had never gotten any farther than Guaymas. They had kept a tight watch on customs revenues while there, but had been of no help in either containing the Apaches on the frontier or forcing the Yaquis and Mayos into submission in the southern part of the state. They had failed to stop the rebels of Plácido Vega from raiding the port, and did not even pursue them. The *pesqueiristas* wanted aid in the form of more money, not federal troops. The task of guaranteeing public security could be far more effectively tackled

---

[46]*Ibid.*, January 9 and 30, 1871. The evidence seems to support the *pesqueiristas'* contention. By 1876 the federal government had built no roads leading into Sonora. The Congress authorized construction of a wagon road from Tepic to Guaymas, but funds were never forthcoming. In the construction of telegraph lines Sonora fared little better. Not until the end of 1872 did the Congress authorize the extension of the telegraph from Mazatlán to Ures; and by 1875 the line still had not even been started. The federal government also provided no assistance in bringing a railroad to Sonora. Cosío Villegas, *República Restaurada–vida económica,* 569, and maps facing 546, 578; *La Estrella de Occidente,* January 27, 1871, Reel 5, and February 28, 1873.

[47]*El Eco de Sonora,* February 20, 1871.

[48]*La Estrella de Occidente,* October 20, 1871.

through the state's initiative.[49] Moreover, they believed that the overgrown federal army was entrapping the country in a vicious cycle: the federal troops were needed to maintain order against political discontent, which arose from impoverishment, which was created by the errant fiscal policy of the federal government, which in turn resulted from thee vast sums needed to maintain the army.[50]

Rather than federal troops, what Sonora needed, in the *pesqueiristas'* view, was the exact and prompt payment of the subsidy for the Apache war, and additional monies for a campaign against the Yaquis and Mayos, without the state government's having to provide an accounting of how it would be spent before it was paid. They also wanted federal assistance in diverse other ways: lower tariffs for the Pacific states, extension of the Free Zone (an area where foreign goods were free of customs duties along the frontier) to include Sonora, good roads and telegraph lines to unite the state with the rest of the country, and a railroad from El Paso through Guaymas to Mazatlán with liberal land concessions. Behind all of these requests for federal funds, or rejection thereof, was the desire for the freedom of all the states to run their own affairs completely. For the *pesqueiristas* this freedom meant no coercion of state sovereignty, no restrictions on state initiative in the pursuance of progress unless clearly prohibited by the Constitution of 1857, while at the same time being left the fiscal resources necessary to attend to their needs.[51]

So great was the dissatisfaction of the *pesqueiristas* with the Juárez government in the matter of the determination and control of economic policy that from among their ranks arose a trial balloon for the 1871 federal elections. That winter some of them began promoting the governor for presdient of the Republic as an alternative to the national liberal interests that had run the country since the Reforma. Being a native of the frontier, they said, Pesqueira would end the favoritism shown the central states and foster the neglected interests of the frontier states. In addition, knowing full well its debilitating effect on the states, he would reverse the growing centralization of power. Furthermore, the Liberal Party was divided into three national factions (those backing Juárez, Lerdo, and Porfirio Díaz), none of which, upon winning the election, would be motivated or able to tackle the demanding task of the

---

[49]*El Eco de Sonora,* January 9, 1871.

[50]*Ibid.,* March 6, 1871.

[51]*Ibid.* The Free Zone, a strip of land twenty-five miles wide in which foreign goods could be introduced free of customs duties, was instituted in Tamaulipas in 1858 to impede emigration from that state into Texas. In 1870 the zone was extended west to Nuevo León, Coahuila, and Chihuahua to encourage the settlement and development of the frontier. Cosío Villegas, *República Restaurada-vida económica,* 283, 290.

social and economic reconstruction of the country with any degree of equanimity. Being a neutral in the post-war contention for national power, his supporters claimed, Governor Pesqueira could reunite the liberal party. He could effectively lead it in meeting the challenge of promoting progress.[52]

This somewhat fanciful but, by its very audacity, perceptive promotion of Pesqueira for the presidency was squelched by the governor's absolute renunciation of any such candidacy.[53] Aware that there was little chance of ever winning such an election, Pesqueira did not want to worsen his already uneasy relations with the Juárez government. The *pesqueiristas* then threw their support to Juárez. They did so on the basis of favoring that candidate whom they perceived most upheld liberalism in the face of the nationalist trend in the absorption of power and prerogative.

Lerdo, Pesqueira's followers said, was the one who had been setting the basic direction of the Juárez administration in the post-war years. Though they did not excuse Juárez from blame, they thought that, if separated from Lerdo, he would attend more to the needs of the country and curb the growing federal interference in state governments—in particular the practice of placing in them persons loyal to the federal executive.[54] The third candidate, Porfirio Díaz, connoted demagoguery in the *pesqueiristas*' minds. Díaz himself was not tyrannical. Rather, he was surrounded by those who had recently instigated disorders, mutinies, and revolts, persons who

... presented themselves as tribunes of the restive common people, scorning informed society, assailing accepted conduct, breaking down doors to seize another's interests and doing other villainies in this manner, introducing into our society, much too strained already, all the horrors of the worst kind of demagoguery.[55]

It was a question for the *pesqueiristas* of which candidate's liberal antecedents were most trustworthy, as a group of the governor's supporters in Ures put it, "to sustain liberal institutions ... [and to] consolidate peace, the respect for guarantees, and the best direction for the progressive march demanded by the necessity for practical improvements from whose lack our actual condition suffers in the highest degree." Though no longer noteworthy, Juárez liberal credentials were judged the most reliable.[56]

Nonetheless, Juárez's reelection in 1871 changed little. The contention between Pesqueira and Mexico City continued unabated. The succession of

---

[52] *El Eco de Sonora,* February 3 and 20, 1871.
[53] *Ibid.,* March 6, 1871.
[54] *Ibid.*
[55] *Ibid.,* March 27, 1871.
[56] *Ibid.*

Lerdo to the presidency the following year, at Juárez's death, intensified the conflict, as seen in the questions involving the railroad, containment of the Apaches, pacification of the Yaquis and Mayos, and the use of the Guaymas customs revenues.

The federal government, in the minds of Pesqueira and his followers, was not solely to blame for the state's woes. More reproachable than Mexico City were the governor's increasingly visible and vocal opponents within the state, and their numbers were growing. The offense the *pesqueiristas* attached to the opposition was that of exploiting local and private interests at the expense of the welfare of the state as a whole. It was the liberal/national contradiction in reverse: decentralization run rampant and devoid of legitimacy. State interests were being undermined by unjustifiable local and private pretentions.

Those deemed the most crass were the instigators of open revolt, knavish sorts who craved public positions to build personal fortunes, having been unable to do so by honorable means. Even worse in its effect on the welfare of the state than the personal greed of such as these were the out-and-out bandits they attracted to their cause, always ready to wrap their crimes in a revolutionary banner. Only slightly a cut above these seditious instigators were the agitators and demagogues who were trying to promote themselves. In doing so, they inhibited economic progress.[57]

The *pesqueiristas* derided less, but fretted more over, those working more covertly and with greater subtlety to undermine the governor's regime and thus obstruct the resumption of the expansion of the state's economy. A group of non-liberals, they contended, those who had never supported the grand liberal coalition, were not trying to break up the liberal party within the state. They were promoting prominent personages in the party as opposition candidates, hoping, thus, to fuse elements of the party to themselves, in order to gain power.[58] Even more threatening were those of the opposition who had once supported and even been part of the Pesqueira administration, but who since had fallen from grace and been expelled. These people, the governor's followers believed, were the ones most responsible for all the misfortunes befalling Sonora. Under the cover of the state's liberal institutions, they had been resisting and undermining the state executive's policies to bring progress to the state. As members of the legislature and municipal officials, they had been stalling the governor's improvement projects and thwarting his requests for more authority to cope with Sonora's ills. In the

---

[57]*La Estrella de Occidente,* December 8, 1871, Reel 6; *El Eco de Sonora,* March 27, 1871.

[58]*El Eco de Sonora,* April 17, 1871. In particular, the *pesqueiristas* cited the promotion of General García Morales for governor in 1871 and 1875.

press, they had been trying to destroy his reputation because it was an obstacle to their own ambitions and local or private interests.[59]

The last scorn was reserved for the affluent fellow-travelers of the opposition, notables of considerable resources who, the *pesqueiristas* claimed, apathetically carped at the state executive from the sidelines. They would not befriend the Pesqueira administration with what it needed most—financial backing. Instead, they blamed the government for the lack of progress and the levying of ever greater taxes. Such carping only lent support to those fomenting discontent and instability.[60]

Pesqueira and his followers may have seen the opposition as fragmentally composed and motivated, but its total effect on the state was clear enough to them. The opposition was keeping Sonora ensnared in the post-war depression. Rather than blame the Pesqueira administration for Sonora's lack of progress, under the guise of the absorption of power by the state executive, those of the opposition should blame themselves. It was was their disruption, cloaked in a corruption of liberal principles, that was stymieing progress. Preoccupied with gaining political power and promoting their own parochial interests, feigning their love of liberty and their horror at what they called "the despotism of Sonora," the opposition leaders had kept the state in such a condition of agitation and uncertainty that capitalists had abstained from investing, businesspeople had curtailed their operations, and the laboring classes had been thrown out of work. They had continually distracted, indeed prevented, the government from attacking the social and economic ills of the state. If the opposition continued to disrupt the state and entrap it in a vicious circle of disorder and economic stagnation, it would succeed only in bringing a return to the pre-Reforma era of civil strife and economic backwardness.[61]

The *pesqueiristas* charged the opposition not only with undermining the state's welfare through a perverted interpretation of liberalism, but also with impairing Sonora's sovereignty under the hypocritical cloak of federalism. Those who sanctified local prerogatives to the detriment of the state executive, at the same time advocated increased federal intervention, which was also at the state administration's expense. Knowing that Sonorans were unwilling to support their petty interests, the *pesqueiristas* contended, the opposition looked for an outside force to assist them in furthering their local and private interests by weakening the power of the state executive. Thus, they called for the sending of more than two thousand federal troops for the frontier and the Yaqui-Mayo valleys as the solution to the security problem. At the same time they criticized the policy favored by the governor of federal

---

[59] *El Defensor del Pueblo* (Guaymas), June 18, 1875.

[60] *El Amigo de Pueblo* (Ures), July 23 and 30, 1875.

[61] *Ibid.*, June 11, 1875; *El Mochuelo* (Ures), August 29, 1873.

subsidies to the frontier states to be spent as they saw fit, arguing that instead the subvention should be administered by an inspector under the orders of the Minister of War. In short, the *pesqueiristas* concluded, the opposition was willing to bargain away the state's sovereignty to strip the governor of any effective power and ultimately force Pesqueira's removal from office.[62]

Both the *pesqueiristas* and the opposition that formed in the post-war years were caught in the liberal-national contradiction as they arrived at conclusions as to why there was no full recovery from the Intervention, no resumption of progress. The harmonization of the national good to the states' individual concerns and of each state's welfare to the interests of the localities within it seemed increasingly unachievable. The depressed economic conditions appeared to negate the assumption on which the Restored Republic rested: that the combination of liberalism and nationalism would at last realize the permanent progress of the nation and its disparate parts.

SINALOA: MAZATLAN AT ODDS

The far more limited sources available for Sinaloa suggest that the liberal/ national contradiction was evident also in that state's economic difficulties, though necessarily the picture there must be drawn less clearly and more restrictively than for Sonora. Mazatlán's commerce was hurt considerably by the forces and interests fostering the creation of a national economy. The completion of the railroad between the national capital and Veracruz gave the Atlantic and Mexico City mercantile interests the competitive advantage in the distribution of goods from Europe and the eastern United States to the interior of the country. Already favored by their greater proximity to these North Atlantic markets, the marked reductions in overland freight created by the railroad enabled Veracruz, Tampico, and Mexico City wholesalers to offer merchants on the eastern side of the Sierra Madre in Chihuahua, Durango, and Jalisco an increasingly better price than their counterparts in the Sinaloan port. Markets further to the east were lost altogether to Mazatlán commerce.[63]

The federal government's support was in great part responsible for the realization of Mexico's first railroad of consequence, to Mazatlán's detriment. Its promotion of steamship navigation on the Pacific coast also had an injurious effect on the port. Mexico City subsidized first North American steamship lines and then some national companies to stop at Pacific ports.[64] These subsidies encouraged the dispersion of trade along the coast away from

---

[62] *El Mochuelo*, August 29, 1973.

[63] Buelna, *Compendio*, 44; Cosío Villegas, *República Restaurada—vida económica*, 609, 661.

[64] Cosío Villegas, *República Restaurada—vida económica*, 543, 549.

Mazatlán, by overcoming that port's natural advantage of central location, and its role as a distributor was undermined.[65] At the same time, Mexico City did little to correct Mazatlán's nautical deficiencies, which handicapped the port in trying to meet the growing competition from Guaymas, San Blas, and Manzanillo. The harbor's vulnerable opening to the Pacific brought shipping to a virtual standstill during the rainy season (from July through September), with its frequent gale force winds coming in off the ocean.[66] The Congress authorized federal funds for port works to conserve the bay and provide greater safety to the harbor in 1868, but such improvements had not materialized by the mid-1870s.[67] "A few thousand dollars would make a safe harbor," commented United States Consul Isaac Sisson, "but neither the Mexican government nor her people can see the great benefit they would derive from such an enterprise."[68] Neither the general Sinaloan public nor the state government could see it either.

Within Sinaloa, the relation of the local interests of Mazatlán versus the more general welfare of the state as a whole had long been the central issue in the promotion of progress. It continued to be so in the post-war years. Port notables, who had always been highly pragmatic in their ideological affinities, were quick to employ liberalism as a justification in the conflict. The principles of decentralized authority and free trade were a solid rationale for the protection of the port's commercial interests. The larger national welfare, whether in the federal or state context, had always worked to constrict Mazatlán's economic expansion. Consequently, general public sentiment in most of the state was not sympathetic to the specific promotion of public improvements, such as the port works, that would enhance the city's economic activity. Moreover, at that time the state government had little, if any, monies to spare. When the capital was transferred to Culiacán in 1873, there was even less likelihood that such state support would be forthcoming, that the port's local interests would be considered a vital part of the state's welfare. Indeed, the transfer of the capital soon after resulted in the removal of the state-run secondary school (Liceo de Rosales) that had been established in the port the previous year.[69]

That Mazatlán underwrote state revenues made the conflict between the state's welfare and the port's interests even more contentious. Denied support for the promotion of its own advancement, Mazatlán was providing the lion's

---

[65] Buelna, *Compendio,* 44-45.

[66] United States Department of State, *Commercial Relations,* 1871, Mazatlán, Consul I. Sisson, 910.

[67] Rubí, 13.

[68] United States Department of State, *Commercial Relations,* 1871, Mazatlán, Consul I. Sisson, 910.

[69] González Dávila, 182, 570.

share of the funding for the rest of the state's progress. In 1873, 140,000 pesos of Sinaloa's total revenues of 165,000 pesos accrued from the port. This huge proportion was the result not only of its economic position in the state, but also because the Sinaloan government relied heavily on *alcabalas* and taxes on commercial establishments for its income.[70] Mazatlán's notables strove to reduce these charges (and the federal government's, too) on their commercial interests as much as possible. They employed their own political representatives, politicians from neighboring districts affiliated with the port's commerce, and ambitious military officers based in the port in varying combinations to accomplish this end. There were few opportunities in the post-war years that Mazatlan's commercial interests and their varied clients did not attempt to exploit.

The temporary success of the La Noria Revolt in and around the port (fall, 1871) resulted in the lowering of a variety of taxes on commerce. Mazatlán commercial interests had encouraged and financially supported the action of the federal garrison in seconding the La Noria rebellion. The provisional governor, Mateo Magaña, a *tepiqueño* merchant established in the port, quickly looked after his commercial kindred. Magaña decreed exemptions from duties on certain articles of commerce, lowered the export tax on precious metals, and abolished several port-use taxes. His successor, Manuel Márquez, a military veteran named by *porfirista* General Donato Guerra, continued granting lower tariffs and duties.[71]

A year later (December, 1872), diputados from the southern districts, generally allied with Mazatlán notables and often residing in the port, found themselves temporarily in the majority. (A good many of the legislators from the northern districts, who had formed a majority supporting Governor Eustaquio Buelna, of Culiacán, were not in attendance at the reconvening of the legislative sessions following the fall recess.) The opposition diputados quickly seized the opportunity to reduce state levies on Mazatlán commerce. They passed legislation forgiving the personal contributions owed by La Noria insurgents, granting other numerous tax exemptions to individuals and businesses, amplifying the forms of credit that could be used in payment of all kinds of state taxes, and suppressing a small government public security force in the port. All these measures resulted in a sharp reduction in state revenues.[72]

Nevertheless, the most flagrant fiscal compromise committed by the opposition diputados was their decree of December 31, ordering that the copper money in circulation be amortized by accepting it at par value as payment of

---

[70] United States Department of State, *Commercial Relations,* 1873, Mazatlán, Consul I. Sisson, 839-840. [71]
[71] Buelna, *Apuntes,* 132, 130-131.
[72] *Ibid.,* 160.

state taxes. These included the federal contribution (a fixed percentage of revenues collected by the states and forwarded to Mexico City), over which they had no right to legislate. A couple of weeks earlier, two commercial houses had begun discounting the copper money at fifty percent rather than the customary ten percent. The other port merchants soon had followed suit. The popular classes, among whom the copper *cuartillas* principally circulated, suffered miserably. It was, thus, not hard for José C. Valadés, a Mazatlán journalist, an ardent *porfirista,* and veteran of the recent La Noria Revolt, to organize throngs of irate, suffering poor into hostile mobs. On December 22, they threateningly demanded that the government insure the acceptance of the *cuartillas* at par. Government officials acquiesced. The merchants went on about their business. They drove down the discount to as much as eighty percent and bought the *cuartillas* at these ridiculous prices; then, in a few days, they used them to pay state taxes as authorized by the legislature on December 31. Sympathetic to the merchants' interests, the temporary opposition majority also feared the continued unrest of the popular classes, who angrily hovered over their deliberations.[73]

The petition of various Mazatlán residents to the federal government for the transfer of the mint from Culiacán provides another example of port notables' keen opportunistic sense in the promotion of their local interests. The revival of the La Noria Revolt in July, 1872, had originated in Culiacán. The port residents in large part justified their request on the grounds that revolutions frequently erupted there. In point of fact, the port itself had been the principal base of support for the La Noria cause, as well as for the several other rebellions localized within Sinaloa. For this reason, as well as for economic and geographic reasons, the petition was denied.[74]

COMMON BINDS

There were several matters in which Sinaloa and Sonora were caught up together in the liberal-national contradiction. In the dispute over the trade in Sonoran wheat, the affected interests in each state argued on both sides of the question. The producers of central Sonora and their shippers in Guaymas and Hermosillo lobbied for a continuation of high tariffs on foreign wheat in defense of their local interests. At the same time, in the national interest, they advocated the free interchange of such products among the states. The high price of Sonoran wheat of which Sinaloans continually complained was the result, the Sonoran producers and shippers said, of the *alcabalas* Sinaloa's state and municipal governments levied on it.[75] In contrast, the Sinaloan

---

[73]*Ibid.,* 158-159.
[74]*El Clamor Público,* November 30, 1872.
[75]*La Estrella de Occidente,* November 22, 1867, Reel 5, and July 5, 1872.

consumer interests (based in Mazatlán) defended such state and local duties on wheat as essential revenues. They located themselves under the national interest by advocating freer foreign trade. Lowering the external tariff would make foreign wheat more competitive and thereby lower the price of domestic wheat nationwide, they contended. Sinaloan solicitations for lower tariffs, though temporarily granted, were never made permanent.[76]

On the question of mining tariffs and taxes, Sinaloan and Sonoran interests were affected similarly. Mining concerns in both states, supported by politicians and journalists in general, called for the fulfillment of the liberal principle of free trade. Plagued with recovery from the war, security problems, high freight rates, and a shortage of capital, the high federal tariffs and the strict requirement of the legal minting of ore were doubly burdensome. Mexico City was being short-sighted in clinging to the heavy charges and restrictions on mineral production as an immediate solution to fiscal deficiencies, Northwest mining interests argued. Free export of ores and lower tariffs would in the long run increase production and stimulate other sectors of the economy to the point where federal revenues would actually in time be much larger.[77] In response to such continuing demands from numerous parts of the country, the Congress approved the export of gold and silver ores in 1871. But the following year the law was modified so as to increase revenues (the tariff was raised from four to five percent) and to better control contraband (through tighter restrictions).[78] When a congressional committee recommended repeal of the export of ores the very next year (1873), strong opposition was expressed in the Northwest.[79] Some even advocated the export of ores with absolute freedom and without any customs duty.[80]

Mexico City was hesitant about promoting the construction of railroads on the northern frontier unless they connected those regions with the center of the country. Lerdo in particular was fearful that United States influence, through railroads linking the frontier with that expanding neighbor, might lead to the eventual acquisition or, at the least, the domination of some or all

---

[76]Cosío Villegas, *República Restaurada–vida económica,* 107-108.

[77]*La Estrella de Occidente,* September 10, 1869, and January 17, 1870, Reel ? . The Sonoran government in 1868 proposed the repeal of the state's tax on mining production, considering it onerous, unfair, and anti-economic since it was levied on only a single branch of production. The legislature repealed the tax a few months later but added a five percent levy on nationalized foreign goods to cover the lost revenue, as the governor had suggested. *Idem,* October 30, 1868, and January 1, 1869.

[78]Cosío Villegas, *República Restaurada–vida económica,* 170-175.

[79]*La Estrella de Occidente,* August 8, 1873. Residents of Alamos sent a solicitation to the President, asking that he work to oppose the proposed repeal of the permission to export ore.

[80]*El Gulfo de Cortes,* September 10, 1873.

of the frontier regions.[81] Yet the rugged western Sierra Madre had long cut off the Northwest from any facile communication with the central core of country. The likelihood that any rail line, given such an elevated cost per square mile and such often monumental obstacles to construction, would be built in the immediate future was highly unlikely. It would be 1912 before a completed rail line—the extension of the Sonora Pacific through Tepic to Guadalajara—crossed the Sierra Madre.

Notables in the Northwest shared the common consensus among politicians and prominent families throughout the nation that the railroad was the key to the rapid expansion of economic activity that would lift the country out of its depressed, disorderly condition.[82] But the realization of such a stimulus to the Northwest's economic expansion could, at that time, come only through a rail linkage with the United States across the basin and range country along the northern Sonoran frontier. Since mid-century, the economies of Sinaloa and Sonora had been gravitating in that direction, expanding in close relation to that market connection. A railroad would help promote and cement those economic links, pulling the Northwest further away from the emerging national economic orbit, which was centered in the interior. The liberal principle of the free flow of investment and economic activity across international boundaries was to the Northwest's immediate and essential benefit in the post-war years. But it was in conflict with what was being articulated in the interior as the nation's welfare.

Liberalism appeared to side with the Northwest in its quest for recovery and progress. Nationalism, at least that defined and emanating from Mexico City, appeared to be a growing obstruction to that endeavor. Finding a place in the nation and a share in its progress was becoming unexpectedly thorny. Difficult too were the efforts of the various localities of Sinaloa and Sonora to secure the harmonious relation between their economic interests and what their respective state executives or legislative majorities deemed the state's general welfare. Progress was entangled in the growing contradiction between liberalism and nationalism. So too was politics.

---

[81] Frank Knapp, *The Life of Sebastián Lerdo de Tejada, 1823-1889* (Austin, 1951), 171.

[82] Cosío Villegas, *República Restaurada—vida económica*, 609-613.

8

The Liberal-National Contradiction: Politics

(1867-1875)

The failure of the anticipated progress to materialize in the post-war years was matched by the inability of the new liberal political order to stabilize. While the economy was stagnant, politics was increasingly agitated. Neither occurrence was expected, and both evoked disappointment and rising discontent. That the Reforma and the Intervention, which had dislocated the economy, entailed a burdensome recovery was easy enough for all to see. Yet it was commonly believed (and, in point of fact, largely true) that these impassioned, costly struggles had rid the country of interior and exterior enemies.[1] Political harmony was, thus, seemingly the natural consequence. The new liberal political order codified in the Constitution of 1857 was now free to evolve, and, as the post-war period began, expressions of the liberal credo were much in evidence in the Northwest, as well as nationwide.

THE NEW LIBERAL ORDER: ILL AT EASE

The government at all levels took a tolerant attitude toward the defeated imperialists. Though there were existing decrees for retaliation, many prisoners were pardoned, and others' sentences were lightened. The decree authorizing confiscation of property was repealed. A precedent was set for granting amnesty to unsuccessful armed opponents.[2] In the Northwest, a parallel to the general pardoning of Santa Anna nationally was the eventual pardon granted to Manuel María Gándara, the venerable opportunist, erstwhile conservative-imperialist affiliate, and bitter rival of Ignacio Pesqueira. Though imprisoned for three years, upon his release he reestablished himself in Sonora. He pursued his economic interests, understanding that his political

---

[1] Cosío Villegas, *Historia Moderna de México: La República Restaurada—la vida política* (México, 1955), 33, 121.

[2] *Ibid.*, 66.

career had ended.[3] Other prominent imperialist supporters reentered politics. Joaquín María Astiazarán, a lawyer and hacendado from Guaymas, had served as a district judge and acting prefect of the entire department of Sonora during the imperialist occupation. Yet he soon became one of Pesqueira's chief political lieutenants. In 1871 and 1873 he was elected to the legislature and to the office of substitute governor; in the latter capacity, he replaced Pesqueira during his increasingly frequent leaves of absence.[4]

Nationally, there was a prevailing tolerance not only of past enemies but of present political opponents as well. Political expression was wide and free—and at times scathing. In both Sinaloa and Sonora a whole string of newspapers with a variety of viewpoints appeared, where previously there had only been an official newspaper and a few ephemeral private publications. Most of the newspapers were personal in operation, combining straight reporting with biased commentary in favor of local interests or of particular political personalities and their associates. Their discussions of public policies and political principles were often far-reaching and sometimes vituperous, as they engaged one another and the official newspapers in lengthy and heated debates.[5]

The extensive free expression reflected the considerable dispersion of political power in the country. Though voting manipulation continued, elections at all levels were now usually real political contests. The closer margins and disputed returns indicate that no person, group, or locality was able to establish clear control over the political structure at whatever level. No one could command; all had to debate, persuade, and deal. This situation was especially true in Sinaloa, where the constitution was as liberal as any in the country. The prefects were chosen by ballot, rather than (as elsewhere) at the governor's discretion. Moreover, both the governor and the prefects were prohibited from immediate reelection.[6]

The dispersal of political power meant that state and federal governments had to respect local sentiment. The shifting alliances in the post-war years revealed that local feelings and interests had to be taken into account, that no one person or group could control the various governmental branches exclusively. The constitutions of both Sonora and Sinaloa had devolved prerogatives and powers to both the municipios and the legislature at the state

---

[3] Almada, 293-294.

[4] *Ibid.*, 90-91; Corbalá Acuña, *Constituciones*, 259-260; *La Regeneración* (Hermosillo), June 14, 1876.

[5] Cosío Villegas, *República Restaurada—vida política*, 33, 66, 492. The proliferation of newspapers published in the two states after the Intervention is manifested in the University of Arizona Microfilm Collection, especially for Sonora.

[6] Buelna, *Compendio*, 61.

executive's expense.[7] Any attempt to recover them provoked prompt and substantial opposition.

Political groupings were based on personalities and specific issues (usually those with direct effects on local interests), rather than on ideology or socio-economic class. There was common agreement that liberalism should be the ideological basis for the society and that such a political order offered social and economic opportunities for all elements to improve their lives. Adolfo Almada's proposal for a minimum wage in the Sonoran legislature was an extreme expression of this generally accepted social attitude.[8] There was one important exception to this harmonious social mood in the Northwest. Throughout the rest of the country (except for the Mayas in the Yucatán), the Indians were being integrated into the national life as full citizens, with direct interests in the nation, who were to be respected by others as such. However, the tribal Yaquis and Mayos in southern Sonora and the Cahita villagers in northern Sinaloa continued to be regarded as obstacles to progress—obstacles to be removed from their hold on fertile lands and made to be submissive to state and local authorities. Only the lack of funds and federal support prevented Sonoran whites and mestizos from undertaking armed subjugation of the two tribes. Sinaloans ignored the guarantees to the northern Indian villagers decreed by General Angel Martínez in 1866.[9]

The liberal impetus for the expansion of public instruction was also manifest in the Northwest. Legislative proposals for schooling were numerous, with laws passed erecting statewide educational structures that were new to Sinaloa and far more integrated, elaborate, and centralized than previously in Sonora. The extension of public instruction was limited only by the inadequacy of funding. Education was seen as the means to train a new generation, which, schooled in liberalism, would bring about sustained social and economic progress. "That longed for future ... do you know from what direction we will see it come to light?" asked one Sinaloan editorial writer rhetorically. "From the direction of youth; from among the masses of young people; from there will come to us the light marking the dawning of our great new day; these poor and insignificant beings whom today we see with indifference, will pronounce the mysterious word, the 'sesame' of our future happiness."[10] Secondary schools to provide the educational, professional, and political leaders of the future were planned in both states. The one actually established in Sinaloa (the Colegio Rosales in 1873) began to have an effect within a decade.

---

[7]*Ibid.,* 60-65; Banderas Rebling,.46-63.

[8]Cosío Villegas, *República Restaurada—vida política,* 459. For details of Almada's proposal see Chapter 6.

[9] See Chapter 6 for details.

[10] *Boletín Oficial del Estado de Sinaloa* (Mazatlán), August 29, 1872.

With such expressions of the new liberal order in evidence, why then was there such growing political agitation, such instability? This question was one for which Sinaloans and Sonorans, along with Mexicans in general, were little prepared. The simplistic answer that increasingly emerged was that the political mismanagement, corruption, or opportunism of one's opponent was responsible for the political discord. Such explanations were often partially correct, but what permitted such political sins against the liberal credo to find the room in which to maneuver and to have such profound effects on the body politic were several underlying conditions emanating from a decade of intense, pervasive warfare.[11]

The continuing economic difficulties left little room for compromise in matters of political economy, straining the trust in opponents' political intentions. The veteran army created by the wars was most troublesome to accommodate into the new liberal order. To discharge the veterans was to return to the society uprooted, unemployed men acquainted with the uses of unrestricted power, accustomed to direct and expedient action. Ambitious, higher-ranking officers in particular entered politics with such habits. The alternative—to retain the veterans due to the necessity of maintaining order in the face of die-hard imperialist subversion and a growing number of local revolts instigated by the electorally unsuccessful—was equally onerous. The cost of maintaining the army sapped the financial wherewithal needed to promote economic recovery. Moreover, the political ambitions of veteran officers were not contained by military positions. On the contrary, such ambitions were stimulated by the knowledge of the increasing reliance of the civilian government on the military to preserve order. The new generation of bandits spawned during the war years complicated this problem even further. The line between political cause and brigandage had worn quite thin.[12]

There was, additionally, a generational complication. The two wars had created opportunities for a large number of young men, especially those who saw military service, to rise to positions of power and prominence at a much more accelerated rate and in much larger numbers than in peacetime. At the same time, the wars extended in office the number of older politicians, who, accustomed to such prolonged power, did not wish to relinquish it so readily. The result was an insufficient political turnover to accommodate the proliferation of political ambitions.[13]

The dilemma for both those in office and those out of power at any given time was how to reconcile liberalism, which formed the conditions in which post-war politics functioned, with centralized authority, which seemed in-

---

[11] Cosío Villegas, *República Restaurada—vida política,* 363-474.
[12] *Ibid.,* 66, 77, 230-261, 305.
[13] *Ibid.,* 85, 485.

creasingly necessary in handling the pressing circumstances generated by the wars.[14] Local liberal interests leaned on the side of liberalism. It offered them considerable leeway in local prerogative and decision-making and underwrote local control. The only restrictions on such local power were those liberal principles commonly agreed to and embodied in the Constitution of 1857 and in the state constitutions. Local liberals generally acted on the premise that strict adherence to these fundamental laws was the surest guarantee of the right of each locality to work out its own future.

National liberals turned increasingly to the relaxation of liberal principles and to the expansion of authority. Coalescing around Juárez, Lerdo, and Díaz into political parties, the imperatives of national politics led them to seek increasing centralization of power and interference at the state and local level in order to insure their position nationally. From time to time they drew the line in defense of liberal principles. Often they did so because they could compromise the ideals of their young adulthood only so far. At other times they did so opportunistically as a pragmatic means to check their rivals. Sometimes both motives intertwined.

Liberals in control of state government found themselves somewhere in between. They espoused liberalism in their resistance to encroachment on their power by national political interests. Yet they advocated greater central authority within the state to promote the general good in their resistance to local efforts to restrict their power. They were caught most in the contradiction between liberalism and nationalism.

SONORA'S LIBERAL TRUSTEE: INCREASINGLY OUT OF FAVOR

Governor Pesqueira and his followers believed, or at least publicly claimed, that *he* was the trustee of liberalism in Sonora. Only the person who implanted liberal principles in the state and institutionalized them, the *pesqueiristas* said, could nurture their growth to full maturity. The people were not yet enlightened enough to preserve these liberal institutions themselves. As a consequence, Pesqueira and his followers concluded, it was essential that he remain in power as a strong executive until the general populace could be educated and habituated sufficiently to manage and maintain these institutions themselves, until enough progress and political stability could be achieved to make that transfer of authority possible.

In contrast, the *pesqueiristas* claimed, the opposition was impeding this slow, difficult process, even threatening to undo it. The governor seems to have had serious doubts about whether the urban notables, with whom he came into conflict in the legislature and the municipios, really had the interests of the general populace at heart. These local liberals from prominent

---

[14]*Ibid.*, 221.

families were concerned only with the promotion of their own private interests and the preservation of their domination over their communities. It was Pesqueira's view that from among their numbers the core of the opposition originated.[15] The disruption that the opposition was fomenting in the state, the *pesqueiristas* said, was preventing the governor from maintaining the peaceful and orderly flow of political life necessary for the people to internalize the liberal principles of the Reforma. It was also impeding the government's efforts to obtain ample revenues to educate the general populace so as to enable them to make the liberal institutions work. Likewise, national liberals were restricting state income by absorbing revenues to educate the general populace so as to enable them to make the liberal institutions work. Likewise, national liberals were restricting state income by absorbing revenues and denying appeals for assistance, while at the same time interfering in state affairs through abuse of authority (Juárez and Lerdo) or demogoguery (Díaz). All these actions were resulting in growing disorder and factionalism.[16]

The *pesqueiristas* did not deny that there were other patriotic, honorable persons among those who wished to rule. But only Pesqueira, they contended, had the prestige and influence necessary to contain the forces for disorder by resisting factionalism within the liberal party, demagoguery among those hungry for personal power, and encroachment by federal authorities.[17] The governor and his followers thus rationalized the need for his continuance in office, for his trusteeship over the new liberal order in Sonora. The opposition, be it national or local, they told the populace (and themselves), threatened to undo all the governor had accomplished in bringing liberalism and progress to Sonora, to prevent him from permanently implanting these values in the state. Pesqueira's growing problem was that the opposition was telling the people a different story, and more and more of them seemed to be listening.

Not surprisingly, the opposition to Pesqueira had germinated among the prominent families of Alamos. Never having dominated state government themselves, the notables of that colonial mining town had always upheld local prerogative and control. They had been among the last to abandon the ill-fated state of Occidente, endeavoring until the end to make it work as an alliance among the various urban centers and districts in the Northwest, which would prevent any one of them from securing its own interests at the others' expense. Such a political union, centered in southern Sonora and northern Sinaloa, had also offered them the most likely support in their relations with the nearby tribal Indians. For the next two decades, the gentry of Alamos had vigorously supported federalism to prevent the centralization

---

[15] *El Eco de Sonora,* March 27, 1871.
[16] *Ibid.,* February 20 and March 6, 27, 1871.
[17] *Ibid.,* March 27 and April 17, 1871.

of power and damage to their interests implied in the alliance of the *gandaristas* with the tribal Indians and centralists. When in the mid-1850s this conflict flared up again and was transformed into a theater of the national civil war between liberals and conservatives, *alamense* notables had formed the cornerstone of Pesqueira's liberal coalition. They contributed liberally in money and supplies and produced a covey of young military officers to assist the governor in his efforts to rid the state of the *gandaristas* and to subdue the tribal Indians. Miguel Urrea, then their titular head, had been made substitute (vice-) governor in 1857 as a symbol of that alliance.[18]

The honeymoon had not endured for long, however. The prominent families of Alamos had concurred with Pesqueira in the importance of securing Sinaloa for the liberal cause as insurance against a conservative counterrevolution in Sonora. More than half the troops, officers, and supplies of the Sinaloan expedition of 1858 to 1859 were furnished by the town. But when the governor proposed to go to Sinaloa to lead the campaign personally, *alamense* notables balked. Led by Urrea and the venerable José María Almada, long the defender of the town's interests, they called the plan extravagant in view of the continuing threats to Sonora's own security, in particular that of another uprising by the Yaquis and Mayos. They had not given Pesqueira a blank check. They were not willing to take on the additional burden.

Among themselves, they began to wonder aloud whether they had not brought to power another Gándara. Why else, they reasoned, would he personally go to Sinaloa to receive the title of provisional governor of that state if not to satisfy his own personal ambition? And where would that ambition lead next? Besides, though they were largely footing the bill, it was people like Manuel Monteverde, Cirilo Ramírez, and the Escalantes of Hermosillo, the Morales brothers of Ures, and the Robinsons of Guaymas who seemed to have Pesqueira's ear. In protest, Urrea refused to take charge of the government during the governor's absence.

Through the official newspaper the government had then begun to label the *alamense* gentry egotists and hypocrites and to question their patriotism for holding back on their underwriting of the state treasury. The following year (1860), Urrea resigned in protest against the administration's policies and the accusations hurled at his friends. *Alamenses,* he said, had over the previous four years contributed more than 85,000 pesos over and above the

---

[18] Almada, 812-813. The aging patriarch of the Almadas, Don José María, had stepped aside in favor of Urrea, the more youthful husband of his niece Justina. During the previous decade Urrea had lived alternately in Alamos and Chínipas, just across the border in Chihuahua. He had acquired the mines of Palmarejo near that Chihuahuan town in 1845 and had set up two *haciendas de beneficio* (ore reduction works). He also had served as the *jefe político* (prefect) of that *canton* (district) for a couple of years and had prepared a statistical survey of mining in that district, which was published in the *Boletín* of the Sociedad Mexicana de Geografía y Estadística. But in the mid-1850s, with the growing struggle for power resuming in earnest in Sonora, he had returned to Sonora.

ordinary contributions assigned them. They were tired of paying the high taxes, extraordinary contributions, and forced loans required to sustain Pesqueira's militant administration, an administration that seemed tailored only to his ambitions and not to their interests.

The next year, with his reelection at stake, Pesqueira moved to close the breach. He again offered the position of substitute governor to Urrea. The latter, supported by the leading figures of Alamos, laid down conditions for his acceptance: after this term, the governor was not to seek further reelection; the secretary of government, Manuel Monteverde, was to be replaced; and the continuous exactions arbitrarily imposed on the commerce and mining of the town (to which the governor had always turned when in fiscal straits) were to cease. Pesqueira acceded to the concessions. Once reelected, however, he pursued his former course of regarding Alamos as an inexhaustible source of government revenues. Thoroughly disgusted, Urrea quit the political arena altogether, retiring to his mining interests in neighboring Chihuahua. Pesqueira from then on viewed the prominent families of Alamos with suspicion and ill-will. The feeling was mutual.

A few months later, Pesqueira committed the ultimate affront to *alamense* notables. In putting down the Estevez Revolt, government forces had captured one of José María Almada's two sons, who had affiliated with the rebels. The other son had been killed in battle. Hotheaded, and lured by the commission of captain, they had unwisely joined the revolt. The governor released all of the prisoners but the young Almada, whom he sentenced to death. The whole town was stunned. An ill-considered choice of political loyalties by a member of a prominent family, especially an Almada, did not warrant capital punishment. Fearing a riot, Pesqueira even refused to allow the condemned youth to take leave of his relatives.

The break with Pesqueira had thereafter been complete for the branch of the Almada family and for many of their in-laws and friends. When the time was right, they joined the imperialist cause, led by the patriarch's son, José María Tranquilino Almada, and succeeded in capturing and holding the district for Emperor Maximilian. The other Almada branches and the vast majority of the *alamense* gentry, including the embittered Urrea in nearby Chínipas, remained loyal to the Republic. They contributed liberally, sending many of their sons and considerable money and supplies to nearby republican forces.[19] Nevertheless, they had fought for Juárez and the liberal constitu-

---

[19] Sources for the above narrative summary of the *alamense* notables' alienation from the Pesqueira administration include: Almada, 812-813; Acosta, 164-165, 181; Miles, 20-25, 32-56; Corbalá Acuña, *Alamos,* 78-80, 90-91; Stagg, *Almadas of Alamos,* 94-107. To add further insult, Pesqueira had arrested José María Almada, charging him with inciting the new Mayo uprising which had recently erupted in response to the Estevez Revolt. Through the active intercession of one of his nephews, Bartolomé E. Almada, recently elected to the Congress, and because of the rather spurious evidence against

tion, not for Ignacio Pesqueira. When Maximilian and the French were defeated and constitutional government once more restored, they turned their attention and efforts toward his retirement from Sonora's political life.

Alamense notables saw people like themselves, the prominent families of Sonora's important communities, as the true defenders of liberalism. The state required no trustee or guardian. What it needed were more upholders of liberal principles like themselves, principles which, they said, were being subverted by the governor for his own political ambitions and self-esteem. *He* was the encroaching "national" authority for them.

There was no challenge to Pesqueira in the 1867 elections. The prestige and popularity resulting from the recent triumph over the imperialists made him too formidable. But the notables of Alamos hoped at least to fence in his ambitions in the legislative chambers. Up to that point the *alamenses* had been the heart and soul of the opposition, and most of its hands and feet as well. Now, in the state legislature their elected representatives found willing allies. Some diputados—such as Domingo Elías González and Ricardo Johnson of Guaymas, and Francisco C. Aguilar of Ures—had by then also broken with the governor. A far larger number, though they continued to support Pesqueira for governor in the elections, did not hesitate to cooperate in curbing the state executive's efforts to enlarge his power and the government's revenues at their own expense and that of the municipios they represented. Chief among them were the veteran liberals Jesús Quijada of Ures and Francisco Morena Buelna of Hermosillo, Román Román of Moctezuma, and a young lawyer from Guaymas, Ramón Martínez, who had previously seen service on the bench.[20]

The third legislature (1867-1869), composed in great part of the leading liberals from the various towns of the state, was quick to demonstrate its independence from the governor. The Sonoran constitution of 1861 had transferred to the legislature the power over judicial appointments, which had formerly been shared by the executive and the now defunct council of government. When Pesqueira made strong observations concerning its appointments to the supreme tribunal and judges of the first instance (state district courts), the legislature overrode his objections. (The several constitutions of Sonora, including that of 1861, empowered the governor to make observations, or objections, to any bills passed by the legislature. He did not, as in United States constitutional law, either veto or approve the whole piece of legislation, though he could in his observations object to all parts of the bills

---

him, the elder Almada succeeded in obtaining his release from jail in a few months, but only after paying the government 10,000 pesos as a "donation." In November, 1864, he moved to Mazatlán, right after that port had been taken by the French.

[20] Almada, 240-636 *passim;* Corbalá Acuña, *Constituciones,* 89, 256-258; Acuña, 97-98.

sent to him for promulgation by the legislature. His vetoing power was, thus, only over those parts of a bill to which he made formal objection. The legislature could override any observations made by the executive.)

The resignation of General García Morales as substitute governor, due to his being named military commander of the state, sparked a struggle over the naming of his successor. The governor wanted Manuel Monteverde, then his principal political associate. A majority of the diputados favored José Pesqueira (a young cousin of the governor's), who was a merchant in Guaymas and an erstwhile soldier in the national guard who had attained the rank of lieutenant colonel. After months of wrangling, including long periods in which the legislature lacked a quorum as a consequence of walkouts on both sides, the governor succeeded in cajoling a bare majority of six to vote for Monteverde.[21]

The disagreements between the executive and the legislature over fiscal matters had political, as well as economic, implications. Surrounding the dispute over who should and would bear what burden of taxation were more fundamental issues: the distribution of political power involved in the procedures for raising the revenues and the possibilities for greater governmental initiative in their expenditures. These underlying points of contention, more than any specific issue that arose through the course of the third legislature's sessions, galvanized dissenting diputados into an opposition group.[22] They began to accuse Governor Pesqueira of absolutist tendencies and of attempting to absorb powers and prerogatives specifically delegated to the legislature and the municipios.[23] In the closing session, they initiated a series of constitutional reforms, which, if given final passage by a succeeding legislature, would profoundly alter the division of political power in the state.[24]

One of the reforms provided for the popular election of the vice-governor (the prior nomenclature having been restored), the magistrates of the supreme tribunal, and the judges of the first instance (all formerly chosen by the legislature), and the prefects (previously appointed by the governor). Of even greater import was the reform which prohibited the immediate reelection of the governor, vice-governor, and prefects. Included in this proscription was an

---

[21] Acuña, 98-99.

[22] *El Pueblo de Sonora* (Ures), February 4, 1868.

[23] Corbalá Acuña, *Constituciones,* 89-90.

[24] *El Pueblo Sonorense* (Ures), December 6, 1872. The constitutional reforms were initiated on May 25, 1869, by the following members of the third legislature: Francisco Moreno Buelna (Hermosillo), president; Ramón Martínez (Ures), vice-president; Francisco C. Aguilar (alternate, Alamos) and Román Román (alternate, Hermosillo), secretaries; Domingo Elías González (Arizpe); Gabriel Corella (Guaymas); Adolfo Esquer (Alamos); Jesús Quijada (Ures); José Aragón (Moctezuma); José María Vélez Escalante (Hermosillo); Ricardo Johnson (Guaymas); and Jesús Morales (alternate, Sahuaripa). For some reason not explained in the sources consulted, Hermosillo district was represented by an extra diputado (three, instead of the normal two) in the third legislature.

even tighter restriction which prevented the vice-governor from seeking the office of governor in the next term. This constraint eliminated the possibility of alternating control of the executive by two individuals. Another important reform was the extension of direct election to all offices of the state. Previously, only local officeholders had been so selected. The power of the executive was also further abridged. One reform restricted its authority to impose correction punishment. Another empowered the president of the legislature to sanction and promulgate laws when the governor failed to do so in the specified time, which the reform also reduced to three days.[25]

The impact of these reforms was far-reaching. Direct elections would sharply curb the state executive's ability to influence, if not manipulate, the elections, and place their conduct much more firmly in the hands of the municipios. The damage done to the Pesqueira regime by the prohibition against immediate reelection of state executive officeholders was obvious, but the most devastating blow to Pesqueira's efforts to extend his control over the state was the reform pertaining to the prefects. Their popular election would shift control over those district executives from the governor to the district towns and the notables who dominated them.

The outcome of the 1869 elections was of great consequence because of the formation of an opposition nucleus in the legislature and the constitutional reforms it initiated. From among this nucleus came a candidate to challenge Pesqueira's reelection. Ricardo Johnson, a diputado from Guaymas, was a mining entrepreneur. Over the previous decade, he had successfully begun to exploit the numerous holdings his father had acquired around San Marcial (east of Guaymas and south of Hermosillo) in the post-independence years. (The elder Johnson, the North American trader based in Oposura who had gained renown as an Indian-fighter, had died on the last of several trips to the California gold fields.)[26] Though now a person of considerable means, young Ricardo lacked the prestige of an established family and prominent service in the liberal, republican cause. More importantly, there was as yet no formal organization to fuse the growing numbers of disgruntled citizens of various parts of the state. Johnson carried only the districts of Alamos and Moctezuma.[27]

---

[25]*Ibid.*, November 29 and December 6, 1872; Corbalá Acuña, *Constituciones*, 108-137.

[26]Strickland, 267, 283-284. An active and expert mining prospector, Ricardo Johnson had inherited and purchased what would become the most important mines in the Minas Prietas mining district: those of Minas Prietas proper and the nearby Creston, Santa Cruz, and Colorado mines. For a number of years, financed by Ortiz Brothers of Hermosillo, he worked the mines with varying degrees of success. In the 1880s, he sold the mines to several North American investors at a handsome profit. The four Minas Prietas mines brought $150,000; the Creston, Santa Cruz, and Colorado mines $200,000. Southworth, *El Estado de Sonora*, 50.

[27]Villa, 310.

Of greater consequence was the setback the opposition received in the voting for the legislature. Only Ramón Martínez (for the district of Sahuaripa), Román Román (for Moctezuma), and Francisco Moreno Buelna (for Alamos) were reelected. They were joined by a new opposition representative from Alamos, Adolfo Almada. The other diputados, all newcomers,[28] proved to be far less contrary to the governor's wishes. They willingly decided to shelve the constitutional reforms in their opening sessions. They explained to the citizenry that they desired to know the opinion of the other branches of government and of the municipalities before taking action on them. The supreme tribunal answered favorably, as did all those ayuntamientos who responded. The executive branch demurred public comment. However, its feelings were conveyed quite plainly to individual diputados. The fourth legislature kept the reforms on the shelf. It did continue to have differences with the governor on fiscal matters, but even there, the budget was permitted to rise by twenty-one percent over the two-year period.[29]

In the next elections, held in 1871, the opposition made a concerted effort to reverse Governor Pesqueira's increasing domination of Sonoran politics. Their candidate was well-known, a potent challenger with credentials as a champion of the liberal cause against the conservatives and imperialists at least as illustrious as Pesqueira's: General Jesús García Morales, the governor's own brother-in-law. The general had been Pesqueira's right arm during the Reform War and the Intervention, a stature acknowledged in his election to the office of substitute governor at the war's conclusion. But his acceptance soon afterwards of the federal appointment as military commander of the state in time eroded their political association. The two former compañeros found themselves more and more on opposite sides of frequent disputes between Mexico City and the Sonoran government. They parted company and went their separate and increasingly conflicting ways.[30] In García Morales, the opposition was able to neutralize Pesqueira's accustomed reliance on his past glories. They could zero in on the issue of no reelection.[31]

Nonetheless, once again organization was pitifully lacking, and García Morales was able to add to Johnson's previous success in the districts of Alamos and Moctezuma only one or two electors in some of the other districts. Pesqueira was reelected by the sizable margin of 165 to 51.[32] The opposition learned from the election that they were not only lacking in organization, but

---

[28]Corbalá Acuña, *Constituciones,* 256-258.

[29]*La Estrella de Occidente,* April 25, 1873; *La Regeneración,* July 20, 1876. See Chapter 7 for details on the fiscal question.

[30]Acuña, 109. Ties were most probably also loosened by the death of Morales's sister in late 1865 and Pesqueira's remarriage two years later. Almada, 578, 583.

[31]*El Eco de Sonora,* April 6, 1871.

[32]Corral, 86.

were also deficient in political muscle. The pesqueiristas' manipulative tactics in the capital itself clearly illustrated that fact.

The oppositionists in Ures had succeeded in winning the municipal elections the previous fall (1870). This victory carried considerable import for state and federal elections, since these were conducted under the auspices of the ayuntamientos. Two years prior to that, the *pesqueiristas*, then in control of municipal government, had issued a prohibition against public parades or demonstrations by political groups. The opposition had observed the ban even though it was directed against them in the previous state elections. Following that precedent, the oppositionist ayuntamiento had passed a few regulations of its own concerning the approaching state elections: political groups were required to notify the municipal authorities of the day and hour of their scheduled meetings so that "the best order might be kept"; the carrying of arms to those meetings was prohibited; anyone trying to disrupt the meetings was to be arrested and fined; and public parades after such political meetings were prohibited. The parades were banned, the ayuntamiento reasoned, because of the difficulty in maintaining the order required of the municipal authorities with the exultations of the political groups in the streets and plazas. It was particularly difficult at that time in view of the strife and ill-feelings it said had arisen in the last municipal elections and the frequent disorders occasioned by the crowing of political groups in the recent past. This was the rationale also given for the other restrictions on the conduct of political meetings and rallies.

The *pesqueiristas* had immediately complained to the district prefect, Rafael A. Corella. Appointed by the governor (and one of his loyal subordinates), Corella ordered the suspension of the regulations. The ayuntamiento then just as quickly appealed to the governor to reject the reelectionists' complaint when it was forwarded to him and, in the meantime, to order the prefect not to interfere in the municipal government's dispositions. The prefect, it contended, had no right to suspend its determinations until the state government had ruled against them and ordered their suspension by the prefect. Not unexpectedly, Governor Pesqueira ordered the dispositions derogated, citing the constitutional right to bear arms and the guarantee of free assembly and interpreting the request for information concerning the time and place of meeting as a requirement of approval by the municipal authorities. Far more damaging was the governor's confirmation of the prefect's order for the prior suspension of the disposition. Worse still, Pesqueira removed from office those members of the ayuntamiento who had approved the electoral regulations. In so doing, he had given his reelectionist supporters control once more over the local government and, thus, the state elections in the capital.[33]

---

[33] *El Voto Libre* (Ures), May 19, 1871.

Following the state primary elections some weeks later, the opposition newspaper in Ures caustically reported that few voters in the capital had participated. In some voting precincts only eight or ten showed up. In others, there were insufficient voters for the elections even to be held. "The citizens," it explained, "no longer have any faith in their rights, because they have been destroyed by the attacks aimed at them." The excesses committed by the reelectionist party, especially those abuses perpetrated against the opposition, the paper said, had convinced capital residents that voting would serve them little, considering the advantage held by the government's partisans.[34]

The gubernatorial electoral effort had proven to be an exercise in futility; for some, one of persecution. Once again Pesqueira had relied on his image as the knightly defender of Sonoran liberalism. Had he not, his supporters reminded the voting public, been the one who had led them out of the chaotic times of Gándara and the civil wars, the one who had turned back the forces of reaction and intervention? And if that was so, was now the occasion to switch leaders in such still troubled times? [35]

The governor's image was becoming tarnished, however. He was finding it more and more necessary to resort to manipulation of the state's liberal political institutions to maintain his governmental authority and political predominance. The electoral struggle in Ures was indicative. Nonetheless, the opposition was as yet unable to convince a majority of the state that he was a power-hungry tyrant to be voted down. The elections were a lesson to the opposition that most Sonorans still might very well accept Governor Pesqueira's justifications for his continuance in office. And even if they did not, as events in the capital seem to connote, it was evident that few yet felt angry enough or pushed around enough to oppose him.

A CONSTITUTIONAL CHALLENGE IN SONORA

Pesqueira's mastery of the state executive would continue, but his relations with the legislature would not be so easy. Despite their losses in the gubernatorial race, the opposition scored major gains in the legislative body. Ardent oppositionists, like Adolfo Almada (Alamos) and Jesús Quijada (Ures), were returned. They were joined by newcomers Jesús Corella (Altar), Leopoldo Gil Samaniego (Alamos), and Francisco Hernández (Moctezuma). Two other diputados, the veteran Ramón Martínez (this time representing Sahuaripa) and first-termer Juan Antúñez (Ures),[36] had supported the combined candidacies of Pesqueira and Juárez in the state and federal elections, as

---

[34]*Ibid.*, June 30, 1871.
[35]*El Eco de Sonora,* March 27 and April 17, 1871.
[36]Corbalá Acuña, *Constituciones,* 258.

members of a political club in the capital (the Asociación de la Paz).[37] Nevertheless, they wasted no time in manifesting their independence, combining with the other five diputados to form a working independent majority. They were able to compromise the executive's railroad concession policies, contain the previous two-year escalation of the budget, and repeal the extraordinary powers granted the governor to assist in quelling the La Noria Revolt in Sinaloa. They succeeded in the latter case, even though Pesqueira was correct in his claim that the rebellion had not yet been completely suppressed.[38]

These successful legislative skirmishes, nevertheless, were over policy matters. They did not fundamentally alter the political power balance. Given their continuing defeats in the gubernatorial elections, the opposition understood that only the constitutional reforms (initiated when they last dominated the legislature) would do that. But the timing for taking up the reforms had to be right. The independent diputados constituted only a bare majority of the thirteen-member legislature. Passage of any constitutional reforms required a two-thirds majority.

In the fall of 1872, the opportunity came. Two of the *pesqueirista* legislators, Pedro García Tato and Próspero Salazar Bustamante, had temporarily taken other offices to assist in the governor's Sinaloan campaign. They were replaced by their *suplentes*, Benigno V. García and Leopoldo Valencia, both independents. Under the 1861 constitution, the candidate with the second highest number of votes (who was often the successful candidate's political rival) became the alternate. In this case, both García and Valencia had been active challengers to the *pesqueirista* slate. Even though Alamos diputado Gil Samaniego was absent that fall also, the addition of the two alternates gave the independents the necessary eight votes to act on constitutional questions. Their task was made easier by the nonattendance of two other *pesqueirista* legislators. Joaquín M. Astiazarán (the substitute governor and now close associate of Pesqueira) had taken a leave of absence, while Joaquín Corella was seriously ill.

In the midst of a fall recess, the president of the legislature, Jesús Quijada, called the body into extraordinary session on November 1 to consider final passage of the constitutional reforms. Rafael Corella, who had been present at the regular sessions, refused to attend. That left Carlos I. Velasco as the lone *pesqueirista* legislator to oppose the adoption of the reforms. Caught off guard by the parliamentary maneuver, he could muster coherent, detailed objections to only some of the reforms. All of the reforms were duly approved that same day and sent to the governor for their promulgation on

---

[37]*El Eco de Sonora,* april 17, 1871.
[38]Corral, 99-100.

December 1, to take effect that day. Even Velasco gave his signature to the sanctioning of the reforms, most likely because of the awkwardness of his situation.[39]

In giving final passage to the constitutional reforms, the independent legislative majority laid down an uncompromisable challenge to Pesqueira's hegemony over the state that made any further coexistence between the governor and the opposition impossible. As a result, most Sonorans, who had remained neutral or indifferent, were forced off the political fence they had been straddling since the Intervention. That fence had also been ideological.

The constitutional reforms were the logical institutionalization of the liberal principles Sonorans had come to accept as the basis for their society. Those of the opposition who had been pushing for their incorporation had come to believe them mandatory for the preservation of the new liberal order in the face of the authoritarian, centralizing tendencies of the state executive. Those of the *pesqueirista* party, who had increasingly tried to table the reforms, had come to believe them decisive in the opposition's deliberate attempt to undermine the balance between liberal principles and the requirements of authority to promote the state's welfare. The neutral majority until then had been able to overlook the extremes of this conflicting interpretation of the political reality and to maintain a common ground between them based on their belief that the state's liberal institutions were not out of harmony with the demands and intentions of its governmental authority. But the sanctioning of the constitutional reforms accelerated and brought out into the open the contradiction that had been emerging since the Intervention, so that it became difficult, if not impossible, to straddle or reconcile that contradiction any longer.

The opposition would no longer tolerate the compromise of one iota of what it considered to be the full institutional expression of liberalism, and it would now employ whatever legal means were available or creatable to root those liberal principles firmly in the political order. Likewise, Pesqueira and his followers were not willing to resort to whatever expedients were required, even if arbitrary, to uphold the government's authority against all challenges. The promotion of what it deemed the state's welfare in the face of what it considered self-interested demagogues now took precedence over the strict adherence to liberal principles. Very rapidly, the middle ground eroded.

The *pesqueiristas* quickly moved to quash the constitutional revolution that had just been pulled off. Diputados García Tato and Bustamante reclaimed

---

[39]*El Pueblo Sonorense,* November 29 and December 6, 1872. Pedro Garcia Tato was temporarily serving as head of the *aduana* in Guaymas in place of the federally appointed administrator, who had been removed by Governor Pesqueira for withholding revenues which the governor claimed rightfully belonged to the state government in recompense for its part in the Sinaloan campaign. Próspero Salazar Bustamante was serving in that campaign as a colonel in the national guard.

their seats. Astiazarán ended his leave of absence, joined by Rafael Corella, who terminated his boycott. Governor Pesqueira astutely utilized the only legal maneuver that might prove defensible. He returned the constitutional reforms with a note of observations on November 14. If the objections were accepted, as with the case of statute law, they would need to be overridden by a two-thirds majority, which the opposition no longer possessed. But the president of the legislature, the experienced Jesús Quijada, was too shrewd to let the maneuver slip through. The next day he countered by proposing the *tramite* (procedural action) of rejecting the governor's observations on the grounds that they were unconstitutional. Nowhere in that part of the existing constitution detailing the procedures for its reform, Quijada argued, could there be found any mention of the governor being empowered to make such observations, as he was specifically entitled to do on statute legislation. The *tramite* called for the observations to be returned to the governor, along with the previously sanctioned constitutional reforms for their promulgation.

The independent diputados had counted heads and knew they had the votes (six to five) to pass Quijada's proposal, since only a simple majority was required for procedural matters. But the *pesqueirista* legislators finessed them. Before a vote could be taken, Velasco walked out, quickly followed by the four other supporters of the governor. They had not been remiss in their arithmetic, either. Since there was now no quorum, no vote on the procedural question could be taken. The *pesqueirista* diputados, however, in their hasty exit had left their opponents one loophole: the right of members of the legislature in session to compel those absent to attend or, upon refusal, to call their alternates. The independents immediately summoned Benigno V. García, the only *suplente* then in the capital (and conveniently a fellow independent), and thereby attained a quorum. The procedural motion was approved the following day (November 16, 1872).[40]

Despite its legality, Governor Pesqueira refused to respect the legislature's action. So the seven independent diputados met on December 5 to promulgate the constitutional reforms. However, the resolve of one of them had weakened. To the chagrin of the other six, the heretofore resolute Juan Antuñez declared that he would not vote to promulgate the reforms because the governor, who normally undertook the official publication of new laws, had not done so. Perhaps he had been treating with the other side. Most likely, as a true independent (not an oppositionist like all the others but Martínez), as a permanent resident of Ures, and as a member of the Juárez-Pesqueira political club during the previous election, he simply could not go

---

[40]*Ibid.;* Corral, 101-102. García was the alternate for Pedro G. Tato. One justification for replacing Tato in particular was his final remark as he walked out of the chambers on the 15th: "Before I will vote for this *tramite*, I will retire and protest, because the reforms are in essence a rebellion, and I will not agree to deal with this matter any further." *El Pueblo Sonorense*, December 6, 1872.

as far as the others politically. Whatever the precise motivation, Antúnez withdrew from the chambers, leaving the others again without a quorum.

Powerless now to do anything, the remaining diputados went public to rally support. They dissolved the legislature and issued a public manifesto explaining that they had done so because the governor's intransigence had, in effect, left the reforms suspended. They then took their case to the general public through an independent newspaper, *El Pueblo Sonorense*, which printed the minutes of the extraordinary session to counter the executive's version of the conflict in the official newspaper. They were seconded energetically by opposition newspapers in Alamos, Guaymas, and Hermosillo.[41] More than three hundred citizens of Alamos sent a vote of thanks through that town's ayuntamiento to the independent diputados who had approved the constitutional reforms.[42] Adolfo Almada and Jesús Corella were sent to Mexico City to consult the noted jurists Rafael Martínez de la Torre, Ezequiel Montes, and Francisco Gómez del Palacio about the constitutional questions involved in the dispute. The three jurists opined that the executive had no power to make observations to any such reforms, and their opinion was widely circulated in the state by the opposition.[43]

The Pesqueira administration, meanwhile, in a similar fashion was trying to mobilize public opinion against the reforms. The official newspaper printed the governor's observations as the core of its case against their necessity and appropriateness. Pesqueira contended that the reforms were conceived in a time of emotion, "when the fever of partisans had replaced disinterested patriotism," and that it was his understanding they had been judged unfavorably by public opinion.

In particular, the governor opposed direct election for state offices because of "the state of learning in which our masses find themselves." The general populace was not fully prepared for the full exercise of liberal institutions. The great majority of the citizenry lacked enough public instruction to judge the aptitudes and qualifications of persons for public office. The electoral colleges were generally composed of "the most enlightened persons of each population, and thus most capable of electing those citizens most qualified for the offices."

Secondly, those reforms limiting the power of the executive, Pesqueira argued, would diminish its authority. That authority was requisite for the protection of constitutional guarantees, for the trusteeship of liberal princi-

---

[41] Corral, 102; *La Estrella de Occidente,* April 25, 1873. The six independent diputados were joined on December 5 by Leopoldo Valencia, the alternate for Próspero S. Bustamante, instead of *suplente* Benigno V. García, who had joined the six on November 16.

[42] *El Pueblo Sonorense,* January 3, 1873.

[43] Corral, 102.

ples that was necessary until the preparation of the general populace was adequate to permit their full institutionalization.

The reform prohibiting the vice-governor from being elected governor in the following term, Pesqueira reasoned, was in fact a circumscription of individual rights. It deprived the person occupying that office of the right granted to every other citizen (except the incumbent) to be governor. This reform, he charged, was aimed only at suppressing the opportunity for the incumbent governor to possibly occupy the office (as acting governor, after being elected vice-governor) during the period between two elected terms. Furthermore, it was being deliberately promoted by a particular party for its own interests. This reform was important to Pesqueira, since in his observations he had not objected to the prohibition against the governor's immediate reelection. He apparently realized that such a concession was by now a political necessity. His continued reelection had become so unpopular that to oppose the prohibition was no longer tenable.

Governor Pesqueira saved the most fire for the reform calling for the election of the prefects. The executive, he said, "ought to have complete freedom to name and remove his agents. In any other manner administrative unity would disappear; the Executive would be impotent to insure that the law was fully observed." What Pesqueira meant in practical terms was that the prefects were the principal agents to do his bidding, to contain and reduce the power of the municipios. In particular this objection connoted the utilization of the prefects to thwart the designs of opponents who, as municipal authorities, could undercut his power and quite possibly prevent his future reelection. The popular election of the prefects, which would deprive the governor of the power to remove them, would make them independent officials from whom the ayuntamientos could secure the support to restrict or circumvent his authority. Indeed, the reforms as a whole, Pesqueira concluded, tended "in their essence to constrict the attributions of the branch which, more than any other, needs complete freedom of action in order to fulfill its ends." [44]

To convince the public of the rightness of its cause, the Pesqueira administration encouraged the ayuntamientos to issue protests against the constitutional reforms. *La Estrella* and the newspapers loyal to Pesqueira attacked

---

[44] *La Estrella de Occidente,* November 22, 1872. The governor also contended that the reform reducing the period for making observations to three days was impractical, since the executive had only one secretary to assist him. Worse still, the power given the president of the legislature to promulgate the law if the governor had not made his observations in the allotted time would obligate the executive to sanction the laws "irremissibly." Furthermore, it infringed on the executive's prerogatives.

In a follow-up editorial in *La Estrella* on February 14, 1873, the example of Sinaloa was given as a case in point of what would happen if the prefects were elected, rather than appointed by the governor. The editorial said such election of prefects was the origin of the revolutions and disorders which had plagued that state almost every year since the Intervention.

them vigorously. The governor pulled out all the stops. He well knew that his seventeen-year domination of state politics was ended if the reforms ever became law in fact.[45]

While the state executive orchestrated its propaganda organs into *allegro fortissimo*, it determined to fashion its own legislature to bestow legitimacy on its actions and illegality on those of its opponents. On December 10, 1872, though they did not constitute a quorum, the five *pesqueirista* legislators called the alternates of three independent legislators and, with them, declared the legislature reconvened. The independent diputados, refusing to participate in what they considered an illegally constituted legislative body, left the capital. The legislature thus formed by the *pesqueirista* diputados declared null and void the procedural motion of November 16 (which had returned the governor's observations) and then sent the observations to committee for study.[46]

The following April the constitutional reforms were brought before the full legislature for consideration, and the committee reported favorably on each of the governor's observations. The effect of the observations was to eliminate all of the major reforms except that prohibiting the reelection of the governor.[47] Meanwhile, independent diputados Martínez, Almada, and Hernández had returned to the legislative sessions. So, too, had Juan Antúnez, who seems to have had another change of heart. All four in most instances voted together to uphold the reforms approved the previous November and to oppose the governor's observations to them (which were approved by the *pesqueirista* majority on April 22).[48] The ambivalent Antúnez, however, joined the six diputados loyal to the governor in signing the new reformed constitution; together they provided the two-thirds majority required for final passage. Martínez, Hernández, and Almada refused to sign. The legitimate reformed constitution, they said, was that approved the previous November. The new, reformed constitution was promulgated May 31, 1873, and was to become effective the following September 16, a day after the newly elected governor would be installed. This arrangement conveniently permitted Pesqueira's reelection.[49]

The governor, after many months, had succeeded in foiling the first serious threat by the opposition to break his tenure over the state executive. He did

---

[45] Corral, 103. The resulting protests against the constitutional reforms came principally from *municipios* in the central and northeast parts of the state, in the districts of Hermosillo, Ures, Arizpe, and Moctezuma. *La Estrella de Occidente*, April 11, 1873.

[46] Corral, 103.

[47] *Ibid.;* Almada, 181.

[48] *La Estrella de Occidente*, May 2, 1873.

[49] Corral, 103; Almada, 181.

not intend to go through such a close call again. In the elections that summer, Pesqueira was determined not only that there be no serious opposition to his reelection, but that, in addition, a legislature subservient to his wishes be selected. Or, as the official newspaper so diplomatically chose to express it in one of its editorials, a legislature that would "clear away from the executive all of the obstacles which have impeded him from unfolding his beneficent action."[50]

The demoralized antagonists of the government could muster little opposition. That part of the citizenry sympathetic to their cause or still neutral had little faith left in election after constitutional reforms had been overturned so high-handedly. The Pesqueira administration, its control over the situation fully restored, used its agents to insure that whatever opposition did muster was only token.[51] In the electoral college Pesqueira received 211 votes. A lone elector from Guaymas voted for a political unknown, Antonio Loustanau.[52] None of the independent diputados was reelected. Even in Alamos district, *pesqueirista* legislators were chosen.[53] The governor's triumph was conclusive.

The contradiction between liberalism and central authority had become so distended that many among the opposition came to believe that the profanation of the former by the Pesqueira regime released them from the obligation to respect the latter. Some concluded that the subversion of the constitutional reforms and the thorough manipulation of the state elections constituted a license to work to overthrow the Pesqueira administration for so abusing state authority. The governor's triumph was thus qualified and increasingly pyrrhic. From then on he ruled less and less by consent, more and more by manipulation and coercion. Professions of commitment to liberal principles became mere empty propaganda. Recourse to the arbitrary exercise of authority became indispensible.

A few days after his inauguration in mid-September, Governor Pesqueira's growing sense of security received a sudden jolt. Carlos Connant, a rather obscure figure, who had seconded the the La Noria Revolt and attained the rank of lieutenant colonel fighting with the *porfirista* rebels in Durango, pronounced against the government in the southern mining center of Promontorios.[54] He and his three hundred or so followers proclaimed the constitutional reforms of November, 1872, to be in force and declared the Pesqueira administration thereby illegal. Connant's forces quickly occupied nearby Alamos, whose numerous oppositionists were sympathetic to the cause of the

[50] *La Estrella de Occidente,* May 30, 1872.
[51] *La Regeneración,* July 20, 1876.
[52] *La Estrella de Occidente,* October 3, 1873.
[53] Corbalá Acuña, *Constituciones,* 259.
[54] Almada, 171-172.

254 *Liberal-National Contradiction: Politics*

rebellion. However, the insurgents were defeated by state troops as they advanced northward. They then took refuge in neighboring Chihuahua, surrendering their weapons to district officials in Chínipas.[55]

Connant had not carefully organized and welded together the disperse elements within his ranks. More importantly, he was almost unknown in the state and lacked the prestige necessary to convince large numbers of recruits of the necessity of armed resistance, and the general public of abandoning all obedience to the Pesqueira government. Alamos district was once more the origin of the governor's troubles. He made sure that his prefect there, José María Loaiza, imposed stern measures on the town to prevent any further such occurrences.[56]

To finance operations against the short-lived revolt, Governor Pesqueira had imposed the rather considerable extraordinary contribution of 35,000 pesos under emergency powers granted him by the legislature; in so doing, he alienated many of the leading businesspeople and professionals of Hermosillo. They had been growing more and more tired of the governor's increasing tendency to resort to forced loans and extraordinary contributions to balance the state's budget. They wrote a letter of protest to the legislature in early November.

These extraordinary levies hurt the businesses of notables like those of Hermosillo because they had to pay the bulk of the ordinary contributions as well. Yet they could live with it, they said, "to conserve the peace of the state." But now, with the revolt crushed, the government had the gall to demand the fulfillment of the twenty-five percent additional tax on the extraordinary contribution. This imposition, they protested, was illegal, since the law levied the twenty-five percent additional tax only on ordinary revenues. "You know as well as, or better than, we do," they told the legislature, "that the people can no longer support more contributions: they have arrived at an extreme of misery and prostration . . . ."[57]

Whether it agreed with the Hermosillo notables' assessment or not, the legislature was not about to cross the governor. It did not, as its three predecessors had done, try to block his "beneficent action." In 1874 the legislature approved a direct ordinary contribution of 110,000 pesos, a sum more than double that levied in 1869. In addition, the governor was empowered to determine the percentage which would apply to each class of property or

---

[55] Acuña, 117-118.

[56] Corral, 105-106, 116.

[57] *La Estrella de Occidente,* November 28, 1873. Those signing the letter included: Francisco Gándara; Florencio Monteverde; José Castro and Company; Espiridión Morales; Fernando Montijo; Benigno V. García; Camou Brothers; Manuel Escalante; Leandro Gaxiola; Luis Nanetti; Gabriel Monteverde; Manuel María Huguez; and José Ortiz.

capital in order to arrive at that figure.[58] Pesqueira was now free to devise pretty much whatever policies he thought necessary. The governor, however, proved fickle. After at last succeeding in obtaining a legislature ready and willing to do his bidding, the bold, innovative executive became an absentee landlord, retiring to his hacienda. At times he left the administration in the hands of his secretary of government and longtime confidant Cirilo Ramírez; at others, he formally entrusted the government to the substitute governor (and far more recent devotee) Joaquín María Astiazarán, who served almost fourteen months during the two-year term.[59]

If the legislature was finally pliant, the agents of the federal government were as nettlesome as ever. Opponents of the government and disgruntled businesspeople from the principal towns in the state—the two groups now were often one and the same—began seeking these federal officials out for protection from the stiffer tax levies and the growing number of arbitrary acts of the Pesqueira administration. One of their zealous accomplices was the federal district judge in Guaymas, Domingo Elías González. An old foe of the governor's, he had left his seat in the legislature in the late 1860s for the federal bench. Elías González always granted the *amparos* (injunctions) these dissenting notables sought against collection both of the *alcabalas* and of a contribution levied on nationalized foreign goods. The judge was actively abetted by the chief federal treasury official in the port, Alfonso Mejía, who was in charge of the customs house. To discourage the Pesqueira administration from its customary habit of resorting to the forceful removal or circumvention of those federal officials who acted strongly to its disliking, were Captain José María Rangel and his substantial federal garrison. (Rangel and his men, as noted in the preceding chapter, had been sent to Guaymas as a permanent federal presence in September, 1872, occasioned by the governor's last such episode in defying the federal bureaucrats in the port.)[60]

Rangel's garrison also made Guaymas a haven for those of the opposition who felt or foresaw the persecutory wrath of the state executive, for the governor began resorting to various repressive tactics to suffocate the persistent resistance to his domineering rule. The central authority of the state could no longer coexist with any semblance of the free exercise of liberal institutions. Freedom of the press was assaulted, opponents persecuted and forced to flee—to Guaymas or some other temporary refuge—or even to emigrate. All possible means were used to obstruct their attempts to seek redress

---

[58]*Ley de contribución directa ordinaria,* December 14, 1874, MAHm, Sonora, Reel 6.

[59]Corral, 106; Almada, 311. Personal tragedies (the deaths of four sons and a sister between 1872 and 1875) undoubtedly contributed to Pesqueira's frequent and prolonged absences. Acuña, 121.

[60]Almada, 644; Corral, 117-118.

in the federal courts. Judge Elías González himself was frequently harassed.[61]

The growing number of *amparos* emanating from the federal district court in Guaymas for relief from the collection of taxes crimped the government's fiscal resources. Counteracting this loss was one of the principal reasons for the government's growing reliance on extraordinary contributions—such as that for 15,000 pesos approved by the legislature in June, 1874—and for the huge rise in the ordinary contribution passed six months later. Rather than alleviate the administration's fiscal bind, however, these tax levies served instead to fan the popular discontent smouldering among Sonorans.[62]

ALTERED CONFIGURATIONS IN SINALOAN POLITICS

Post-war politics in Sonora was largely self-contained. The political contradiction between liberalism and nationalism (or centralized authority) involved the federal dimension only marginally and, at that, not until the mid-1870s. The arena was wholly the state. The conflict was between local liberals in most of that state's urban centers on the one hand and the state executive and its adherents on the other. In Sinaloa the federal dimension, a carryover from the Intervention itself, was present from the beginning, and it intensified during the post-war period.

A federal garrison was present in Guaymas only after 1872, but one had been stationed in Mazatlán since the early 1840s. Its principal function had been to protect the revenues due the national government, but it often had honored this duty more in the breach than in the observance. The Intervention had enlarged the garrison greatly, as the port became the focal point of military operations in the Northwest. This role declined minimally during the post-war years. Manuel Lozada, who had generally allied with the conservatives and imperialists during the decade of war, continued his struggle to make neighboring Tepic autonomous. Thus, the military establishment that had congregated in Mazatlán during the Intervention in large part remained. Most of the officer corps were non-Sinaloans, as were a good share of their troops. Their political ambitions had been aroused by the positions of prominence they had acquired during the several years of military rule.

Many of these outsiders were *tepiqueños,* emigrés from the federal military district controlled by Lozada.[63] Consequently, they were associated not

---

[61]*La Regeneración,* July 20, 1876.

[62]Corral, 118; Villa, 324.

[63]Garibay, *passim.* A canton of Jalisco, Tepic was converted into a military district on August 7, 1867, dependent on the federal government. In 1884 it was made a federal territory, and in 1917 it became the state of Nayarit. See Jean Meyer, "El ocaso de Manuel Lozada," *Historia Mexicana* 18 (April-June, 1969), 535-568, for a thorough study of Lozada's autonomous movement.

only with other veteran officers from neighboring states serving in the military establishment resident in Sinaloa, but also with a community of refugees centered in Mazatlán who had become very much involved in the port's commerce and the state's politics while waiting to return to their homeland. Of primary concern to the *tepiqueños* was the campaign against Lozada designed to restore their white-*mestizo* domination of Tepic and of the Indian villagers (whom Lozada had succeeded in uniting). They sought federal and state officials who would conduct and support this campaign vigorously. They also had largely imbibed the economic interests and political inclinations of the *mazatlecos* and other Sinaloans in neighboring southern districts.

The ambitions of General Ramón Corona, commander of the Army of the West (the 4th Division) headquartered in Guadalajara, went beyond the state. Corona had risen through the ranks of the federal military establishment in Sinaloa during the Reforma and the Intervention to command all of the liberal forces operating in west-central Mexico. After the war he continued to oversee the federal units in the state. A native *tepiqueño*, he had ties to the refugee community. As an outsider, Corona had judged his own accession to the governorship of Sinaloa unwise in 1864. Nonetheless, he wanted a state executive who would be subordinate. When General Rosales had proved too independent, the general had forced him to step down. General Rubí had then served loyally as governor through the final defeat of the Empire. Corona's post-war interest in Sinaloan politics was the usefulness of a dependent governor to his higher aspirations.[64]

These new elements altered, but did not transform, the basic political configuration that had been operating in the state since the late 1830s. The contention for political power remained fundamentally that between the notables of Mazatlán and Culiacán. But the traditional alignment was now much more clearly statewide in its scope and complexity, made so by the politicization of large segments of the citizenry of other districts and by the addition of the non-native elements. The political mobilization of large segments of the state's population occasioned by the Reform War and the Intervention meant politics in the post-war years would no longer continue in the simplified terms of the Mazatlán merchants and garrison versus the Culiacán gentry, nor would it principally be a matter (as it was in Sonora) of local liberals resisting an aggressive state executive and his personal followers. Rather, Sinaloan post-war politics centered around the efforts of local liberals in the north-central two-thirds and southern one-third of the state trying to prevent one another from dominating the state executive to the detriment of their particular interests. Groups from both areas staunchly avowed the supremacy of liberal principles over the claims of centralizing authority, whether at the state or federal level.

---

[64] Cosío Villegas, *República Restaurada—vida política,* 509-511, 609.

The prominent families of Culiacán and their allies in the other northern (and central) district towns considered themselves stalwart defenders of liberalism, those most responsible for its triumph. They had stood firm as control over the southern third of the state had wavered back and forth between liberals and conservatives, imperialists and republicans. The previously loose—at times non-existent—political ties among them were tightened into a common political understanding. It was based upon a commitment to the principles and institutions contained in the very liberal state constitution of 1861 (a document they were most responsible for designing) and on a deference in leadership to those among the Culiacán gentry (generally civilians) who had risen to prominence in the liberal ranks during the decade-long struggle. In the previous political balance such regional unity would have given these notables in the northern districts the edge, but the *tepiqueños* and the veterans of the federal military establishment based in Mazatlán had added a powerful new element to Sinaloan politics, a fact not lost upon the port's merchants.

The foreign merchants of Mazatlán had reconciled themselves to the fact that there was no longer a future in the conservative cause several years before most fellow sympathizers elsewhere in the nation succumbed with the demise of the Empire. The northern and central sections of the state had become staunchly liberal. The Mexican component of the port's commerce had steadily expanded at the middle levels, and the children of these business-people had returned from their education in Mexico City and Guadalajara with a pronounced attraction for the tenets of liberalism. Members of the port's commercial establishment were, thus, united in their endorsement of a liberal Mexico, for they saw in liberalism's upholding of local prerogatives an exploitable advantage to their economic interests. The Mazatlán business community looked to the *tepiqueños* and the veteran military units for political allies to counter predominance in state politics by the prominent families of the northern and central district towns.

The 1867 elections returning the state to constitutional government manifested the altered political alignment, yet they also revealed that it would take several years for such an alignment to crystallize. Four candidates vied for governor. General Rubí, the acting governor, was supported largely by native Sinaloans—especially those in the south and his old companions in arms—and by almost all employees in the state. Rubí's candidacy, which was more personal than geographical, was supported by General Corona from Guadalajara. Mazatlán merchants and their clients in the southern districts chose to back the candidate of the *tepiqueños*, General Angel Martínez, the chief of federal forces in the state.[65] There was likewise a split in northern

---

[65]*Ibid.,* 511-517; Buelna, *Apuntes,* 99. General Corona's role in the 1867 elections is not fully clear. According to Cosío Villegas, Corona sent out Irineo Paz to manage Rubí's provisional administration as secretary of the government before the elections and

Sinaloa. The candidacies of two ardent liberals emerged: that of Manuel Monzón, prefect of Culiacán since the French invasion of the state; and that of Eustaquio Buelna, who had just resigned as federal district judge to campaign.[66]

Notables in the north, led by the prominent families of Culiacán, could least afford a division within their ranks. They had far less means of political manipulation. The partisans of Martínez committed electoral abuses with the aid of detachments of the Army of the West then under his command in the state. These federal troops, most of whom were from Jalisco and soon to be discharged, bolstered the *tepiqueño* party.[67] Rubí used the full powers of the provisional government, and then some, to influence the elections. He removed his opponent Monzón on the ironic and hypocritical grounds that since Monzón was running for governor, there would be a greater guarantee of free elections in Culiacán if he were not prefect there.[68] In spite of these finaglings—or perhaps because of them—no candidate received a majority, and the selection of the governor was thrown into the legislature.

The newly elected diputados approved by a slim majority the proposal by a northern legislator (Roberto Orrantia) that Rubí and Martínez be eliminated from consideration. The grounds were that as active soldiers and federal employees they were constitutionally ineligible and that, more importantly, they had used their offices to influence the election. The proposal reflected the reliance of northern liberals on strict adherence to liberal institutions: in this case, the vote provided by the narrow edge their representatives held in the legislature. Their move temporarily brought the southerners together. The partisans of Rubí and Martínez, who predominated in Mazatlán (then the state's capital), made common cause to force the legislature to reverse the

---

to convince the vacillating Rubí that he should be a candidate. The former mine worker seems to have had doubts about his abilities to conduct the office on a permanent basis. When Paz began using official correspondence to promote Rubí's candidacy, the latter was forced to ask for his resignation, but Rubí declared him a Sinaloan citizen at the same time. Meanwhile, Francisco Sepulveda, head of the federal *aduana* in Mazatlán and closely tied to Corona, and Francisco Azcarate, a Corona protégé in the military and at that time Rubí's private secretary, successfully worked to convince the provisional governor that he should run for permanent office.

At the same time, Martinez's candidacy had surfaced and was endorsed by Paz and his friends, who considered him better qualified than Rubí. Most of the *tepiqueño* and other non-Sinaloan officers backing Martínez had risen through the ranks as Corona's loyal lieutenants during the Reforma and Intervention, along with Rubí and his Sinaloan comrades. This association made Corona's support of Rubí difficult, as it meant opposition to his colleagues' candidate. It also limited the effective means at Corona's disposal to assist Rubí: as commander of the 4th Division in Guadalajara, his main tools to influence the election in Rubí's favor were the federal troops whose immediate commanders were the veteran officers supporting Martínez.

[66]Buelna, *Apuntes,* 99.

[67]Mena, II, 244.

[68]Jorge L. Tamayo, ed., *Documentos, discursos, y correspondencia de Benito Juárez,* Vol. 12 (Mexico, 1967), 59, 64-65.

resolution. Rowdy demonstrations were held. Threatening crowds gathered outside the legislative chambers and individual diputados' residences. This plebeian pressure wore down enough northern legislators to repeal the resolution and reach a compromise. Martínez was unacceptable to a majority of the legislature: he was not a citizen of the state. Rubí was at least a native, and had shown himself to be independent of the *tepiqueño* military chiefs who had elevated him to power two years before. To appease the north, Monzón was elected vice-governor.[69]

Governor Rubí walked a tightrope, caught in the middle of the new political alignment. The *tepiqueño* party was tired of raising to power native Sinaloans who then turned independent. This feeling explained why they had backed Martínez in the elections and why, in January, 1868, some of their veteran officers engineered a revolt calling for new elections and recognizing Martínez as provisional governor. Colonels Jorge G. Granados and Adolfo Palacios first pronounced in Culiacán with national guard detachments (January 4), recognizing Vice-Governor Monzón as provisional governor. They hoped to enlist northern liberals in their attempt to remove Rubí. Monzón did not cooperate in any way, nor did any other prominent northerners. The two colonels then joined General Jesús Toledo, who pronounced January 9 in Villa Union (near Mazatlán), promising new elections and recognizing General Martínez as provisional governor. The provisional office would give Martínez a decisive edge in the proposed elections. Before accepting it, however, he waited to see what General Corona's intentions were.[70]

The commander of federal forces in the western states had left for Sinaloa the day the rebels declared themselves in Culiacán (January 4), apparently acting on instructions from his superiors in Mexico City. Based on his correspondence with Rubí and Martínez, he still believed that the two had reached an understanding. They were the official conduits of his influence in the state, so it was much to his anguish to find upon his arrival on January 17 that the discord between them had reached the point of belligerency. He soon recognized the grave difficulty of trying to conciliate the opposing interests. Conversations with the diputados convinced him that the legislature supported Rubí and would oppose any measure that sought to remove him. At the same time, he discerned that Mazatlán merchants were eager to profit from a revolutionary change of government, while veterans, who had voluntarily resigned or had been discharged by the reorganization of the army, saw an opportunity to receive their severance pay with official funds commandeered by the revolt.

Despite these difficulties—or perhaps because of them—Corona conducted negotiations and attempted to arrange solutions that exceeded his authority.

---

[69] Buelna, *Apuntes,* 99-101; Cosío Villegas, *República Restaurada—vida política,* 517-520.

[70] Buelna, *Apuntes,* 106-111; Cosío Villegas, *República Restaurada—vida política,* 520-523.

He proposed to Rubí that he resign, that the president of the supreme tribunal become interim governor, and that new elections be held. Rubí refused. To give in to such a forceful imposition, in the face of the apparent abandonment by his political benefactor, he said, would be a disgrace and a humiliation, as much for the state as for himself. Corona then went to the leader of the rebels, General Toledo, asking for an end to the rebellion. Toledo accepted, but said Martínez would have to make the ultimate decision. The latter apparently judged in his subsequent meeting with the division commander that Corona's position was compromised and that he would, at worst, remain neutral.

Martínez's calculation seemed initially correct. Corona did not relieve him of his command, though he did entrust the command of some of the federal troops to Bibiano Dávalos to protect the interests of the federal government (primarily the customs revenues in the port). On January 27, Corona left for Guadalajara, consigning to Manzanillo a large supply of arms and munitions in order to prevent their use by the rebels. The day after Corona's departure, Martínez publicly accepted the insurrection's leadership. He also wrote Lerdo, the Interior Minister, assuring him that his provisional government expressed the will of the people and respected completely federal interests and officials in the state.[71]

Notification of the federal government was tangential to what Martínez and the other rebels considered the critical factor to their success: Corona's neutrality. Their confidence was in that neutrality and in their judgment that his command was the decisive external consideration. It was a trust misplaced. On February 11, Lerdo curtly informed Martínez that Mexico City would not countenance the insurrection against a duly elected constitutional government and that the Minister of War already had orders to send a federal detachment to Sinaloa to suppress the rebellion. General Corona implemented the orders by dispatching troops under the command of General Donato Guerra, who decisively defeated Martínez in early April. Martínez went into exile in California. The other rebel leaders were eventually pardoned. Corona, having alienated both Rubí and the *tepiqueños*, lost much of his influence in the state.[72]

Armed insurrections continued during the remainder of Governor Rubí's term,[73] and both the federal executive and General Corona lent aid to suppress them. *Tepiqueño* officers Adolfo Palacios and Victoriano Cruz pronounced against Rubí the following year (1869), repeating the call for new

---

[71] Cosío Villegas, *República Restaurada—vida política,* 523-527. Corona went grudgingly to Mazatlán as an intermediary. He had indicated to Júarez two weeks before his wish not to go there, since he did not want to appear to be supporting either claimant to the governorship. Tamayo, 871.

[72] Cosío Villegas, *República Restaurada—vida política,* 527-537.

[73] Buelna, *Compendio,* 17.

elections, but they were soon driven from the state.[74] The next year the governor had to contend with incursions from Tepic by small bands sent by Placido Vegas trial balloons in preparation for his return to power. But protected and abetted by Lozada, whom Sinaloans had come to detest, Vega's trial balloons fizzled.[75]

The notables of northern district towns did not wish Rubí any good fortune either. Nevertheless, they did not cooperate with the *tepiqueño* revolts to remove him from office, nor did they promote any of their own. Rather, they determined to respect constitutional authority and oppose Rubí's administration in the legislature when they could. Though a Sinaloan, and not a *tepiqueño,* the governor was nonetheless a southerner. If he were forced to choose, they believed he would side with the business community of Mazatlán and their *tepiqueño* allies. Led by Eustaquio Buelna of Culiacán and Manuel Inzunza of Mocorito, the northern notables' representatives pushed through a series of constitutional reforms. According to the only available source, which does not give specifics, these reforms were designed to clarify certain governmental prerogatives and make the executive more accountable. Governor Rubí opposed some of the reforms and (as Pesqueira did in Sonora) asserted the right of observation, a ploy the legislative majority resisted. Introduced in the 1867-1869 legislature, the reforms were given final approval in January, 1870, by its successor. The following May, the new legislature passed a law instituting the direct election provision provided for in the 1861 constitution.[76]

THE FEDERAL DIMENSION IN SINALOA

The 1871 elections, operating under the new, most open electoral procedures in the country, were a barometer of the relative strength of the two major parties in the new political alignment in Sinaloa. While in the preceding election there had been several candidates, this time there were only two. The choice of the *tepiqueño* party was General Manuel Márquez de León, who was vigorously backed by the Mazatlán business community. A native of Baja California, Márquez had been a prominent young liberal politician and militia officer before service, during the Reforma and Intervention, in the Army of the West brought him to Sinaloa.[77] Opposing the veteran southern officers was the united candidacy of the northern party, in the person of Eustaquio Buelna. The veteran lawyer and civil servant was a most apt choice to weld solidly together the notables of Culiacán and their counterparts in the northern and central district towns. Buelna was from a prominent family of Moco-

---

[74] Acuña, 104.
[75] Mena, II, 252.
[76] Buelna, *Apuntes,* 107, 110.
[77] Gaxiola, F.J., 497.

rito, but had attended secondary school in Culiacán and had settled there upon returning from legal training in Guadalajara. He quickly had become a leader of the Culiacán gentry, serving in various administrative offices during the Reforma and the Intervention. His liberal reputation was second to none. After the war he had served as a federal district judge and magistrate of the state's supreme tribunal. In 1869, he had been elected to the legislature. A fervent partisan of the liberal political order, diputado to the convention that drew up the Constitution of 1857, Buelna had played a leading role in 1870 in the passage of constitutional reforms that liberalized even further the state's already open political system.[78]

Governor Rubí was prevented from running by the prohibition against immediate reelection, but he and his largely personal following could have an impact on the outcome nonetheless. By throwing his weight to one candidate, he might improve his chances for reelection in 1875. To the miscalculations of the northern party, he chose *their* candidate. Buelna's commitment to strict adherence to liberal principles, which was well known, would offer the least strictures against Rubí's candidacy in the next elections. In contrast, the *tepiqueños'* frequent resort to armed force and political manipulation bespoke the possibility of a closed election in four years. Influential in the governor's decision to support Buelna was the strong urging to do so by President Juárez. Rubí was in the President's debt for the federal support he had received in putting down the series of revolts that had threatened his government. The northern party, in turn, had decided to align itself with Juárez in the presidential contest.[79]

Márquez's partisans were more tightly linked to the national electoral struggle. They were firmly committed to Porfirio Díaz, who enjoyed considerable popularity in the state. (Lerdo had little, if any, support in Sinaloa.) The close ties with the *porfiristas* were forged on the basis of a full extension of liberal institutions and a vigorous promotion of economic activity. The Mazatlán business community whole-heartedly endorsed both positions. Díaz, wrote the editor of a Mazatlán newspaper, was the only possible guarantee for the preservation of the liberties won during the Reforma. Then was begun the immense task of equalizing human rights, ending the old privileges of class and family, "approaching the state of social perfection in which law ought not to rule more than reason and justice, nor aristocracy more than virtue, work, and knowledge." However, it was not only a question of the *porfiristas* being people who searched for the faithful observance of the law and who were committed to the progress of the nation: "Civilization advancing, always full of life, and the status quo, opposing all such advances, are two

---

[78] González Dávila, 65.
[79] Cosío Villegas, *República Restaurada—vida política,* 607-608; *La Voz del Pueblo* (Mazatlán), June 13, 1871.

principles in perpetual conflict . . . . The party which proclaims Díaz represents civilization; that which desires the reelection of Juárez is the stationary party, the enemy of all innovation."[80]

A speech by a young Journalist, José C. Valadés, to a meeting of port residents which endorsed Díaz and Márquez elaborated these themes:

> To be interested but not want public employment is an aberration for many; people ask us what our ambition is, and, if we do not have it, they say that we lie. No, we do not want offices; we desire the well-being of the nation. In order to have work we want movement and numerous commercial transactions; we want metals from the mines to be exported, minted and circulated; artisans to have plenty of work and be well paid, and industry and the sciences to be protected, so that they might progress. The general good today involves the solution of a political question . . . .
>
> The people must correct these political deformities, must search out a man who will work out our reconstruction, . . . save the country from this marasmus, and do what must be done . . . so that our institutions will not be a lie, progress a fantasy, the people a beast with two feet—the fodder of cannon, the food of the few, that thing which our governments until now have believed their own . . . . We say to the present government that Mexico awakens, and that it wants liberty, that it wants honor, that it wants progress, that it wants democracy, and that it sees the past as a terrible nightmare; that it is willing to pardon errors, if their authors do not persist in them, because it desires union and because the epoch of greatness and happiness has arrived.[81]

The candidacies of Márquez and Díaz were joined not only through common ideological affinities, but also through the two aspirants' own personal connections. Long an enthusiastic admirer of the general, Márquez in the post-war years had become one of a circle of Díaz's close political friends and agents. Through him, a growing number of *tepiqueño* (and Jaliscan) officers were acquiring ties to the *porfirista* party nationally. Their concern went beyond the elections to contingency preparations in the eventuality of their electoral defeat. Such intentions would bring with them the direct intrusion of national political interests in the contest for control of the state.[82]

The results of the presidential election in Sinaloa mirrored those nationally: 88 electoral votes for Juárez, 58 for Díaz. Buelna ran more strongly in the gubernatorial race, defeating Márquez 25,000 to 11,000.[83] The compara-

---

[80]*La Voz del Pueblo,* June 13, 1871.

[81]*Ibid.*

[82]Cosío Villegas, *República Restaurada—vida política,* 180, 575-588.

[83]*Ibid.,* 670.

tive results were an indication of Buelna's prestige in the state, the unity of the northern party, and the added support of Rubi's followers. The initial response of the *tepiqueño-mazatleco* opposition was local in vision, similar to that of four years previous.

In early September (1871), Francisco Cañedo and General Eulogio Parra initiated armed resistance. Cañedo, a native of Tepic, was just completing his term as prefect of Culiacán. Parra, a former commander of federal troops in the state, had retired to a ranch in the district of San Ignacio. Their plan was to prevent the newly elected diputados, in particular those from the north, from assembling in Mazatlán to certify the election results. Such action would create a situation favorable to Márquez, especially since a strong minority of opposition legislators had been elected in the south. However, national guard units within a month thoroughly routed the two rebel bands, the plan to obstruct the certification of the elections was foiled, and Buelna duly assumed control of the government.[84]

All the while, Márquez publicly feigned neutrality toward the local insurrection, but he was in communication with the inner *porfirista* circle, awaiting the declaration of a national rebellion. The commander of federal forces in Sinaloa was also anticipating that revolt. In agreement with state authorities, Colonel José Palacios had mobilized his troops to help suppress Cañedo and Parra's armed efforts. But learning of the national uprising planned for late October from his compadre, General Donato Guerra, he thereafter became increasingly inclined toward joining it. When he was replaced by General Rubí in mid-November (the federal executive had begun to doubt his loyalty), Palacios declared his adhesion to the La Noria Revolt, backed by the federal garrison. So, too, now did Márquez.[85]

The defeated candidate had been quietly collecting supplies and enlisting local support. Palacios' declaration gave the prior armed opposition to the election results a national character, a challenge to the federal, as well as state, authorities. That opposition thereby acquired an ideological cause and the tactical support of other rebel nuclei. The Mazatlán *aduana*, then possessing substantial revenues, offered a handy source of funds, as did the Mazatlán business community.[86] Port merchants readily supported the revolt, with

---

[84]*Ibid.*, 670-672. According to Buelna, Cañedo had offered to work for Buelna's election by using his influence as prefect. But in return he wanted Buelna to replace the current judge of the first instance, Manuel Manzón, with his friend Francisco Ferrel. Buelna had refused the deal.

For his instigation of the revolt, Cañedo was sentenced to death. After considerable lobbying by his friends, the legislature agreed to commute the sentence to ten years imprisonment. Buelna made no observations to the law commuting the sentence. Soon after, with Palacios's declaration for the Plan of La Noria, Cañedo escaped from prison. Buelna, *Apuntes*, 116, 122.

[85]Cosío Villegas, *República Restaurada—vida política*, 672.

[86]*Ibid.*, 672, 675.

prospects of customs duties being arranged to enhance their profits. They were joined by the *tepiqueños,* native southern district veterans and politicians allied with the port, and Cañedo, who had finagled his way out of incarceration. General Donato Guerra, designated by Díaz as the commander of the western zone, arrived in early December to organize officially the movement in Sinaloa and named Márquez governor and military commander.[87]

Within two months, the central and southern districts had fallen under the rebels' control. Mexico City, its martial resources stretched thin, did not at first have sufficient forces to aid Buelna and had temporarily left his government to fend for itself. With the assistance of Sonoran Governor Pesqueira, Culiacán was retaken in late February, 1873, and with the arrival of federal troops under General Feliciano Rocha in April, the Buelna government was able to regain general control over the state by late May.[88] Nonetheless, the governor's political troubles were far from over.

External meddling in Sinaloan politics had not ended. It had merely been altered in its sponsor. Along with federal troops, General Rocha brought a federal declaration of siege (decreed March 9, 1873, but not published until the general's capture of Mazatlán). Rocha named General Rubí governor and military commander of the state. Though given the command of federal forces of the previous November, the ex-governor and loyal *juarista* had done little in the way of combat, since the large majority of his troops had adhered to the Plan of La Noria.[89] Rubí was no more effective in holding the state after Rocha's departure at the end of May.

By early September, the rebels had re-entered Sinaloa and regained control of a majority of the districts, including the capital of Mazatlán. They had outmaneuvered Rubí, who had come out from the port to engage them. Only the arrival in October of federal contingents under General José Ceballos (sent to Mazatlán) and General José Carbó (sent to Culiacán) terminated the rebellion; their actions were aided by President Lerdo's amnesty declaration, which sapped the rebels' resolve and unity. After more than a year, the armed efforts to reverse the results of the 1871 elections had finally been suppressed. However, General Ceballos prolonged the state of siege, even though he carried with him a presidential decree of September 14 lifting it. He assumed the post of governor and military commander of the state.[90]

To the northern party, and to Buelna in particular, it looked as though they had been sold out by the federal government. Rubí's appointment had provoked great disillusionment and discontent among their sympathizers, and

---

[87] Buelna, *Apuntes,* 123-131.

[88] Mena, II, 265.

[89] Buelna, *Apuntes,* 135, 141-142.

[90] Cosío Villegas, *República Restaurada—vida política,* 713, 715, 747, 752; Buelna, *Apuntes,* 144-157.

they blamed Mexico City and its agent, Rubí's provisional government, for the resurgence of the rebels. Furthermore, the supporters of the Buelna government believed the state of siege to be an attempt by a national political interest to control their state's politics. Instead of vigorously hunting down the remaining dispersed bands, they charged, the provisional government had delayed and diddled to prolong the state of siege and, thus, to provide time for the federal executive to build a new party, unconditionally loyal to it, in order to ensure future electoral victories. For the *buelnistas* and their sympathizers in the north, Rubí was the willing accomplice of these external designs, who was trying to attract those who had backed the rebellion, especially the business people, other notables, and clients of Mazatlán.

The northerners' distrust of the motives of the federal executive had increased with Lerdo's succession to the presidency in 1872 (following Juárez's death in July). Juárez had at least been popular in the state and his close relations with Rubí were well known. But Lerdo had no following in the state. It was, thus, quite plausible that he was trying to create one in Sinaloa: by prolonging the state of siege, he could ensure the success of his clients in the next election. General Ceballos had not bothered to retain a prominent Sinaloan politician as provisional governor—not even one as distrusted by northerners as Rubí.[91]

Not until Buelna arrived in Mexico City in mid-November to protest to Lerdo the continuance of the state of siege was it finally lifted. (A few days after their meeting, the federal executive ordered General Ceballos to publish the decree raising it.) Vice-Governor Angel Urrea managed the government until Buelna's return in early February (1873).[92]

The attempts of national political interests to gain predominance in Sinaloan politics—whether carried out, planned, or only intended—had failed. The northern party had successfully ridden out the various external pressures to overturn its triumph in the 1871 elections. The notables of the northern district towns, led by Buelna, were also now free of Rubí and his personal following—at least for the time being. The ex-governor had been discredited

---

[91] Buelna, *Apuntes*, 142-143. According to Buelna, Rubí's appointment was promoted by interested persons from Mazatlán who gained Rocha's ear soon after he landed in the port. Rubí's political circle, led by Jesús Río, president of the supreme tribunal, and José D. Martínez, Rubí's secretary of government, hoped, thus, to return to power. The *tepiqueño* party, represented by Francisco Sepulveda, former administrator of the *aduana* and Corona's faithful steward during the Intervention, preferred the ambivalent Rubí far more than the *tepiqueños'* arch-opponent Buelna. The Mazatlán merchants were eager to delay Buelna's return, if not to replace him permanently, in order to avoid the fiscal retaliation they expected with the return of his government.

Buelna claims in his historical account that the Secretary of War had instructed General Ceballos not to publish the decree, though he does not say if that order came from above.

[92] *Ibid.*, 157.

and politically weakened by his apparent opportunism and military ineffec-
tiveness during the La Noria rebellion. But the *mazatlecos* and their *tepiqueño* allies were tenaciously determined to undermine the Buelna government in whatever way they could, despite their long series of setbacks.

Southern diputados exploited the advantage of their proximity to the
capital with the reconvening of the legislature on December 4, 1872, after the
termination of the state of siege. While many of the legislators from the
northern districts were making their way to Mazatlán, the southerners passed a
number of laws that undercut the power and resources of the state executive,
while promoting the financial interests of their own most prominent constituents. Through various fiscal measures they curtailed government revenues;
in doing so, they lined the pockets of numerous individuals and businesses.
Through the impoverishment of the treasury, they rendered the national
guard ineffective, suppressed a small police force in the capital employed by
the government to ensure public order, and forced the absence from office of
numerous unpaid civil servants. By shackling the official newspaper, they
even deprived the state executive of the means to defend its policies publicly
at a time when the opposition press was attacking them rudely and often
calumniously.[93] By the time of Buelna's return from Mexico City, the northern *diputados* had regained the upper hand in the legislature. But the intense
political pressures then at work in the capital made the maintenance of their
position quite trying.

The potential power of public persuasion had been demonstrated in the
copper money amortization affair in December, 1872 (see Chapter 7). José C.
Valadés, who had led the popular demonstrations that had forced the legislature then to accept the copper coins at par value even though merchants were
driving their price down by as much as 80 per cent in business transactions,
was one of numerous young port notables who could impassion and direct a
crowd with fiery oratory. Schooled in letters, Valadés had made public
speeches on the glories of liberalism as early as the age of fourteen. By the
time he was twenty, he had joined the ranks of the southern opposition and
had acquired an ambition to become a state legislator. He had helped form the
porfirista club in Mazatlán and had participated in the last armed phase of
the recent revolt. With family assistance, he had since established a newspaper
that was blatantly attacking the Buelna government.[94]

Governor Buelna reached the conclusion that as long as his administration
and, correspondingly, the interests of the notables of the northern district
towns were within the immediate, hostile reach of the Mazatlán business
community and the clientele that did its bidding, his and their fortunes would

---

[93]*Ibid.*, 160-161.
[94]Valadés, 41-44; Cosío Villegas, *República Restaurada—vida política*, 713.

continue to be threatened. The governor resolved to transfer the capital out of the port, back to Culiacán. The exodus of *tepiqueños,* beginning that spring, was a valuable aid in doing so. The federal government's campaign from March through May (1873) succeeded in the complete destruction of Lozada's autonomous movement, and the *tepiqueño* emigrés immediately began returning home. For more than a decade they had been the principal political allies of the *mazatlecos* and the main recruiting source for revolts instigated or sponsored by the port's merchants and politicians. Their departure seriously weakened the port's political strength.[95]

In August (1873), following the state elections for the legislature, Governor Buelna left Mazatlán for Culiacán, ostensibly to make an inspection tour of the districts along the way. In reality, he was arranging the transfer of the capital. The governor reached agreement with the newly elected diputados (principally those from the northern districts). Meanwhile, the permanent deputation of the out-going legislature, which had come from Mazatlán a short time after Buelna, convoked the installation of the new legislature in Culiacán on September 16.[96] Four days later, the latter declared that city the new capital of the state.[97]

The Buelna administration now had more freedom of action and, with the solid support of the northern majority in the legislature, could dictate fiscal measures which would notably improve the condition of the treasury by restoring lost revenues.[98] Also signifying the shift in the balance of political power was the removal of the state-run secondary school to Culiacán in March, 1874. Established in Mazatlán the year before at Buelna's initiative, the school was renamed the Colegio de Rosales by the governor, who also upgraded it by adding professional instruction.[99] Such a school, then the only one of its kind in Sinaloa, would attract young notables from districts throughout the state, as he had been drawn from Mocorito by the parochial Seminario Tridentino some thirty years before. Buelna had remained to become an important leader among the Culiacán establishment. So, too, would those who were drawn to the Colegio Rosales thereafter.

---

[95] Buelna, *Apuntes,* 161.

[96] *Ibid.,* 162-163.

[97] *Boletín Oficial del Estado de Sinaloa,* October 4, 1873. Governor Buelna and the new legislature also had a strong legal justification for transferring the capital. On July 22, 1867, President Júarez, having experienced serious problems resulting from the residence of state governments in ports opened to foreign commerce, had expedited a decree ordering the transfer of all state capitals so located to an interior city or town, preferably close to the center of the state. Mena, II, 285.

[98] Buelna, *Apuntes,* 163.

[99] González Dávila, 561-562, 570-575. The *colegio's* professional instruction prepared its students for the following careers: teaching, bookkeeping, engineering (mechanical, metallurgical, and civil), assaying, law, medicine, pharmacy, dentistry, surveying, and agronomy.

In June, 1874, Governor Buelna undertook a visita through the northern districts, aimed at putting diverse administrative branches in order and promoting the establishment of primary schools legislated several months before. The following January he made a similar visita to the southern districts, with the added objective of reconciling what differences he could there. A beginning was also made in reforming and modernizing the administration of justice, in particular by adopting the codes of the Federal District.[100]

Buelna and the northern party he led were firmly in control of the government after the transfer of the capital to Culiacán. Yet the underlying tension between the exercise of liberal institutions and the demands of political control continued. There was no military draft conducted by the Buelna administration; full civil guarantees were respected. The governor claimed that freedom of the press reached its greatest extension yet in the state, even though the opposition frequently abused it. Still, there were limits. The peppery young Valadés was jailed for infractions of the press law in the fall of 1874. The liberal law prescribed a limited number of cases where such correction or fine could be imposed. The Mazatlán editor carried a counter-claim to a congressional court of inquiry (*gran jurado nacional*), accusing the governor of misusing his office. But the Congress absolved the governor unanimously of any wrongdoing.[101]

The decentralization of authority within the state government was also a problem, in at least one important instance. In late September, 1873, the governor suspended the state treasurer, Tomás Gómez, for three months on the grounds of irregular procedures and disobedience to his dispositions. The aging civil servant, who had served in the treasurer's post on various occasions, had remained behind in Mazatlán when the state executive and the legislature had shifted the seat of government to Culiacán. In the port Gómez had tried to make payments from the treasury with complete independence from the governor. When the latter had asked him for a daily accounting of treasury transactions (to know the quantity which the government could dispose of the following day), he had balked, contending such a request was contrary to his alleged independence in making disbursements. Buelna claimed Gómez was trying to obstruct his efforts to order the state's fiscal affairs. In retaliation, the suspended treasurer brought a complaint of wrongdoing before the legislature, which absolved the governor of the charge in a court of inquiry on December 29.[102]

The Buelna administration also faced impediments to its policies in the courts. Mazatlán notables began employing the tactic of asking for injunctions against various government dispositions, especially those relating to fiscal

---

[100] Buelna, *Apuntes,* 165-166, 169-170.
[101] *Ibid.,* 166.
[102] *Ibid.,* 164.

matters. The governor claimed that the port merchants were doing so to undermine the government and make improper acquisitions of merchandise. Sometimes, the Buelna administration was upheld, as when the Supreme Court in May, 1873, rejected the *amparo* petitioned by the merchants to halt the collection of the thirty-three percent levy on the taxes they had paid to the rebels the previous year. But more often the courts did not support the government. Federal district judges regularly decided in the merchants' favor and the Supreme Court generally upheld their rulings. The governor believed that corruption was involved in many of the suits, in particular those instigated by the wealthy Spanish merchants residing in Mazatlán.[103]

The contradiction in politics between liberalism and nationalism, between the practice of liberal institutions and the inclinations toward the centralization of authority, between the demands of local liberal interests for a large measure of self-determination and the advantages to state and national interests of a greater concentration of political power, was more and more evident in the postwar years. It increasingly unsettled and impassioned public life. Factionalism grew and the resort to armed force and manipulation became more and more adopted as a means to defend one's interests. By the mid-1870's, how long the contradiction could be maintained was open to serious question in the Northwest, as elsewhere in the nation. A two-year long struggle ensued to try to resolve the contradiction.

---

[103]*Ibid.,* 161, 169-170.

9

Cross Purposes: The Tuxtepec Revolution
(1875-1877)

By 1875 the Lerdo administration had come to embody the liberal-national contradiction to such a point that the contradiction was no longer reconcilable. Devoid of his predecessor's prestige, Lerdo's fortunes rested solely on his policies. (Frank A. Knapp's biography of Lerdo provides the best detailed discussion to date of his policies and objectives.) Lerdo wanted a strong national government, dominated by a powerful president, whose cabinet would serve as administrators, not formulators of policy. Far less cautiously than Juárez, Lerdo moved to extend his control over the states by replacing opponents and even neutrals with friendly governors. Toward this end, the creation of the national Senate in 1874, with its power of intervening in the states when it judged their governments not to be functioning properly, gave the President concentrated leverage. Through such beholden governors—and the intervention of a subordinate army when necessary—cooperative federal diputados who would acquiesce in his programs could be elected and the executive could become the initiator of most major legislation.

Yet Lerdo's commitment to legality, to the strict adherence to many of the Reforma's liberal principles, undermined his efforts to centralize authority. He tolerated a vociferous press. He granted generous amnesties, most notably that following the La Noria Revolt. His commitment to a rigid implementation of the Reform Laws (making them constitutional amendments and enforcing them to the letter) incurred the wrath of the clericalists. His tendency toward governmental passivity with respect to the economy and nationalistic hesitancy in treating with foreign investors led to his being blamed for the sluggish recovery of the economy, which bred disillusionment and discontent after expectations of progress had been so high. At the same time, he was held culpable by many whose local interests had been injured by the national economy that had begun to take shape.

THE TUXTEPEC COALITION

The contradiction between liberalism and nationalism contained in Lerdo's policies had alienated most political elements in the country by the last year of his term. Even his strong support among professionals, among those of considerable property and social prominence, and among much of the bureaucratic element (which Lerdo had elevated to government posts during his long tenure as chief of the Juárez cabinet) had begun to wane. Disappointed office-seekers, dissatisfied businesspeople, and disillusioned intellectuals were withdrawing their support as the President laid plans for his reelection.

The numerous political groups in outright opposition to Lerdo were now beginning to coalesce around Porfirio Díaz. The Oaxacan veteran's effort to unseat Juárez and Lerdo in the La Noria Revolt had been premature. Now the alienation had become widespread and had gone past the point of tolerating any further attempts from Mexico City to dictate politics. Yet what Díaz was soon to lead was only a coalition, not a movement. There was no single identifiable program—though Díaz's Plan of Tuxtepec had as its slogan "No Reelection! " There was, rather, a collection of groups, each of which had its own particular grievance against Lerdo. Personifying so vividly the contradiction between liberal principles and centralizing authority, Lerdo had alienated groups on all sides.

Prominent among the opposition were ambitious veteran officers, people like Díaz himself, who had risen to prominence (from obscurity in many cases) through the opportunities offered by the long years of war and who craved the recognition and reward they felt they had coming to them. They had become accustomed to positions of leadership and power, and the discharge of two-thirds of the army in the post-war years had left them adrift in the states where the last campaigns of the war had sent them. Some were in their home regions, or returned there. But many had found themselves in a new locale, had sought out local allies, had gotten to know local issues and gripes, and had then frequently led electoral fights—and even insurrections, when they had been unable to win at the ballot box. Issues were not their real concern, though they could parley slogans when necessary. Their real interest was pragmatic political power, and who was going to have it. They wanted to be in on it. Porfirio Díaz was one of them, and they knew it.

Veteran radical liberal politicians had been the official opposition for more than a decade. They resided in Mexico City, with many having power bases out in the states and regions; theirs had been purist voices calling on the Juárez and Lerdo governments to be true to the Constitution of 1857, to all the principles that they had committed their public lives to since mid-century. Politicians such as Vicente Riva Palacio, Ignacio Luis Vallarta, and Ignacio Ramírez had vigorously resisted the growing shift of power away from the localities and from the Congress, which comprised their representatives, toward the federal executive. They had expressed outrage at electoral manipulation. They had insisted on free trade and the following of other liberal economic principles. These strict constitutionalists saw in Porfirio Díaz an unwavering hero of the Intervention who could throw the lerdista rascals out.

The opposition also attracted young liberals, both those trained in Mexico City and those out in the principal cities of the states, who had come of age and begun to enter politics. Educated to liberalism, in many cases imbued with Auguste Comte's liberal positivism, their young minds were attuned to progress, to a future in which they could prosper and make their mark. That future seemed stalled, and they blamed the economic passivity of Lerdo's administration for it. Porfirio Díaz seemed a public figure not mired in status quo thinking, but rather one open to new ideas, new approaches. The young José Valadés had said as much four years before in a speech in Mazatlán:

> ... Mexico is not what it ought to be in this age .... The spectacle that the country presents is very sad—so lamentable that it even threatens our existence as a nation .... [These difficulties] make us appear to be a people lacking in civilization and progress. Are all the rules here unheard of? ... Does Mexico have a budget? On what is it spent? Is it employed well? Is its credit firm? Do we have public improvements, expositions, shipping? Do we have, finally, any prospects? Where is our place in the world? Is our nation an island in the Ocean or is it a civilized nucleus which has obligations and ought to fulfill them? ... The people must correct these political deformities, must search out a man who will work towards our reconstruction ....[1]

The clericalists had been rudely awakened by Lerdo's strict implementation of the Reform Laws, in particular the closing of convents and the prohibition of public ceremony. The feeling that their prior assumption of Lerdo's pro-clericalist leanings had been betrayed made them all the more bitter. There had been minor disorders and riots in the preceding two years in the states of the central corridor (from Puebla to Jalisco) and a revolt even in Michoacán, though the clergy was not directing them. For the clericalists, anyone seemed better than Lerdo. The overtures of the pragmatic Porfirio Díaz made them feel relief was possible.

If there was any sense of a movement in the Tuxtepec coalition, it came from local liberal politicians and military veterans. They had believed that their victory in the Intervention would assure a national liberal framework premised upon local prerogative and the dispersion of political power. The growing encroachment of the federal executive, and Lerdo's manipulations in

---

[1] *La Voz del Pueblo* (Mazatlán), June 13, 1871.

particular, had antagonized them. Porfirio Díaz for them, as Juárez before, was a means by which they could come together and a symbol of their cause. They would see the ensuing Tuxtepec Revolt primarily as another national movement of local groups to preserve local control by adhering strictly to the principles of the Constitution of 1857.[2]

Local liberals in the Northwest were part of the growing resistance to Lerdo's efforts to impose his clients in the state governments, through whom he could dictate national politics from Mexico City. In their resistance they linked up with national political interests to dismantle the growing centralization of authority. In Sonora local liberals sought to end the long control of state government by Ignacio Pesqueira. Only afterward did they see the necessity of opposing attempts from Mexico City to reverse their efforts. In Sinaloa resistance was wholly to Lerdo's attempt to impose a client. In both states the 1875 elections were the prologue to the two-year-long struggle that was about to follow.

ELECTORAL IMPOSITION

After a decade of contention, the balance of power in Sinaloan politics had swung to the notables of the northern district towns. Southerners, led by the business community of Mazatlán, still disputed their control, but they were at present too weak to mount a serious electoral challenge. Instead, it came from Mexico City. The Lerdo administration had seemingly toyed with intervention in the state's politics three years before through the prolongation of a state of siege in connection with the La Noria Revolt. Now it determined, with far less discretion, to impose electorally a loyal friend in the state executive.

The candidates for the 1875 state elections narrowed down to José Rojo and José María Gaxiola for governor, Antonio H. Paredes and General Domingo Rubí for vice-governor. Rojo and Paredes were the choices of the northern districts and Rosario. The candidacies of Gaxiola and Rubí, which predominated in the remaining southern districts, were principally sustained from Mazatlán in the person of General Francisco Arce, commander of the federal forces in the state. Southerners did not really field a serious candidate. Thus, general opinion in the state was that Gaxiola's and Rubí's candidacies were merely the vehicle by which the Lerdo government intended to impose its will on the state through its federal agents in order to assure support for the presidential elections the coming year.

---

[2] The villagers of Morelos were one such local liberal interest group, as John Womack, Jr., so humanly relates in his *Zapata and the Mexican Revolution* (New York, 1969), 8, 73.

Gaxiola, though a native of Sinaloa and active politically during the Ayutla and Reforma period, had resided outside the state for a number of years. He had recently returned to Sinaloa as a federal district judge, but had then resigned the office shortly afterwards, because federal employees were prohibited from holding office by the state's constitution. He retained his position as judge of the criminal court of Mexico City, however, since he had taken leave of absence to come to Sinaloa. This action nurtured doubts about the location of Gaxiola's prime interests and loyalties. Rubí was still a soldier and employee of the federal government. Moreover, his cooperation with the previous effort of the Lerdo administration to intervene in Sinaloa's politics was still fresh in the public's mind. With General Arce sending federal detachments to the districts most hostile to their candidacies, general opinion seemed to be right.

Rumors circulated that Gaxiola would stay in office only long enough to assure the reelection of Lerdo the following year. Rubí would then manage the government for the remainder of the term. Such rumors, and the mounting evidence that seemed to bear them out, turned public opinion against their candidacies in most parts of the state. Governor Buelna resigned so he would not be associated with the anticipated electoral imposition. His successor, Vice-Governor Angel Urrea, apparently was far less concerned about such an association.[3]

Professing neutrality, Urrea remained in office. Yet he was silent in the face of numerous abuses committed by General Arce's federal troops. One of the most blatant occurred in Rojo's home district of Sinaloa, the strongest center of his support. After a brawl between Rojo and Gaxiola partisans in the *cabecera*, Colonel Maximo Velasco, sent by Arce to take command of the federal soldiers there during the electoral period, arrested various *rojista* supporters in order to intimidate the local populace. Those arrested included the candidate himself. Detachments were sent out into the countryside to accomplish the same purpose. Several *rojistas* were forced to flee from persecution because of their influence in the villages. The chief local authorities of Ocoroni, Bacubirito, and Bamoa were jailed. Urrea's response was to illegally dismiss from office the elected prefect of the district under the pretext of such electoral disorders and to replace him with a loyal subordinate until the elections were over.[4]

Despite such assistance, Gaxiola garnered only a little more than a thousand-vote majority, winning only in the districts of Mazatlán, Cosalá, and San Ignacio. Elsewhere, only the open manipulative pressures of federal troops and the acting state executive held down the *rojista* vote. In the capital,

---

[3] Buelna, *Apuntes,* 166-167, 169.
[4] *Ibid.*, 171-172.

notwithstanding the federal garrison's threats and obstructions, the *rojista* supporters stood firm and Gaxiola lost badly. But in Sinaloa district, so great were the oppressive tactics employed by federal soldiers that the *rojistas* had little hope of winning. In a silent protest by his many supporters there not a single vote was cast for Rojo. When the out-going legislature decreed that elections be conducted in the villages of that district in which they had not been held on the appointed day, Urrea opposed it. When the legislature then asked the district's political authorities to execute the decree, the acting governor instructed them not to do so.

The electoral imposition in Sinaloa had succeeded. Federal forces were soon after withdrawn from the districts and returned to Mazatlán. Gaxiola and Arce were confident of their control over the state.[5]

In Sonora, the concern of most local liberals was not the prospect of dictation of state politics from Mexico City, but the continued dictation of state politics by Ignacio Pesqueira. For two years he had held complete mastery over the government with the concurrence of a submissive, hand-picked legislature. His administration had grown increasingly arbitrary in removing any obstacles to its centralization of authority. The price—a rapid loss of prestige and a growing alienation from the general populace—bolstered the ranks of the opposition. Indeed, so strongly had the opposition recovered from their crippling setback at Pesqueira's hands two years before that they were ready to challenge him once again at the polls.

There was good reason for the opposition leader's optimism. For the first time in twenty years, Pesqueira would not be running for governor. This concession was the only one the political boss had tolerated in quashing the previous legislature's constitutional reforms. However, he had no intention of surrendering his hegemony over the state. He aimed to impose his cousin, José Pesqueira, in his stead and presented himself as a candidate for the newly created Senate, as well as for substitute governor. From the executive office he could respond effectively to any significant difference with his successor or any crises the latter could not handle. Nevertheless, the opposition would not have to run directly against Don Ignacio's name and past reputation, which he had always presented to the voters as a claim against them for his continuance in office.[6] More significantly, much of Pesqueira's prominent support was eroding.

---

[5] *Ibid.*, 172-173. According to Buelna, many southerners associated with the *porfirista* party voted for the *lerdista* candidate because they considered his government much more likely to topple afterwards. Events would prove their calculation correct.

In the federal elections (July 11, 1875), Rojo won soundly as a congressional candidate in the electoral district of Ocoroni (the far north, including Sinaloa district). This victory demonstrated that his failure to win a single vote in the earlier state elections was due to a silent protest by the *rojista* party.

[6] Corral, 119.

Many politicians, such as Román Román and Jesús Quijada, had often resisted Pesqueira's policies in the legislature but, nonetheless, had declined to oppose his reelection openly. Now they were actively working for his defeat. Even the governor's friends had begun to desert him. Ismael Quiroga owed his meteoric rise in politics in large part to Pesqueira. The governor had made him his private secretary while Quiroga was still in his teens and then had appointed him editor of the official newspaper. After a term in the legislature (1869-1871), he had been elected to the Congress at the age of twenty-six. Now, having just turned thirty, he was turning his back on his political mentor. The Monteverde brothers of Hermosillo were also calling it quits— even Manuel, who had been Pesqueira's chief political associate until he retired from the political scene to his mines in Zubiate after his term as substitute governor had ended in 1869.[7]

Aware that lack of cohesion had contributed notably to their earlier defeats, the opposition leaders moved to channel the growing anti-Pesqueira sentiment into a well-organized adversary in the elections. Political clubs were organized by notables in the district towns to choose and campaign for a slate of local candidates, including those for the legislature.[8] A state convention was called for mid-May (1875) to select candidates for governor and the Congress. Not surprisingly, Guaymas was chosen as the host town, since it was under the friendly and protective eye of Captain Rangel's federal garrison. The convention, composed of delegates from the opposition clubs formed in the principal urban centers, again turned to General Jesús García Morales to lead their banner. García Morales, they declared, "symbolizes order, respect for the law, the death of nepotism, guarantees to all parties, and the most loyal, sincere, and positive adherence to the constitutional system; [he is] the only one who can lead us along the broad path of progress to general well-being . . . ."[9]

---

[7] Almada, 636, 638.

[8] Corral, 118.

[9] *El Convencional* (Guaymas), June 4, 1875. Among those attending the convention were Jesús Quijada, Ismael Quiroga, Francisco C. Aguilar, and Román Román from the Arizpe-Ures area; Gabriel Monteverde, Leonides G. Encinas, and Benigno V. García from Hermosillo; Adolfo Almada, Manuel Moreno, and Francisco Cevallos from Alamos district; and Francisco Mears and Wenceslao Iberri from the port of Guaymas.

Besides García Morales, the convention declared for the following candidates: substitute governor, Francisco Serna (to be chosen by the new legislature); senators, Manuel Monteverde and Jesús A. Almada; their alternates, Jesús Quijada and Domingo Elías González; federal diputados, Alfonso Mejía and Captain José María Rangel (Hermosillo electoral district); and their alternates, Ismael S. Quiroga and Rafael Ruiz (Ures). No federal deputy was endorsed for the Alamos electoral district because its delegates lacked instructions for proposing such a candidate.

The independents in the district of Alamos later selected a slate of candidates: for federal diputado, Felix Almada, with Santiago Goyenche as alternate; also Adolfo Almada and Manuel Moreno for the state legislature, and their alternates, Aristides Verdugo (a nephew of Miguel Urrea and at that time manager of his uncle's business affairs) and Quirino Corbalá. *El Fantasma* (Alamos), July 16, 1875.

The local liberals of the opposition still believed that the full exercise of liberal institutions and effective state authority were compatible if the most capable and principled persons held office. The convention's manifesto laid the blame for the state's economic stagnation and social decadence squarely on the ineptitude and indolence of the Pesqueira regime.[10] The opposition newspapers, blossoming forth as desert flowers after a sudden downpour, quickly went on the offensive, picking up the manifesto's theme and adding to it other grievances. Governor Pesqueira, the opposition press said, was a poor administrator, who spent his time savoring the accumulation of power at his hacienda, Las Delicias, rather than attending to the needs of the state. His underlings, the prefects, were even worse. They were little more than henchmen, many of dubious origin, who did little more than suppress municipal independence and individual rights for the political perpetuation of the regime.[11]

The opposition claimed that the administration had fostered the social progress of the state only minimally, for it demonstrated little concern for education. The primary schools, it said, yielded only a fraction of what was needed to provide those attending them with a real future. Even worse, there was not a single *colegio* where one could acquire a profession, and the laboring classes lacked the funds to send their children outside the state to learn a career:

> Here only the child of a rich man can be somebody; the child of a poor man, though he has talent superior to that of the former, will be forced to see such talent undeveloped until the hour of his death, because in nineteen years of administration the men who form the government have not taken the time to establish a *colegio* of professional instruction.[12]

The prostration of the economy was the direct result of the Pesqueira regime's inattention and ruinous fiscal policies, the opposition papers charged. Commerce, "the thermometer of public wealth," was crippled by the government's high consumption taxes, excessive personal contributions, incessant extraordinary levies, and lack of guarantees. The money accruing from such fiscal policies had gone to line the pockets of the governor's friends and underlings and to underwrite the questionable military exploits of "El General," while public improvements and education cried out for want of funds.[13]

---

[10] *El Convencional,* June 4, 1875.

[11] Manuel R. Uruchurtu, *Apuntes biográficos del Señor D. Ramón Corral, 1854-1900* (México, 1910), 13, 15-23; *El Independiente* (Hermosillo), May 13, 1875.

[12] *El Convencional,* June 4, 1875.

[13] *Ibid.*

At the root of the problem, the opposition preached, was Pesqueira's betrayal of the liberal principles of the Constitution of 1857 and the Reforma. The days when progressive ideas were the inheritance of a few illustrious and patriotic persons were gone. Since the promulgation of the Constitution, the way of progress and reform had been opened to the sight of all. Yet the post-war years had shown that those who were entrusted as guardians of the people's newly won rights had tried to convert themselves into their tutors, and in so doing had become their enemies. The Pesqueira administration had become despotic, had broken faith with the liberal traditions of the Reforma.[14]

One had only to look at the governor's inner circle, the opposition said, to verify such charges. His advisor and chief assistant since 1871, Joaquín M. Astiazarán, had supported Gándara and had served as prefect of the Imperial Department of Sonora. He had then dropped out of politics after the Empire's defeat, a beneficiary of the general mood of toleration. But when Pesqueira's support among his former allies had begun to wane, Astiazarán had presented himself as a decided partisan of the governor's becoming successively a diputado, the leader of the *pesqueirista* faction in the legislature, and acting governor. Now he was a candidate for the Senate. In addition, one of the two *pesqueirista* candidates for alternates to that office, General Miguel Blanco, was an old reactionary general who had abandoned Hermosillo in the face of Raousset's first filibustering expedition, fought under the conservative banner, and served the Empire. Pesqueira was the one who had prevailed previously in securing his election as a federal diputado, in spite of his poor reputation in the state.[15]

Governor Pesqueira and his followers mounted a concerted campaign of their own. Political clubs were formed in most of the principal towns, slates of candidates were chosen, and newspapers were established to counter the opposition's propaganda barrage. The *pesqueiristas* also resorted to more tainted means. In Hermosillo they paid a bunch of riffraff to break up a rally in favor of the opposition's candidates by shouting "Long live Pesqueira and death to the rich" and by roughing up some of the opposition's supporters, with the assurance of immunity.[16] Similar tactics were employed in Ures. As some of the members of the opposition's club were entering a meeting hall one night, they were attacked by a band of *pesqueiristas*, led by the state treasurer, Juan M. Salcido, and some local police. Nine were wounded and

---

[14] *El Independiente*, May 13, 1875. Some of the leading writers in the opposition press were Jesús Quijada, Adolfo Almada, Román Román, Ismael S. Quiroga, Jesús Corella, Francisco Elías González, Miguel Urrea, Aristides Verdugo, and Ramón Corral. *El Amigo del Pueblo*, June 11, 1875.

[15] *La Regeneración*, June 11, 1875.

[16] Villa, 324.

most of those who had gathered were dispersed. When the opposition leaders tried to begin the meeting anyway, the meeting hall was invaded by the *pesqueirista* band, and it became impossible to proceed. Ciriaco Martínez and Jesús Quijada went to the chief of police, demanding guarantees for their right to hold the meeting, but he excused himself, saying he could not keep order. He refused to disperse the *pesqueiristas* from the hall, and the meeting was cancelled.[17]

A similar fate befell the opposition in the elections. They won the districts of Arizpe, Altar, Magdalena, and Alamos and gained a near split in the district of Moctezuma. The government triumphed in Sahuaripa, Hermosillo, Guaymas, and Ures. The opposition claimed the government won the latter three districts—important because of their large numbers of electors—through fraud and abuses. They cited the refusal of election officials, named by ayuntamientos loyal to Pesqueira, to give opposition supporters their ballots, as well as their use of public revenues to pay them for their services. In addition, when the secondary elections were held in those three districts, illegal Pesqueira electors were admitted to the polls, while oppostion electors were prevented from entering.[18]

Even with its triumph in five of the nine districts, the government preferred not to take chances. In early August the out-going, subservient legislature declared void the elections in the districts of Alamos, Altar, and Arizpe. José Pesqueira thus easily obtained a clear majority and the *pesqueirista* candidates triumphed in the elections for the Congress (save for the electoral district of Alamos) and for the legislature (excepting the districts of Alamos, Arizpe, and Altar).[19]

ARMED RESISTANCE SEEKING OUTSIDE ASSISTANCE

In both Sonora and Sinaloa there soon followed armed resistance to the electoral impositions. They were two of numerous insurrections which began to surface around the country, most in reaction to President Lerdo's efforts to insure his reelection in 1876 by intervening in state politics. These local revolts in time became linked in varying degrees and durations with the national revolution initiated by Porfirio Díaz in January, 1876, with the publication of the Plan of Tuxtepec. Still, many local liberals turned to armed resistance outside of his leadership. Most acted without his orders. Thus, the Tuxtepec Revolt was quite loose and local in the character of its operations.[20]

---

[17] *El Pueblo Independiente* (Ures), June 4, 1975.

[18] *El Amigo del Pueblo*, July 30, 1875; *El Fantasma*, July 16, 1875.

[19] Corral, 119-120; Corbalá Acuña, *Constituciones,* 259-260.

[20] Cosío Villegas, *República Restaurada—vida política,* 814, 824-825.

The air of control surrounding the *lerdista* circle in Sinaloa, emanating from the results of the state elections, was not long in dissipating. The new administration's position eroded quickly. In mid-October Gaxiola was conceded extraordinary powers on account of the approach of rebel forces under Susano Ortiz (an early leader in the La Noria Revolt in Sinaloa), who had pronounced against the new government in neighboring Durango. An extraordinary contribution of one-half percent was decreed, along with a military draft; both actions provoked discontent. Many public employees of the former administration were dismissed because they were not *lerdistas.* Public instruction was neglected. By the following July, the secretary of the government (Jesús Bringas) had resigned in disgust, small rebel bands had begun cropping up in several parts of the state, and federal elections could be held in only two of the five electoral districts (those that could be manipulated by General Arce).[21]

That same July, the links with the Tuxtepec Revolt were forged. One of Díaz's closest collaborators, General Donato Guerra, had slipped into Sinaloa from Tepic in late June to promote the Plan de Tuxtepec. As Díaz emissary, Guerra had particularly sought out Colonel Francisco Cañedo, whom the Oaxacan general had decided was their most likely and effective connection in Sinaloa.[22] On July 11 Cañedo and Manuel Inzunza, commander of the national guard in the capital, declared for the Plan de Tuxtepec in Culiacán. Since both enjoyed the governor's confidence, they caught Gaxiola off guard and confined him to his residence. Cañedo was immediately seconded in the northern districts, including Cosalá.[23]

There was hardly any prominent family that did not take part in, or at least support, the revolt in Culiacán and the other district towns. The decision was not easy, however. The northern party had supported the legal constitutional government—both that of Sinaloa and that of the nation in Mexico City—against the series of revolts that had surfaced since the Intervention. Their partisanship toward the Juárez-Lerdo regime had progressively cooled to the point of suspicious neutrality. Yet whatever differences that had arisen

---

[21]*Ibid.*, 824, 880-881; Buelna, *Apuntes* 173-194. Rumors of poisoning surrounded the October 30 death of José Rojo (the defeated gubernatorial candidate the previous summer) in his home town of Sinaloa. An immense throng from that town and neighboring villages attended the funeral. Buelna, *Apuntes,* 174.

On February 27, 1876, Pedro Betancourt pronounced against the government in Villa Unión; he was succeeded, after his death in March, by Gerardo Ocampo. Rafael Partida in Cosalá district (April 7) and Feliciano Roque in San Ignacio (May 29) led others in revolt against the government. Buelna, *Apuntes,* 174.

[22]Cosío Villegas, *República Restaurada—vida política,* 824, 853, 882; Mena, v.2, 318.

[23]Buelna, *Apuntes,* 176. The federal forces had just left the capital days before to pursue those already in revolt. It was widely rumored that General Arce had ordered them to do so because he knew of Gaxiola's growing unpopularity and hoped to provoke a state of siege by leaving the governor exposed to a revolt in the capital.

or grievances they had suffered had not provoked them to armed resistance. They had observed constitutional legality in their opposition. But now their forbearance with manipulation had reached a limit. Such constitutional scruples were of much less concern to southerners who endorsed the revolt: many who had supported Gaxiola in the elections believed his manipulative policies on behalf of Lerdo's interests had gone too far; *porfiristas* quite possibly had anticipated what, indeed, transpired.[24]

On July 20 (1876) President Lerdo declared Sinaloa in a state of siege and named General Arce provisional governor. The general was considered even more of a despotic instrument of Lerdo than Gaxiola, and this feeling only fueled the growing alienation. Federal forces spread out from Mazatlán, recovering control over much of the state by October. Guerra was hunted down near the Chihuahua border and later shot while trying to escape. Cañedo retired. Inzunza kept a small band of guerrillas operating in the foothills of the sierra. Arce moved all the state offices and archives to Mazatlán.[25]

Tuxtepec rebels in Sinaloa shared the fate of most others throughout the north and west of the country. Díaz was forced to abandon the revolt along the northern frontier and return to Oaxaca. But the centers of guerrilla resistance were so widespread and so localized that the federal government's resources had become stretched too thin to end the revolution nationwide. With a second revolt, which was instigated by José María Iglesias (the Chief Justice of the Supreme Court and next in line to the presidency) and supported by numerous *lerdistas* who could not abide the blatant rigging of the federal elections, and a Díaz-led offensive from Oaxaca that decisively defeated federal forces at Tecoac, Lerdo's position in Mexico City became untenable by late November, and he left for the United States. The ex-president was joined within a month by Iglesias, whom Díaz had handily defeated in Querétaro.[26]

Timing his pronouncement conveniently with Lerdo's abdication on November 25, the military commander and prefect of Culiacán, Lieutenant Colonel Jesús Ramírez, went over to the rebels' side and quickly united the scattered bands behind his leadership. By late January (1877) his forces controlled the state. General Arce's conversion to the Tuxtepec Plan was too late and artificial.[27]

---

[24]*Ibid.*, 172, 176-177.

[25]*Ibid.*, 177-181.

[26]Cosío Villegas, *República Restaurada—vida política*, 825-826, 886-924.

[27]Buelna, *Apuntes*, 182-187. Besides uniting those already in active rebellion, Ramírez was seconded by Colonel Andres L. Tapia, Lieutenant Colonel Manuel Inzunza, Lieutenant Colonel Cleofas Salmón (the prefect and military commander of Cosala), and Lorenzo Torres, who had returned to the district of Fuerte from Sonora, where the year before he had helped bring an end to the Pesqueira regime.

Unlike the fallen Governor Gaxiola in Sinaloa, Ignacio Pesqueira had suspected that at least some of his opponents would not passively accept the revised results of the elections. Preparations for such an eventuality were made while he still officially occupied the governor's office. In late June (1875) the out-going legislature had granted him extraordinary powers on the pretext of the tense situation then reported in the Río Yaqui. The governor used these powers a month later to decree an extraordinary contribution of 35,000 pesos and to issue an executive order for the mobilization of the national guard.[28]

Pesqueira's political senses were accurate. In early August, a day or two after the legislature's declaration of the *pesqueiristas'* electoral victory, a revolt broke out in the districts of Altar and Magdalena, repudiating the results of the recent elections. The leaders called upon President Lerdo to install an interim governor until new elections were held, by virtue of the extraordinary powers with which he had been recently invested. Francisco Serna, the administrator of the *aduana* of the coastal landing of Libertad in Altar district, was proclaimed head of the insurrection. Serna's principal collaborators were also federal employees in that region: Francisco del Río and Manuel Barreda, respectively administrators of the frontier *aduanas* of Altar and Magdalena.[29] Their reputation and social standing, as well as the widespread sympathy favoring their objectives, attracted many of the notables of those districts to the revolt. However, the government's advanced preparations enabled it to quickly counter and defeat the rebels, who wisely retired to Arizona.[30]

On September 1 Don Ignacio handed over the government to Don Pepe with the insurrection quelled. Nevertheless, the new Governor Pesqueira was not granted a grace period. The Yaquis and Mayos had begun to renew their long-enduring struggle to regain some of their lands while the state was preoccupied with the *sernista* revolt. The tribes were led by a new young chief with vision, steadfastness, and a knack for organization. Born José María Leyra, he had become commonly known as Cajame.[31] Granted emergency powers, the new governor decreed an extraordinary contribution of 30,000 pesos in early October and launched a vigorous campaign against the tribes, believing that the uprising was being promoted by his political enemies. He had the legislature extend his emergency powers a month later and levied another extraordinary contribution, this time one of 40,000 pesos. The total of extraordinary taxes had, thus, reached 105,000 pesos in a little more than

---

[28]Corral, 119-120.
[29]*La Estrella de Occidente,* August 20, August 27, and September 24, 1875, Reel 6; *idem.,* August 27, 1875.
[30]Corral, 120-121.
[31]*Ibid.,* 122-123.

three months, and the amount provoked great disgust among the notables and the general public.[32]

In the meantime, rebel bands had begun reappearing in the northern part of the state, taking advantage of the government campaign against the Yaquis and Mayos. Serna, with the help of sympathetic emigrés in Arizona, had recruited and equipped a new force and had returned to operate in the northwest part of the state, where the revolt had been initiated. At the same time, Juan C. Escalante had raised a rebel band in the east in the district of Arizpe. In late December the two were joined by rebel bands in the districts of Hermosillo and Ures. Led by Francisco E. González and Antonio Palacio, the rebels succeeded in briefly occupying both towns before being driven off by superior state forces.[33]

The Pesqueiras' archenemies on Alamos had not been idle, either—only cautious. The government was keeping a watchful eye on its foremost antagonists. They had been entreating Lorenzo Torres, a *porfirista* of long standing in northern Sinaloa, to come to initiate armed resistance in that district, which the town's prominent families promised to support and protect. In mid-January (1876) Torres seconded Serna's plan in the mining center of Promontorios, reciting a litany of the *alamense* opposition's accumulated grievances against the Pesqueira regime. Torres succeeded in taking and holding Alamos for nearly three weeks before being driven south by a more numerous state contingent.[34]

Though General Don Ignacio in the north and Governor Don Pepe in the south triumphed in the great majority of encounters with the rebels, they could not crush the insurrection. They ill-advisedly cracked down hard on opposition notables in the principal towns, even those not actively supporting the revolt, through confiscation of property, imprisonment, and suspension of rights. This repression and the resort to the increasingly intolerable extraordinary contributions only intensified the determination and swelled the ranks of the opposition.[35]

Even more damaging, the Pesqueiras' poor relations with the federal government and its bureaucracy now had come home to roost. When they asked President Lerdo to order the federal forces in the state to help the state executive put down the rebellion, Lerdo diplomatically complied. But his commander there was hardly one who would seriously lend assistance: General García Morales, the Pesqueiras' opponent in the last two elections. Moreover, the President provided his general with an out. García Morales was to

---

[32] *La Estrella de Occidente,* November 26, 1875.

[33] Corral, 121-126.

[34] *Ibid.,* 129-130; *La Estrella de Occidente,* February 11 and 18, 1876, Reel 6.

[35] Corral, 125, 128-131; *El Susurro* (Guaymas), August 1, 1877.

lend aid in restoring peace, but only if it did not interfere with the principal obligations of the federal forces: to protect the Guaymas customs house and defend the frontier against the Apaches. The general informed the governor that he had barely enough troops to carry out these assignments.[36]

The Pesqueira regime then cut off what few ties remained with Mexico City. Not only was the federal bureaucracy refusing to help as requested, the government charged angrily in retaliation, but it was directly aiding the rebels. General García Morales, it said, gave the rebels entrance to the military colonies on the frontier while denying entry to state troops. The officials of the Guaymas *aduana* were remitting arms and supplies to the rebel forces. Moreover, the government claimed, opponents of the regime were successfully seeking refuge in that port, protected from persecution by Captain Rangel with the general's blessing.[37]

The rebels had also sought federal intervention, reaching the conclusion that only in this way, after a decade of legal and, more recently, armed setbacks, could they bring the Pesqueira regime down. But to them, such intervention connoted the sending of a federal representative to take control temporarily of the state government and convene new elections: "The Independents have never wanted to impose governors in Sonora, inasmuch as in their political plan they solicited federal intervention in order that new elections might be convoked."[38] In late January, with the opposing forces seemingly locked into a stalemate, conditions were propitious for Lerdo to act. Furthermore, with the eruption of the Tuxtepec Revolution and the approach of federal elections, the President needed all of the firm allies he could muster. The two Pesqueiras, in his eyes, had proven themselves nothing but troublesome upstarts in recent years, so Lerdo sent General Vicente Mariscal to restore order and arbitrate the conflict.

Mariscal arrived in Guaymas on March 1 (1876), calling for an end to hostilities and proceeding at once to Alamos to confer with Governor Pesqueira. Federal officials and military officers in Guaymas painted the Pesqueira regime in dark colors, and Mariscal took note of the enthusiastic receptions shown him in the villages along the way to Alamos, and especially in the city itself. The conference between the federal envoy and the governor was evidently stiff and unproductive. Pesqueira immediately left for Ures with his troops. Mariscal on March 14 declared Sonora in a state of siege, assuming the political and military command of the state. When the governor protested, Mariscal ordered the rebel forces under Torres and Serna to serve as auxiliaries to his own federal troops. Mariscal then marched from Alamos

---

[36]Corral, 125, 128-129.

[37]*La Estrella de Occidente,* January 28 and 31, and February 18, 1876, Reel 6.

[38]*Ibid.,* February 25, 1876 (the reprint of an article in *La Hoja Suelta* [Tucson]).

through Guaymas to Hermosillo, collecting these auxiliary forces and receiving tumultuous welcomes in each town. On March 21 President Lerdo ratified Mariscal's state of siege declaration. General Don Ignacio and Governor Don Pepe, who had been gathering their forces in Ures, recognized the handwriting on the wall. They dismissed their troops and submitted to the interim governor.[39]

TESTING LINKAGES

The Pesqueira era had finally drawn to a close. However, its demise had made national political interests a part of Sonoran politics as they had never been previously. Though the assumptions about local prerogatives and dispersion of authority remained, reliance on connections with Mexico City and the political groups who based themselves there, or sought to establish themselves there, became accepted by local liberals, whether independent or *pesqueirista*. The interim period and the elections of 1877 revealed the new order of things.

Sonorans received the new provisional government of General Mariscal warmly. He had delivered them from the long rule of the Pesqueira regime. Votes of thanks poured in from ayuntamientos throughout the state, expressing their deep gratitude to Mariscal and the federal government for declaring the state of siege that deposed the Pesqueiras and for the opportunity they now had to enter a new era of regeneration and progress.[40] Though President Lerdo had been none too popular in the state, many Sonorans approved of Mariscal's support of Lerdo's reelection. The President, they acknowledged, had been the one who had sent Mariscal to end the civil war.[41]

Sonorans went along with the provisional governor as he nimbly switched his recognition from Lerdo to Iglesias to Díaz during the Tuxtepec Revolution, putting down a die-hard attempt of the Pesqueiras to regain power in the process.[42] In a year in office, Mariscal had restored full civil guarantees, placed many of the leaders of the independent party in the highest public positions, cracked down on the lawless elements whom the Pesqueiras had

---

[39]Corral, 132-134.

[40]*Boletín Oficial del Estado de Sonora* (Ures), April 21 and 28, and June 23, 1876, Reel 6.

[41]*Los Cinco Vocales* (Guaymas), June 10, 1876.

[42]Corral, 135-139; *La Voz de Alamos* (Alamos), March 13, 1877. Mariscal had astutely sent his secretary of government, Jesús Quijada, to Mexico City to keep him abreast of political developments and to serve as an authorized agent in the interior if and when Lerdo fell from power. With the decisive *porfirista* victory at Tecoac in late November (1876), Mariscal had switched his allegiance to Iglesias. The Pesqueiras, who had previously backed Lerdo to uphold the principal of reelection, had likewise recognized Iglesias, claiming that with Lerdo's fall, Mariscal no longer had any authority to serve as provisional governor. This reasoning provided the rather shaky justification for their revolt in December. Almada, 447.

tolerated as an occasional source of support, put public administration and the treasury in some semblance of order, and tried to foment public instruction and public improvements.[43]

The new president, Porfirio Díaz, did not view Governor Mariscal in quite such a favorable light. The *lerdista* appointee had not sworn adhesion to the Tuxtepec Plan until almost three months (February 5, 1877) after the triumph of Tecoac, and he had been the last holdover governor to do so. Díaz had serious doubts about Mariscal's loyalty, as he had about that of the remaining *lerdista* governors who had adhered to his provisional government. He determined to replace them when he could. The time was not yet appropriate in Sonora, however: Mariscal could count on the firm adhesion of his troops, and reports filtering back to Díaz indicated that he was still well thought of in the state.[44]

Three months later, however, the President seems to have changed his mind about the possibilities for Mariscal's replacement. Feeling more secure since he had been constitutionally elected, and being threatened only by possible *lerdista* expeditions from Texas, in late May Díaz named General Epitacio Huerta provisional governor and military commander of Sonora.[45] The general left for the state accompanied by none other than Ignacio Pesqueira. The ex-governor had abandoned his aloofness from national political interests. They had been instrumental in bringing about his fall from power. He concluded that they were now essential to his hopes to recover it. Since his defeat the previous winter, Pesqueira had vigorously pleaded his case with Díaz, while his friends had conducted a whispering campaign in the Mexico City press, alleging Mariscal's disloyalty to the Tuxtepec Revolution.[46] With no local political group having as yet mounted a serious challenge to Mariscal, the *pesqueiristas* were the only viable nexus to Sonoran politics then available to the President.

---

[43] *Boletín Oficial de Sonora*, April 14, 1876, Reel 6; *La Voz de Alamos*, February 27 and March 6, 1877.

[44] Cosío Villegas, *Porfiriato—vida política interior*, vol. 1, 159, 166, 301.

[45] *Ibid.*, 302. There is considerable uncertainty among available sources concerning the exact powers with which General Huerta was entrusted by Díaz. Cosío Villegas and the newspapers in the following two citations seem to agree that General Huerta came to Sonora both as provisional governor and as military commander of the state, implying that Díaz had acted on the premise that Mariscal might still be legally considered only a provisional governor and, thus, subject to replacement by the federal executive until state elections were held. Yet Governor Mariscal had convoked state elections April 20, more than five weeks before Díaz named General Huerta. This time should have been enough for word to have reached the President of the impending state elections in early June. Perhaps he sent Huerta with what *La Prensa* of Guaymas termed "discretional" powers to test the political waters to see if Mariscal's removal might be possible before the finalization of the elections. However, Huerta's arrival came a week after the new legislature's certification of the results and Mariscal's inauguration.

[46] *La Reconstrucción* (Hermosillo), May 8, 1877.

When General Huerta and Pesqueira arrived together in Guaymas in mid-July, Don Ignacio's old followers spread rumors that Díaz had sent Huerta to depose Mariscal and soon their *jefe* would resume control of the government again. General Huerta in no way disclaimed these rumors; rather Pesqueira continued at his side as he proceeded to Ures.[47] Nevertheless, the President's power to secure friendly governors was limited by two critical considerations. The Plan of Tuxtepec had given him authority to replace only provisional governors freely. It left completely to the states the process of the restoration of constitutional government and any alterations in their constitutions that they might determine. Secondly, Díaz had to proceed with prudence in promoting candidates for state elections. He did not know well the local interests in the vast majority of states, interests that were always varied and numerous, sometimes contradictory, occasionally very potent. He and his agents had to respect them.[48]

Whatever General Huerta's precise instructions and intentions were, the reception he received in Sonora did not take long to force their alteration. The carriage in which he and Pesqueira were riding through Hermosillo was surrounded by large crowds, harangued, and even stoned. No less hostile manifestations greeted them in Ures. The official reception in the capital was also antagonistic, though more refined. Mariscal had convoked state elections April 20 (1877) and had just been duly elected constitutional governor. The new legislature rallied to his defense. Led by Carlos Ortiz, it declared that the federal executive had no constitutional authority to intervene in state elections, whether to nullify their results, or depose and replace state officials resulting from them. It warned that it would brook no federal interference in Sonora's internal affairs. To do so, it said, would diminish the state's sovereignty.[49] The representatives of the independent party, which overwhelmingly dominated the legislature, were reiterating the narrow limits of the anti-Pesqueira movement's acceptance of federal intervention: to restore the free exercise of liberal institutions, nothing more.

The political waters had been tested unproductively, and Díaz was quick to restore good relations with the elected state government. General Huerta, without doubt on instructions from Mexico City, within a month recognized Mariscal's administration as legitimate.[50] Huerta himself was removed from the scene in a few months and replaced by General Bibiano Dávalos, who struck up warm relations with the governor.[51]

[47]*Boletín Oficial de Sonora,* July 27, and August 10, 1877; *La Prensa* (Guaymas), July 23 and August 19, 1877.
[48]Cosío Villegas, *Porfiriato—vida política interior,* vol. 1, 293, 455, 459.
[49]*Boletín Oficial de Sonora,* August 17, 1877; Corral, 139-143.
[50]Corral, 143.
[51]Cosío Villegas, *Porfiriato—vida política interior,* vol. 1, 302.

The closing of ranks behind the governor in the face of General Huerta's arrival seemed to exhibit a political consensus in Sonora. Almost all those politically active in the state save the *pesqueiristas* had stood behind him in relations with Mexico City. In reality, however, there was far from a consensus on political matters within the state. Governor Mariscal had disturbed a large segment of the independent party by declining to promulgate and observe the Reformed Constitution of 1872. Twenty-seven *ayuntamientos* had called upon him to do so the previous summer.[52] Instead, in convoking the state elections, he had declared that the newly elected legislature would be constituent with ninety days to formulate a constitution and had used the Pesqueira-dictated electoral law of 1875 as the basis for their effectuation. The latter action meant principally that there would be no direct election nor electoral selection of prefects.[53]

Some, especially those in Alamos, chose to support the governor's candidacy in spite of these failings. They did so on the assumption that by also promoting Francisco Serna for vice-governor and by electing responsible diputados, they could ensure that the constitutional reforms of 1872 would be adopted and any personal ambitions the governor might have would be thwarted. Their sense of gratitude for his appearance in Alamos to end the revolution and his decision to remove the Pesqueira regime from office apparently outweighed their prior political experiences. Once more they were entrusting their commitment to liberalism to an outsider.[54]

There were others of the independent party with a more immediate sense of alarm, and perhaps a touch of sour grapes as well. It seemed clear to them that, in fact, the governor favored the constitution and electoral law that was in force during Ignacio Pesqueira's last administration (both of which they considered illegal) and that he favored neither the election of the prefects nor direct elections. Perhaps, they surmised, he opposed them for the same reasons that Pesqueira had: because they were serious obstacles to his ambitions to centralize power in his hands. Nevertheless, they duly acknowledged the accomplishments of Mariscal's provisional government and politely argued against his candidacy on the grounds that he lacked the constitutional re-

---

[52]*Boletín Oficial de Sonora*, June-August, 1876, Reel 6, and August 24, 1877, Reel 7; *La Regeneración*, July 20, 1876.

[53]*Boletín Oficial de Sonora*, April 20 and May 4, 1876, Reel 6. Mariscal rejected the petitions of the ayuntamientos, which included most of those of the state's principal urban centers, on the grounds that there were three state constitutions with more or fewer claims to legitimacy and that he did not have the authority to declare any one of them in force. Critics from the independent party questioned how he could then pick and use parts of the three constitutions, without recognizing any one of them, to compose the convocation of the elections and the rules under which the constituent legislature was to operate.

[54]*La Voz de Alamos*, August 13, 1878.

quirement of Sonoran citizenship and that, as an outsider, he did not adequately understand the state's needs.[55] The point of their argument was simply why an outsider, especially one about whom they had serious reservations, should reap the rewards of office that a person like Serna, whom they were promoting in the elections, so richly deserved for having led the revolutionary struggle against Pesqueira. In the back of their minds was the fear that Mariscal would become another Don Ignacio.

The backers of Governor Mariscal responded to *sernista* critics by saying that the governor's record over the previous year spoke for itself. Even his opponents acknowledged his accomplishments. If he had not done more, it was because he lacked the revenues to do so. The economic sectors were beginning to recover from the dislocations occasioned by the revolution. Mariscal, they concluded, had brought peace to the state, had restored full civil guarantees, had begun to tackle the state's pressing problems, and, thus, should be elected so that he might continue what he had commenced.[56]

The *sernistas* lost the June elections, but the margin was close: 113 to 86. They swept the districts of Hermosillo and Altar, won the district of Sahuaripa, and split in Moctezuma.[57] That elections were not held in Guaymas (the reasons for which are not evident in the sources) hurt the *sernista* cause, since the port was one of their strongest centers. Also damaging was the fact that, despite Serna's popularity in the district of Alamos, all of its electors voted for Mariscal for the reasons noted earlier. Serna was elected vice-governor, having been endorsed for that office by the *mariscalistas*. The *sernistas*, however, did win both seats from Alamos and Hermosillo, as well as those from Altar and Sahuaripa, to give them a slim majority in the legislature (with the absence of legislators from Guaymas).[58]

The linkage with national political interests was more pervasive in Sinaloa. The ties had been developing gradually through the post-war years. The *tepiqueño* emigrés and non-Sinaloan veterans had served as intermediaries initially. By the early 1870s, the notables of Mazatlán and other southern district towns had come to rely on connections with national political elements in their efforts to gain control of state politics, or at least to prevent the northern party from doing so. Increasingly, they had become allies of the *porfiristas*. Their support of the state of siege in 1872 and of the *lerdista* candidate in the 1875 elections had been tactical moves to block the continued dominance of the northern party and to open the way for their own return to power. In both they had failed.

---

[55] *El Club de Reforma* (Hermosillo), May 6 and 27, 1877, *El Plan de Tuxtepec* (Guaymas), May 11 and 18, 1877.

[56] *La Reconstrucción*, May 15, 1877.

[57] *Boletín Oficial de Sonora*, July 20, 1877.

[58] *La Voz de Ures*, June 15, 1877; *La Voz de Alamos*, August 13, 1878.

The gentry of the northern urban centers had steadfastly opposed outside intervention in Sinaloan politics. Mutual endorsement of candidates between local and national liberals was one thing—they had supported Juárez in 1867 and 1871—but the efforts of interests centered in Mexico City to secure state executives beholden to them was quite another. Such subordination was unacceptable to the northern party. They had opposed every such attempted imposition and had done so successfully. It is, thus, ironic that in the election following the armed expulsion of the *lerdista* imposition, the very connections with national political interests which northerners had so stubbornly resisted were forged to such a point that thereafter they became permanent.

At first, the leader of the triumphant Tuxtepec rebels, Colonel Ramírez, toyed with the idea of running for governor in the state elections scheduled for April (1877). As was the case with Ramón Corona a decade earlier, however, he soon abandoned the intention after considering the obstacles to it. He was persuaded that his election would arouse strong opposition because of the constitutional question raised by his current status as a professional soldier and employee of the federal government. In this he mirrored the recent exploits of Gaxiola and General Arce in most Sinaloans' eyes. Instead, he settled on Andrés L. Tapia, an active *porfirista* and former legislator from Cosalá, with close ties to Mazatlán. Tapia had organized and led the revolutionary effort in Cosalá district. However, his affiliations with the port alone made public opinion in the north generally cool to his candidacy. The northern party suspected that he would try to transfer the government back to Mazatlán, since his disaffection from the permanence of the capital in Culiacán was well known. The question of his religious beliefs also raised doubts among much of the nominally Catholic populace. He was a Mason. Critics said he was an atheist.[59]

Tapia's only opponent, Francisco Cañedo, was not the overwhelming expression of the popular will either. His skittish and yet, at the same time, often barefaced conduct in the recent revolution (as well as in previous ones) had cast a shadow over his reputation. So too did the widely held suspicion that he was partly responsible for the death of General Donato Guerra. From the time of Guerra's arrival as Díaz's agent for the western states, conflict had arisen between the two men. Cañedo wanted to keep control over the revolt within the state in his own corner, rather than hand it over to an outside superior. He had resisted Guerra's assumed authority and frequently refused to go along with the latter's military plans. The rebel movement had collapsed

---

[59]Buelna, *Apuntes,* 187. Tapia charged that Joaquin Redo, a close ally of Cañedo's, had spread around the accusation that he was an atheist. Cosío Villegas, *Porfiriato—vida política interior,* vol., 1, 461.

within two months and Guerra's flight to Chihuahua City had been intercepted by federal troops.[60]

It was commonly said that if there had been an alternative candidacy, both Tapia and Cañedo would have been rejected. But that was not the case. Why the members of the northern party did not field a candidate of their own is not clear. Quite possibly, it was because they did not count among themselves any prominent *porfirista* and revolutionary leader. In the wake of the Tuxtepec triumph, that quality was an important consideration in promoting a candidacy. They did select Roberto Orrantia, veteran Fuerte legislator who had long represented their interests, to run for vice-governor.[61] Nevertheless, since they had not endorsed a candidate for governor, the choice for the northern party members was between the lesser of two evils. And in that case, Cañedo had the clear advantage. True, he had supported the La Noria Revolt, but his ties to Mazatlán were far less clear then Tapia's, and the latter's candidacy had a strong impositionist character. Colonel Ramírez was an outsider, recently brought to military power. Cañedo, by contrast, had been a resident of the state for more than two decades and had developed ties with a number of prominent Culiacán families, in particular the Vegas. Consequently, the northern party largely backed Cañedo; to this support he added his substantial popularity in the south, which was due to his /porfirista and La Noria affiliations.[62]

To counter Cañedo's greater popularity, Provisional Governor Ramírez supported Tapia with all the resources at his command. He called village authorities to meet him on some or another pretext and then tried to persuade them to work for Tapia, threatening them if they would not agree.[63] He was assisted by the chief of federal forces in Sinaloa—a Corona protégé recently arrived from Jalisco, General Francisco Tolentino—who lent the full weight of his office in Tapia's favor.[64]

Despite such tactics by the provisional government, Cañedo obtained two-thirds of the vote. Tapia charged that Cañedo's own illegal tactics had brought about the electoral triumph. Lorenzo Torres, the defeated candidate said, had manufactured votes in the northern districts, while Joaquín Redo

---

[60]Buelna, *Apuntes,* 178-180, 187-188. Without Cañedo's cooperation, Guerra had soon been soundly defeated by federal forces and had decided to retire to the city of Chihuahua, traveling practically alone. Cañedo had agreed to send notices ahead of Guerra to protect and assist him along the way. Near that city, Guerra had been arrested and then shot while trying to escape.

[61]*Ibid.,* 188. A decade earlier Orrantia had sought to throw out the candidacies of Generals Rubí and Martínez for final selection by the legislature.

[62]*Ibid.,* 187-188; González Dávila, 82-83.

[63]Buelna, *Apuntes,* 187-188.

[64]Cosío Villegas, *Porfiriato—vida política interior,* vol. 1, 461.

had purchased them in the south.[65] *Cañedista* inspectors at the polling stations in Culiacán had vigorously opposed the provisional governor's attempt to obtain the vote for federal troops in the capital. Ramírez was forced to let Eustaquio Buelna arbitrate, and the ex-governor, though no fond admirer of Cañedo, ruled that they should be prohibited from voting because the express conditions of the state electoral law did not permit it. President Díaz had likewise assisted Cañedo by ordering the federal garrison of Mazatlán to abstain from voting in accordance with the state election law, despite their commander's decided support of Tapia.[66]

STRIKING A DEAL WITH DON PORFIRIO

Both Cañedo and Tapia had believed they enjoyed the favor of the President. In the end, each saw Díaz as the unofficial, but ultimate arbiter of the elections. It was primarily to him that Tapia addressed his charges of electoral fraud. It was to him that Cañedo explained his victory as such an absolute triumph that no one could doubt it.[67] And it was to him that General Toletino complained diplomatically about the lack of *porfirista* support for Tapia: "It is difficult, my general, to say in a letter all the machiavellian things that have happened in Sinaloa; but I can assure you that the friends of the government have not complied as expected."[68] Cañedo enunciated the factor judged most crucial by both candidates. He desired above all that the President know "who has been your most constant defender in these parts."[69]

The support of the northern party had been important. But ultimately the fate of the election, these three concluded, had rested with Díaz's judgment about the security of and prospects for his connections with them, then the most politically powerful figures in Sinaloa. Perhaps their conclusion about Díaz's decisive ability to intervene in Sinaloan politics was as yet unwarranted. (Certainly in Sonora the new President had been proven limited in his influence.) Local liberals, in particular those of the northern party, might very well have still been the dominant element in Sinaloan politics. But those most prominent in the electoral contest—Cañedo, Ramírez, Tapia, Tolentino—no longer thought so. Connections with Mexico City were essential by then for them.

---

[65]*Ibid.*, 461-462. Tapia's accusations went unanswered from Mexico City. Díaz recognized that Cañedo had won an overwhelming majority of the vote and had done so in the face of the active intervention of the provisional government and federal commander against him.

[66]Buelna, *Apuntes,* 188.

[67]Cosío Villegas, *Porfiriato—vida política interior,* vol. 1, 461.

[68]*Ibid.*

[69]*Ibid.*

The President had subtly made known his preference in the elections. Ramírez was a hesitant latecomer to the Plan of Tuxtepec. Though an early defector to the revolution, Tolentino had proven to be a collaborator whose ambitions were hard to subordinate. Tapia was a *porfirista* of good standing, but he owed his rise to Ramírez. That left Cañedo, who had been cultivating connections with the national *porfirista* circle as long and as carefully as almost any other figure then of influence in the state's politics.[70] Yet Cañedo was not the typical *porfirista* who had ultimately scaled the ladder successfully in the scramble for political power during the Restored Republic. He was not a distinguished military *jefe* of the Reforma or the Intervention. He was no man of jurisprudence or letters. Rather, Cañedo had risen to the top in Sinaloa through his political savvy, the suppleness of his commitments, and a keen sense of which way the winds were blowing.

Cañedo did not have the advantage of established family connections. He was born in an out-of-the-way ranchería in the municipio of Acaponeta on the Tepic side of the Río de las Canas. While still a youngster, he had gone to Mazatlán, where he found work as an errand boy in the commercial house of Vasabilbaso Brothers, cleaning and sweeping floors. He later became a clerk there. After serving in the republican cause against the Intervention, Cañedo moved on to Culiacán, taking a similar position in the store of Manuel Izurieta and then setting up a small business of his own, which floundered.[71] But in a few short years there he had gained the acquaintance of some notables, including members of the Vega family, and succeeded in being elected prefect. In 1871 he promoted the rather unrealistic candidacy of Alberto Vega for vice-governor, freely spending the money accruing from Vega's commercial establishment.[72]

The *tepiqueño* migrant pronounced against the results of those elections, but kept quiet his ambitions of becoming provisional governor of the state;[73] when the insurrection fizzled, Cañedo was captured and sentenced to death. By the grace of the legislature, and the concurrence of Governor Buelna, the sentence was commuted to ten years imprisonment, which Cañedo succeeded in escaping with the collusion of an escort transferring him to Mazatlán. Cañedo immediately cast his lot with the revolt of the *tepiqueño* party in support of the Plan of La Noria.[74] Operating generally in the northern districts, he was accused of seizing livestock, crops, money, and personal valuables, and of making forced loans.[75] When the revolt's fortunes waned, he

[70]*Ibid.*, 461-462; *idem, República Restaurada—vida política*, 824.
[71]González Dávila, 82-83.
[72]Buelna, *Apuntes,* 207-208.
[73]*Ibid.*, 116.
[74]*Ibid.*, 115-124.
[75]*El Clamor Público,* December 7, 1872.

knew when to get out, quickly arranging amnesty terms with General Ceballos.[76]

Cañedo then sat out of the political arena for a while, but he remained always alert to read the signs of change. He watched as the pendulum in the struggle between the two regions of the state swung back in the northern party's favor, with the return home of his fellow *tepiqueños*. Accordingly, he loosened his ties with the dwindling *tepiqueño* party and their *mazatlecan* allies and moved to patch up his relations with the Culiacán establishment. He maintained the close ties with Díaz that had been forged during the latter's retreat through Sinaloa at the close of the La Noria Revolt, and bided his time.[77]

The opportunity came with the 1875 elections. Cañedo feigned his support of Gaxiola, correctly perceiving that his imposition on the state by President Lerdo would promote the conditions of discontent favorable for another attempt to sit in the governor's chair. As Díaz's principal contact in Sinaloa, he broke open the Tuxtepec Revolt in the state. But he retired from action when the going got sticky, unwilling to subordinate his leadership to Guerra, much to the disgust of the other local *jefes*. Nevertheless, with Ramírez's resuscitation of the revolt, Cañedo returned to the fighting, mending fences with the revolutionary *jefes* and building support for the upcoming state elections.[78]

A singular opportunist, Cañedo had found a home in the *porfirista* camp. He had struggled long and hard to gain political control over the state, and like his political benefactor, Don Porfirio, he did not intend to give it up soon. Both men seemed to understand one another, to perceive similarly the new possibilities taking shape in the wake of the Tuxtepec Revolt. Local liberals like Cañedo could insure their own success in state politics by establishing permanent connections with national liberals of the *porfirista* circle, who had come to dominate public affairs at the federal level. In turn, the cooperation of such local liberals in state office could greatly assist *porfirista* liberals in achieving long-term tenure in Mexico City.

Such political possibilities were immediately pursued. The manipulative tactics of General Tolentino on Tapia's behalf could prove a serious obstacle to the Cañedo government, if continued. The experiences of the past ten years had demonstrated that very well. Without any delay after the confirmation of his electoral victory by the legislature, Cañedo asked Díaz to replace Tolentino as commander of the federal forces in Sinaloa with General Eguiluz. The President readily complied. Furthermore, Díaz made it clear to

---

[76] Buelna, *Apuntes,* 156.
[77] Hector R. Oléa, *Breve historia de la Revolución en Sinaloa, 1910-1917* (México, 1964), 5.
[78] Buelna, *Apuntes,* 176-187.

Ramírez and Tapia that Cañedo's large majority was proof enough for him of the validity of the election.[79] The political bond was sealed.

Díaz's choice of connection was an astute one. Cañedo needed him. He lacked a well-established family or regional base in Sinaloa. Though he was currently popular because of the Tuxtepec triumph, that popularity was temporary and shallow. There were few genuinely loyal to him. His commitments had been none too abiding, his principles none too exemplary for that. The rest sought him out pragmatically, in calculation, just as he approached them. Cañedo was firmly a part of state politics, not considered an outsider, and yet he was freer than almost any other prominent Sinaloan liberal from the local interests that limited maneuvering in making connections with national political circles. That Cañedo and Díaz found one another, that political ties between them were cemented so quickly and so solidly, is quite understandable.

There was no such immediate, optimum connection in Sonora following the triumph of the Tuxtepec Revolution. Díaz had discovered that fact rudely enough. General Huerta had been considered wholly an intruding outsider. Ignacio Pesqueira had lost almost all public respect. General Mariscal, though not a native, had come to the state in the most favorable circumstance of liberator from local despotism and, through success in the state elections, had acquired a general popularity and political base of his own. No other prominent local liberals as yet were either willing or sufficiently prepared to forge close working political ties with the *porfiristas* in Mexico City. Consequently, Díaz had to wait, but not for long.

The notables of the independent party in Sonora had begun choosing sides. The recent election had divided them between those who endorsed the continuation of the Mariscal government in light of its provisional success and those who suspected in it the possible formation of another centralizing regime that would pamper its partisans while neglecting the needs of the state, as the Pesqueira government had done. The latter group had united behind the candidacy of Francisco Serna to oppose, unsuccessfully, Mariscal's election. They shared common perceptions about the governor and those who decided to support and work with him.

The *sernistas* in part judged Mariscal by those closest to him. They saw the governor's support as coming principally from the northeastern districts, which had long dominated Sonoran politics. Ures was its focal point, where políticos from the Northeast and other sections of the state had come to be close to, and to share in, the source of political power that was located in the state capital. Politicians such as Lauro and Jesús Morales, Adolfo Almada, Ismael S. Quiroga, Manuel M. Corella, Cirilo Ramírez, Francisco C. Aguilar,

---

[79] Cosio Villegas, *Porfiriato—vida política interior,* vol. 1, 462.

Domingo Elías González, Leocadio Salcedo, Román Román, Jesús Quijada, and Rafael Corella were people who (whether as independents, ex-*pesqueiristas* turned independents, or even *pesqueiristas*) had been in and out of government, guiding the fortunes of the state since the Reforma. Their record, the *sernistas* believed, was a sorry one. They had become tired men, with a *juarista-lerdista* bureaucratic mentality, more preoccupied with holding office than with the urgency of political and administrative reforms or the vigorous promotion of the economy necessary to relieve the people of their impoverishment. They had compromised liberal principles without having brought progress in recompense. It was prominent persons such as these who had the governor's ear, the *sernistas* said.[80]

Sernista sentiment was strongest among the notables of Hermosillo, Guaymas, and Altar, towns in which Serna had lived, made his fortune, and acquired his public prestige.[81] Born in Altar district in 1832, Serna had acquired a hacienda and mining interests there. But in time, he had made his home in Hermosillo, where he had also engaged in commerce. Serna had risen to public prominence because of his unwavering opposition to the Intervention, after which he was elected municipal president and then named prefect of the district. He had then returned to Altar as a federal customs employee, from where he was endorsed for vice-governor in 1875 and then initiated the revolt that brought down Pesqueira.[82] With Serna, the business circles of the northwestern districts, and to a lesser extent Guaymas, had hoped to end the domination of the state by those from Ures and the northeast.[83]

These mostly business-oriented notables of the northwestern urban centers were generally not politicians themselves. They were entrepreneurs seeking a political group who could manage the government without undue burden on their private interests and with effective promotion of economic activity, in which those interests could prosper. Just such a political circle was then emerging among the *sernistas*: a small group of young newcomers, based in Alamos, who had risen to prominence in the revolt against Pesqueira.[84] This ambitious coterie wanted to bring about thorough-going administrative and fiscal reforms and the energetic promotion of the economy. They sought to do so by injecting new blood and modern ideas into the government, and they thought themselves most qualified.[85] Furthermore, these young políticos perceived that a political connection with Mexico City was necessary to

[80]*El Club de Reforma*, May 27, 1877; *El Plan de Tuxtepec*, May 11, 1877.

[81]*La Reconstrucción*, June 5, 1877; *El Club de Reforma*, April 29, May 13.

[82]Alamada, 740-741; *La Voz del Estado* (Magdalena), March, 1889 in MAHm, Sonora, Reel 9.

[83]*La Reconstrucción*, June 5, 1877.

[84]*El Club de Reforma*, May 6 and 13, 1877.

[85]*Ibid.*, May 27, 1877; *La Constitución* (Hermosillo), April 18, 1879.

bring about that substitution of governmental personnel and secure the requisite assistance in solving the state's lingering security problems and in stimulating economic activity.

The circle was led by an outsider, but one who had rapidly acquired prestige in the southern part of the state because of his aid to the beleaguered *alamense* notables in their resistance to the Pesqueira regime. Luis Torres was a tough veteran of the *porfirista* revolutions in Sinaloa. The military life was practically all he had ever known since moving to northern Sinaloa from his native Chihuahuan mining center of Guadalupe y Calvo during the Intervention: he had enlisted in the republican ranks in 1862 at the age of eighteen. He had risen to the rank of lieutenant colonel, but had gambled his commission away on the unsuccessful 1868 Martínez revolt. He then had become a *porfirista,* and with the Oaxacan general's rise to power, his own fortunes had revived. Torres had become acquainted with anti-Pesqueira elements in Alamos while serving in that district during the Intervention and had maintained and strengthened those ties from across the border in the years following. His election in 1875 as alternate federal diputado from Alamos electoral district[86] was an indication of the esteem in which by then he was held in southern Sonora. Torres, thus, had a base from which to court a connection with national political interests.

After taking part in the Tuxtepec Revolution in Sinaloa in 1876, Torres returned to Alamos the following year and was elected federal diputado for the southern part of the state. In Mexico City he quickly became a personal friend of President Díaz and established close, working political relations with him. With the connection realized, Torres went back to Sonora to animate his political circle and prepare for its coming to power. Then only thirty-four himself (in 1878), Torres' principal collaborators were Ramón Corral (24) and Carlos Ortiz (27), both of Alamos. Corral was a talented journalist from modest origins; Ortiz was the polished, European-educated, eldest son of one of the town's most prominent families. They were the two diputados from that district and leaders of the *sernista* opposition in the legislature. Other scions of the *alamense* gentry were members of Torres' coterie. Though Alamos was his base, Torres wisely began to integrate into his political circle the sons of prominent families from the central and northern part of the state who had been on the outside of Sonoran politics looking in for at least a decade. Some newcomers to the state were also included.[87]

---

[86] Almada, 792-793.

[87] *Ibid., passim.* Among Torres's young collaborators in Alamos were Carlos Ortiz's brothers, José María, Alfonso (25), and Agustín (22); Rafael Izabal (24); Felizardo Torres (30); and José T. Otero (44). Those from the northwest part of the state included Francisco, Victór (30), and Dr. Fernando Aguilar (22)—all sons of former governor José de Aguilar, who had unwisely cooperated too closely with the imperialist occupation; Francisco Gándara (41), son of the discredited Manuel María Gándara; and Antonio

Francisco Serna continued as titular head of the opposition to the Mariscal administration. He provided the respected name and the state-wide reputation needed to facilitate the transfer of real power in the state to the group of young politicians surrounding Torres, who were maneuvering into a position of dominance over Sonoran politics. Within five years, Torres would come to head a triumvirate that would rule Sonora for three decades, closely linked to the Díaz regime. Its control was on a par with that of the regime fashioned by Francisco Cañedo in Sinaloa.

For more than a half century the Northwest had been on the fringes of national life. The urban notables who dominated local society in Sonora and Sinaloa had at first remained somewhat aloof, preoccupied with the pressing problems of their new states. The nation's retrogression, brought on by the struggle between centralism and federalism, had left them with feelings of being hamstrung yet neglected, meddled with yet ignored. Some had even begun to lose a sense of identity with the country. The Reforma and the Intervention had then served as catalysts to reintegrate them—and the general populace politicized by the wars—into the nation, to confirm their right to full participation in the national life, to firmly establish in them a sense of national belonging.

The post-war years had not brought the expected fulfillment of the promises of progress and the unrestricted exercise of liberal institutions and local prerogatives. But rather than despair and withdraw, as the previous generation had done, those in Sonora and Sinaloa had found themselves drawn increasingly into the national life by the very economic problems and ideological contradictions that confronted them. In the aftermath of the Tuxtepec Revolution, some among them had reached the conclusion that the promotion of local interests necessitated the forging of close, working connections with those who directed the nation's politics in Mexico City. In the years following the region would become an integral part of the political machine erected by Porfirio Díaz and, in time, would come to dominate the nation for a decade and a half after the Revolution of 1910 that ended the long reign of the *Porfiriato*. After a century, the periphery would be at the center.

Escalante (43). Among the newcomers were Lorenzo Torres (42), a compañero from the *porfirista* revolts in Sinaloa, and Dr. Prisciliano Figueroa (32), who had recently completed medical school and was serving as doctor for the federal garrison in Guaymas.

Bibliography

Particularly noteworthy for the study of Sonora and Sinaloa are two microfilm collections, used extensively in this work: the Microfilm Collection of the Instituto Nacional de Antropología y Historia, Museo de Historia y Antropología in Mexico City (abbreviated MAHm); and the Mexican Newspaper Miscellany, 1837-1886 (Film 828), in the University of Arizona Library (abbreviated UAm), from the Bancroft Library at the University of California at Berkeley. The collections of newspapers in the Hemeroteca Nacional and official gazettes in the Biblioteca de la Secretaría de Hacienda (both in Mexico City) are also a rich source of material for the post-intervention years. The Archives of the State of Sonora up to 1900 are found in the Biblioteca y Museo del Estado in Hermosillo. Despite repeated attempts, the State Archives of Sinaloa for the period could not be located. Local historians, including Antonio Nakayama, indicate there are simply none available, a fact confirmed by archival officials in the state capitol. There is no state library at work collecting and preserving documents and other contemporary sources as in Sonora.

MANUSCRIPTS

Informaciones Matrimoniales, 1799-1894. Compiled from the Archivo Histórico de la Catedral de Hermosillo by the Biblioteca y Museo de Sonora (Hermosillo).
Selections from the *Archivo General de Gobierno del Estado de Sonora, Justicia Civil, Actos de Martrimoniales.* Compiled by the Biblioteca y Museo de Sonora.

PUBLIC DOCUMENTS

Aguilar, José de (Governor). *Memoria del Estado de Sonora.* Ures, 1850.
_____. *Memoria del Estado de Sonora.* Ures, 1851.
Almada, Antonio, and Espinosa de los Monteros, José de. *Manifiesto del comisión de Occidente sobre su división en dos estados.* Mexico, 1829. In MAHm, Sonora, Reel 2.
Balanza general del comercio marítimo por los puertos de la República Mexicana, 1825-1826. México, 1827, 1828.
Departamento de la Estadística Nacional: Sonora, Sinaloa, Nayarit. México, 1928.
Espinosa de los Monteros, Carlos. *Exposición sobre las Provincias de Sonora y Sinaloa.* México, 1823. In MAHm, Sonora, Reel 2.

Gándara, Manuel Maria (Governor). *Memoria del Estado de Sonora* (1849). In MAHm, Sonora, Reel 3.

Gaxiola, José María. *Exposición sobre el estado actual de la administración pública del Estado de Occidente.* Guadalajara, 1829. In MAHm, Sonora, Reel 23.

Paredes, Mariano. *Proyectos de leyes sobre colonización y comercio en el Estado de Sonora.* México, 1850.

Pesqueira, Ignacio (Governor). *Memoria del Estado de Sonora.* Hermosillo, 1870.

Riesgo, Juan M., and Valdés, Antonio J. *Memoria estadistica del Estado de Occidente.* Guadalajara, 1828. In MAHm, Sonora, Reel 2.

Rubí, Domingo (Governor). *Informe del Gobernador de Sinaloa al Congreso del Estado de Sinaloa.* Culiacán, 1869.

Selected articles, circulars, commissions, constitutions, decrees, documents, *exposiciones, informes,* letters, *leyes,* manifestos, *noticias,* petitions, *proyectos, reglamentos,* reports, and *representaciones.* In MAHm, Sonora, Reels 1-24.

United States Department of State. *Report on the Commercial Relations of the United States with All Foreign Nations.* Washington, 1855-1902.

Zúñiga, Ignacio. *Memoria sobre el permiso de la navegación de los ríos Fuerte y Yaqui.* México, 1841. In MAHm, Sonora, Reel 2.

CONTEMPORARY GEOGRAPHIES AND TRAVEL JOURNALS

Bartlett, John Russell. *Personal Narrative of Explorations and Incidents in Texas, New Mexico, California, Sonora, and Chihuahua.* London, 1854.

Buelna, Eustaquio. *Compendio histórico, geográfico y estadístico del Estado de Sinaloa.* México, 1877.

Escudero, José Agustín de. *Noticias estadísticas de Sonora y Sinaloa.* México, 1849.

Estrada y Zenea, Ildefonso. *Manual de gobernadores y jefes políticos.* México, 1878.

Fleury, Colonel Ernesto de. *Noticias geológicas, geográficas y estadísticas sobre Sonora y Baja California* (n.p., 1864). In MAHm, Sonora, Reel 12.

Gilliam, Albert. *Travels in Mexico.* Aberdeen, 1847. Reprinted in *Viajes en México—crónicas extranjeras, 1821-1855,* edited by Secretaría de Obras Públicas. México, 1964.

Gregg, Josiah. The *Diary and Letters of Josiah Gregg: Excursions in Mexico and California, 1847-1850.* Edited by Maurice Garland Fulton. Norman, 1944.

Guillet, Captain. "Las notas sobre Sonora del Captain Guillet, 1864-1866." Translated by Ernesto de la Torre Villar. *YAN—Ciencias Antropológicas,* no. 1 (México, 1953), 46-59.

Hardy, R.W.H. (Lieutenant). *Travels in the Interior of Mexico, 1825-1828.* London, 1829. (Reprinted by the Rio Grande Press, 1977.)

Morfí, Juan Agustín (Padre). *Descripción (1778) por Padre Morfí, sobre Arizpe, Sonora, capital fué de las Provincias Internas.* México, 1949.

Mowry, Silvester. *Arizona and Sonora.* Revised Edition. New York, 1864.

Ortega, José (Padre). *Historia del Nayarit, Sonora, Sinaloa y ambas Californias.* México, 1887. (Originally published in Sevilla, 1754.)

Pavía, Lázaro. *Los estados y sus gobernantes.* México, 1890.

Pérez Hernández, José María (General). *Compendio de la geografía del Estado de Sonora.* México, 1872.

Pfefferkorn, Ignaz. *Sonora—A Description of the Province.* Translated by Theodore E. Treutlein. Albuquerque, 1949.

Reid, John C. *Reid's Tramp; or, A Journal of the Incidents of Ten Months of Travel through Texas, New Mexico, Arizona, Sonora, and California.* Selma, Alabama, 1858.

La relación de Sahuaripa de 1778, edited by R.H. Barlow. México, 1947.

Southworth, John R. *El Estado de Sonora—sus industrias, comerciales, mineras y manufacturas.* Nogales, Arizona, 1897.

Spring, John. *John Spring's Arizona.* Edited by A.M. Gustafson. Tucson, 1966.

Stone, Charles P. *Notes on the State of Sonora.* Washington, 1861.

Velasco, José Francisco. *Sonora.* Translated by William F. Nye. San Francisco, 1861. (An abridged translation of Velasco's *Noticias estadísticas del Estado de Sonora,* which was published in Mexico City in 1850.)

Ward, Henry G. *Mexico.* 2 vols. México, 1829.

Zúñiga, Ignacio. *Rápida ojeada al Estado de Sonora, Territorios de California y Arizona, 1835.* México, 1948. (Originally published in México, 1835.)

NEWSPAPERS

El Amigo del Pueblo (Ures) 1875. UAm, Reel 3.

Boletín Oficial del Estado de Sinaloa (Mazatlán, Culiacán), 1870-1873. Biblioteca de la Secretaría de Hacienda.

Boletín Oficial del Estado de Sonora (Ures), 1844. MAHm, Sonora, Reel 3; 1876-1879, MAHm, Reels 6-7 (1876-1878 also in the Biblioteca de la Hacienda).

El Centinela (Ures), 1845. MAHm, Sonora, Reel 11.

Los Cinco Vocales (Guaymas), 1876. UAm, Reel 2.

El Clamor Público (Culiacán), 1872-1873. UAm, Reel 1.

El Club de Reforma (Hermosillo), 1877. UAm, Reel 3.

El Conciliador (Guaymas), 1845. MAHm, Sonora, Reel 11.

La Constitución (Hermosillo), 1879. Biblioteca de la Secretaría de Hacienda.

El Convencional (Guaymas), 1875. UAm, Reel 2.

El Defensor del Pueblo (Guaymas), 1875. UAm, Reel 2.

El Eco de Sonora (Ures), 1870-1871. UAm, Reel 3.

La Estrella de Occidente (Ures), 1859-1876. MAHm, Sonora, Reels 3-6, 12-13, and the Biblioteca de la Secretaría de Hacienda.

El Fantasma (Alamos), 1875. UAm, Reel 1.

El Fenix (Mazatlán), 1872-1873. UAm, Reel 1.

El Golfo de Cortes (Guaymas), 1873. UAm, Reel 2.

El Independiente (Hermosillo), 1875. UAm, Reel 3.

La Integridad Nacional (Ures), 1856. UAm, Reel 3.

El Iris de Paz (Ures), 1845. MAHm, Sonora, Reel 11.

El Látigo (Guaymas), 1872. UAm, Reel 2.

El Mochuelo (Ures), 1873. UAm, Reel 3.

El Nacional (Ures), 1854-1855. MAHm, Sonora, Reel 11.

Periódico Oficial del Departamento de Sonora (Ures), 1865-1866. MAHm, Sonora, Reel 5, and UAm, Reel 3.

El Plan de Tuxtepec (Guaymas), 1877. UAm, Reel 2.

La Prensa (Guaymas), 1877. UAm, Reel 2.

El Progreso (Culiacán), 1857. UAm, Reel 1.

El Pueblo de Sonora (Ures), 1867-1868. UAm, Reel 3.

El Pueblo Independiente (Ures), 1875. UAm, Reel 3.

El Pueblo Sonorense (Ures), 1872-1873. UAm, Reel 3.
La Reconstrucción (Hermosillo), 1877. UAm, Reel 3.
La Regeneración (Hermosillo), 1876. UAm, Reel 3.
El Siglo Diez y Nueve (México), 1842. MAHm, Sonora, Reel 3.
El Sinaloense (Culiacán), 1847. MAHm, Sinaloa, Reel 4.
El Sonorense (Ures), 1846-1859. MAHm, Sonora, Reels 3, 10, 11.
El Susurro (Guaymas), 1877. UAm, Reel 2.
Uno de Tantos (Ures), 1863. UAm, Reel 3.
El Voto de Sonora (Ures), 1845. MAHm, Sonora, Reel 10.
El Voto Libre (Ures), 1871. UAm, Reel 3.
La Voz de Alamos (Alamos), 1876-1878. UAm, Reel 2.
La Voz de Sonora (Ures), 1855-1857. MAHm, Sonora, Reels 3, 10, 11, 24.
La Voz del Estado (Magdalena), 1889. MAHm, Sonora, Reel 9.
La Voz del Pueblo (Mazatlán), 1871. UAm, Reel 1.
La Voz del Pueblo (Ures), 1851. UAm, Reel 3.

SECONDARY WORKS

Acosta, Roberto. *Apuntes históricos sonorenses—la ciudad de Alamos en la época de las guerras de Reforma y del Imperio.* México, 1945.
Acuña, Rodolfo. *Sonoran Strongman: Ignacio Pesqueira and His Times.* Tucson, 1974.
Allen, Mary Jane. "The Story of the Southern Pacific Railroad of Mexico." Master's thesis, University of Southern California, 1946.
Alamada, Francisco R. *Diccionario de historia, geografía y biografía sonorenses.* Chihuahua, 1952.
Bancroft, Hubert H. *The History of the North Mexican States,* 1531-1800. San Francisco, 1884.
——. *The History of the North Mexican States and Texas,* 1801-1889. San Francisco, 1889.
Banderas Rebling, Elsa. *Semblanza histórica crítica de las constituciones políticas del Estado de Sonora.* Hermosillo, 1964.
Beltrán Martinez, Ramón. "Apuntes para la historia de la casa de moneda en Culiacán." In *Estudios Históricos de Sinaloa,* edited by Congreso Mexicano de Historia. México, 1960.
Brading, David A. *Miners and Merchants in Bourbon Mexico, 1763-1810.* Cambridge, 1971.
Brassea Escalante, Bertha. "Historia de la educación en Sonora." Bachelor's thesis, University of Sonora (Hermosillo), 1953.
Brinckerhoff, Sidney B. "The Last Years of Spanish Arizona, 1786-1821." *Arizona and the West* 9 (Spring, 1967), 5-20.
Buelna, Eustaquio. *Apuntes para la historia de Sinaloa, 1821-1882.* México, 1924.
Calvo Berber, Laureano. *Nociones de historia de Sonora.* México, 1958.
Carlisle, Charles R., and Fontana, Bernard L. "Sonora in 1773—Reports of Five Jaliscan Friars." *Arizona and the West* 9 (Spring-Summer, 1969) 39-56, 179-190.
Chase, Russell E. Jr. "Mexico, 1821-1867: The Apocalyptic Vision." Paper presented to the Northern Great Plains Historical Conference (Winnipeg, Oct. 21, 1972).
Cline, Howard F. "The 'Aurora Yucateca' and the Spirit of Enterprise in Yucatán." *Hispanic American Historical Review* 27 (1947), 30-60.

_____. "The Sugar Episode in Yucatán, 1825-1850." *Inter-American Economic Affairs* 1 (1948), 30-51.

Congreso Mexicano de Historia, ed. *Estudios históricos de Sinaloa.* México, 1960.

Corbalá Acuña, Manuel Santiago. *Alamos de Sonora.* México, 1968.

_____. *Sonora y sus constituciones.* Hermosillo, 1972.

Corral, Ramón. *Obras históricas.* Hermosillo, 1959. (Originally published in *La Constitución* [Hermosillo], 1885-1886).

Cosío Villegas, Daniel, ed. *Historia moderna de México: El Porfiriato–la vida económica.* 2 vols. México, 1965.

_____. *Historia moderna de México: El Porfiriato–la vida política interior.* 2 vols. México, 1970.

_____. *Historia moderna de México: La República Restaurada–la vida económica.* México, 1955.

_____. *Historia moderna de México: La República Restaurada–la vida política.* México, 1955.

_____. *Historia moderna de México: La Republica Restaurada–la vida social.* México, 1955.

Cowdery, Richard B. "The Planning of a Transcontinental Railroad through Southern Arizona, 1832-1870." Master's thesis, University of Arizona, 1948.

Dabdoub, Claudio. *Historia de el valle del Yaqui.* México, 1964.

de la Torres Villar, Ernesto. "La política americana durante la Intervención francesa en México." *Revista de Historia de America,* Nos. 63-64 (January-December 1967), 13-67.

Domínguez, Miguel. *La Guerra de Independencia en las provincias Sonora y Sinaloa.* Hermosillo, 1949.

Donohue, John A., S.J. *After Kino–Jesuit Missions in Northwest New Spain, 1711-1767.* St. Louis, 1969.

Dunne, Peter M. *Black Robes in Lower California.* Berkeley, 1968.

Ezell, Paul H. "Indians Under the Law–Mexico, 1821-1847." *America Indígena* 15 (July, 1955), 199-213.

Flores Caballero, Romero. *La contra-revolución en la independencia.* México, 1973.

Font Rius, J.M. *Instituciones medievales españoles.* Barcelona, 1949.

Forbes, Robert H. *Crabb's Filibustering Expedition into Sonora, 1857.* Tucson, 1952.

Galaz, Fernando. *Dejaron huella en el Hermosillo de ayer y hoy.* Hermosillo, 1971.

Garibay, K., Angel María, Director. *Diccionario Porrúa de historia, biografía y geografía de México.* 2nd ed. México, 1965, and supplement, 1966.

Gaxiola, Francisco Javier. *Revista histórica del Estado de Sinaloa, 1856-1865.* México, 1894.

González Dávila, Amado. *Diccionario geográfico, histórico, y estadístico del Estado de Sinaloa.* Culiacán, 1959.

Hale, Charles A. *Mexican Liberalism in the Age of Mora.* New Haven, 1968.

Hamnett, Brian. *Politics and Trade in Southern Mexico, 1750-1821.* Cambridge, 1971.

Harris, Charles. *The Sánchez Navarros; A Socio-Economic Study of a Coahuilan Latifundio, 1846-1853.* Chicago, 1964.

Hastings, James Rodney. "People of Reason and Others–The Colonization of Sonora to 1767." *Arizona and the West* 3 (Winter, 1961), 321-340.

Hernández, Fortunato. *Las razas indígenas de Sonora y la guerra del Yaqui.* México, 1902.

Herr, Richard. *The Eighteenth Century Revolution in Spain.* Princeton, 1958.

Herring, Patricia. "A Plan for Colonization of Sonora's Northern Frontier—The Parades *Proyectos* of 1850." *Journal of Arizona History* 10 (Summer, 1969), 103-114.

Hill, James M. "America Looks Southward, 1830–1860." Master's thesis, University of Missouri, 1950.

Hinton, Thomas B. *A Survey of Indian Assimilation in Eastern Sonora.* Anthropological Papers of the University of Arizona, no. 4 (Tucson, 1959), 1-32.

Ibarra, Alfredo. *Sinaloa en la cultura de México.* Mexico, 1944.

Kessell, John L. *Friars, Soldiers, and Reformers: Hispanic Arizona and the Sonoran Mission Frontier, 1767-1856.* Tucson, 1976.

Knapp, Frank. *The Life of Sebastián Lerdo de Tejada, 1823-1889.* Austin, 1951.

Ladd, Doris M. *The Mexican Nobility at Independence, 1780-1826.* Austin, 1976.

Lister, Robert, and Lister, Florence. *Chihuahua: Storehouse of Storms.* Albuquerque, 1966.

Lockhart, James, and Altman, Ida. *Early Provinces of Mexico.* Los Angeles, 1977.

Lynch, John. *The Spanish-American Revolutions, 1808-1826.* New York, 1973.

Manson, Clara. "Indian Uprisings in Sonora, Mexico." Master's thesis, University of Southern California, 1963.

Mattison, Ray H. "Early Spanish and Mexican Settlements in Arizona." *New Mexico Historical Review* 21 (October 1946), 273-327.

Mena Castillo, José. *Historia compendiada del Estado de Sinaloa.* 2 vols. México, 1942.

Mendizabal, Miguel O. de. *La evolución del Noroeste de México.* México, 1930.

Meyer, Jean. "El ocaso de Manuel Lozada." *Historia Mexicana* 18 (April-June, 1969), 535-568.

Miles, Carlota. *Almada of Alamos—The Diary of Don Bartolomé.* Tucson, 1962.

Moorehead, Max L. "Spanish Deportation of Hostile Apaches—The Policy and Practice." *Arizona and the West* 17 (Fall, 1975), 205-220.

Nakayama, Antonio. *Documentos para la historia del Rosario, Sinaloa.* Culiacán, 1955.

————. *Documentos ineditos e interesantes para la historia de Culiacán.* Culiacán, 1952.

Navarro García, Luis. *Las Provincias Internas en el Siglo XIX.* Sevilla, 1965.

————. *Sonora y Sinaloa en el Siglo XVII.* Sevilla, 1967.

————. *La sublevación del Yaqui en 1740.* Sevilla, 1966.

————. *José de Gálvez y la Comandancia General de las Provincias Internas del norte de Nueva España.* Sevilla, 1964.

Ocaranza, Fernando. *Los Franciscanos en las Provincias Internas de Sonora y Ostimuri.* México, 1933.

————. *Parvu crónica de la Sierra Madre y las Pimerías.* México, 1942.

Oléa, Hector R. *Breve historia de la Revolución en Sinaloa, 1910-1917.* México, 1964.

Polzer, Charles W., S.J. "The Evolution of the Jesuit Mission System in Northwest New Spain, 1600-1767." Doctoral dissertation, University of Arizona, 1972.

Poston, Charles D. "Building a State in Apache Land." *Overland Monthly* 24 (August and September, 1894), 203-213, 291-297.

Pradeau, Albert Francisco. *La Expulsión de los Jesuitas de las Provincias de Sonora, Ostimuri y Sinaloa en 1767.* México, 1959.

————. *Sonora y sus casas de moneda.* México, 1959.

Priestly, Herbert I. *José de Gálvez—Visitador General of New Spain, 1765-1771.* Berkeley, 1916.

Quintero, F.L. "Historia panorámica de le región del Fuerte." In *Estudios Historicos de Sinaloa,* edited by Congreso Mexicano de Historia. México, 1960.
Reed, Nelson. *The Caste War in Yucatán.* Stanford, 1964.
Rippy, J. Fred. "Anglo-American Filibusters and the Gadsden Treaty." *Hispanic American Historical Review* 5 (May, 1922), 155-180.
_____. "The Indians of the Southwest in the Diplomacy of the United States and Mexico, 1848-1853." *Hispanic American Historical Review* 2 (August, 1919), 363-396.
Sauer, Carl. *Aboriginal Population of Northwest Mexico.* Ibero-Americana, No. 10. Berkeley, 1935.
Schmitt, Karl M. *Mexico and the United States: Conflict and Coexistence.* New York, 1974.
Shull, Dorothy Boe."The History of the Presidios in Sonora and Arizona, 1695-1810." Master's thesis, University of Arizona, 1968.
Simmons, Marc. "Spanish Attempts to Open a New Mexico-Sonora Road," *Arizona and the West* 17 (Spring, 1975), 5-20.
Smith, Ralph A. "The Indians in Mexican-American Relations Before the War of 1846." *Hispanic American Historical Review* 43 (February, 1963), 34-64.
Sobarzo, Horacio. *Crónica de la aventura de Raousset-Boulbon en Sonora.* México, 1954.
_____. *Crónicas biográficas.* Hermosillo, 1949.
Stagg, Albert. *The First Bishop of Sonora: Antonio de los Reyes, O.F.M.* Tucson, 1976.
_____. *The Almadas and Alamos.* Tucson, 1978.
Stevens, Robert C. "Mexico's Forgotten Frontier: A History of Sonora, 1821-1846." Doctoral dissertation, University of California at Berkeley, 1963.
Strickland, Rex. "The Birth and Death of a Legend—The Johnson 'Massacre' of 1837." *Arizona and the West* 18 (Autumn, 1976), 257-286.
Tamayo, Jorge L., ed. *Documentos, discursos y correspondencia de Benito Juárez,* vol. 12. México, 1967.
Uruchurtu, Manuel R. *Apuntes biográficos del Señor Ramón Corral,* México, 1910.
Valadés, José C. *Mis confesiones.* México, 1966.
Vicens Vives, Jaime. *Approaches to the History of Spain.* Berkeley, 1970.
_____. *Manual de historia económica de España.* Barcelona, 1965.
_____, ed. *Historia social y económica de España y America,* vols. 3 and 4. Barcelona, 1957, 1959.
Villa, Eduardo W. *Educadores sonorenses biografías.* n.p., n.d. (In the Biblioteca y Museo de Sonora [Hermosillo].)
_____. *Galería de sonorenses ilustres.* Hermosillo, 1948.
_____. *Historia del Estado de Sonora.* Hermosillo, 1951.
Villicana, Ernesto Lemoine. "Historia geográfica-política del Estado de Sonora." *YAN–Ciencias Antropológicas,* No. 1 (1953), 60-63.
Womack, John Jr. *Zapata and the Mexican Revolution.* New York, 1969.
Wyllys, Rufus K. *The French in Sonora, 1850-1854.* Berkeley, 1932.
Zúñiga Sánchez, Luis. *Apuntes para la historia de Mazatlán.* Mazatlán, n.d.

Acknowledgments

Many people and institutions in varying degrees have assisted in the creation of this book. Extensive research in Mexico would not have been possible without the generous grant of a Traveling Fellowship by Harvard University, and supplemental assistance from the State University of New York Research Foundation. The State University College at Plattsburgh generously provided clerical time for the typing of the manuscript, principally in the person of Carol Hall, whose composure and efficiency in the midst of many rushed deadlines was greatly appreciated. The University of Arizona Press is acknowledged for effecting publication of this work.

The location and perusal of archival materials was facilitated by the courteous assistance of the directors and staffs of the Widener Library, the Houghton Library (in particular, the Papers of the United Church Board for World Missionaries and the American Board of Commissioners for Foreign Missionaries), the University of Arizona Library, the Arizona Heritage Center, and the Library of Congress in the United States; and in Mexico, the *Hemeroteca Nacional,* the *Biblioteca Nacional,* the *Biblioteca de Hacienda,* the *Biblioteca del Museo de Antropologia y Historia,* the *Biblioteca del Colegio de México,* the *Archivo General de la Nación,* the *Biblioteca y Museo de Sonora,* the *Archivos del Estado de Sonora,* and the *Biblioteca del Congreso del Estado de Sinaloa.* Special archival direction was provided by Luis Pompa y Pompa, Ernesto de la Torre Villar, Hector Aguilar Camín, and Daniel Cosío Villegas, who also generously shared with me his manuscript of the politics of the Porfiriato, and his wisdom on the larger questions of the chosen subject. For interviews which provided important biographical and familial backgrounding, I thank Antonio G. Rivera, Rafaela Marcor, Martín Salido, and Emilia Almada. For geographic illustrations, I am most grateful to Kathe Fairweather, whose cartographical skills are such that the conversion of information to maps was rendered not only facile, but instructive as well.

There are also those whose support has been more subtle, yet enduring. It is to them, above all, that I wish to pay special recognition. Collectively, they are the important legacy of my past, the base from which this book has been shaped. I am indebted to my uncle, James M. Hill, who first made history come alive for me through a myriad of stories that connected our family with the historical experience of this country, and who demonstrated that the on-going study of history can be an abiding source of fascination and wisdom; to my parents (Leonard A. Voss, Vesta S. Voss, and Marthann Hill Voss), who constantly have held out before me the value of learning, have celebrated my accomplishments in it, and yet have allowed me the utmost freedom in pursuing it; to Harold Woodman, who, at a critical time of career choice in my life, revealed to me the responsibilities and satisfactions in being a professional historian, and who ever since has shown me the full potential for the relationship that begins between professor and student; to Bernard Bailyn, who confronted me with the analytical approach that history entails not the choice of certain causal factors to the exclusion of others, but their integration into a meaningful pattern of varying priorities to understand the movement of human experience through time; to John Womack, Jr., who offered the comments, questions, and suggestions that stimulated me to make far more of this manuscript than otherwise would have been possible, and who taught me that history is an organic, caring reality that must be felt if it is to be properly and fully understood; to my children, who gave up a portion of their childhood years with a parent—time in their lives which I can never repay; to my wife, whose assistance in research and proofreading was most helpful, who, as a sounding board has played devil's advocate and comforter during times of stress and decision, and whose abiding companionship has provided my professional work with a continuing renewal of energy and a proper perspective.

S.F.V.

Index

Agriculture, 4-9 *passim*, 23-24, 35, 40-42
  in Sinaloa, 42, 189-190
  in Sonora, 40-42, 107, 108 n.51,
    188-189, 192
Aguilar (family), 299-300 n.87
  Francisco A., 108, 139
  Francisco C., 241, 278 n.9, 297
  Francisco J., 136, 139
  José (de)
    economic activity of, 118, 156
    education and professional career
      of, 74, 110 n.61
    political career of, 110-112,
      136-139, 173 n.136
  Victores, 28 n.100, 74, 92
Alamos. *See also* Yaquis and Mayos
  as a center of federalist sympathy,
    86-87
  cost of political loyalties in, 100, 174,
    240, 254
  description of, 29-30, 47
  development of, 29-30, 46-47, 86, 199,
    201
    obstacles to, 107, 111, 159-160,
      191-192
  economy of, 23, 29, 39, 46-47
  flood of 1868 in, 192
  opposition to Pesqueira in, 238-241,
    250, 253-254
  as origin of Torres circle, 299
  political involvement in, 238-239
  population estimate for, 17 n.61,
    160 n.99, 199 n.90
  and the state of Occidente, 58-60
  support of liberalism in, 139, 159,
    239-241

Almada (family), 26-27, 31 n.108, 39, 98,
  100, 159
  Adolfo
    legislative proposal of, 182, 182-183
      n.26, 235
    political career of, 244, 246, 250,
      252, 278 n.9, 280 n.14,
      297
  Antonio (father), 26, 31, 31 n.109
  Antonio (son), 58, 74, 98, 100
  Bartolomé, 138 n.15, 139, 167,
    240-241 n.19
  Gregorio, 74, 112 n.75
  Ignacio, 31 n.109, 111
  José, 26, 31
  José María
    business activities of, 86, 100,
      107 n.49, 159
    political career of, 58, 86, 99-100,
      239-240
Altar, 17, 47, 106, 111, 198, 200
Altata, 78, 123, 124, 126, 128, 163
Apaches. *See also* Crown policies;
  Government policies, Sonora
  depredations of, 71-72, 105-106,
    110-111, 158-159, 178
  raiding by, 5, 9-10, 20 n.69, 66-72
  U.S. responsibility for, 110, 178-179
Arce, Francisco, 275-277, 282-283
Arizpe. *See also* Apaches, depredations of
  description of, 22 n.81, 113, 198
  development of, 22 n.81, 28, 47,
    73-74, 106, 113, 198
  political involvement in, 20, 30,
    64-65, 85-86, 96-98, 100
  population estimate for, 47

Arizpe, Intendancy of, 20, 24 n.90, 28, 34, 35
Astiazarán, Joaquín A., 41-42
Astiazarán, Joaquín María, 214-215, 233, 247, 249, 255, 280
Ayutla Revolt, 133, 135-137, 142-144

Banderas, Juan (Juan Ignacio Jusacamea), 51-52, 66-67
Blanco, Miguel, 118, 143-144, 280
Bourbons. *See* Crown policies
Buelna, Eustaquio
    administrative policies of, 201-203, 268-271
    and election of 1871, 259, 262-265
    as governor, 180, 220, 265-271, 276, 295
    as liberal leader, 144, 147, 262, 294
Bustamante, Prospero S., 139, 247-248

Cahitas, 2, 4
Camou, Hermanos, 140, 156, 157 n.82, 173 n.136, 254 n.57
Cañedo, Francisco, 265-266, 282-283, 292-297, 300
Capital location controversy
    in Occidente, 57-58
    in Sinaloa, 76, 128, 143, 146, 268-269, 292
    in Sonora, 64-65, 100, 109
Carbó, José G., 266
Centralism-federalism conflict, 80-82
    in Sinaloa, 83-84, 98-99, 121-129
    in Sonora, 82, 84-94, 95-105 *passim*
the Church (Roman Catholic). *See also*
        Franciscans; Jesuits
    dioceses of, 20-22, 26-27, 29, 81 n.48
    post-independence weakness of, 33, 49-50, 72, 80-81
Colonization, 115-119, 150-151, 179
Commerce, 5, 9, 24, 35-44 *passim*, 106, 192-193, 223, 230-231. *See also*
        Apaches, depredations of; Economic relations of the region; Yaquis and Mayos, depredations of
    in Sinaloa, 42, 75, 79, 190-191
    in Sonora, 40, 44-45, 107, 191
Concordia (San Sebastián), 2, 34, 47, 76, 174, 177
Connant, Carlos, 253-254
Conquest, colonial, 2-3
Conservatism-liberalism conflict. *See also*
        Relations of the region with national

politics; Rivalry of Culiacán and Mazatlán
    in Sinaloa, 142-148, 162-165, 174-175
    in Sonora, 135-142 *passim*, 147-148, 174-175
Constitution of 1857 (federal), 133-135, 145, 204-206, 217, 237, 275, 280.
        See also Relations of the region with national politics
Constitutions
    for Occidente, 49, 52-53
    for Sinaloa, 75, 161-162, 234
    for Sonora
        from 1831 to 1848, 68-69, 105 n.39, 107 n.50
        from 1861 to 1872, 160, 208 n.4, 241-242, 247-252, 251 n.44, 290
Consular reports (U.S.) on economic activity
    for Sinaloa, 181, 186-187, 195 n.78
    for Sonora, 176, 181 n.22, 182
Contraband, 40, 55, 119, 128, 152 n.61
    role of, in Culiacán-Mazatlán rivalry, 46, 78, 80, 83-84, 123-127 *passim*, 186
Corella, Joaquín, 139, 247
Corella, Rafael, 139, 245, 247, 249, 298
    military career of, 165-170, 257, 260-261
    political involvement of, 170-171, 257-261 *passim*, 258-259 n.65, 261 n.71
Corral, Ramón, 147 n.42, 280 n.14, 299
Cosalá, 28, 39, 47, 57-58, 76-77, 193
Crabb, Henry, 130-131, 138-141
Crabb expedition. *See* Crabb, Henry
Crown policies
    and Bourbon reforms, 18
    effect of, on independence, 34, 48, 50, 55, 63
    for the frontier, 10-11, 16-20
    on missions, 3-4, 10
    for the promotion of urban hispanic society, 22-24, 27, 31
Cubillas, Fernando, 118, 156, 158
Culiacán. *See also* Capital location controversy; Contraband; Rivalry of Culiacán and Mazatlán
    development of, 2, 28-29, 46, 143-144, 163, 194
    economy of, 28, 42, 46, 124
    political involvement in, 46, 57-58,

76-78, 143, 163, 257-258
population estimate for, 194, 195

de la Huerta, Torcuato, 139, 158
de los Reyes, Antonio, O.F.M., 25-27,
    30-31
Díaz, Porfirio, 223-224, 263-264, 273-275
    and the forging of regional alliances,
        288-289, 294-297, 299-300
    and the La Noria Revolt, 220, 265-266
    and the Tuxtepec Revolt, 281-283,
        287-288
Duque, Francisco, 104

Economic relations of the region with
    other areas. *See also* Commerce;
    Consular reports (U.S.) on economic
    activity
    Arizona, 152 n.61, 156-157, 182-183,
        191
    Baja California, 5, 38, 40, 195
    Bordering Mexican states (Chihuahua,
        Durango, Jalisco), 3, 5, 6, n.18,
        38-42 *passim*, 153, 195, 227
    California, 23-24, 111, 113-114, 128,
        156, 192, 196
    China, 37, 40, 156, 196
    Europe, 37-38
    Interior Mexican states, 24, 29, 35,
        153, 182, 195-196, 227
    Mexican Pacific coast, 24, 40, 196
    New Mexico, 38, 40, 68
    United States, 37-38, 232
Education, 30-31, 72, 235
    in Sinaloa
        primary, 128-129, 185, 197,
            199-203
        secondary, 124, 143-144, 185, 200,
            269
    in Sonora
        primary, 72-73, 98, 112 n.75,
            152-153, 160, 200-201,
            279
Elías González (family), 29-31, 41 n.21,
    85-86, 97
    Domingo, 220, 241, 255-256, 278 n.9,
        298
    José María, 69 n.14, 85, 98, 100
    Juan, 50, 86
    Rafael, 85-86
    Simón, 52, 58 n.80, 65, 85, 97, 100
Escalante, Leonardo, 65-66, 92, 98-99
Escalante y Arvizu, Manuel, 65 n.4, 66, 92

Escalante y Moreno, José María, 136-137
Espejo, Pedro, 119, 136-137, 146
External contact, 36-37, 43 n.32, 48,
    62-64, 113. *See also* Economic
    relations of the region with other
    areas
    colonization, 115-119
    filibusters, 114-119 *passim*, 117 n.92,
        130-131, 138-141, 153-154
    foreign investors, 180-181
        in Sinaloa, 181, 186-187, 195 n.78
        in Sonora, 181-182, 186, 213-216
    foreign merchants, 35-44 *passim*, 48,
        68, 71, 139-140
        in Mazatlán, 80, 83-84, 123-129,
            163, 174, 195-196, 258,
            271
    markets, 36-37, 128
    North American migrants, 114
    war with the U.S., 110, 125, 126 n.109

Family Networks
    formation of, 29-32, 43-44
    political influence of, 52-53
        in Occidente, 56-61 *passim*
        in Sinaloa, 77-78, 83, 121-124,
            143-146
        in Sonora, 65, 68-69, 72, 84-94
            passim, 116 n.87, 208,
            237-241, 298-299
Federalism. *See* Centralism-federalism
    conflict
Filibusters, 114-119 *passim*, 117 n.92,
    130-131, 138-141, 153-154
Fiscal problems (state)
    in Occidente, 54-55
    in Sinaloa, 165, 184-185
    in Sonora, 64, 70-71, 112, 184, 210,
        219 n.41
Flood of 1868, in Sonora, 192
Foreign merchants and investors. *See*
    External contact
Franciscans
    and the decline of missions, 20-22, 49,
        54-55, 81
    frontier expansion by, 19-20
French Intervention. *See* Intervention
    (French)
Fuerte, 47, 57-58, 76

Gálvez, José de, 19-20, 22-23, 26, 29
Gándara (family), 92 n.79, 299 n.87
    Jesús, 137-138, 147

Gándara *(continued)*
  Juan, 92
  Juan Bautista, 101, 104, 111
  Manuel María
    economic activities of, 92, 100-101,
      118
    political career of, 92-93, 97-105
      passim, 110, 136-139,
      174 n.139
    role of, in revolts, 92, 99-104
      passim, 103 n.34, 138,
      139 n.18, 148, 172
Gandaristas, 105, 115, 138-139, 147-148,
  172, 174
García Morales, Jesús
  economic activities of, 150-151
  military career of, 139, 165, 172, 179,
    209, 212, 242
  as opposition candidate, 244, 278, 281,
    285-286
  as provisional governor of Sinaloa,
    167-170
Gaxiola, José María, 275-277, 282-283
Gaxiola (family), 58-59
  José María, 59-60, 104
  Manuel María, 59-103
  Nicolas María, 59
González, Dionisio, 156, 157 n.82, 173
  n.136
Government policies, Sinaloa
  on administrative reorganization, 270
  for the promotion of education, 168
    n.123, 201-203, 270
  on taxation and commercial regulation,
    126-127, 163, 228-230, 267
    n.91, 268-269 (*see also* Vega
    [family])
Government policies, Sonora. *See also*
    Pesqueira, Ignacio; Centralism-
    federalism conflict
  on Apache raids, 68-71, 98, 150,
    209-211
  on colonization, 116, 150-151
  on fiscal matters, 216-219, 254-256
  for the promotion of economic
    activities, 98, 102
  for the promotion of education, 72-73,
    98, 152-153, 201
  on transportation and communications,
    151-152, 212-216
  on the Yaqui and Mayo valleys,
    150-151, 212
Guaymas. *See also* Contraband; Filibusters
  description of, 43, 108

development of, 24, 107-112 *passim*,
  199, 201
economy in, 37 n.7, 42-43, 104 n.36,
  157-158
political involvement in, 172-173,
  179-180, 255, 278
population estimate for, 47, 160 n.99,
  199 n.90
relations of, with national government,
  108, 255, 286
Guerra, Donato, 261, 266, 282-283,
  292-293

Hermosillo, José María González, 34
Hermosillo (Pitic)
  description of, 45
  development of, 44-45, 107-108, 156,
    199, 201
  economy of, 107-108, 156-157
  political involvement in, 64-65,
    172-173
  population estimate for, 160 n.99,
    199 n.90
Horcasitas (San Miguel de), 17, 28, 47
Huerta, Epitacio, 288-289
Huidobro, Manuel Bernal, 15

Iberri (family)
  José, 108, 139
  Wenceslao, 108, 139, 278 n.9
Independence
  effect of, on region, 34-37
  limited war for, in region, 34-35
Indians. *See names of individual tribes;*
  Tribal Indians
Industry, 188
  in Sinaloa, 78 n.41, 188
  in Sonora, 93 n.83, 157, 188
Iñigo, Manuel
  business activities of, 41, 93, 101-102,
    108-109 n.56, 157
  political maneuvering by, 93-94, 101,
    104
Intendancy of Arizpe, 20, 28, 34, 35
Intervention (French)
  economic problems caused by,
    176-178, 181-184
  politics of, 149, 165, 168-173
Inzunza, Manuel, 262, 282, 283 n.27
Iriarte, Francisco, 39, 43, 58-60, 77

Jesuits
  conflict of, with settlers, 7-13, 16 n.51
  conflict of, with tribal Indians, 8 n.27,
    13-16

expulsion of, 18-19, 19 n.66
mission concept of, 3, 7-8, 10-12
and mission society, 4-6, 14
pacification of the region by, 4, 10
Johnson, John, 43-44 n.37, 71
Johnson, Ricardo, 243-244
Johnson "Massacre" (1837), 71
Juárez, Benito
political intervention by, 263-265, 267
presidential policies of, 165, 169,
179-180
and the state-federal conflict, 165-167,
219-225
Jusacamea, Juan Ignacio (Juan Banderas),
51-52, 66-67

Kino, Eusebio, S.J., 4, 7, 9

La Noria Revolt, 229, 265-266
León, Fortino, 147 n.43, 164 n.109,
166-167
Lerdo de Tejada, Sebastián
political career of, 223-225, 266-267,
272-273
political intervention by, 266-267,
275-277, 281-283, 285-287
presidential policies of, 180, 205,
210-211, 220, 231, 272-275
Liberalism. *See* Conservatism-liberalism
conflict
Lozada, Manuel, 161, 165-168, 177,
256-257, 262

Magdalena, 159, 198, 200
Mariscal, Vicente, 286-291, 297, 300
Márquez de León, Manuel, 164, 167-168,
262-266
Martínez, Angel, 173, 189, 258-261
Martínez, Ramón, 215, 241, 244, 246,
249, 252
Martínez de Castro, Agustín, 78 n.39,
143, 145
Mayos. *See* Yaquis and Mayos
Maytorena, José María, 108
Mazatlán. *See also* Contraband; External
contact, Foreign merchants; Rivalry
of Culiacán and Mazatlán
description of, 43, 79 n.42, 80, 128
development of, 42-43, 76-80, 128-129,
190-191, 194-200 *passim*,
227-228
economy in, 42-43, 78-80, 128,
188-192, 195-196, 227-228

federal garrison in, 75, 82, 124-125,
127, 256
political involvement in, 163, 170,
228-230
population estimate for, 47, 128, 195,
196
Military, the, 33, 81-82, 236, 273. *See also*
Crown policies; Presidios; Relations
of the region with national politics
and the *comandancia general*, 67-68,
81, 102 n.30, 146 n.41
and federal military colonies, 111,
209-211
and the federal garrison in Mazatlán,
75, 82, 124-125, 127, 256
and military *jefes* in Sinaloa, 163-164,
256
and the militia-national guard, 54,
59-60, 111-112, 209
Mining, 6 n.15, 23, 35, 38-40, 186-188,
231. *See also* Mint
in Sinaloa, 2, 6, 39, 75-76, 186-187
in Sonora, 6, 39-40, 156, 186
Mint
in Sinaloa, 124, 186 n.41, 187, 194
in Sonora, 71, 108, 152, 186 n.41
Missions. *See* Franciscans; Jesuits
Moctezuma (Oposura), 47, 71, 198
Monteverde (family), 74, 139, 173 n.136,
254 n.57, 278
Francisco, 45, 74
Manuel
as acting governor, 210, 212,
218-219, 242
economic activities of, 137 n.14,
156, 278
education of, 74
political career of, 136-137, 240,
242, 278
Monzón, Manuel, 259-260, 265 n.84
Morales, Antonio, 136-137
Municipios, 196-197, 200. *See also*
Constitutions; Education
in Sinaloa, 161-162, 193, 197-198,
201-202
in Sonora, 72-73, 112, 160, 197-201
passim, 207-208, 217-218

Nationalism, 130, 135, 140-141, 151-154
passim, 171-174
Notables. *See also* Capital location
controversy; Family networks;
Progress
base of, in towns, 44, 68-69, 208-209

Notables *(continued)*
  concept of, 24-27
  confrontation of problems by, 52,
      62-64, 72-74, 79-83, 99, 115-120
      passim
  political predominance of, 54-56,
      68-69, 109, 121-123, 208
  and the sense of national identity,
      62, 114-115, 131, 173-174,
      203-204
Nueva Galicia, 2, 3 n.2
Nueva Vizcaya, 2, 3 n.2

Occidente (state of)
  constitution of, 49, 52-53
  creation of, 35
  division question for, 57-61
  fiscal penury in, 54-55
  politics in, 55-61
  problems to resolve in, 52-55
Opatas
  accommodation of with whites, 17,
      22 n.81, 66-67, 91
  alliance of, with *gandaristas*, 99, 102,
      138, 148, 172-173
  as laborers, 41, 91
  uprisings by, 103 n.34
Oposura (Moctezuma), 47, 71, 198
Ortiz, Carlos, 289, 299
Ortiz, Celedonio, 140, 156, 157 n.82,
  173 n.136
Otero, José T., 106-107 n.47, 139, 299
  n.87

Palacios, Adolfo, 260-261, 265
Palomares, Crispin S. de, 139, 151, 179
Papagos, 4, 16, 99, 102, 103 n.34, 106
Paredes y Arrillaga, Mariano, 58, 60, 99,
  125
Periphery
  in formation of Mexican nation,
      62-63, 119 n.98, 204
  Sinaloa and Sonora as, 1-2, 80, 95, 300
Pesqueira, Ignacio, 74
  administrative policies of, 148-156,
      207-220 *passim*
  conflict of, with legislature, 214-219,
      241-244, 247-252
  criticism of opponents by, 221-227,
      237-238
  economic activities of, 136-137, 152
    n.59
  military service of, 137, 147-148, 172,

    179-180, 266
  opposition to, 238-250, 253-256,
    277-281
  political career of, 136-142, 147-148,
    171-173, 223-224, 244 n.30
  removal of, from office, 284-289, 297
Pesqueira, José, 242, 277, 281, 285-287
Pesqueiristas, 221-227, 237-238, 245-253
  passim, 280-281, 288-290, 298
Pimas Altos, 4, 9, 16, 88
Pimas Bajos
  as laborers, 41, 91
  missions of, 4, 16-17, 22 n.81
  uprisings by, 9, 16, 102
Pimería Alta, 4, 6 n.18, 17, 22, 67, 81
Pitic (Hermosillo). *See* Hermosillo (Pitic)
Political policies. *See* Government policies,
  Sinaloa; Government policies, Sonora
Population estimates
  Alamos, 17 n.61, 160 n.99, 199 n.90
  Altar, 47
  Arizpe, 47
  Concordia (San Sebastián), 47
  Cosalá, 47
  Culiacán, 194, 195
  Fuerte, 47
  for groups of towns, 17 n.61, 47
  Guaymas, 47, 160 n.99, 199 n.90
  Hermosillo, 160 n.99, 199 n.90
  Horcasitas (San Miguel de), 47
  Intendancy of Arizpe, 24 n.90
  Mazatlán, 47, 128, 195, 196
  Oposura (Moctezuma), 47
  for the region, 6-7, 17 n.61, 183
  Sahuaripa, 47
  San Ignacio, 47
  Sinaloa, 47
  Ures, 47, 199 n.90
Presidios. *See also* Crown policies;
  Relations of the region with national
  government
  colonial, 9-10, 17, 19, 28 n.100
  post-independence, 48-49, 54, 68,
    69 n.14
Progress
  notables' concept of, 29
  notables' vision of
    for region, 63, 65, 115, 131, 204
    for Sonora, 82, 84-94, 95-105
      passim
  obstacles to, 82-83, 94, 105, 110,
    113, 176-178, 203
Province of Sonora and Sinaloa,15,20,31,33

Quijada, Jesús
    as legislator, 241, 246-247, 249
    as opposition leader, 278, 280 n.14, 281
    as secretary of government, 287 n.42,
        297
Quiroga, Ismael, 278, 280 n.14, 297

Railroads, 213, 216, 231-232. *See also*
    Transportation and communications
    in Sonora
Ramírez, Cirilo, 139, 255, 297
Ramírez, Jesús, 283, 292-296
Raousset de Boulbon, Gaston, 117-119
Redo, Joaquín, 293-294
Relations of the region with national
    government. *See also* Pesqueira,
    Ignacio; Relations of the region with
    national politics
    colonization, 116-117, 150 n.53, 179
    combatting armed insurrections,
        261-262, 265-266, 285-286
    commerce, 106, 192-193, 223,
        230-231
    Indian policy, 50-52, 209-212, 222-223
    military, 82, 236, 273. *See also*
        Military, the
    political intervention, 255-256,
        266-267, 270-271, 275-277,
        281-289, 291-300
    post-independence neglect
        of the region, 48-49, 67, 84-85,
            90-91
        of Sonora, 82, 84-94, 95-105 *passim*
    railroads, 213, 216, 231-232
    revenues, 54, 219-223, 231
    state prerogatives, 148-149, 208-216,
        220-227 *passim*, 236-237
    subsidization of economic activity,
        223, 227-228
    territorial transfer (of Sonora), rumors
        of
        to the U.S., 114, 119, 135, 141-142
        to France, 168, 172
Relations of the region with national
    politics. *See also* Relations of the
    region with national government
    centralist-federalist conflict, 80-84
        passim, 94-95, 101, 103-105,
        121-129
    conservative-liberal conflict, 126-128
        passim, 132-148, 162-165,
        174-175

French Intervention, 149, 165,
    168-173
post-independence years, 62-64
Restored Republic, 204-207, 221-225,
    227, 233-237, 271-275
Tuxtepec Revolt, 281-284, 287-289
Rivalry of Culiacán and Mazatlán, 121-129,
    142-143, 194-195, 257-271,
    291-294. *See also* Centralism-
    federalism conflict, Conservatism-
    liberalism conflict, Relations of
    region with national politics
Robinson, John A., 140, 156, 158
Rojo, José, 275-277, 282 n.21
Rosales, Antonio, 144-145, 164, 167-168,
    170-171
Rosario
    description of, 45
    development of, 28, 45, 76, 193
    economy of, 23, 28, 39, 45, 186-187
    political involvement, 34
Rubí, Domingo
    as governor, 171, 259-262
    military career of, 164 n.109, 171, 266
    political maneuvering by, 257-258,
        262-263, 265-268, 275-276

Sahuaripa, 47, 198
Salido (family), 50, 107 n.47
    Bartolomé, 29-31
    Martín, 192
San Ignacio, 34, 47, 76
San Miguel de Horcasitas, 17, 28, 47
San Sebastián (Concordia), 2, 34, 76, 174,
    177
Santa Anna, Antonio López de
    political career of, 133, 233
    political intervention by, 77, 96-97,
        101, 123, 128
    presidential policies of, 119
Seris, 4-5, 9, 67, 102
Serna, Francisco, 278 n.9, 284-286,
    290-291, 297-300
Sernistas, 290-291, 297-299
Sinaloa (town), 47, 76
Spanish settlement, 6-7, 17 n.61, 22,
    24-32, 27-28 n.98-99. *See also*
    Franciscans; Jesuits; Subsociety
    competition
Spence, Tomás, 43-44, 140
Subsociety competition, 1-2, 11, 18-22,
    31-32. *See also* Franciscans; Jesuits;
    Spanish settlement

Tapia, Andres L., 283 n.27, 292-297
Taxation and commercial regulation.
    See Government policies, Sinaloa
Tepiqueños, 164-166, 169-170, 175, 196,
    256-269 *passim*, 267 n.91, 291.
    See also Rivalry of Culiacán and
    Mazatlán
Territorial transfer (Sonora). *See* Relations
    of the region with national
    government
Tolentino, Francisco, 293-296
Torres, Lorenzo, 283 n.27, 285-286, 293,
    299-300 n.87
Torres, Luis, 299-300
Transportation and communications.
    See Government policies, Sonora
Trías, Angel, 151, 213
Tribal Indians, 33, 41, 48-51, 99, 102-103,
    235. *See also* Apaches; Cahitas;
    Opatas; Papagos; Pimas Altos; Pimas
    Bajos; Seris; Yaquis and Mayos
    of northern Sinaloa, 34-35 n.2, 74, 189
Tuxtepec Revolt, 281-284, 287-289

Urban growth, 24, 27-30, 42-47, 75, 138,
    197-198. *See also individual towns*
    concentration of, in Sinaloa, 75-76,
        193-194, 197-198
Ures
    Apache raids on, 110, 158
    description, 158
    development, 47, 107-109, 158-159,
        199, 201
    economy, 47, 158-159
    political involvement, 100, 109, 138,
        245-246, 297
    population estimate for, 47, 199 n.90
Urrea, Angel, 267, 276-277
Urrea, de (family)
    José, 76-77, 96-104
    Mariano, 96-97 n.4
    Miguel, 98, 239-240, 278 n.9, 280 n.14
U.S. consular reports on economic activity
    for Sinaloa, 181, 186-187, 195 n.78

for Sonora, 176, 181 n.22, 182
U.S., war with, 110, 125, 126 n.109

Valadés, José C., 144 n.33, 230, 264,
    268, 270, 274
Valdés, Pedro, 127-128
Vega, de la (family), 46, 77-78, 83-84,
    121-128 *passim*, 143-146, 293-295
    Francisco, 78, 126-128, 162, 169
    Joaquín, 78, 145-146
    Manuel, 77-78
    Plácido, 147-148, 162-168, 262
    Rafael, 78, 123, 126
Verdugo, Pomposo, 123, 143-145

War with the U.S., 110, 125, 126 n.109

Yáñez, José María, 119, 136, 145-147
Yaquis and Mayos. *See also* Progress,
    notables' vision of; Cahitas
    conception of autonomy for, 13-14,
        41, 65-66
    depredations of, 17-18, 53, 106-107,
        159
    resistance of, to political subordination,
        51, 66-67
    resistance of, to territorial encroach-
        ment, 41-42, 51, 65-66, 88,
        106-107 n.47, 159, 179,
        191-192
    uprisings by
        of 1740-1741, 15-17, 19
        of 1825-1827, 51-54 *passim*
        of 1832-1833, 65-67
        during the Gandara-Urrea civil
            wars, 99-103 *passim*
        during the conservative-liberal
            struggle, 138, 148, 148
            n.46
        during the Intervention, 172-173
        from 1867 to 1875, 179, 284-285
Yucatán, 33, 173, 235

Zúñiga, Ignacio, 87-91, 102-103